AF683842

Proceedings of the Fourth

International Conference Massively Parallel Processing Using Optical Interconnections

Proceedings of the Fourth

International Conference Massively Parallel Processing Using Optical Interconnections

June 22-24, 1997

Montreal, Canada

Edited by

J. Goodman, S. Hinton, T. Pinkston, and E. Schenfeld

Sponsored by

IEEE Computer Society Technical Committee on Computer Architecture

In cooperation with

ACM Special Interest Group on Architecture (SIGARCH)

The IEEE Lasers and Electro-optics Society (LEOS)

The Optical Society of America (OSA)

The International Society for Optical Engineering (SPIE)

IEEE COMPUTER SOCIETY

Los Alamitos, California

Washington • Brussels • Tokyo

Copyright © 1997 by The Institute of Electrical and Electronics Engineers, Inc.
All rights reserved

Copyright and Reprint Permissions: Abstracting is permitted with credit to the source. Libraries may photocopy beyond the limits of US copyright law, for private use of patrons, those articles in this volume that carry a code at the bottom of the first page, provided that the per-copy fee indicated in the code is paid through the Copyright Clearance Center, 222 Rosewood Drive, Danvers, MA 01923.

Other copying, reprint, or republication requests should be addressed to: IEEE Copyrights Manager, IEEE Service Center, 445 Hoes Lane, P.O. Box 133, Piscataway, NJ 08855-1331.

The papers in this book comprise the proceedings of the meeting mentioned on the cover and title page. They reflect the authors' opinions and, in the interests of timely dissemination, are published as presented and without change. Their inclusion in this publication does not necessarily constitute endorsement by the editors, the IEEE Computer Society, or the Institute of Electrical and Electonics Engineers, Inc.

IEEE Computer Society Order Number PR07974
ISBN 0-8186-7974-3
ISBN 0-8186-7975-1(case)
ISBN 0-8186-7976-X (microfiche)
IEEE Order Plan Catalog Number 97TB100152
Library of Congress Number 97-72014

Additional copies may be ordered from:

IEEE Computer Society
Customer Service Center
10662 Los Vaqueros Circle
P.O. Box 3014
Los Alamitos, CA 90720-1314
Tel: + 1-714-821-8380
Fax: + 1-714-821-4641
E-mail: cs.books@computer.org

IEEE Service Center
445 Hoes Lane
P.O. Box 1331
Piscataway, NJ 08855-1331
Tel: + 1-908-981-1393
Fax: + 1-908-981-9667
mis.custserv@computer.org

IEEE Computer Society
13, Avenue de l'Aquilon
B-1200 Brussels
BELGIUM
Tel: + 32-2-770-2198
Fax: + 32-2-770-8505
euro.ofc@computer.org

IEEE Computer Society
Ooshima Building
2-19-1 Minami-Aoyama
Minato-ku, Tokyo 107
JAPAN
Tel: + 81-3-3408-3118
Fax: + 81-3-3408-3553
tokyo.ofc@computer.org

Editorial production by Deborah Plummer/Ian Torwick

Cover design by Alexander Torres

Printed in the United States of America by Braun-Brumfield, Inc.

IEEE COMPUTER SOCIETY

IEEE

Table of Contents

Message from the General Chair

Welcome to this, the fourth meeting on Massively Parallel Processing using Optical Interconnects. We hope you will find the program stimulating and of help in this highly interdisciplinary field.

A major goal of the conference is to bring together researchers in the rather separate fields of computer architecture and photonics. Computer architects are in the best position to identify the most important interconnect problems to face the computer industry, and are generally quite familiar with the capabilities and limitations of electrical approaches to solving such problems. Those working in the field of photonics have a good sense of the unique attributes of optics as an inter connect medium, and can project what the capabilities of such approaches may ultimately be, as well as identify the outstanding photonic device and systems problems that require further development.

The computer architecture field finds itself at a juncture where different philosophies compete for the future. The massively parallel machine remains of high interest, but to a smaller number of companies than ever before. Interest in networks of workstations as a parallel-computing paradigm appears to be growing. Tight coupling of machines through networks with low-protocol overheads are important, as are new schemes for maintaining cache coherency. The bandwidth demanded of interconnects continues to rise dramatically, and the pressure to keep latencies low is extremely strong.

In the photonics area, significant progress has been made over the past few years in developing low-cost parallel fiber links for interconnections over distances of the order of ten meters (or less). Photonics appears poised to move a level lower in the interconnect hierarchy, perhaps entering a single machine. Whether this is at the backplane or board level is uncertain, and will be influenced greatly by the costs of photonic solutions. Wavelength division multiplexing, which is having a profound impact on long-distance links in the national networks, may find a role at shorter distances as well.

All these developments (and more) make this an exciting time in the field covered by this conference. I am confident that this excitement will be felt by those attending, and hopeful that this meeting can serve a useful purpose in furthering progress in this field.

Joseph W. Goodman
Stanford University
General Chair

Message from the Program Co-Chairs

Welcome to Montreal and the fourth MPPOI conference. Indeed, it has been our pleasure serving as program chairs for this important cross-disciplinary meeting which brings together top researchers in the fields of parallel processing and optical interconnects. To reflect the current state of the art in this research area we have encouraged authors to submit manuscripts demonstrating original unpublished research in the following topical areas.

-Optical Interconnections and Reconfigurable Architectures.
-Interconnection Networks.
-Embedding and Mapping of Applications and Algorithms.
-Packaging and Layout of Optical Interconnections.
-Electro-Optical and Opto-Electronic Components.
-Relative Merits of Optical Technologies (free-space, fibers, wave guides).
-Passive Optical Elements.
-Data Distribution and Partitioning.
-Characterizing Parallel Applications-Cost/Performance Studies.

The review process required submitted papers were reviewed by at least three different reviewers with the final decisions being made by the program chairs based on the recommendations given by the program committee members. The result of this review process is a program consisting of two tutorial speakers, ten invited talks, and twenty regular papers.

To encourage cross-disciplinary education we have included two tutorial sessions, one at the beginning of each day, covering the key issues and latest advancements in "high-performance opto electronic physical layers in systems" by Tony Levi (USC) and "switching techniques, adaptive routing and deadlock handling in interconnection networks" by Jose Duato (U. Valencia). We have also included two panel sessions to provide an opportunity for open discussion. The first panel discussion, organized by Frank A.P. Tooley (McGill) and Julian Bristow(Honeywell), focuses on "The Evaluation of Optical Interconnects Capabilities, Limitations, and Markets." The second panel discussion, organized by D. Scott Wills (GaTech) and Julian Bristow (Honeywell), focuses on "Interconnect Architectural Issues." We also have included a few more invited talks this year so that this conference can be a bit more focused on the themes presented in the tutorial sessions. Each session follows a theme set by the invited talk(s). Regular papers are grouped together within sessions as they related to these themes.

We thank the hard work and dedication of the program committee who are listed in these proceedings. We also thank D. Scott Wills, Frank Tooley, and Julian Bristow for organizing the two panel sessions. We acknowledge the help of Eugen Schenfeld (NEC Research Institute) in keeping things running smoothly, and we are grateful to Sue Bredhoff (NEC Research Institute) for facilitating administrative duties. Finally special thanks go to Joe Goodman (Stanford), the general chair, for guiding us to another successful conference.

Enjoy the conference!

H. Scott Hinton
University of Colorado at Boulder

Timothy M. Pinkston
University of Southern California

Message from Steering Committee Chair

Welcome to the fourth meeting on Massively Parallel Processing Using Optical Interconnections (MPPOI'97). We, the MPPOI Steering Committee, strive to maintain and build this forum as the prime interaction conference, between computer and optical scientists and engineers. The role technology plays in computer and communication industry is a prime one. Optics is an emerging technology. It seems that optics is well based in the telecommunication domain, as well starting to have a role in the shorter distances of 10-100 meters. Computer systems were historically most influenced from technology that was primarily introduced in related products. Such was the case for the punch cards (to program weaving machines for the cloth industry), relays (used first in the telephone switching industry), vacuum tubes (many consumer applications such as radios, telephones, etc.), transistors, integrated circuits, micro-processors, etc. Through history, it seems that the first emerging technology was for consumer applications, and then computer architects and engineers, look at ways to use these consumer technology for computation.

What is the next to happen consumer technology to affect computation? As the scope of this conference suggest, we think it will be a mix of cheap consumer commodity communication that will allow the connections of 100's to 1000's single-chip DRAM+CPU+Communication components, into a scalable computation system.

There are many problems to overcome, and we as scientists and engineers should be happy that there are problems (so we can suggest solutions!). From addressing the issue of packaging of optical network (alignment, cheap consumer production, etc.) to programming paradigms, network architectures and new algorithms, that will cleverly take advantage of the new optical technology yet avoiding any possible pitfalls.

The MPPOI steering committee wishes to welcome all of you to the 4th conference and looks forward to your future participation, suggestions and comments.

I would like to thank all the authors and the participants for contributing to the success of this conference. Special thanks go to J. Goodman, MPPOI'97 General Chair, and to Scott Hinton and Tim Pinkston MPPOI'97 Program Co-Chairs for their many contributions and extensive work towards putting together a very successful program. I would also like to thank all the many people that helped with the conference, including the session chairs and the IEEE Computer Society personnel. Last, but not least, I would like to thank my secretary, Ms. Susan Bredhoff who was so helpful, patient and kind during the process of putting the conference together, and kept everything in order and under check.

Eugen Schenfeld
MPPOI Steering Committee Chair
NEC Research Institute

CONFERENCE COMMITTEES

CONFERENCE CHAIR

Joseph W. Goodman
Stanford University

PROGRAM CO-CHAIRS

H. Scott Hinton
University of Colorado

Timothy M. Pinkston
USC

PUBLICITY and PUBLICATION CHAIR

Eugen Schenfeld
NEC Research Institute

STEERING COMMITTEE

Chair
Eugen Schenfeld
NEC Research Institute

J. Goodman, *Stanford University*
L. Johnsson, *University of Houston*
S. Lee, *University of California at San Diego*
R. Melhem, *University of Pittsburgh*
P. Wang, *George Mason University*

PROGRAM COMMITTEE

J. Chrostowski, *NRC, Canada*
H.-A. Choi, *George Washington University, USA*
J. Duato, *University of Valencia, Spain*
A. Ferreira, *CNRS, LIP - ENS Lyon, France*
K. Ghose, *SUNY at Binghamton, USA*
M. Haney, *George Mason University, USA*
K. Huang, *Hong Kong University, USA*
M. Ishikawa, *University of Tokyo, Japan*
N. Jokerst, *Georgia Tech, USA*
K. Kasahara, *NEC Corp., Japan*
F. Kiamilev, *University of N. Carolina, Charlotte, USA*
R. Kostuk, *University of Arizona, USA*
C. Kuznia, *University of Southern California, USA*
A. Krishnamoorthy, *Lucent Technologies, USA*
A. Lentine, *Lucent Technologies, USA*
K. Li, *Princeton University, USA*
A. Louri, *University of Arizona, USA*
F. McCormick, *UCSD, USA*
J. Midwinter, *University College London, UK*
D. A. B. Miller, *Stanford University, USA*
L. Ni, *Michigan State University, USA*
A. Nowatzyk, *Sun Microsystems, USA*
H. Ozaktas, *Bilkent University, Turkey*
D. Panda, *Ohio State University, USA*
D. Plant, *McGill University, USA*
J. Rowlette, *AMP, USA*
A. Sawchuck, *University of Southern California, USA*
S. Scott, *Cray Research, USA*
B. Shoop, *US Military Academy, USA*
C. Stunkel, *IBM T.J. Watson Research, USA*
T. Szymanski, *McGill University, Canada*
H. Thienpont, *Vrije Universiteit Brussel, Belgium*
F. Tooley, *McGill University, Canada*
A. Walker, *Heriot-Watt University, UK*
D. S. Wills, *Georgia Tech, USA*
H. Wilmsen, *Nortel, Canada*
S. Yalamanchili, *Georgia Tech, USA*

Tutorial Session I

High-performance Optoelectronic Physical Layers in Systems

A. F. J. Levi
University of Southern California
Los Angeles, California 90089-1111
alevi@usc.edu

Abstract

A number of companies have been developing low-cost very high-performance parallel fiber-based optoelectronic interconnects [1-7] as an alternative to copper-based interconnect solutions. Potential applications include the replacement of parallel electrical interfaces such as SCI [8] and HIPPI-6400 [9]. In addition to copper replacement, the remarkable atributes of this new optoelectronic technology hold promise for future novel system optimization and design.

A typical parallel fiber-optic port consists of 8 data lines each signaling at the rate of 1 Gbps or greater and capable of synchronous transmission over several hundred meters of low-skew [10] ribbon fiber. While such high-density high-bandwidth interconnect technology is attractive for insertion into advanced systems, there is a mismatch between the high signaling rates of low-cost optoelectronic components such as Vertical Cavity Surface Emitting Lasers (VCSELs) and that which is achievable with conventional CMOS circuitry. Future system integration of parallel fiber-optic interconnects requires that a cost-effective bridge be established between these two technologies. Hence an important challenge is to leverage low-cost, high integration CMOS technology and directly interface to parallel fiber-optic transceiver modules.

This talk will describe some of our experiences working with Hewlett Packard as part of an on-going DARPA-sponsored program to explore the new technology. The USC effort has been building on an existing experimental Gbps fiber-optic physical layer as well as developing a new multi-Gbps high-speed VLSI CMOS host interface [11] for the HP-POLO parallel fiber-optic interconnect module. A follow-on program will explore an increased level of system integration and the possibility of inserting optoelectronic solutions into practical systems on interconnect length scales of less than 1 m. The possibility of using free-space optical interconnects for very short links will also be discussed.

References

[1] M. Lebby et al. Characteristics of VCSEL Arrays for parallel Optical Interconnects. IEEE 1996 Proceedings 46th Electronics Components and Technology Conference, 279-291, May 1996. IEEE Cat# 96CH35931. ISBN# 0-7803-3286-5

[2] J. D. Crow et al. The Jitney Parallel Optical Interconnect. IEEE 1996 Proceedings 46th Electronics Components and Technology Conference, 292-300, May 1996. IEEE Cat# 96CH35931. ISBN# 0-7803-3286-5.

[3] Y. M. Wong et al. OptoElectronic Technology Consortium (OETC) Parallel Optical Data Link: Components, System Applications, and Simulation Tools. IEEE 1996 Proceedings 46th Electronics Components and Technology Conference, 269-278, May 1996. IEEE Cat# 96CH35931. ISBN# 0-7803-3286-5.

[4] S. Swirhun et al. The P-VixeLink Multichannel Optical Interconnect. IEEE 1996 Proceedings 46th Electronics Components and Technology Conference, 292-300, May 1996. IEEE Cat# 96CH35931. ISBN# 0-7803-3286-5

[5] Y. S. Lui et al. Polymer Optical Interconnect Technology (POINT) - Optoeletronic Packaging and Interconnect for Board and Backplane Applications. IEEE 1996 Proceedings 46th Electronics Components and Technology Conference, 308-315, May 1996. IEEE Cat# 96CH35931. ISBN# 0-7803-3286-5.

[6] T. Nagahori et al. 1-Gbyte/sec Array Transmitter and Receiver Modules for Low-Cost Optical Fiber Interconnection. IEEE 1996 Proceedings 46th Electronics Components and Technology Conference, 255-258, May 1996. IEEE Cat# 96CH35931. ISBN# 0-7803-3286-5.

[7] K. Hahn et al. Gigabyte/s Data Communications with POLO Parallel Optical Link. IEEE 1996 Proceedings 46th Electronics Components and Technology Conference, 301-307, May 1996. IEEE Cat# 96CH35931. ISBN# 0-7803-3286-5.

[8] 'IEEE Standard for Scalable Coherent Interface (SCI)', The Institute of Electrical and Electronics Engineers, Inc., New York, IEEE Std 1596-1992, 1992.

[9] 'High-Performance Parallel Interface - 6400 Mbit/s Physical Layer (HIPPI-6400-PH)', Technical Committee of Accredited Standards, X3T11, April 1997.

[10] A. P. Kanjamala and A. F. J. Levi. Sub-picosecond skew in multimode fiber ribbon for synchronous data transmission. Electronics Letters 31(16): 1376-1377, August 1995.

[11] B. Sano, B. Madhavan, and A. F. J. Levi. 8 Gbps CMOS interface for parallel fiber-optic links. Electronics Letters 32(24): 2262-2263, November 1996.

SESSION I

Guided-Wave Optical Interconnects

Chair

J. Rowlette
AMP

Parallel Optical Interconnection for Massively Parallel Processor RWC-1

Takashi Yoshikawa
Optoelectronics-NEC laboratory, Real World Computing Partnership(RWC)
34 Miyukigaoka Tsukuba, Ibaraki, 305, Japan
t_yoshi@obl.cl.nec.co.jp

Hiroshi Matsuoka, Takashi Yokota, and Junich Shimada
Tsukuba Research Laboratory, Real World Computing (RWC)
Mitsui-building 16F, Takezono 1-6-1, Tsukuba, Ibaraki, 305, Japan
matsuoka@trc.rwcp.or.jp

Abstract

A GByte/sec-class optical interconnection subsystem for a parallel computer was developed, and it operated stably in the testbed system of a parallel computer, Real World Computer-1 (RWC-1). Although it consisted of MMF parallel links, data was transmitted over 1 km because of deskew operation of +/- 15 ns. Random packets were transmitted without error over 17.5 hours, corresponding to a BER of 10^{-14}.

1. Introduction

Optical interconnections are in high demand for connecting nodes of parallel computers. For example, our machine, Real World Computer (RWC-1) has 1,024 nodes connected by hierarchical Multidimensional Directed Cycles Ensemble (hMDCE) network (Fig. 1)[1]. It demands high-capacity and rather long interconnections which needs

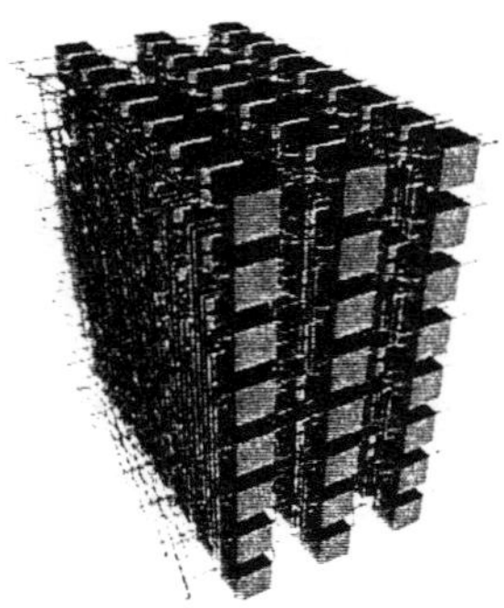

Figure 1: hierarchical Multidimensional Directed Cycles Ensemble (hMDCE) network

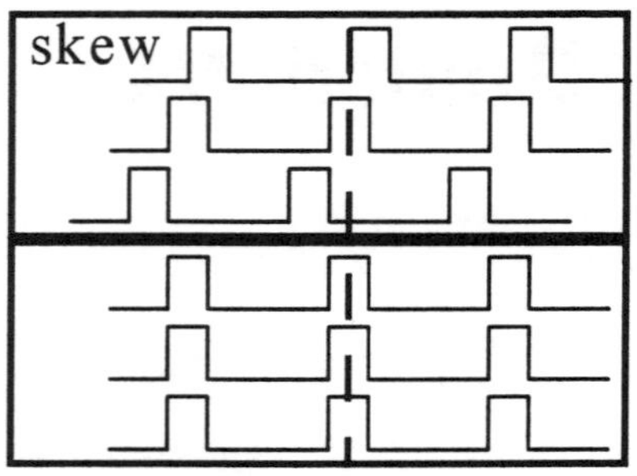

Fig. 1 Degradation of parallel data by skew.

elaborate works for assembling by electronic interconnections. For optical interconnection in parallel computers, the following are requested, in general. (i) GByte/sec class throughput. From a cost consideration, Multi Mode Fiber (MMF) parallel optical links are suitable for achieving this throughput. (ii) A link length of 1 km [1]. This enables some of the node of Parallel computers to be placed over several floors. To achieve a 1-km link by an MMF parallel link, a deskew of about 10 ns is necessary, provided the fiber skew is 10 ps/m.(Fig. 2) (iii) Reconfigurable. For parallel computers, sometimes the node link is reconfigured. At such times clock distribution is mostly affected. To avoid this, the clock is transmitted by the clock recovery function without maintaining a specially prepared clock transmission line. (Fig. 2) (iv) Small and light weight connectors and cables. A baud rate of 1 Gbit/s with 10:1 mux greatly reduces the weight and volume of connectors/cables. A 144-core electrical connector/cable can be replaced by an optical 8MPO connector/cable.

0-8186-7974-3/97 $10.00 © 1997 IEEE

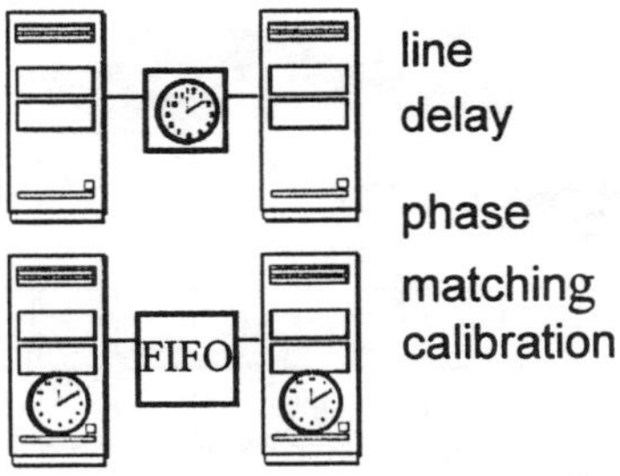

Fig. 2 Clock delivery limits reconfigurability.

2. Interconnection subsystem

The interconnection configuration is shown in Fig. 4. Each transmitting and receiving function was assembled on a 15 cm x 15 cm small card (Fig. 5) Here, 48 x 100 Mbit/s parallel data is divided into 6 ch x 8 bits. After 8B10B coding, coded 6 x 10 bits data were 60:6 multiplexed and transmitted through GI/62.5 MMF ribbon by 6 x 1 Gbit/s array optical modules [2](Fig. 6). The output wave form of the receiver module (ECL) and BER measurement of the optical array module are shown in Fig. 7. Skew was compensated using inserted control character of Fibre Channel, K28.5- characters. When K28.5- is detected, it is compared with the timing of that of the master channel and deskew operation is performed using a First-In-First-Out (FIFO) memory (Fig. 8). The cable length of channel A (slave channel) is intentionally set two-meters longer than that of channel B (master channel) creating 10-ns skew.

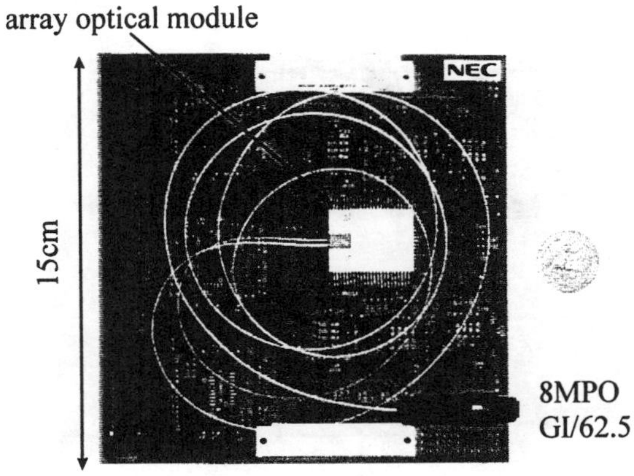

Figure 5: Gbyte/s Transmitting card.

Figure 6: 8 x 1 Gbyte/s array optical module.

This skew is satisfactorily compensated by a newly developed IC. Provided the skew is 10 ps/m for the MMF

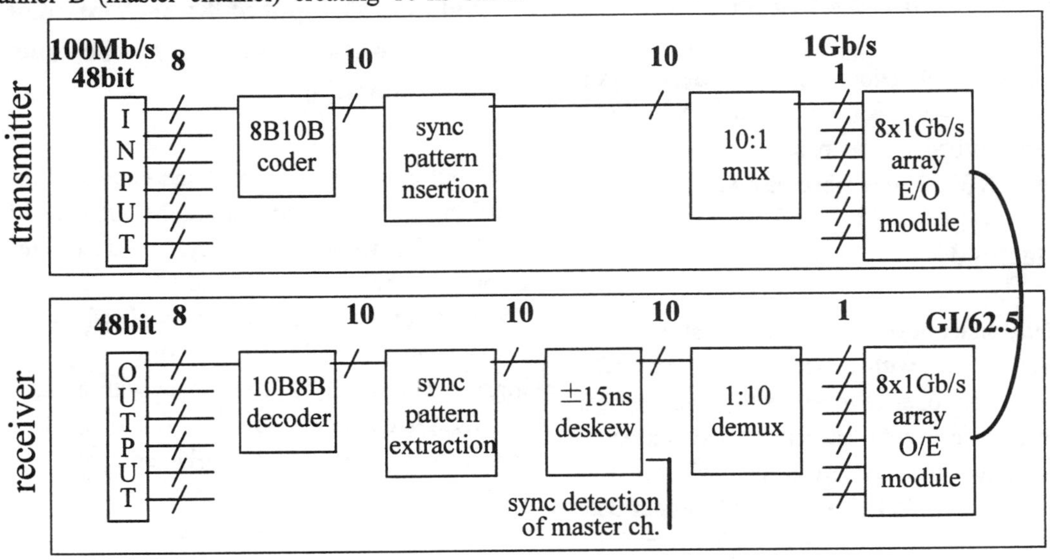

Figure 4 Functional block of the optical interconnection subsystem.

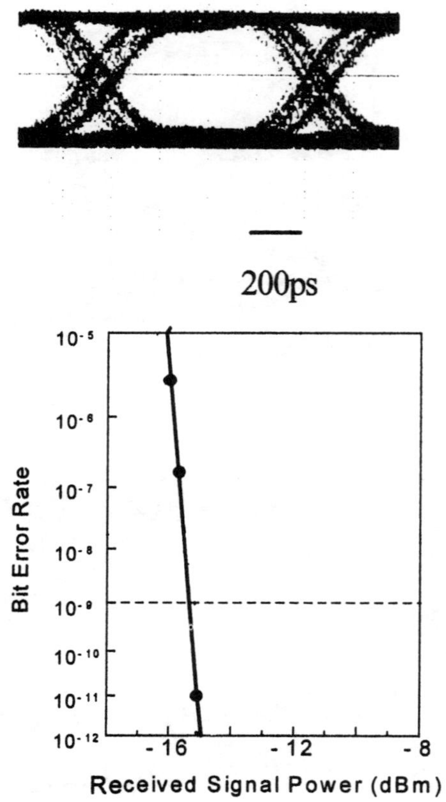

Figure 7: Receiver output (ECL) and BER of the array optical module with all channel operating. Sensitivity is -15.3 dBm at the BER of 10^{-9}.

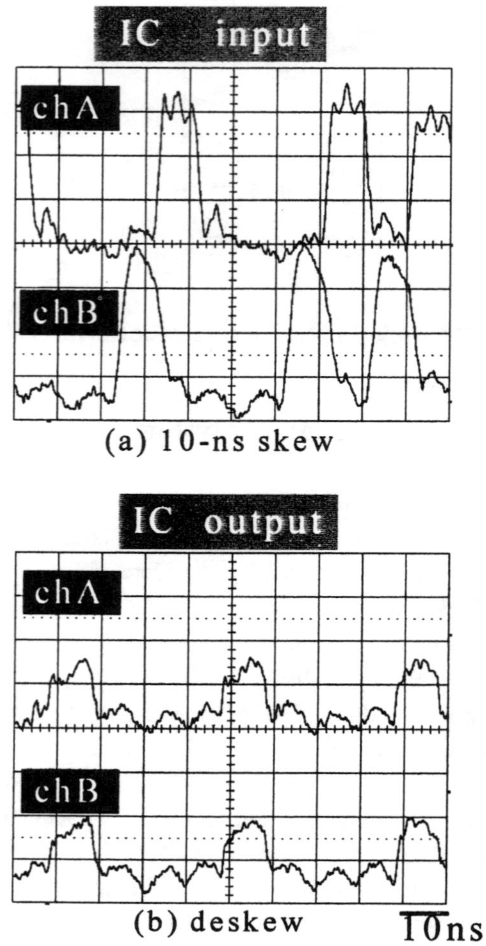

Figure 8: Deskew operation of the newly developed IC. Input of the ch.A intentionally had 10-ns skew(a). The skew was successfully compensated(b).

ribbon, this deskew function enables over 1-km transmission, which was confirmed in the node-networking-system testbed of the parallel computer Real World Computer-1 (RWC-1) described below.

3. RWC-1 testbed

RWC-1 is currently under development. It consists of 1,024 Processor Elements (PEs) with a newly proposed RICA architecture, which can operate even with asymmetrical node connection distances with intensified networking of PE nodes[3]. For now, only testbed is available for data link experiments. From a Work Station (WS), output data was written in the output buffer of the IC called Switching Unit (SU), which controls the communication between PEs including data transmission. After data transmission, the input buffer of the SU is read and expressed on the control panel on the WS. By comparing the output and input buffer of the SU, we can see whether data transmission is completed or not (Figures 9 and 10).

The data format of RWC-1 is 24-bit width data and 4-bit width control signals, such as strobes. First, burst mode transmission of 72-bit length data with a packet length of 12-bits was examined. In spite of using MMF ribbon, data transmission was satisfactorily completed over 1 km because of deskew function. Next, the continuous transmission mode was evaluated. Random packets generated by the SU was continuously transmitted. In this mode, we could not examine the contents of the SU buffers without stopping the data transmission. Therefore, the CRC

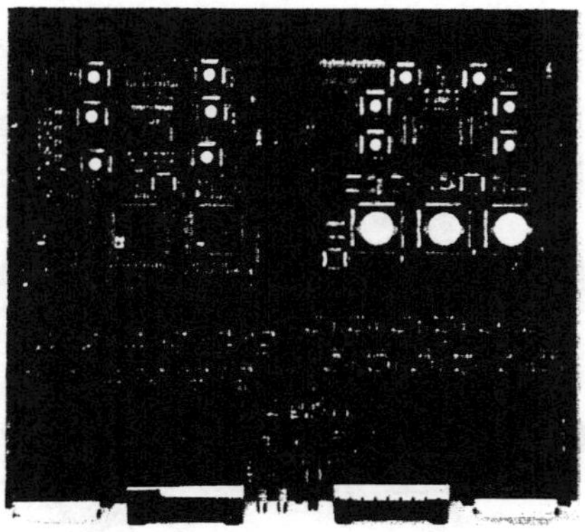

Figure 8: Optical Interconnection subsystem. It has transmitting card and receiver card and electric connectors and buffers to use testbed system designed for electric interconection.

bit was monitored. Once it goes high (error is detected), it never falls until a reset signal is sent to the SU. The monitoring window is shown in Fig. 10. A packet receiving signal was used for the trigger. It operated 17.5 hours without error, corresponding to a BER of less than 10^{-14}. Although it was not examined because of the prohibition of overnight operation, this subsystem is designed for a BER of 10^{-22} in the power-loss budget.

The size of this subsystem is for now, six-inches by six-inches in each transmitting and receiving card. It can be attached to a processor board directly. With more size reduction, the interconnection subsystem will be able to be mounted directly on the PE board. Also electrical 144 pin connector and cables were replaced by only a fiber ribbon with MPO connector. (Fig. 11).

Although many array modules have been developed, there are few examples of operating them in a system [4]. This is a good example of application of an array module at the point that it showed very stable operation in a parallel computing testbed system. It can be applied to the Hippi-6400 or Fibre Channel with a little modification.

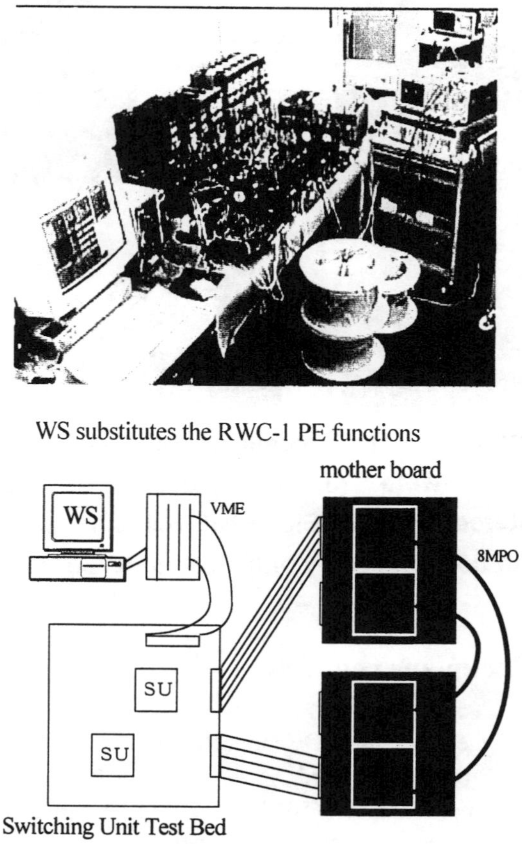

Figure 9: A Photograph and configuration of the RWC-1 PE network testbed. A workstation sent and received the RWC-1 format data using router IC named switching unit (SU). The output and input memory were examined after sending buurst data. 1 Km

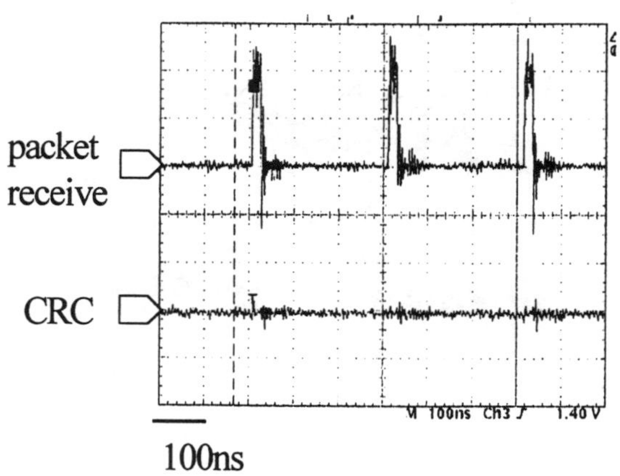

Figure 10: Parallel optical interconnecting subsystem was stably operated for 17. 5 hours without error.

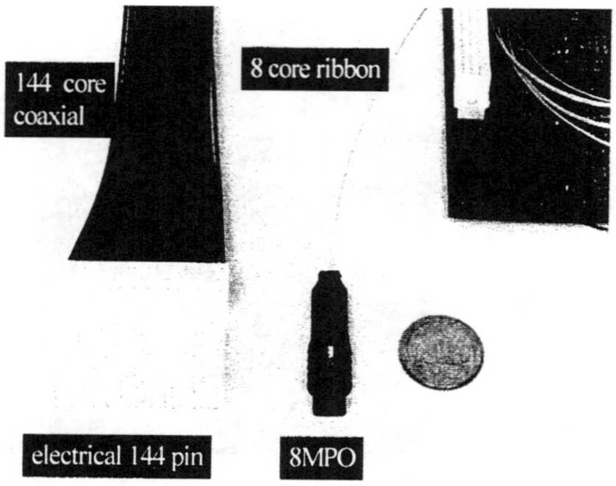

Figure 11: The volume of the connector and cable were greatly reduced by optical interconnection. Electrical 144 pin connector can be replaced by only one 8MPO connector.

4. Backplane connector

Eight piece of 8MPO connector are assembled on a RWC-1 processor board. To attach the PE board to the back plane of the RWC-1 flame, all MPO connector must

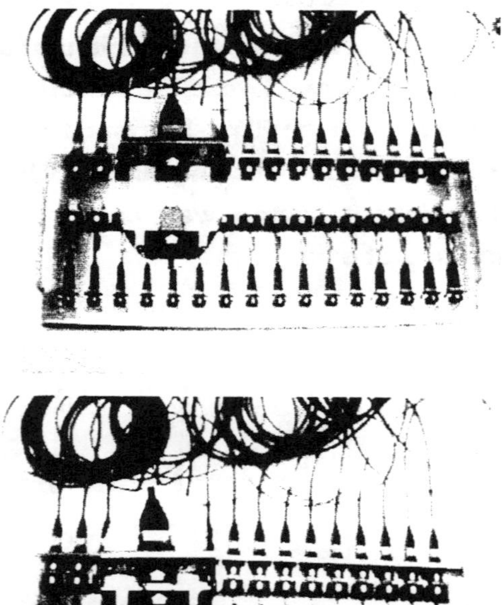

Figure 12: Sixteen piece of MPO connector were inserted into backplane at a time. Before (upper photo) and after (lower photo) insertion.

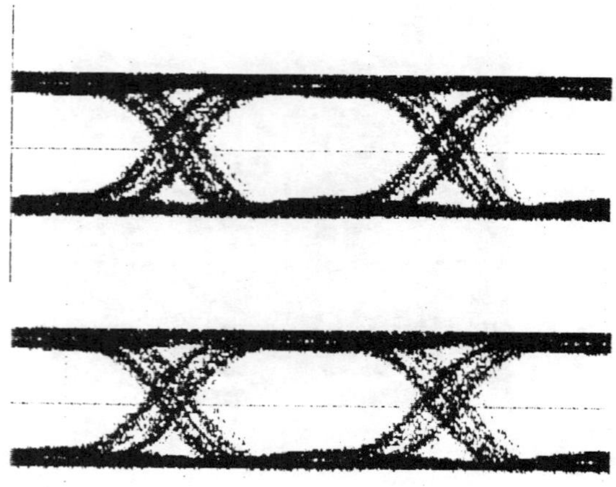

Figure 13: Receiver output of the 1Gbps array optical module through backplane connector. No degradation was observed for 16 piece connection (lower eye pattern) comparing with one piece connection(upper eye pattern).

be connected at a time. The loss and the degradation of the signal waveform were measured experimentally. An test board with sixteen piece of push-pull type MPO connector were connected to the backplane connectors (Fig. 12) The average loss was only 0.5 dB because of large core of the GI-50 MMF. Receiver waveform was compared with that of only one connector (Fig. 13). No degradation was obsereved.

5. Schedule

RWC-1 is now under development. Fundamental operation was realized by electrically connected test system (Fig. 14). The total computing system will be realized first by electrically connected machine in this year with improved PE and SU Ics(Fig. 15). Then optically connected version of RWC-1 will be completed with CS of the PE IC.

Conclusion

A GBytes/sec class optical interconnection subsystem for parallel computers has been developed. It consists of 6 X 1Gbit/sec array optical transceiver modules. It has +/- 15 ns-deskew to sustain parallel data over 1 km transmission through Multi Mode Fiber ribbon. Data was transmitted over 1 km in the system of a parallel computer, the Real

Figure 14: Test system of the RWC-1. All interconnection are electrical.

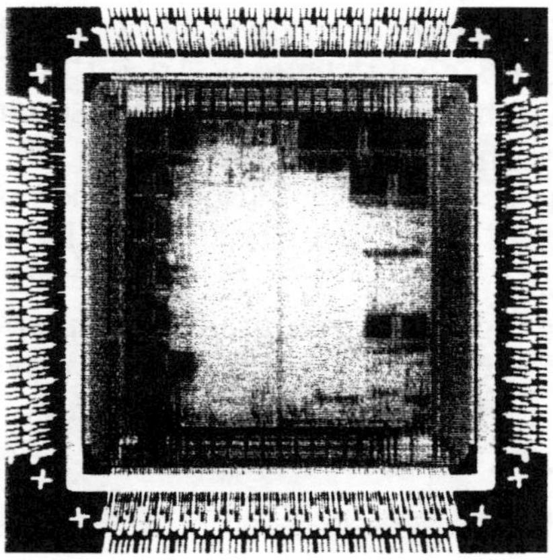

Figure 15: Route IC named SU. This SU has differential ECL interface to send data for 10 m by electrical cable. For optically connected version, SU has made of 0.35μm rule CMOS and has LVTTL interface.

World Computer (RWC-1), using its node-network testbed. It operated over 17.5 hours without error, corresponding to a BER of less than 10^{-14}.

Acknowledgments:

The Authors would liked to thank K. Kobayashi and J. Namiki, M. Shikada, K. Kasahara, and Y. Sugimoto for their continuous encouragement, and S. Araki, K. Miyoshi, Y. Suemura, T. Nagahori, and T. Shimizu for their helpful discussions.

References

[1]Yokota , T., Matsuoka, H., Okamoto, K., Hirono, H., Hori, A., and Sakai, S., 'A Proto-type Router for the Massively Parallel Computer RWC-1, Proc. ICCD'95, pp. 279-284, 1995

[2]Chesson, G., 'HIPPI-6400 Overview', Extended Abstract on HOT Interconnects IV symposium, Stanford CA, pp.121-128, 1996

[3]Nagahori, T., Miyoshi, K., Hatakeyama, I., Arabia, S., Yoneda, I., Kimura, N., Fukushima, K., and Itoh, M., '1-Gbyte/s Array Transmitter and Receiver Modules for Low-cost Optical Fiber Interconnection', 46th Electronic Components and Technology Conference (ECTC), Florida, 28-31 May 1996.

[4]Sakai, S., Okamoto, S., Matsuoka, H., Hirono, H., Kodama, Y., and Sato, M., 'Super-Threading: Architectural and Software Mechanisms for Optimizing Parallel Computation', Proc. ICS93, pp.251-260, 1993.

[5]Engebretsen, D. R., Kuchta, D. M., Booth, R. C., Crow, J. D., and Nation, W. G., 'Parallel Fiber-Optic SCI Links' IEEE Micro, 1996, pp. 20-26

Si CMOS Process Compatible Guided-wave Multi-GBit/sec Optical Clock Signal Distribution System for Cray T-90 Supercomputer

R. T. Chen[1], L. Wu[1], F. Li[1], S. Tang[2], M. Dubinovsky[1], J. Qi[1], C. L. Schow[1], and J. C. Campbell[1], R. Wickman[3], B. Picor[3], M. Hibbs-Brenner[4], J. Bristow[4], Y. S. Liu[5], S. Rattan[6] and C. Noddings[6]

[1]Microelectronics Research Center
JJP Research Campus
University of Texas, Austin
Austin, TX 78758
raychen@uts.cc.utexas.edu

[2]Radiant Research
Braker Lane Suite 420
Austin, TX 78759

[3]Cray Research
1050 Lowater Road
Chippewa, WI 54729

[4]Honeywell Technology Center
3660 Technology Drive
Minneapolis MN 55418

[5]GE Research and Development Center
1 River Rd. Schenectady, NY 12345

[6]MCC
Braker Lane Suite 420
Austin, TX 78759

Abstract

We report the formation of polyimide-based H-tree waveguides for a multi-GBit/sec optical clock signal distribution in a Si CMOS process compatible environment. Such a clock distribution system is to replace the existing electronic counterpart associated with high-speed supercomputers such as Cray T-90 machine. A waveguide propagation loss of 0.21 dB/cm at 850 nm was experimentally confirmed for the 1-to-48 waveguide fanout device. 1-to-2 splitting loss and bending loss were measured to be 0.25 dB and higher. The planarization requirement of the optical interconnection layer among many electrical interconnection layers makes the employment of tilted grating a choice of desire. Theoretical calculation predicts the 1-to-1 free-space to waveguide coupling with an efficiency as high as 95%. Currently, a coupling efficiency of 35% was experimentally confirmed due to the limited index difference between guiding and cladding layers. Further experiments aimed at structuring a larger guiding/cladding layer index differences are under investigation. To effectively couple an optical signal into the waveguide through the titled grating coupler, the accuracy of the wavelength employed is pivotal. This makes the usage of the vertical cavity surface-emitting lasers (VCSELs) and VCSEL arrays the best choice when compared with edge-emitting lasers. Modulation bandwidth as high as 6 GHz was demonstrated at 850 nm. Such a wavelength is compatible with Si-based photodetectors. Temperature dependence of the threshold current up to 155 °C was measured which will determine the power dissipation issue of the optoelectronic packaging. Finally, the first fully monolithic Si-MOSFET integrated receiver was made as the optical clock signal detector. To further enhance the bandwidth of such a detector, a resonant cavity structure with Si/SiO_2 as the bottom mirror was employed. The measured demodulation bandwidth is over 10 GHz. A fully integrated guided-wave optical clock signal distribution system having planarized grating couplers, H-tree Si-CMOS process compatible waveguides, VCSELs and Si-based photoreceivers will be demonstrated in the near future.

1.0 Introduction

The speed and complexity of integrated circuits are increased rapidly as integrated circuit technology advances from very large scale integrated (VLSI) circuits to ultra large scale integrated (ULSI) circuits. As the number of components per chip, the number of chips per board, the modulation speed and the degree of integration continue to increase, electrical interconnects are facing their fundamental bottle-necks, such as speed, packaging, fanout, and power dissipation. Multichip module (MCM) technology is employed to provide higher clock speeds and circuit densities[1,2]. However, the state-of-the-art technologies based on electrical interconnects fail to provide the required multi-

0-8186-7974-3/97 $10.00 © 1997 IEEE

GBit/sec clock speed and communication distance in intra-MCM and inter-MCM hierarchies.

For a multiprocessor computer system, such as a Cray T-90 supercomputer, it is extremely difficult to obtain high-speed (>500 MHz) synchronous clock distribution using electrical interconnections due to large fanouts (48x2) and long interconnection lengths (>15 cm)[3-7]. A fanout chip is required to provide the massive electrical fanout. The synchronous global clock signal distribution is highly desirable to simplify the architecture and enable a higher speed performance. High-speed, large-area massive fanout optoelectronic interconnects may overcome many of the problems associated with electrical interconnects in this interconnection scenario[3-11]. An array of novel optical interconnect architecture has been proposed and then demonstrated by earlier researchers[11-14], which may partially satisfy the above requirements for a massive clock signal distribution in intra-MCM and inter-MCM hierarchies.

In this paper, we report the development of a planarized guided-wave optoelectronic interconnect network for optical clock signal distribution on a board-level multi-processor system, as shown in Fig. 1(a). For comparison, the electrical interconnect network currently employed by Cray Research is shown in Fig. 1(b) which shows the existing 500 MHz 1-to-48 clock signal distribution (one side) realized in one of the 52 vertical integration layers within the Cray-T-90 supercomputer board. To further upgrade the clock speed, an appropriate optical interconnect scheme has to be incorporated. In this paper, an integrated board-level optoelectronic interconnection layer is constructed by using polyimide-based optical channel waveguides in conjunction with tilted waveguide gratings. This guided-wave optoelectronic interconnect network is to be inserted into the Cray supercomputer boards to become an additional optical interconnection layer among many other electrical interconnection layers. As a result, the future

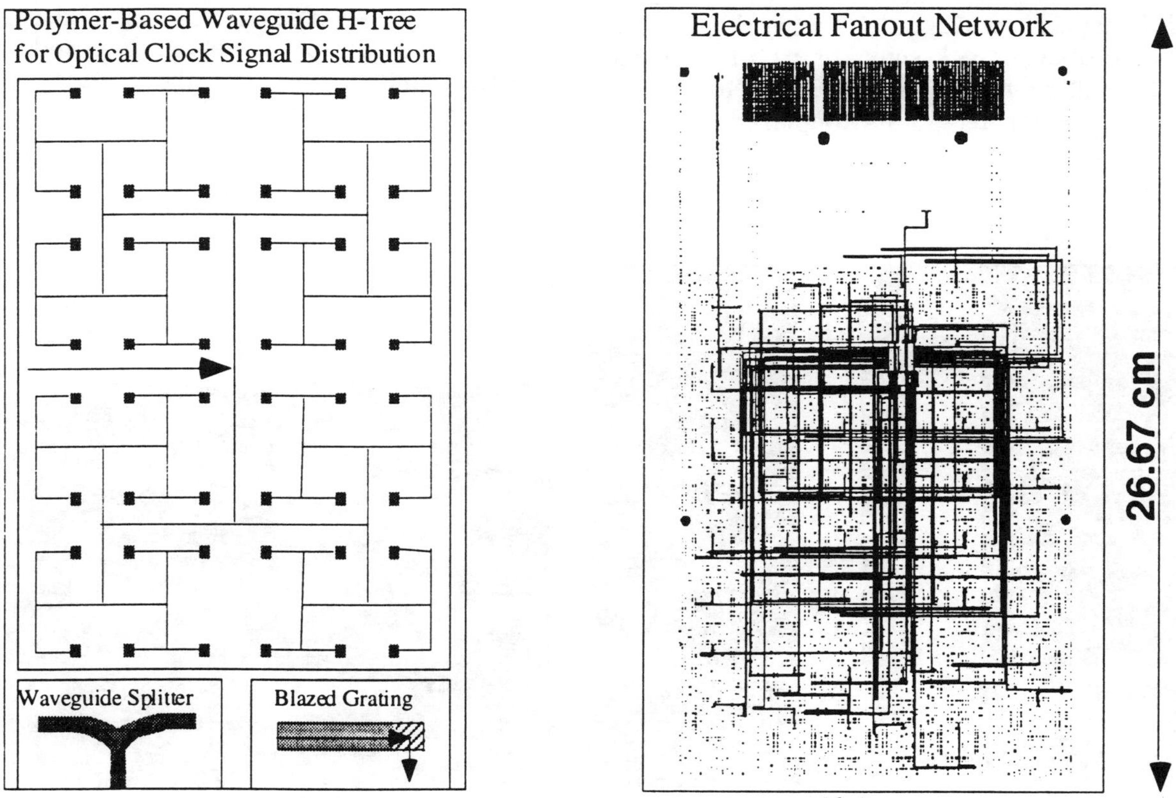

(a) (b)

Fig. 1 Schematic diagrams of massive clock signal distribution networks using (a) an optical waveguide H-tree and (b) an electrical clock signal transmission line network that forms one of the 52 layers of Cray T-90 Supercomputer board. The holes indicate the feed-through marks of the on-board three-dimensional interconnections.

supercomputer system may have a clock speed more than ten times higher than current systems.

To further delineate the existing Cray T-90 system, the two sides of the Cray T-90 supercomputer board consisting of 52 vertical electrical interconnection layers with the board size of 14.48 x 26.67 cm^2 is shown in Figure 2. Our approach is to construct an additional optoelectronic interconnection layer (OIL) for the high-speed optical clock signal distribution using polymer-based guided-wave devices. The selection of guided-wave approach is mainly based on the system alignment and reliability concerns[15]. During the course of research, Si CMOS process compatibility and planarization of the OIL are the two major technical concerns. As shown in Fig. 1(a), a polymer-based waveguide H-tree system is employed to replace the existing electrical fanout interconnect network shown in Fig. 1(b). The optical clock signal delivered by an optic fiber will be coupled into the OIL using an input surface-normal tilted grating coupler, and distributed through out the board by the polymer-based channel waveguide network. The distributed optical clock signal at each fanout end will be coupled into a Si photodetector by an output surface-normal grating coupler.

The building blocks required to necessitate such an optical H-tree system include high performance low-loss polymer-based channel waveguides, waveguide gratings, 1-to-2 3 dB waveguide splitters and 90° waveguide bends. These components allow the formation of a waveguide H-tree for the required optical clock signal distribution, where all the optical paths have the same length to minimize the clock skew problem. The employment of optical channel waveguides and surface-normal waveguide gratings provides a compact, mechanically reliable system. Due to the nature of massive fanouts (48x2) over a large area, the waveguide propagation loss must be minimized while the waveguide grating coupling efficiency has to be maximized. These two factors are very important to ensure enough optical power at the end of photodetectors for high-speed operation. We have employed the highly purified version of the commercially available polyimides in order to fabricate low-loss polymeric waveguides. To improve the waveguide grating coupling efficiency, tilted waveguide gratings are employed to provide the required 1-to-1 surface-normal coupling. Note that a simple 45° waveguide end mirror is not suitable in this case because of the requirement of planarization imposed on the vertical integration of the other electrical interconnection layers[16,17].

(a) (b)

Fig. 2 (a)Photograph of a Cray T-90 multi-processor supercomputer board and (b). 52 on-board electrical interconnection layers affiliated with the board.

While fiber optics technology has successfully implemented among cabinets as replacements for coaxial cable point-to-point link, its application inside a cabinet on the MCM system is severely limited due to the bulkiness of fibers, fiber connectors, and significant labor and cost involved in parallelism of the interconnects. Polymer optical waveguide technology, on the other hand, is particularly suitable for wafer-scale MCM interconnect applications for its large area waveguide formation and potential low costs. It can be viewed as an optical equivalent of electrical printed wiring board technology in which the fabrication cost is independent of the interconnect functionality and complexity. In order to take the advantages of the polymer waveguides, we must be capable of implementing optoelectronic devices such as laser diodes, and photodetectors in the same MCM package. If optical waveguides can be fabricated, integrated, and packaged into the MCM with existing electronic MCM fabrication technologies, the insertion of optical interconnects becomes an acceptable approach to upgrade the microelectronics-based high performance computers.

In this paper, several building blocks needed to realize the high speed optical clock signal distribution are presented. In section 2.0, the formation of polyimide-based tilted grating couplers is introduced. Planarization and high coupling efficiency are two primary concerns. Both theoretical and experimental results to achieve these goals are provided. Polyimide-based multimode channel waveguide fabrication is delineated in section 3.0 where the H-tree waveguide structure having a 1-to-48 fanout is portrayed. Both the waveguides and the tilted gratings are polyimide-based to provide the high temperature processing requirement associated with Si CMOS fabrication. The modulation source that converts electrical signals to optical signals is described in section 4.0 where packaged vertical cavity surface emitting lasers (VCSELs) and VCSEL arrays with a modulation bandwidth of 6 GBit/sec is presented. The power budget consideration is also investigated with appropriate light source allocations to meet the bit error rate (BER) requirement. The demodulation scheme aimed at providing a high-speed Si CMOS process compatible photoreceiver is presented in section 5.0. We have developed the first fully monolithic Si-MOSFET integrated receiver. To upgrade the demodulation bandwidth while reducing the absorption thicknesses, a resonant cavity structure is built. A 3-dB bandwidth of 10 GHz is experimentally confirmed. All these building blocks including the planarized grating couplers, polyimide waveguides, high speed VCSELs and Si-based photo-receivers will be integrated into an optical clock signal distribution system to upgrade the system clock speed of the existing high performance computers such as the Cray T-90 supercomputer. Finally, the concluding remarks are given in section 6.0 where future research plans and projected results are summarized. The success of future system integration relies not only on the maturity of all the device technologies but also on the compatibility of these technologies to the existing Si CMOS fabrication processes.

2.0 Formation of Planarized Tilted Grating

To efficiently couple optical signals from free-space to a polymer waveguide, the planarized grating coupler is the most crucial element that needs to be thoroughly investigated first. There are a large number of publications in grating design[18-22]. However, the surface-normal 1-to-1 coupling scenario in optical waveguides has not been carefully investigated so far. We are interested in a tilted grating profile in a planar structure within a thin waveguide layer upon which other microlithographically defined electrical interconnection layers can be built. Such a configuration requires the insertion of optical interconnect layer to be planarized. The tilted grating profile greatly enhances the coupling efficiency in the desired direction. The gratings under investigation are fabricated by the well-established microfabrication processes. They are mass-producible with excellent accuracy and reproducibility.

The phenomenon of grating-coupled radiation is widely used in guided-wave optical interconnects. Very often coupling in a specific direction is required. To achieve this unidirectional coupling the tilted grating profile is selected as a high-efficiency coupler. A very important aspect of manufacturing of such a coupler is the tolerance interval of the profile parameters, such as the tooth height, the width and the tilted angle.

Consider the grating structure shown in Fig. 3 where the guided-wave optical interconnection layer (layer 4) is sandwiched among other six electrical interconnection layers. For a transverse electric TE guided mode, the E-field is along the z-direction and satisfies:

$$\frac{\partial^2 E_z}{\partial x^2}+\frac{\partial^2 E_z}{\partial y^2}+k^2(x,y)E_z=0 \qquad (1)$$

where a time dependence $\exp(-i\omega t)$ has been omitted, $k(x,y)$ is the wave vector with $k(x,y)=k_0 n(x,y)$, $k_0 = 2\pi/\lambda$, λ is the free space wavelength and $n(x,y)$ is the refractive index.

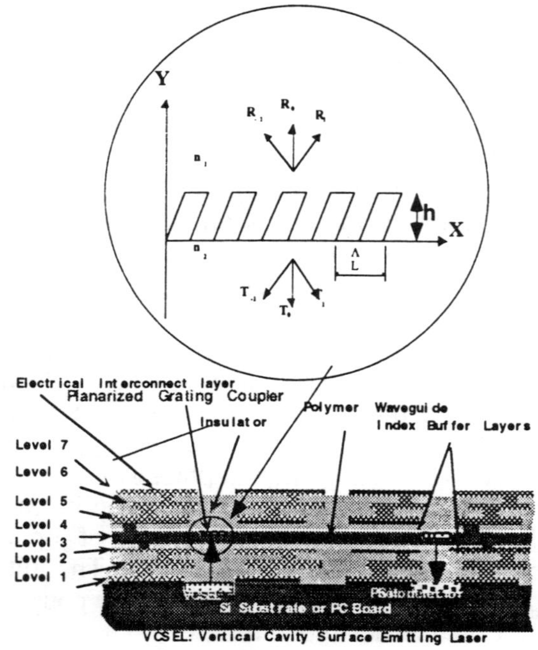

Fig. 3 The grating structure under consideration. The corresponding 3-D integration structure is also shown.

We can express field E_z as an Floquet's infinite summation of partial waves:

$$E_z(x,y)=\sum_{m=-\infty}^{\infty} E_m(y)\exp(i\alpha_m x) \qquad (2)$$

where: $\alpha_m = \alpha_0 + m\frac{2\pi}{\Lambda}$ and Λ is the grating period, α_0 is a phase constant.

Outside the groove region, in the area $y>h$, using Rayleigh expansion we can write:

$$E_{m1}(y)=\delta_m \exp(i\beta_1 y)+R_m\exp(i\beta_{m1}y) \qquad (3)$$

where: $\beta_{m1}=\sqrt{k_1^2-\alpha_{m1}^2}$, $\delta_m=1$ when m=0 and δ_m=0, otherwise.

Below the groove region, in the area $y>0$, the electric field can be written for each corresponding m as :

$$E_{m3}(y)=T_m\exp(-i\beta_{m2}y) \qquad (4)$$

where:

$$\beta_{m2}=\sqrt{k_2^2-\alpha_{m2}^2}$$

Inside the groove region $0<y<h$, $k^2(x,y)$ is periodic in the x direction and can be represented by a Fourier series of

$$k^2(x,y)=\sum_{m=-\infty}^{\infty} C_m(y)\exp(2\pi imx/\Lambda) \qquad (5)$$

Upon substituting (2) and (5) into equation (1) and collecting all terms with the same x-dependence, we can obtain equation at the region $0<y<h$:

$$\frac{\partial^2 E_{m2}(y)}{\partial y^2}-\alpha_m^2 E_{m2}(y)+\sum_q C_{m-q}(y)E_{q2}(y)=0 \qquad (6)$$

By solving Eq.(6) for each of q under the boundary conditions of E_z and $\partial E_z/\partial y$ being continuous at y=h and y=0 (Figure 3), we are able to derive all the diffracted lights under consideration. The details of deriving the solutions for Eq.(6) will be presented at a separate publication. In principle, the diffraction grating period is selected to make the angle of the first diffraction order α_1 equal to the bouncing angle of the waveguide fundamental mode and cut off all other higher diffraction orders. The diffraction grating has a period equals to 0.9 of the wavelength value. The simulation provided is based on a cladding index of 1.45 and a guiding layer index of 1.56. Tooth width is selected to be one-half of the grating period. Fig. 4 is a plot of coupling efficiencies of different diffraction orders versus tooth height (in μm) in the case of a rectangular grating profile. As we can see that the coupling efficiency in this case can be as high as 95% at an etching depth of 1.1 μm.

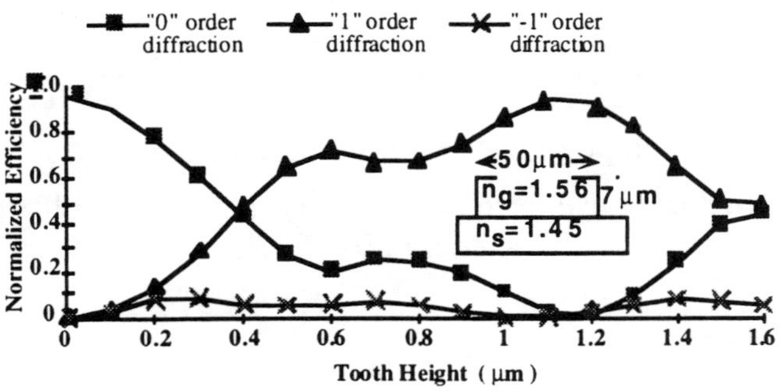

Fig. 4. Plot of coupling efficiency (represented by "▲") versus tooth height for a tilted grating.

We have employed an accurate analytical solution technique to calculate radiation from tilted diffraction grating. The result demonstrates optimum gratings parameter values to maximize coupling in one diffraction order. Based on the result shown in Figure 4, a diffraction efficiency as high as 95% into the waveguide fundamental mode is achievable with a tooth depth of 1.1 μm. Figure 4 is the simulation result based on a multimode channel waveguide having waveguide parameters shown in the inset of Figure 4.

It is clear to us that to provide effective free-space to waveguide and waveguide to free-space conversions, the microstructure of the surface-normal grating coupler shall be tilted to provide the needed phase-matching condition at one waveguide propagating direction rather than two. The tilted angle of the grating corrugation determines the vertical component of the grating **K** vector to be built to provide the required phase-matching condition. In the following, we report the progress in fabrication of the tilted waveguide grating.

The polyimide waveguide can be fabricated on different substrates such as PC board, Si, glass and others by spin-coating. An A600 primer layer was spin-coated first on the substrate with a spin speed of 5000 rpm, and prebaked at 90 ^{0}C for 60 seconds. The Amoco polyimide 9120D was then spin-coated with a speed of 2000 rpm. A final curing at 260 ^{0}C in nitrogen atmosphere was carried out for more than three hours. Typical thickness of the waveguide was 7 μm. The planar waveguide has also been successfully fabricated on Si substrate by inserting a high index polyimide layer (n=1.56 - 1.76) between the 9020D cladding layers.

In order to fabricate the grating coupler by reactive-ion-etching (RIE), a thin aluminum metal mask was deposited on top of the polyimide-based planar guide. The schematic diagram for the fabrication process is shown in Fig.5. First, a 500-Angstrom aluminum layer was coated on top of the waveguide by electron beam evaporation, followed by a layer of 5206E photoresist with a spin speed of 3000 rpm. The grating patterns on photoresist were recorded by interfering two beams at λ=442 nm (a He-Cd laser line). To record a grating with a period of Λ, the cross angle θ of the two interference beams is determined through the formula of $\sin(\theta/2) = \left(\lambda/\Lambda\right)$. After the sample had been developed, a postbake at 120^{0}C for 30 minutes was followed. To transfer the photoresist grating patterns to aluminum, we used RIE to remove the aluminum in the window region of the photoresist pattern. The gases used were $BCl_3/SiCl_4$ with a pressure of 20 millitorr. However, it was found that there were still some photoresist residuals in the grating groove which could block the aluminum RIE process. In order to clean these residuals, an additional step of RIE etching using oxygen was applied before removing the Al layer. To form the tilted grating pattern on the polyimide waveguide, we used a RIE process with a low oxygen pressure of 10 millitorr to transfer the grating pattern on aluminum layer to the polyimide layer. In order to get the tilted profile, a Faraday cage was used[23]. The final step was to remove the aluminum mask by another step of RIE process. Microstructures of the tilted grating having a periodicity varying from 0.5 μm to 3 μm have been fabricated. Fig. 6 shows one of many gratings from a scanning electron microscope (SEM) picture.

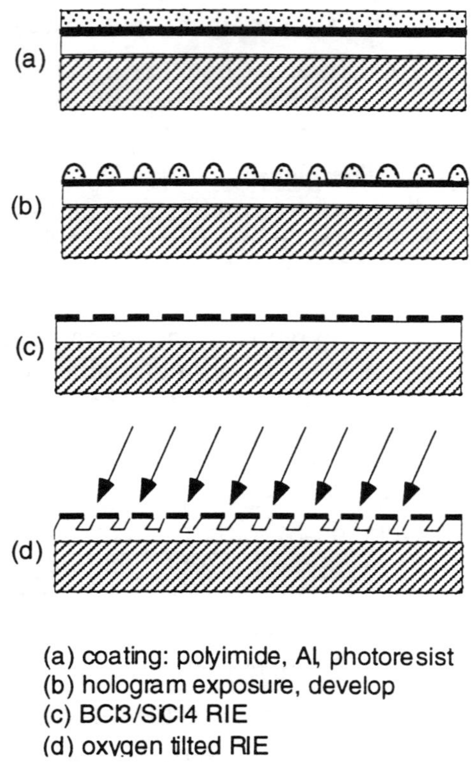

Fig. 5 The schematic diagram for the fabrication of tilted grating on polyimide waveguide.

Fig. 6 SEM picture of a tilted grating which has a tilted angle of 32°. Grating periods from 0.5 μm to 3 μm have been successfully fabricated with an aspect ratio of 1.1.

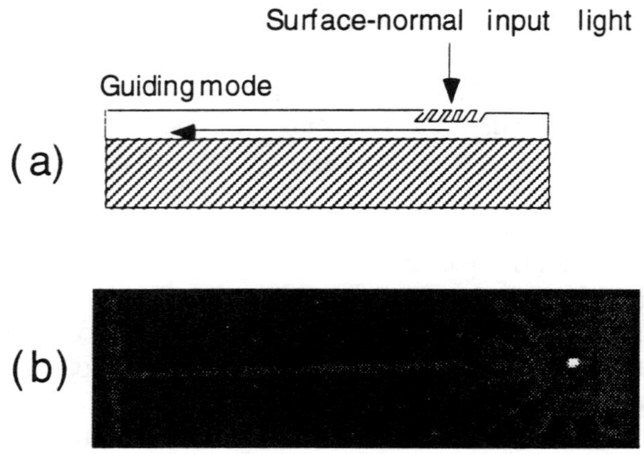

Fig. 7 (a) The schematic of coupling a surface-normal input light into waveguide using the tilted grating. (b) The experimental photograph of coupling a surface-normal input 632.8 nm He-Ne light into the polyimide waveguide.

A test waveguide sample with a tilted grating as the surface-normal input coupler was built using 632.8 nm as the operating wavelength. The schematic of coupling a surface-normal input light into a waveguide using the device fabricated is shown in Fig. 7(a), together with an experimental photograph in Fig. 7(b). The grating is designed to surface-normally couple the laser beam into the waveguide with an operating wavelength at 632.8 nm. The coupling to the planar waveguide with the unidirectional propagation can be clearly observed with a measured efficiency of 35%. This is our first device employing the surface-normal waveguide input coupling. Note that the index difference between the guiding layer and the substrate layer is less than 0.03 for the device shown in Figure 7. Theoretical result shows that the index difference between the guiding and the cladding layers plays an important role in enhancing the coupling efficiency. Further research aimed at providing a larger index difference to increase the coupling efficiency is under investigation.

3.0 Polyimide-based Channel Waveguide Evaluation

A large variety of organic polymers is attractive microelectronic and optoelectronic materials with potential applications as interlayer dielectric, protective overcoat, α-ray shielding, optical interconnects, or even conductive electrical interconnects. In addition to their ease of processing, they possess favorable electrical and mechanical properties such as high resistivity or good conductivity, low dielectric constant, lightweight and flexibility. Compatibility with the microelectronic fabrication, however, is the thermal requirement for the polymer material to survive wire-bonding and metal deposition processes. A specialized class of polyimides stands out in this aspect as they exhibit thermal stability to above 400 ^{0}C.

The polyimide PMDA/ODA, prepared from pyromellitic dianhydride and 4,4'-oxidianiline, is a typical commercially available polyimide coating. Kapton, the first aromatic polyimide commercialized by DuPont in 1960, is physically stable over a wide range of temperatures (-270-400 ^{0}C) and has excellent hear resistance, chemical resistance and therefore provides the required Si CMOS process compatibility. Other high index polyimides (n~ 1.75) at 850 nm are also under investigation.

For optical interconnect applications, PMDA/ODA and other rigid rod polyimides are not the best candidates. They are anisotropic and also tend to be highly colored due to intra-molecular charge transfer complexes that formed between the electron rich diamine and electron deficient dianhydride. These properties result in high optical absorption and scattering losses. Recent investigations to produce "colorless" polyimides by interrupting the planarity of the polyimide chain have focused on polyimides based on 2,2-bis (dicarboxyphenyl) hexafluoropropane dianhydride (6FDA), into which the hexafluoro group has been incorporated to reduce the optical anisotropy.

Because the Cray supercomputer board is 26.67 cm in length, which is beyond the field size of the in-house microlithography, large-area optical waveguides are required to build an optical clock signal distribution layer. To meet the size requirement, a laser beam direct writing was employed to solve the problem. The laser-beam writing system consists of a dual-wavelength HeCd laser (λ_1 = 325 nm and λ_2 = 442 nm), beam-shaping optics, an electronic shuttle and a computer-controlled X-Y-Z translation stage with a stroke of 30 x 30 x 2.5 cm^3. The stage translation speed was continuously adjustable below 1.0 cm/s. The positioning resolution is 0.5 μm and 0.01 μm for the X-Y axes and Z axis, respectively. The Z-stage was employed to precisely control the focused laser beam sizes. Fig.8 shows the schematic diagram of the laser waveguide writing system.

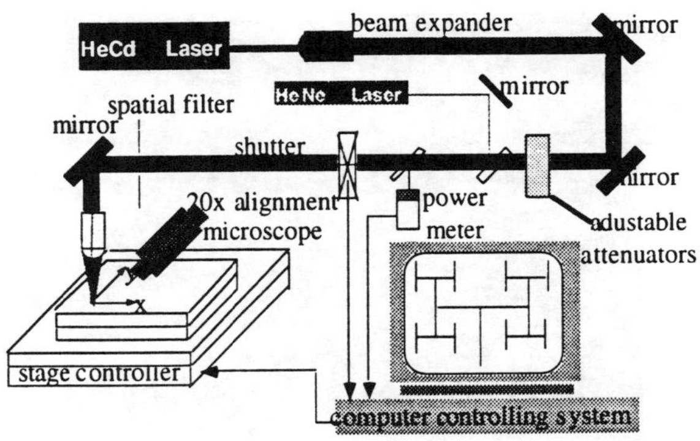

Fig. 8. Schematic of a laser waveguide writing

To ensure the desired electrical and mechanical properties imposed on the Cray supercomputer board, and to meet the required optical properties for the low loss waveguide formation, the photosensitive polyimide provided by Amoco Chemicalswass used for the waveguide fabrication[24]. The polyimide employed has an excellent thermal stability (Tg = 400 °C) and optical transparency when they are thermally or photochemically cross-linked. To fabricate the channel waveguides, the photosensitive polyimide was first spin-coated on the substrate, followed by a soft-cured process to remove the solvent. The exposure was conducted by a focused HeCd UV laser beam (λ = 325 nm) writing, directed by a computer controlled X-Y-Z precision microtranslation stage. The photo-crosslinked polyimide film was finally etched using organic solvent developers into the desired channel patterns. The fabricated waveguides was post-baked at 300-350 °C to remove residual solvent and to improve the solvent resistance.

Fig. 9(a) is the photograph of a 1-to-2 3 dB waveguide splitter (part of the H-tree system) based on polyimide channel waveguides fabricated with a channel width of 50 μm which is compatible with the core size of a multimode glass fiber. The waveguide thickness was measured to be 7 μm. Fig. 9(b) is a 90° waveguide bend fabricated. This device component is useful to direct all fanout beams into a single direction at the end of waveguide in an optical H-tree system. As a result, only one waveguide grating shape is required to couple the optical signal from the waveguide to photodetector surface-normally.

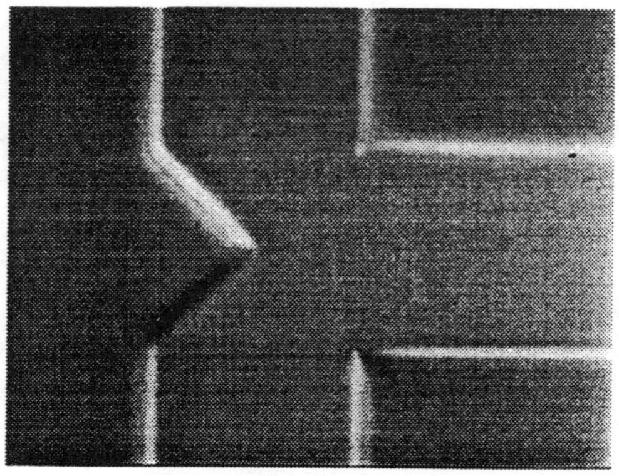

(a)

(b)

Fig.9 (a) photograph of 1-to-2 3 dB waveguide splitter, (b) a 90° waveguide bend.

During the course of research, we have developed a semiautomatic method for quickly measuring the optical loss using a video camera combined with a laser beam analyzer. Our method has no mechanical operation in the measurement system, which leads to accurate and reproducible measurement, and can be used with all kinds of waveguides employed in this research project. We have employed this measuring system to characterize the propagation properties of various polyimide-based waveguides.

The waveguides under test were mounted on a precise six-axis prism coupling. A laser beam profile analyzer (Model Spiricon LBA-100A) was arranged to observe a light streak of the excited mode in the waveguide from the front. The output video signal of the camera was analyzed by the system to provide the waveguide propagation loss.

There are two ways to sample the light intensity of the streak for loss measurement using a video camera, i.e., longitudinal and transverse scan samplings. The peak intensity variations along the streak can be ascertained by scanning along the propagation direction, and the loss value can be directly acquired from the longitudinal change. However, this 1-D scanning applies only to the straight guides; also, setting the sampling line along the streak requires precise adjustment. Hence we scan transversely to the light streak. Repeating the same procedure along the streak, we can obtain 2-D information of the intensity distribution

Based on the loss measurement setup developed, the polymer-based waveguide loss was measured. Repeating the integration of the data along each sampling line, we obtain the longitudinal variation of the mode intensity in the waveguide as shown by the dots in Fig. 10. The solid lines are the least-mean-square fits to a decreasing exponential, the slope of which yields the power loss coefficient. The propagation loss of the TE fundamental mode of the channel waveguide is 0.21 dB/cm at 850 nm and 0.48 dB/cm at 632.8 nm.

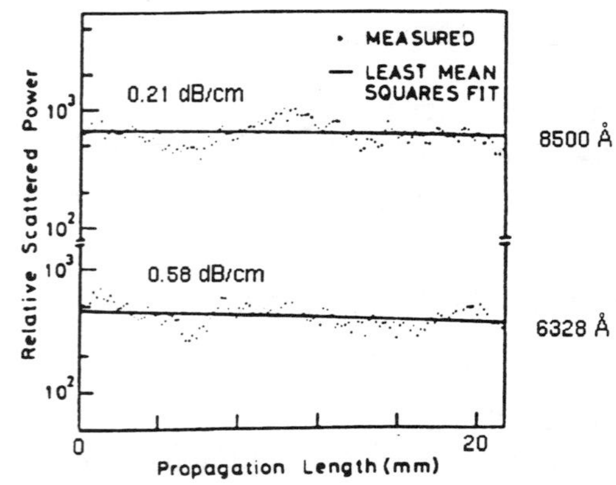

Fig. 10 Loss Measurement of the polyimide Waveguide at (a) 850 nm, (b) 632.8 nm

An optical H-tree fanout network based on polyimide channel waveguides was fabricated for optical clock signal distribution in a Cray multi-processor supercomputer board. The fabricated 1-to-48 H-tree waveguide structure equivalent to that of Figure 1(a) was evaluated. Figure 11 shows the sections of such an H-tree waveguide structure. The corresponding portions are illustrated using the H-tree pattern as references. The measured bending losses for each 1-to-2 splitters and 90-turns were 0.25 dB and higher. The employment of the H-tree waveguide structure is to equalize the propagation delays of different locations where Si-based clock detectors were located. We are in the process of investigating the feasibility of further reducing the bending losses by using curved waveguides which have lower bending losses than the present structure. Further experimental results will be presented in a separate publication.

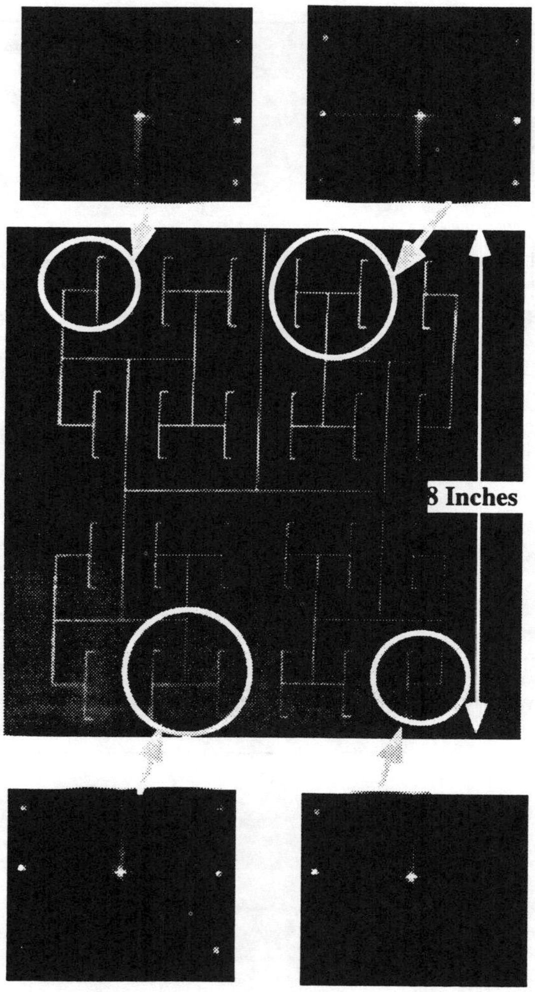

Fig. 11 Portions of the Polyimide-based H-tree Waveguide Structure for the Optical Clock Signal Distribution of Cray T-90 Supercomputer Board

4.0 Vertical Cavity Surface Emitting Lasers and Laser Arrays

To make the optical clock signal distribution system compatible with Si photodetectors, 850 nm is chosen to be the operating wavelength. Both edge and surface emitting lasers are available at this wavelength. High performance vertical cavity surface emitting lasers (VCSELs) are available with the output wavelength of 850 nm provided by Honeywell and MCC[25]. These laser devices, compared to conventional edge emitting lasers, offer a very low threshold current (1~3 mA) with much less temperature sensitivity, moderate optical power (few mW), very high direct modulation bandwidth (> 14 GHz), wide operating temperature range (-55 to +125 °C), and ease of packaging due to the unique surface-normal output configuration. To provide a high coupling efficiency using the proposed tilted gratings, the control of the emitting wavelength is pivotal and which makes VCSELs the best choice due to the large separation of the adjacent longitudinal modes implied by the short cavity length. The VCSELs were delivered by Honeywell and packaged by MCC (single VCSEL modules) and GE (linear VCSEL arrays). To provide the required fanouts with a bit error rate of 10^{-9} at 5 GHz, a laser diode with enough modulated power is needed to compensate -2 dB coupling loss, -6 dB waveguide propagation loss, -17dB fanout loss, -3 dB bending loss and -3 dB power margin. A single high power VCSEL or a linear array of VCSELs that can provide the modulated power are required. In the case of the array approach, the modulated signals have to be synchronized and each VCSEL is employed to provide a sub-H-tree delay-equalized fanout.

Planar configuration of VCSELs allows these devices to be fabricated, wafer scale tested with conventional microelectronics manufacturing processes. The unique surface-normal emitting nature of the device allows us to use exactly the same packaging scheme for coupling light from VCSEL into waveguide as that used for coupling light from waveguide into photodetector. In order individually address each VCSEL in an array, each anode was contacted separately and attached to individual bonding pads upon which a synchronized driving signal shall be applied. Fig. 12 shows the microphotographs of (a) a single VCSEL and (b) a 1x32 linear VCSEL array packaged and assembled by MCC and GE, respectively.

The modulation bandwidth of the VCSEL has a modulation bandwidth as high as 6 GBit/sec. Fig. 13(a) is the plot of the CW output power versus forward current of the VCSEL and the eye-diagram corresponding to 6 Gbit/sec encoding speed is shown in Figure 13(b). Low threshold current was obtained at ~3 mA. The maximum output power can be reached at 5 mW. Fig. 14 shows the temperature stability of the VCSEL tested. The high stability of operating characteristics at high temperatures potentially allows operation without a continuous photodiode feedback control, simplifying drive circuits considerably. The I-V curve of the VCSEL (not shown) concluded that the driving voltage was less than 2.5 volts.

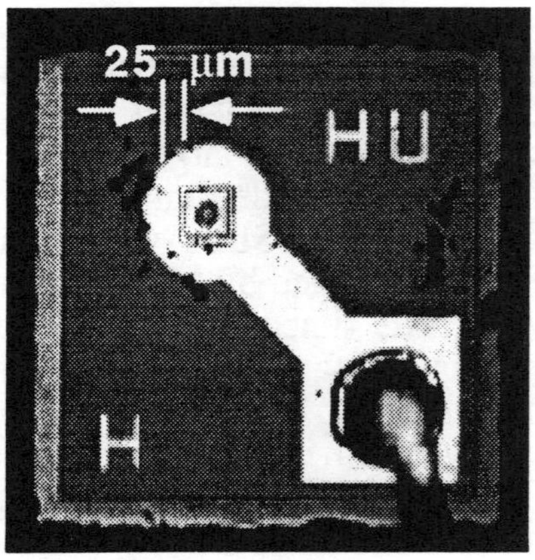

(a)

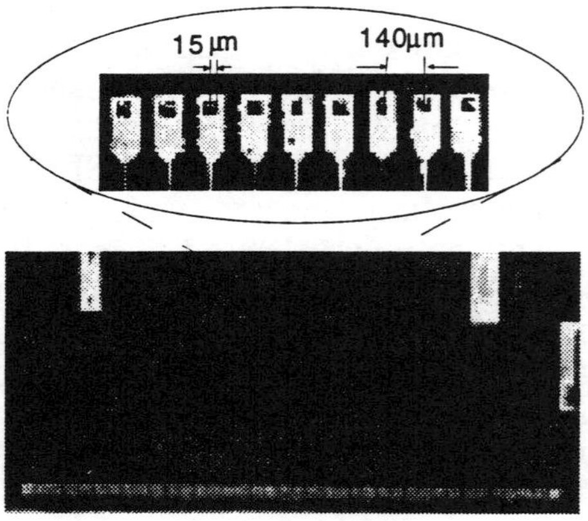

(b)

Fig. 12 Microphotographs of (a) a single VCSEL, and (b) an 1x32 linear VCSEL array.

5.0 Si-based Integrated Optical Receiver as the Clock Signal Detector

It is clear that optoelectronics will be a technology for numerous applications in both the private sector and the military. To date, optoelectronic circuitry for optical transmission has utilized III-V compound materials because their materials characteristics yield higher speed and lower noise.[26,27] However, Si integrated circuit technology is mature, compact, inexpensive, and has demonstrated high reliability. These characteristics make Si-based integrated circuit technology very attractive for multiuser networks, high density arrays, and optical

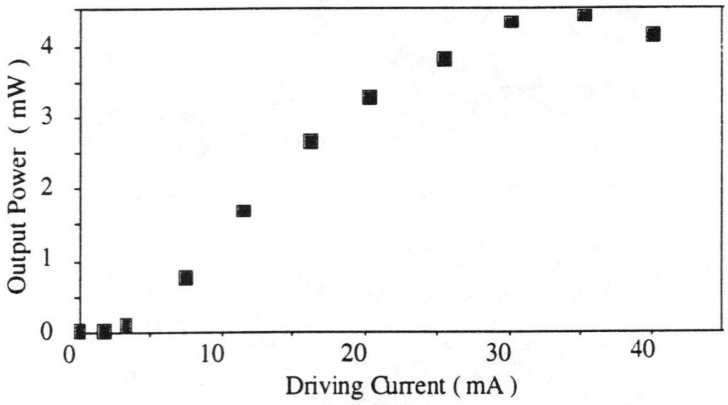

(a)

(b)

Fig. 13. (a) Plot of CW output power versus forward current. (b). 6 GBit/sec eye diagram

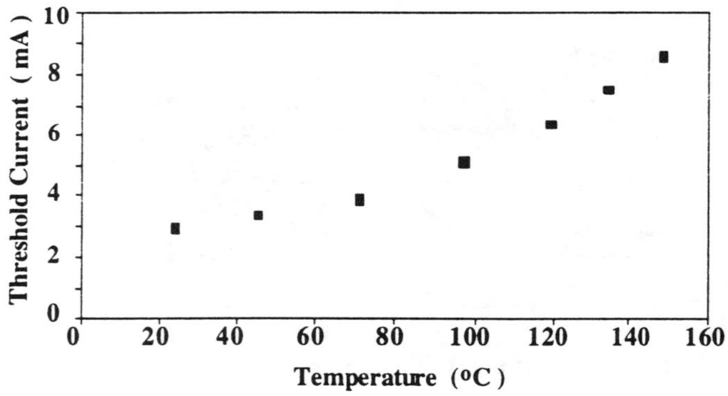

Fig. 14 VCSEL temperature stability.

interconnects where manufacturability and cost are key factors.

For optical clock signal distribution, we have developed the first fully monolithic Si-MOSFET integrated receiver[28,29] and the measured result is shown in Figure 15. The receiver sensitivities for a bit error rate of 10^{-9} were -25 dBm and -32.5 dBm at bit rates of 300 MBit/s and 155 MBit/s, respectively. This represents the best speed-sensitivity performance reported for a monolithic integrated Si optical receiver by any Si technology. As discrete chip devices evolve into high-density arrays of similar devices or circuits, power dissipation in optical receivers has become a concern. In these arrays, the power budget per element must be significantly reduced in order to maintain the total power dissipation at reasonable levels. This problem has been compounded by recent developments in optical transmitters where the optical sources will, in most instances, be arrays of very low threshold lasers, eg., native oxide, vertical-cavity, surface-emitting structures. The ultra-low thresholds of these lasers has significantly reduced the power requirements for the transmitters but this has been achieved at the cost of low output powers. On the other hand, at the receiver output there is still a need to have signal levels near 1V for compatibility with the following electronic circuits. The resulting need to increase the gain in the receiver has, in a sense, shifted the "power problem" from the transmitter to the receiver. In the present implementation of our 300 MBit/s receivers, the power dissipation is 10.5 mW. Recently, we have redesigned the output stage of these receivers to incorporate enhancement-mode MOSFETs. Simulations show that the power dissipation in these circuits will be decreased to approximately 0.6 mW.

In order to increase the speed of these receivers it will be necessary to develop Si photodiodes with much higher bandwidths than those that are presently available. The reason for the relatively low bandwidths of Si photodiodes is that the absorption coefficients of indirect bandgap semiconductors are much smaller (10x) than those of direct bandgap III-V compounds. As a result, in order to achieve high quantum efficiency, Si photodiodes require long absorption thicknesses. This leads to long transit times and low bandwidths. Such a responsivity/bandwidth tradeoff can be circumvented with a resonant-cavity photodetector structure shown in figure 16.[30-33] This structure increases the absorption through multiple reflections between two parallel mirrors in a Fabry-Perot cavity. The lower mirror is an integrated Bragg reflector consisting of

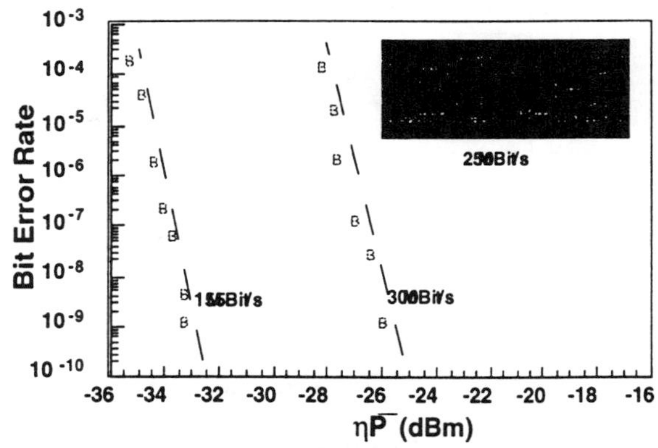

Figure 15 Receiver sensitivity of Si NMOS optical receiver.

alternating λ/4 epitaxial layers similar to that used in vertical-cavity surface-emitting lasers. The top mirror is usually a high reflectivity dielectric stack that can be deposited after fabrication and initial characterization. Previously, using a $Ge_{0.3}Si_{0.7}/Si$ asymmetric Bragg reflector for the bottom mirror we have demonstrated a Si-based resonant-cavity photodiode with a quantum efficiency and a bandwidth of 15GHz.[33] More recently, we have developed an interdigitated PIN polysilicon resonant-cavity photodiode, which employs a Si/SiO_2 Bragg reflector, that is more compatible with standard Si processing technology.[34,35] For an absorbing region thickness of only 0.5 μm a peak quantum efficiency of 40% was achieved and the dark current was < 60 nA at 10 V. For 2μm x 2μm finger width and spacing the bandwidth was measured to be 10 GHz as indicated in Figure 17. System integration involving VCSELs, an H-tree Waveguide Structure and high speed Si-based photodetectors are currently under investigation. Further results will be presented in a separate publication.

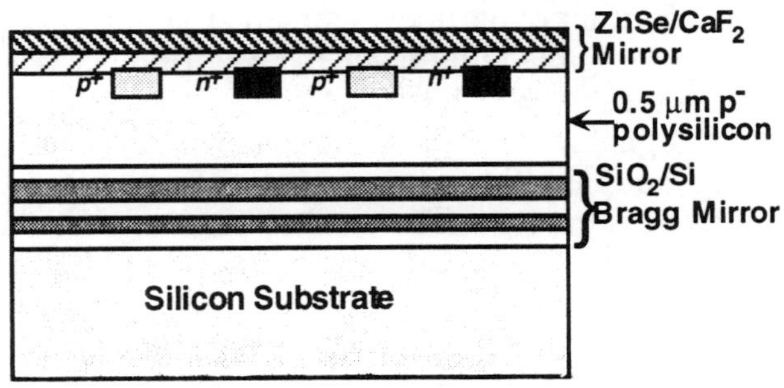

Figure 16 Cross section of Si/SiO_2 resonant-cavity polysilicon photodiode

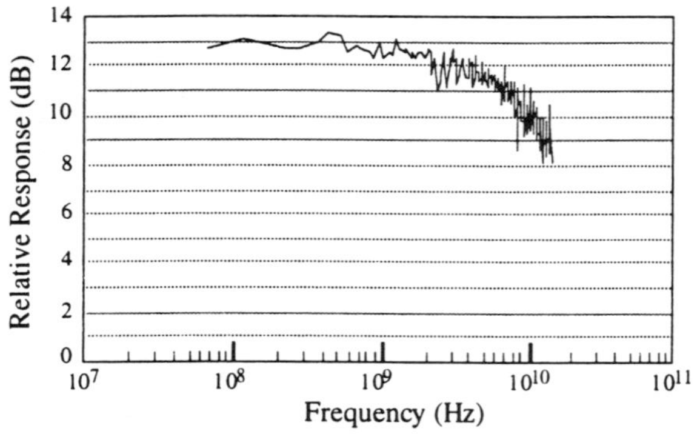

Figure 17 Frequency response of Si/SiO_2 resonant-cavity polysilicon photodiode

6.0 Conclusion

In summary, we report the formation of polyimide-based H-tree waveguides for high-speed optical clock signal distribution in a Si CMOS process compatible environment. A waveguide propagation loss of 0.21dB/cm at 850 nm was experimentally confirmed. Both 1-to-2 splitting loss and bending loss were measured to be 0.25 dB and higher. Curved waveguides which have the potential to further reduce the bending loss were also considered and are currently under investigation and further results will be presented at a separate publication. The planarization requirement of the optical interconnection layer among many electrical interconnection layers makes the employment of tilted grating a better choice. Theoretical calculation predicts that a 1-to-1 free-space to waveguide coupling efficiency as high as 95% is achievable. Currently, a coupling efficiency of 35% was experimentally confirmed due to the limited index difference between guiding/cladding layers. Further experiments aimed at structuring a larger guiding/cladding layer index differences are under investigation. To effectively couple an optical signal into the waveguide through the titled grating coupler, the accuracy of the wavelength employed is pivotal. This makes the usage of the vertical cavity surface-emitting lasers (VCSELs) and VCSEL arrays the best choice due to the well-defined spectrum of a VCSEL when compared with edge-emitting lasers. Modulation bandwidth as high as 6 GHz was demonstrated at 850 nm which is compatible with Si-based photodetectors. Temperature dependence of the threshold current up to 155°C was measured which will determine the power dissipation issue of the optoelectronic packaging. Finally, the first fully monolithic Si-MOSFET integrated receiver was made as the optical clock signal detector. To further enhance the bandwidth of such a detector, a resonant cavity structure was employed while maintainning the demodulation bandwidth at 10 GHz. A fully integrated guided wave optical clock signal distribution system having planarized grating couplers, H-tree Si-CMOS process compatible waveguides, VCSELs and Si-based photoreceivers will be demonstrated in the near future.

This research is sponsored by ONR, BMDO, DARPA's center for optoelectronics science and technology, the ATP program of the state of Texas, 3M Foundation, Cray Research, GE, Honeywell and MCC.

7.0 References

1. D. P. Seraphim and D. E. Barr, "Interconnect and packaging technology in the 90's," Proc. SPIE 1390, pp. 39-54, 1990.
2. C. Neugerbauer, R. O. Carlson, R. A. Fillion, and T. R. Haller, "Multichip module designs for high performance applications," in Multichip Modules, Compendium of 1989 Papers, pp. 149-163, International Electronic Packaging Society, 1989.
3. J. W. Goodman, F. I. Leonberger, S. Y. Kung, and R. A. Athale, "Optical interconnections for VLSI systems," Proc. IEEE 72, pp. 850-866, 1984.
4. M. R. Feldman, S. C. Esener, C.C. Guest, and S. H. Lee, "Comparison between optical and electrical interconnects based on power and speed considerations," Appl. Opt., vol. 27, pp. 1742-1751, 1988.
5. Founad E. Kiamilev, Philippe Marchand, Ashok V. Krishnamoorthy, Sadik C. Esener, and Sing H. Lee, "Performance comparison between optoelectronic and VLSI multistage interconnects networks," IEEE J. of Light. Technol., vol. 9, pp. 1674-1692, 1993.
6. Paola Cinato, Kenneth C. Young, Jr., "Optical interconnections within multichip modules," Opt. Eng., vol. 32, pp. 852-860, 1993.
7. Bradley D. Clymer and Joseph W. Goodman, "Optical clock distribution to silicon chips," Opt. Eng., vol. 25, pp. 1103-1108, 1986.
8. Suning Tang, Ray T. Chen and Mark Peskin, "Packing density and interconnection length of a

highly parallel optical interconnect using polymer-based single-mode bus arrays," Opt. Eng., vol. 33, pp. 1581-1586, 1994.
9. Ray. T. Chen, Suning Tang, T. Jannson and J. Jannson, "A 45 cm long compression molded polymer-based optical bus," Appl. Phys. Lett., vol. 63, pp. 1032-1034, 1993.
10. Ray T. Chen, "Polymer-based Photonic Integrated Circuits," (Invited Review Paper), *Optics and Laser Technology*, Vol. 25, pp. 347-365(1993).
11. Ray. T. Chen, H. Lu, D. Robinson, Michael Wang, Gajendra Savant, and Tomasz Jannson, "Guided-wave planar optical interconnects using highly multiplexed polymer waveguide holograms," IEEE J. Light. Technol., vol. 10, pp. 888-897, 1992.
12. R. W. Wickman, "Implementation of optical interconnects in GibaRing supercomputer channel", Proc. SPIE, vol. CR62, pp. 343-356, 1996.
13. M. R. Feldman, "Holographic optical interconnects for multichip modules," Proc. SPIE, vol., 1390, pp. 427-433, 1990.
14. Suning Tang and Ray T. Chen, "1-to-42 optoelectronic interconnection for intra-multichip-module clock signal distribution," Appl. Phys. Lett., vol. 64, pp. 2931-2933, 1994.
15. Sunny Bains, "Optical interconnects are taking off as the data transport of tomorrow," OEM Magazine, pp. 48-53, July 1996.
16. Y. S. Liu, W. Hennessy, R. Wojnarowski, J. Bristow, Y. Liu, J. Rowlette, J. Stack, J. Yardley, L. Eldada, R. M. Osgood, R. Scarmozzino, S. H. Lee and S. Patra, "Optoelectronic Backplane Interconnect Technology Development," Proc. SPIE, Optoelectronic Interconnects and Packaging IV, Editor: Ray Chen and P. Guilfoyle, pp.2-10, Vol.3005, 1997.
17. K. S. Giboney, "Parallel-optical Interconnect Development at HP Laboratories," Proc. SPIE, Optoelectronic Interconnects and Packaging IV, Editor: Ray Chen and P. Guilfoyle, pp.193-201, Vol.3005, 1997.
18. Toshiaki Suhara and Hiroshi Nishihara, "Integrated optics components and devices using periodic structures," IEEE J. of Quantum Electronics, vol. QE-22, no. 6, pp. 845-867, 1996.
19. D. Brundrett, E. Glystis, and T. Gaylord, "Homogeneous layer models for high-spatial-frequency dielectric surface-relief gratings," Appl. Opt. vol. 33, no. 13, pp. 2695-2760, 1994.
20. D. Y. Kim, S. K. Tripathy, Lian Li, and J. Kumar, "Laser-induced holographic surface relief gratings on nonlinear optical polymer films," Appl. Phys. Lett., vol. 66, no. 10, pp. 1166-1168, 1995.
21. Ray T. Chen, Feiming Li, Micheal Dubinovsky, and Oleg Ershov, "Si-based surface-relief polygonal gratings for 1-to-many wafer-sacle optical clock signal distribution," IEEE Photonics Technol. Lett., vol. 8, no. 8, 1996.
22. R. K. Kostuk, J. W. Goodman, and L. Hesselink, "Design considerations for holographic optical interconnects," Appl. Opt., vol. 26, pp. 3947-3953, 1987.
23. G.D.Boyd, L.A.Coldren, F.G.Storz, "Directional reactive ion etching at oblique angles", Appl. Phys. Lett., vol. 36, no. 7, pp. 583-585, 1980.
24. Suning Tang, Ting Li, Feiming Li, Linghui Wu, Micheal Dubinovsky, Randy Wickman and Ray T. Chen, "An 1-GHz clock signal distribution for multi-processor super computers,"IEEE Third International Conference on Massively Parallel Processing using Optical Interconnections, pp.186-191, 1996. andRay T. Chen, Suning Tang, Ting Li, F. Li, Micheal Dubinovsky, and Randy Wickman, "Board-Level Optical Clock Signal Distribution Based on Guided-Wave Optical Interconnects in Conjunction with Waveguide Holograms," SPIE vol. 2891, pp. 111-117, 1996.
25. Y. Liu, J. Bristow, K. Johnson, A. Peczalski, T. Marta, S. Bounnak, W. Goldberg, and B. Hanzal, "Polymer optical waveguide technology for multichip modules and board level interconnects," SPIE, vol. 2891, pp. 88-95, 1996.
26. O. Wada, *Optoelectronic Integration: Physics, Technology, and Applications*, Norwell, Massachusetts, Kluwer Academic, 1994.
27. M. Dagenais, R. F. Leheny, and J. D. Crow, *Integrated Optoelectronics*, San Diego, CA, Academic, 1995.
28. L.D.Garrett, J.Qi, C.L.Schow, and J.C.Campbell, "A silicon-based integrated NMOS-p-i-n photoreceiver", *IEEE Trans. Electron Devices,* vol. 43, pp. 411-416 (1996).
29. J. Qi, C. L. Schow, L. C. Garrett, and J. C. Campbell, "A Silicon NMOS Monolithically Integrated Optical Receiver," Photon. Tech. Lett., May 1997.
30. A. Chin and T. Y. Chang, "Multilayer reflectors by molecular-beam epitaxy for resonance enhanced absorption in thin high-speed detectors," J. Vac. Sci. Technol., vol. B8, pp. 339-342, 1990.

31. M. S. Ünlü, K. Kishino, J.-I. Chyi, L. Arsenault, J. Reed, S. Noor Mohammad, and H. Morkoc, "Resonant cavity enhanced AlGaAs/GaAs heterojunction phototransistors with an intermediate InGaAs layer in the collector," Appl. Phys. Lett., vol. 57, pp. 750-752, 1990.
32. R. Kuchibhotla, A. Srinivasan, J. C. Campbell, C. Lei, D. Deppe, Y. S. He, and B. G. Streetman, "Low voltage high gain resonant cavity avalanche photodiode," IEEE Photonics Technol. Lett., vol. 3, pp. 354-356, 1991.
33. S. S. Murtaza, H. Nie, J. C. Campbell, J. C. Bean, and L. J. Peticolas, "Short-wavelength, high-speed, Si-based resonant-cavity photodetector," IEEE Photon. Tech. Lett., vol. 8, pp. 927-929, 1996.
34. D. C. Diaz, C. L. Schow, J. Qi, J. C. Campbell, J. C. Bean, and L. J. Peticolas, "Si/SiO_2 resonant-cavity photodetector," Appl. Phys. Lett., vol. 69, pp. 2798-2800, 1996.
35. J. C. Bean, J. Qi, C. L. Schow, R. Li, H. Nie, J. Schaub, and J. C. Campbell, "High-Speed Polysilicon Resonant-Cavity Photodiode with SiO_2/Si Bragg Reflectors," to be published in Photon. Tech. Lett.

Experimental Verification of the Pulse Shepherding Concept in Dispersion–Shifted Single–Mode Fiber for Bit–Parallel Wavelength Links

L. Bergman, J. Morookian, C. Yeh and S. Monacos
Jet Propulsion Laboratory
California Institute of Technology
Pasadena, California 91109

Abstract

A new way to dynamically control in–flight pulses by a co-propagating shepherd pulse in a wavelength division multiplexed (WDM) single–mode fiber system was proposed at the MPPOI '96 Conference. That system functionally resembles an optical fiber ribbon cable, except that all the bits pass on one fiber optic waveguide. This single fiber bit parallel wavelength link can be used to extend the (speed x distance) product of emerging cluster computer networks, such as, the MyriNet, SCI, Hippi–6400, ShuffleNet, etc. Here, we shall present the first experimental evidence that this pulse shepherding effect can be observed in a commercially available Corning DS (dispersion–shifted) fiber. Computer simulation results will first be presented for the case observed in the laboratory setup. A discussion of the experiment setup and measurement procedures will be given. Experimental results will then be compared with computer generated results. Excellent agreement is observed. Future experiments dealing with the shepherding effect among more than two co–propagating pulses will be performed.

I. Introduction

The concept of using a shepherd pulse to promote time-alignment of co-propagating pulses in a bit-parallel wavelength division multiplexed system [1] for a single-mode fiber was presented at the MPPOI '96 Conference [2]. The proposed concept is based on the cross phase modulation (CPM) effects [3] caused by the nonlinearity of the optical fiber in a wavelength division multiplexed (WDM) system. These CPM effects occur when two or more optical beams co-propagate simultaneously and affect each other through the intensity dependence of the refractive index. This CPM phenomenon can be used to produce an interesting pulse shepherding effect to align the arrival time of pulses which are otherwise misaligned. This same CPM effect can also be used to generate time-aligned co-propagating pulses on different wavelength beams.

An example of the pulse shepherding effect [4] is shown below:

Let us assume that two gaussian pulses on two different wavelength beams with wavelengths of 1.55 μm and 1.546 μm, originating in an aligned position as shown in Fig. 1(a), begin to separate from each other due to slight difference in the group velocities for these two beams. Without the presence of a shepherd pulse, these beams will be approximately 1/2 pulsewidth apart at 50 km downstream as can be seen from Fig. 1(a). With the shepherd pulse of 2 exp $(-0.5\ \tau^2)$ on a third beam with wavelength 1.542 μm, originally aligned with the two shepherded pulses and propagating at the same velocity as the pulse on beam #1, at 50 km downstream, the shepherded pulses are still aligned as shown in Fig. 1(b).

What this means is that through the introduction of a shepherd pulse on a separate wavelength beam, it is possible to dynamically manipulate, control and reshape pulses on co-propagating beams in a WDM system. This dynamic control feature from a shepherd pulse will enable the eventual construction of a time-aligned bit-parallel wavelength link as an interconnect with exceptionally high speed, low latency, simplified electronics interface (with no speed bottleneck), and extensibility to all-optical packet networks.

Here, we shall present the first experimental result showing the existence of this pulse shepherding effect.

0-8186-7974-3/97 $10.00 © 1997 IEEE

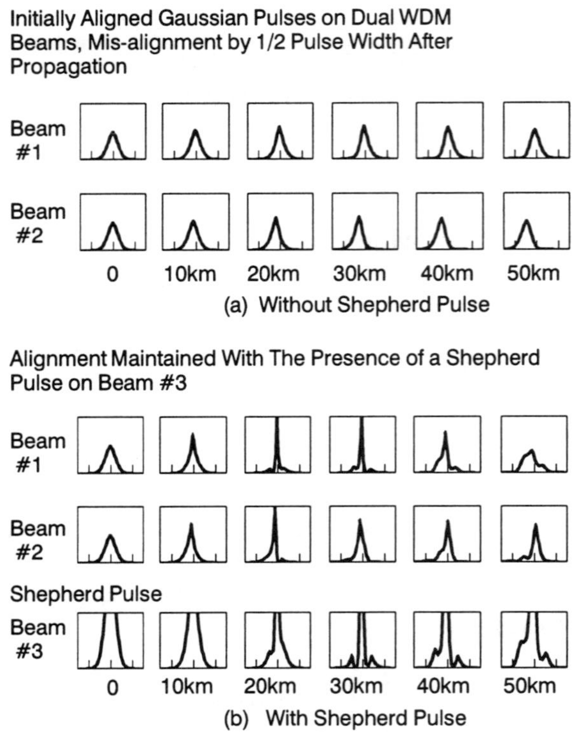

Fig. 1. Evolution of two initially aligned gaussian pulses on the WDM beams. (a) After propagation, separation occurs for pulses on beam #1 and beam #2 without shepherd pulse on the third beam.(b) Alignment maintained for pulses on beam #1 and beam #2 with shepherd pulse on the third beam.

A review of the theoretical background will first be given. Computer simulation results for the case corresponding to that observed in the laboratory will be presented. Experimental setup and measurement procedures will then be discussed. Measured results will be compared with computer results. Evidence of the shepherding effect will be presented. Finally, a discussion on future experiments dealing with the shepherding effect among more than two co-propagating pulses will be given.

II. A Review of the Theoretical Foundation

The fundamental equations governing M numbers of co-propagating waves in a nonlinear fiber including the CPM phenomenon are the coupled nonlinear Schrodinger equations [3,4]:

$$\frac{\partial A_j}{\partial z} + \frac{1}{v_{gj}}\frac{\partial A_j}{\partial t} + \frac{1}{2}\alpha_j A_j = \frac{1}{2}\beta_{2j}\frac{\partial^2 A_j}{\partial t^2}$$

$$- \gamma_j \left(|A_j|^2 + 2\sum_{m \neq j}^{M} |A_m|^2 \right) A_j$$

$$(j = 1,2,3, ... M) \tag{1}$$

Here, for the jth wave, $Aj(z,t)$ is the slowly-varying amplitude of the wave, v_{gj}, the group velocity, β_{2j}, the dispersion coefficient ($\beta_{2j} = dv_{gj}^{-1}/d\omega$), α_j, the absorption coefficient,

$$\gamma_j = \frac{n_2\omega_j}{c\ A_{eff}} \tag{2}$$

is the nonlinear index coefficient with A_{eff} as the effective core area and $n_2 = 3.2 = 10^{-16}$ cm^2/W for silica fibers, ω_j is the carrier frequency of the jth wave, c is the speed of light, and z is the direction of propagation along the fiber.

Introducing the normalizing coefficients

$$\tau = \frac{t - (z/v_{g1}}{T_0}$$

$$d_{1j} = (v_{g1} - v_{gj})/v_{g1}v_{gj},$$

$$\xi = z/L_{D1},$$

$$L_{D1} = T_0^{\,2}/|\beta_{21}|, \tag{3}$$

and setting

$$u_j(\tau,\xi) = (A_j(z,t)/\sqrt{P_{0j}})\ \exp(\alpha_j L_{D1}\xi/2) \tag{4}$$

$$L_{NLj} = 1/(\gamma_j P_{0j})$$

$$L_{Dj} = T_0^{\,2}/|\beta_{2j}| \tag{5}$$

gives

$$i\frac{\partial u_j}{\partial \xi} = \frac{sgn(\beta_{2j})L_{D1}}{2L_{Dj}}\frac{\partial^2 u_j}{\partial \tau^2}$$

$$- i\frac{d_{1j}}{T_0}L_{D1}\frac{\partial u_j}{\partial \tau}$$

$$- \frac{L_{D1}}{L_{NLj}}\left[\ \exp(-\alpha_j L_{D1}\xi)\ |u_j|^2\right.$$

$$\left. + 2\sum_{m \neq j}^{M} exp\ (-\alpha_m L_{D1}\xi)\ |u_m|^2\right] u_j$$

$(j = 1,2,3, ... M)$ (6)

Here, T_0 is the pulse width, P_{0j} is the incident optical power of the jth beam, and d_{1j}, the walk-off parameter between beam *1* and beam j, describes how fast a given pulse in beam *j* passes through the pulse in beam *1*. In other words, the walk-off length is

$$L_{w(1j)} = T_0 \ / \ |d_{1j}|. \tag{7}$$

So, $L_{W(1j)}$ is the distance for which the faster moving pulse (say, in beam *j*) completely walked through the slower moving pulse in beam 1. The nonlinear interaction between these two optical pulses ceases to occur after a distance $L_{W(1j)}$. For cross-phase-modulation (CPM) to take effect significantly, the group-velocity mismatch must be held to near zero.

It is also noted from Eq. (6) that the summation term in the bracket representing the cross-phase-modulation (CPM) effect is twice as effective as the self-phase-modulation (SPM) effect for the same intensity. This means that the nonlinear effect of the fiber medium on a beam may be enhanced by the co-propagation of another beam with the same group velocity.

Equation (6) is a set of simultaneous coupled nonlinear Schrodinger equations which may be solved numerically by the split-step Fourier method, which was used successfully earlier to solve the problem of beam propagation in complex fiber structures, such as, the fiber couplers [5], and to solve the thermal blooming problem for high energy laser beams [6]. According to this method, the solutions may be advanced first using only the nonlinear part of the equations. And then the solutions are allowed to advance using only the linear part of Eq. (6). This forward stepping process is repeated over and over again until the desired destination is reached. The Fourier transform is accomplished numerically via the well-known Fast Fourier Transform Technique.

III. Computer Simulation Results

Based on the above numerical technique, computer simulation is carried out for the case corresponding to that performed in the laboratory.

Two beams with wavelength separated by 5 nm (nano–meter) are launched into a single mode fiber: One beam carries a 20 ps gaussian pulse while the other beam carries a 200 ps gaussian pulse to simulate the cw signal in the experiment. The evolution of the two pulses on these two co-propagating beams is the focus of our simulation. It is noted that the four wave mixing effect is negligible for this case. Let us label the initial 20 ps gaussian pulse carried by one of the beam as the shepherd (S) pulse and the other 200 ps pulse on the other beam as the primary (P) pulse. The parameters that we use for the simulation are:

L = length of fiber = 50 km
β_2 = dispersion coefficient = 2 ps^2/km
λ_1 = operating wavelength of beam #1 = 1.55 μm
λ_2 = operating wavelength of beam #2 = 1.545 μm
γ = nonlinear index coefficient = 20 $W^{-1}km^{-1}$
α = attenuation or absorption of each beam in fiber = 0.2 dB/km
v_g = group velocity of the beam = 2.051147 x 10^8 m/sec
d_{12} = walk-off parameter between beam #1 and beam #2 < 1 ps/km
T_0 = pulse width = 20 ps.

Shown in Fig. 2 is the evolution of these two pulses on two different wavelength beams as they propagate in this single mode fiber. Since both pulses are operating in the positive dispersion region, i.e., the dispersion coefficient β_2 is positive, neither pulse will undergo pulse–compression. Since the dispersion coefficient is quite small, for the distance considered, neither pulse will experience significant pulse-broadening.

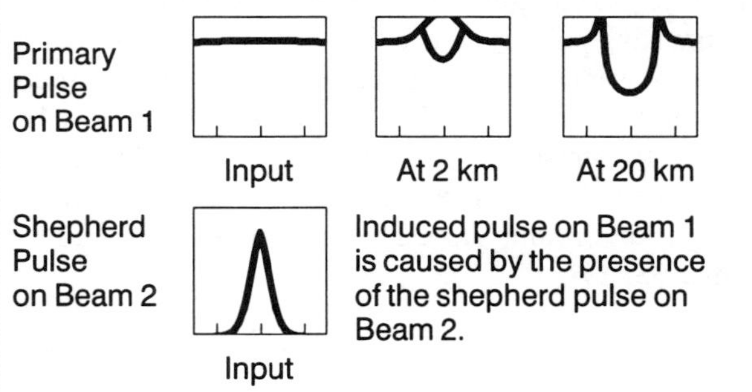

Fig. 2. Computer simulation results for the case of a 20 ps pulse (the shepherd pulse) co-propagating with a 200 ps pulse (approximating a cw primary pulse) in a 20 km dispersion shifted fiber with negligible walkoff. A dip on the 200 ps pulse appeared at the end of the fiber indicating the presence of the shepherding effect.

One notes that in the absence of the shepherding effect (i.e., the CPM effect) these pulses will propagate independent of each other. However, due to the presence of the shepherding effect, very significant changes are observed on the 200 ps primary pulse. On that primary pulse, a dip appears at the location which is aligned with the 20 ps shepherd pulse. This dip appears to grow deeper and broader as both pulses propagate down the fiber, eventually reaching the shape of an inverted 20 ps gaussian pulse. This inverted guassian pulse is superposed over the 200 ps primary pulse. This inverted gaussian pulse on a long plateau looks very much like a dark soliton pulse. Also noted is a narrow rim around this dip. Due to the averaging technique used in the experimental measurement, this narrow rim will not appear in the measured picture of the induced primary pulse; only a dip will appear in the picture.

The effect of the small walk-off is to shift the induced inverted pulse on the 200 ps primary beam slightly. The shepherding effect also skews slightly the symmetry of both the shepherd pulse and the induced inverted pulse on the primary pulse.

This very distinctive feature of an induced inverted pulse on a broad primary pulse which is clearly caused by the shepherding effect has been used to experimentally verify the existence of the shepherding effect.

IV. Experimental Setup and Procedures

A schematic block diagram of the experimental setup is shown in Fig. 3. The pulse source is an Erbium Doped Fiber Ring Laser (EDFRL), producing a 100 MHz train of pulses 20 ps in length at a wavelength near 1551 nm. This Erbium Ring pulse is named the shepherd pulse, operating at peak power of higher than 200 mW. The primary source is a DFB laser diode at 1545 nm operated under a dc bias well above threshold. This cw output from the primary laser diode source is about 1 mW which is amplified through an Erbium Doped Fiber Amplifier (EDFA) to around 33 mW.

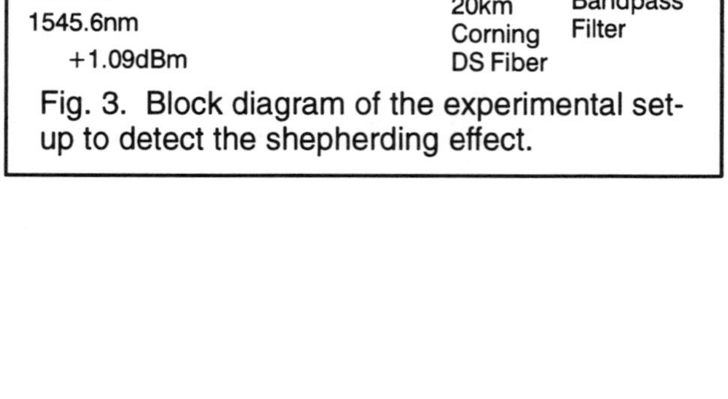

Fig. 3. Block diagram of the experimental set-up to detect the shepherding effect.

As shown in Fig. 3, signals from these two sources of two different wavelengths are then combined using a 2 to 1 fiber coupler. The combined output is sent through a 20 km spool of Corning DS fiber. At the output end of the fiber, an optical bandpass filter is used to reject the pulse signal from the ring laser. The signal from the laser diode is detected and viewed on an oscilloscope. A picture of this output is shown in Fig. 4. A dip on the cw signal is observed indicating the presence of the shepherding effect as predicted by the computer simulation result.

This is the very first time that this shepherding effect has been observed. This experiment also shows that for the length of fiber that we used, i.e., 2 km long, the walk-off effect of this commercially available Corning DS fiber [7] is less than 1 ps/km.

V. Discussion and Future Research

The pictures shown in Fig. 4 clearly demonstrate not only the existence of an induced inverted pulse which can only come about because of the shepherding effect but also the growth of this induced pulse as the interaction distance grows longer as predicted by our computer simulation.

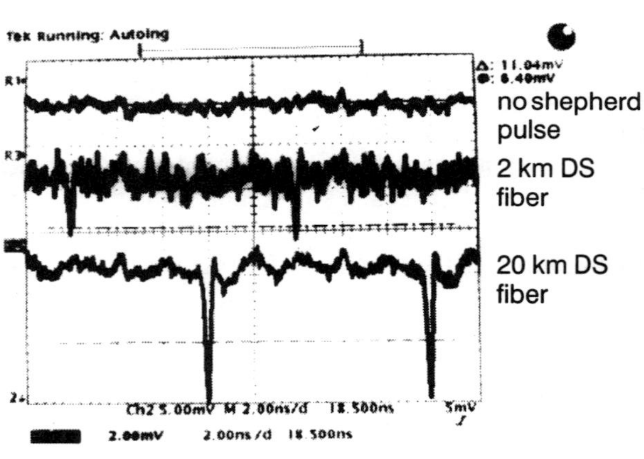

Fig. 4. Picture of the output of the cw primary source. The first line represents the output of the cw primary source signal without the presence of the shepherd pulse. The second line represents the output of the primary pulse with the presence of the shepherd pulse for a 2 km long Corning DS fiber. The third line represents the output of the primary pulse with the presence of the shepherd pulse for a 20 km long Corning DS fiber. A dip is seen indicating the successful interaction of the shepherd pulse with the primary signal.

That this shepherding effect is observable in a commercially available Corning SMF–DS fiber [7] (a dispersion shifted fiber) is worth noting. This means we are now in a position to perform further experiments corresponding to the cases produced by computer simulations without waiting for the production of an idealized fiber.

From a practical point of view, it is worth noting that this single fiber bit parallel wavelength link with shepherding pulse(s) can be used to extend greatly the (speed x distance) product of emerging cluster computer networks, such as, the MyriNet, SCI, Hippi–6400, ShuffleNet, etc. The distance may exceed many kilometers, a distance much beyond the capability of fiber ribbons.

Acknowledgements

The research described in this paper was performed by the Center for Space Microelectronics Technology, Jet Propulsion Laboratory, California Institute of Technology, and was sponsored by the Ballistic Missile Defense Organization, Office of Innovative Science and Technology, through an agreement with the National Aeronautics and Space Administration.

References

[1] L. A. Bergman, A. J. Mendez, and L. S. Lome, "Bit–parallel wavelength links for high performance computer networks", in SPIE Critical Review of Optical Science and Technology, *Optoelectronic Interconnects and Packaging*, edited by Ray T. Chen and Peter S. Cuilfoyle, vol. CR62, p.p. 210–226, (1996).

[2] L. A. Bergman and C. Yeh, "Dynamic alignment of pulses in bit-parallel wavelength links using a shepherd pulse in nonlinear fibers for massively parallel processing computer networks", Presented at the Third International Conference on Massively Parallel Processing Using Optical Interconnections (MPPPOI'96), Maui, Hawaii, October 27–29, 1996

[3] G. P. Agrawal, *Nonlinear Fiber Optics*, Academic Press, New York (1989); J. R. Taylor, Ed., *Optical Solitons – Theory and Experiment*, Cambridge Studies in Modern Optics 10, Cambridge University Press, Cambridge (1992).

[4] C. Yeh and L. A. Bergman, J. Appl. Phys. 80, 3174 (1996).

[5] C. Yeh, W. P. Brown, and R. Szejn, Appl. Opt. 18, 489 (1979).

[6] C. Yeh, J. E. Pearson, and W. P. Brown, Appl. Opt. 15, 2913 (1976).

[7] "Single-mode dispersion", MM26, Opto-Electronics Group, Corning Inc., Corning, NY 14831, (1/96)

SESSION II

TDM and WDM Optical Interconnects

Chair

Steve Scott
Cray Research/SGI

On Wavelength Assignment in WDM Optical Networks*

Eric J. Harder[1†] Sang-Kyu Lee[2] Hyeong-Ah Choi[1]

[1]Department of Electrical Engineering and Computer Science
The George Washington University
Washington, DC, 20052
e-mail: {eharder,choi}@seas.gwu.edu

[2]Computer Science Department
Sookmyung Women's University
Seoul, Korea
e-mail: sanglee@sookmyung.ac.kr

Abstract

We address the problem of assigning wavelengths to paths (connections) in optical wavelength division multiplexed networks. The problem is formulated as follows: given the physical topology of a network with each edge of two opposite directed fiber links and a set of directed paths with no more than L paths over any fiber link, we assign a wavelength to each path in such a way that no two paths are assigned the same wavelength if they share a directed physical link. In this paper, we first prove that the problem is NP-complete for arbitrary network topologies. Our NP-completeness result is obtained through a polynomial time reduction from the graph k-colorability problem. This reduction implies that no polynomial time algorithm can solve the problem with the number of wavelengths bounded by a constant times L for the class of network topologies including meshes. We then consider tree topologies. For star networks (i.e. the length of any path is bounded by two), we give a polynomial time algorithm that requires L wavelengths. For trees with path lengths larger than two, we show that the problem is NP-complete and present a heuristic algorithm based on the polynomial time algorithm for star topologies. Our heuristic algorithm may require $2L$ wavelengths in the worst-case, but the simulation result shows that the average-case performance significantly outperforms the worst-case bound. This suggests that fewer excess wavelengths are required when most of the load is local.

*This work was supported in part by NSF grant MIP-9628468.
†Research supported by an ARCS graduate scholarship

1. Introduction

Wavelength division multiplexing (WDM) is one of the techniques used to exploit the huge optical bandwidth of fiber. In WDM, the spectrum is divided into multiple optical channels with each channel operating with peak electronic rate, where data can be simultaneously transmitted on different wavelength channels on the same fiber.

A wavelength routing network is composed of wavelength-selective elements that can route, switch, and convert wavelengths. The main idea of wavelength-routing networks is the reusability of wavelengths. In general, such a network consists of routing nodes interconnected by point-to-point fiber links. At any time, each node may have logical connections, i.e., light paths, with other nodes. Each path between a pair of nodes is carried on a certain wavelength. If any two light paths do not share a physical link, they can be on the same wavelength. The routing pattern between any two nodes can be fixed (a fixed-routing architecture), or it can be dynamically changed (a dynamic-routing architecture). The former is called non-reconfigurable, and the latter is called reconfigurable which requires optical switches. A routing node can take a signal on a given wavelength and send it out at a different wavelength if wavelength converters are available.

In this paper, we consider non-reconfigurable wavelength routing networks without wavelength converters. An important issue in such a network is to assign a wavelength to each light path in such a way that no two light paths are assigned the same wavelength if they share a physical link. This problem may be stated as the

- **Wavelength Assignment Problem:**

Given: a graph G representing a physical topol-

0-8186-7974-3/97 $10.00 © 1997 IEEE

ogy of the network with each edge of two opposite directed fiber links and a set P of directed paths in G corresponding to connection requests such that the largest number of paths using any directed link is denoted by L,

Objective: to assign a wavelength to each path using the minimum number of wavelengths in such a way that no two paths are assigned the same wavelength if they share a directed physical link.

The wavelength assignment problem under various network models has been considered in [15, 3, 16]. Several heuristics have been proposed based on the framework of linear programming formulation. Recent work has focused on obtaining bounds on the number of wavelengths required for a variety of network and routing scenarios. The work in [2] considered arbitrary networks, with and without switches, and deduced, using an information-theoretic argument, a lower bound on the required number of wavelengths to perform permutation routing. The work in [1], using probabilistic techniques, deduced the existence of a switchless non-oblivious permutation network that provides an upper bound on the number of required wavelengths.

In [13], several network topologies were considered: undirected tree, cycle, and mesh. Directed networks were first considered by Mihail, Kaklamanis, and Rao [10], and an algorithm for tree topologies was presented using $15L/8$ wavelengths. This $15L/8$ bound was improved to $7L/4$ due to Kumar and Schwabe[9] and more recently to $5L/3$ by Jansen[8].

In this paper, we first prove that the problem is NP-complete for arbitrary network topologies. Our NP-completeness result is obtained through a polynomial time reduction from the graph k-colorability problem. This reduction implies that no polynomial time algorithm can solve the problem with the number of wavelengths bounded by a constant times L for the class of network topologies including meshes. We then consider tree topologies. We give a polynomial time algorithm that requires L wavelengths. We show that the problem is NP-complete and present a heuristic algorithm based on the polynomial time algorithm for star topologies. Our heuristic algorithm may require $2L$ wavelengths in the worst-case, but the simulation result shows that the average-case performance significantly ouperforms the worst-case bound.

The rest of this paper is organized as follows: Section 2 discusses the complexity result for arbitrary network topologies. Section 3 presents an algorithm for star topologies. The NP-completeness result and a heuristic algorithm for tree networks are discussed in Section 4. Concluding remarks are given in Section 5.

2. Complexity Result

In this section, we address the complexity of the wavelength assignment problem for arbitrary network topologies.

Theorem 1 *The wavelength assignment problem is NP-complete for a class of network topologies including meshes.*

Proof. The decision version of the wavelength assignment problem (DWAP) may be stated as: given a network topology G', a set P of directed paths, and a positive integer k', decide whether there exists a proper assignment of wavelengths to paths using no more than k' wavelengths.

A non-deterministic algorithm for DWAP need only guess an assignment of wavelengths of size k' for the paths in P and check in polynomial time that no pair of paths assigned the same wavelength share a directed link in G'. Hence the decision version of the wavelength assignment problem is $\in$ NP. In the following, we show a polynomial time reduction from the well known NP-complete problem, namely, the *graph k-colorability* [7] problem to the DWAP.

Graph k-Colorability Problem:

Instance: A simple graph G and a positive integer $k \leq |V(G)|$.

Question: Is there an assignment of colors to vertices of G such that no two adjacent vertices share the same color and the number of used colors is bounded by k ?

Let G be the simple graph and k be the positive integer in an arbitrary instance of the graph k-colorability problem. We construct a directed graph G' and a set P of paths so that G is k-colorable if and only if there exists a proper wavelength assignment for P using k wavelengths (we have set $k' = k$).

For each vertex of G, we associate a path and a directed mesh in our construction of an instance of DWAP. We first show how to construct the meshes and paths, then how to connect the meshes to form G'. The key idea is to transform the vertex adjacency information in G into path adjacency information in G'.

Let $n = |V(G)|$ and label the vertices $V(G) = \{1, 2, \ldots, n\}$ in *breadth-first search* order, with children

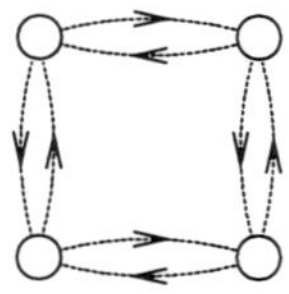

Figure 1: Mesh M^1 for $n = 2$.

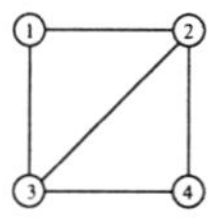

Figure 2(a): Graph G

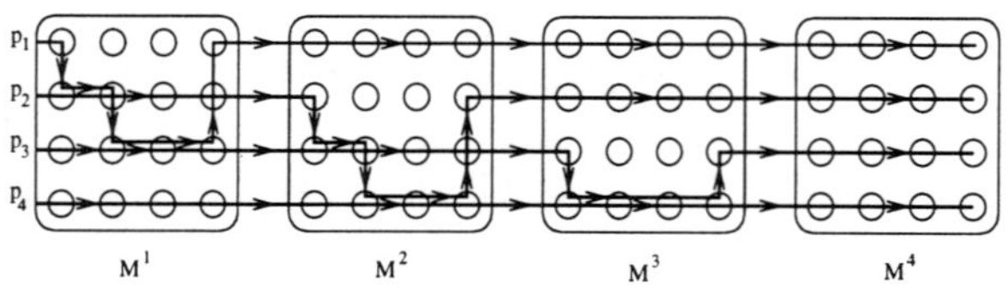

Figure 2(b): Graph G' with 4 paths.

of a given vertex being labeled in least to greatest order. Define M^i, $1 \leq i \leq n$, as an $n \times n$ directed mesh. Denote a vertex of M^i by $m^i_{j,k}$. The links of M^i are, for $1 \leq j, k \leq n-1$,

$$\{(m^i_{j,k}, m^i_{j,k+1})\} \cup \{(m^i_{j,k+1}, m^i_{j,k})\} \cup$$
$$\{(m^i_{j,k}, m^i_{j+1,k})\} \cup \{(m^i_{j+1,k}, m^i_{j,k})\},$$

where $(m^i_{j,k}, m^i_{j+1,k})$ is a directed link. In essence, we have pairs of vertical links between each vertex in a column (except the boundary vertices), and pairs of horizontal left-and-right links between each vertex in a row(except boundary vertices). In the construction of the paths, however, we do not use any of the right-to-left links $\{(m^i_{j,k+1}, m^i_{j,k})\}$. Figure 1 shows a mesh M^1 for $n = 2$. The construction of the paths in G' proceeds as we traverse the vertices of G in the labeled order we determined previously, forming partial paths in each mesh, and later connecting the partial paths and meshes to form the final paths and G'. Let p_i, $1 \leq i \leq n$ denote the paths in the set P, and $p_{i,j}$, $1 \leq i,j \leq n$ denote the partial path of path p_i in mesh M^j. For instance, the path p_1 is composed of partial paths $p_{1,1} \cup p_{1,2} \cup \cdots \cup p_{1,n}$. Each partial path $p_{i,j}$ begins in mesh M_j at vertex $m^j_{i,1}$ As we traverse G, we transform the adjacency information of the currently visited vertex, say v_k, into partial paths in the mesh M^k in the following way:

- each partial path $p_{i,k}$, $i \neq k$, consists of vertices (and the intervening directed links) $m^k_{i,1}$, $m^k_{i,2}$, $\cdots$, $m^k_{i,n}$.
- for each vertex v_s that is adjacent to v_k and has not yet been visited, we let the partial path $p_{k,k}$ traverse vertical down links to row s, and traverse a horizontal link, thus sharing a link with the partial path $p_{s,k}$ (The restriction to unvisited vertices prevents us from re-encoding adjacency information). Since we have labeled $V(G)$ as described above, v_s an unvisited vertex adjacent to v_k implies $k < s$, so only down vertical links are needed to extend the path. If v_s is the qth such unvisited vertex in G, then the partial path has been extended to a vertex in the qth column of mesh M^k. Suppose the partial path is in row $r \leq n$ at this point. Then $p_{k,k}$ is at vertex $m^k_{r,q}$. We now extend the path to vertex $m^k_{s,q}$, traversing the $r - s$ vertical links, and we extend the path to vertex $m^k_{r,q+1}$ to cause $p_{k,k}$ to share a link with $p_{k,q}$. Since each mesh is $n \times n$, we can repeat this procedure for every vertex adjacent to each vertex in G. When the last adjacent vertex is transformed, we extend the path to the end column and traverse vertical links to return to row k (the originating row for the partial path $p_{k,k}$.

Finally, when each vertex in G has been visited and adjacent vertices have been transformed, we connect mesh M^i to M^{i+1}, $1 \leq i \leq n-1$, via directed links

$$(m^i_{j,n}, m^{i+1}_{j,1}).$$

Each partial path $p_{i,j}$ is similarly joined to partial path $p_{i+1,j}$ by including the above link.

Figure 2(a) shows a simple graph G and Figure 2(b) a completed directed graph G'. Note that we have ignored the directed links in G' to better display the paths. We can follow the construction given in the proof by concentrating on how the path p_1 is constructed. Within mesh M^1, p_1 consists of the partial path

$$m^1_{1,1}, m^1_{2,1}, m^1_{2,2}, m^1_{3,2}, m^1_{3,3}, m^1_{3,4}, m^1_{2,4}, m^1_{1,4}.$$

By the construction, p_1 shares the link $(m^1_{2,1}, m^1_{2,2})$ with path p_2, and link $(m^1_{3,2}, m^1_{3,3})$ with path p_3. In the other meshes, the partial paths for p_1 remain along the first row since there are no other adjacencies involving v_1 to transform.

Observe that a path p_i shares a link with path p_j, for $i \neq j$, if and only if vertex v_i is adjacent to vertex v_j in G. So we can properly assign wavelengths to the set P of paths with k wavelengths if and only if we can properly color the vertices of G.

To complete the proof, note that this is a polynomial time reduction since

- the labeling of $V(G)$ can be performed in polynomial time, and
- each path is wholly contained in $n \times n$ meshes, of which there are n.

■

In our reduction from the graph k-colorability problem (for an arbitrary value k), the parameter L of the input to DWAP always has the value two even if G' may require more than k wavelengths. Suppose there exists an algorithm $\mathcal{A}$ for the wavelength assignment problem such that the number $\mathcal{A}(G', P, L)$ of wavelengths used by $\mathcal{A}$ for the input G', P, and L is bounded by cL for a constant c. (Without loss of any generality, assume that c is an integer.) Consider a complete graph G on $2c+1$ vertices (i.e., G has $2c+1$ vertices and every vertex is connected to $2c$ other vertices; hence, G is not $2c$-colorable). Let G' and P be the input the wavelength assignment problem constructed using the method discussed in the proof of Theorem 4.1. Then, G' is a mesh and the value of L is two. Applying algorithm $\mathcal{A}$ to this input, we should have $\mathcal{A}(G', P, 2) \leq 2c$, which implies that G is $2c$-colorable, a contradiction. The following results are consequently established.

Corollary 1 *The required number of wavelengths for a proper wavelength assignment has no relation to the value of L.*

Corollary 2 *There exists no algorithm for the wavelength assignment problem which guarantees the number of wavelengths bounded by a constant times L even if L is two and the network topology is a mesh.*

3. Star Networks

In this section, we consider star networks and show that a proper wavelength assignment can be done using L wavelengths. Similar results for star networks were independently optained in [14, 4].

Theorem 2 *For a star network T, a proper wavelength assignment can be done using L wavelengths.*

Proof. Let $V(T) = \{r, v_1, \cdots, v_n\}$ denote the set of nodes in T, where r is the root and v_i for $1 \leq i \leq n$ are leaf nodes. Partition the set P into P_1, P_2, and P_3 such that

(i) $P_1 = \{p \in P \mid p \text{ is a path from } v_j \text{ to } v_k\}$ for some j, k,

(ii) $P_2 = \{p \in P \mid p \text{ is a path } r \text{ to } v_i\}$ for some i, and

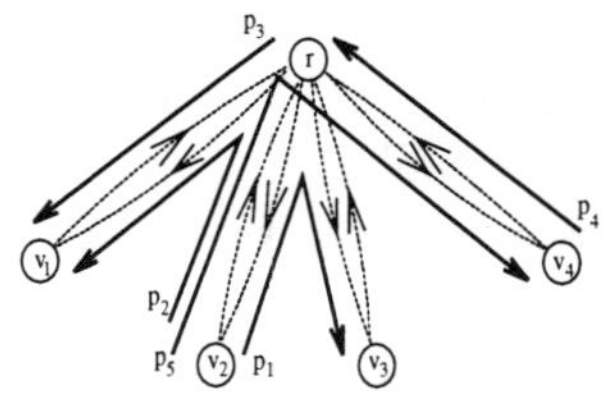

Figure 3(a): T **and** P

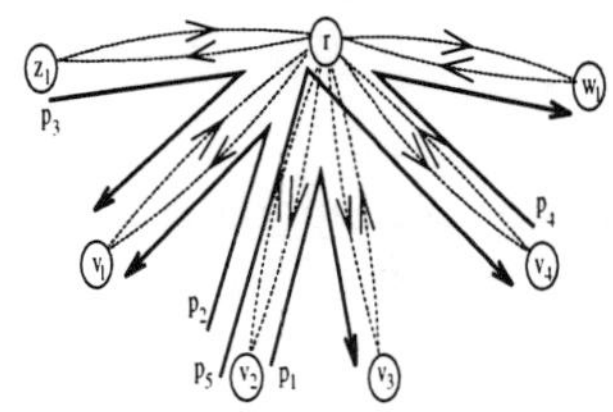

Figure 3(b): T' **and** P'

(iii) $P_3 = \{p \in P \mid p \text{ is a path from } v_i \text{ to } r\}$ for some i.

We then construct a new star network T' and a new path set P' from T and P as follows. Let $V(T') = V(T) \cup \{z_j \mid 1 \leq j \leq |P_2|\} \cup \{w_j \mid 1 \leq j \leq |P_3|\}$, where r is the root node and nodes in $V(T') - \{r\}$ are all leaf nodes such that each leaf node and the root are connected by two directed links in opposite directions. The path set P' is defined such that

(i) $P_1 \subseteq P'$,

(ii) for each $p \in P_2$, if p connects from r to v_j, a new path connecting from z_k to v_j belongs to P' instead of p, and

(iii) for each $p \in P_3$, if p connects from v_j to r, a new path connecting from v_j to w_l belongs to P' instead of p.

Note that each path in P_2 corresponds to exactly one node z_k and each path in P_3 corresponds to exactly one node w_l. Figure 3(a) shows a star network T with four leaf nodes and the set P of five paths, and (b) shows a new star networks T' and the set P' of five paths. Observe that one can easily find a proper wavelength assignment for P from any proper wavelength

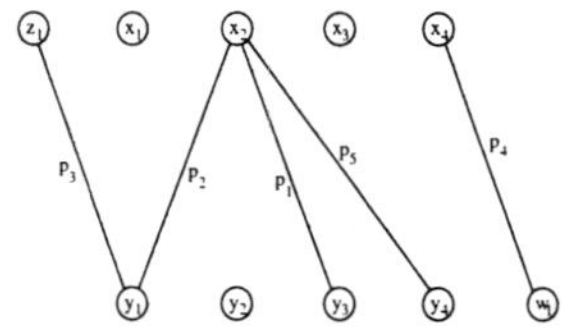

Figure 3(c): G

assignment for P'. In the following, we discuss a proper wavelength assignment for P' using the result for edge-coloring bipartite graphs.

Define a bipartite graph $G(V_1, V_2; E_0)$ such that

(i) $V_1 = \{x_1, \cdots, x_n\} \cup \{z_1, \cdots, z_{|P_2|}\}$,

(ii) $V_2 = \{y_1, \cdots, y_n\} \cup \{w_1, \cdots, w_{|P_3|}\}$, and

(iii) $E_0 = \{(x_i, y_j) \mid (v_i, v_j) \in E(T')\} \cup \{(z_k, y_j) \mid (z_k, v_j) \in E(T')\} \cup \{(x_j, w_l) \mid (v_j, w_l) \in E(T')\}$.

Figure 3(c) shows a bipartite graph G constructed from the instance shown in part (b) by following the above discussion. It is noted that the maximum degree of G is equal to L, and the *edge-coloring* of G can be done using L colors in $O(|E_0| \log |V_1 \cup V_2|)$ time due to [6]. Consequently, a proper wavelength assignment for P in T can be done using L wavelengths in $O(m \log m)$ time, where m denotes the number of paths in P. This completes the proof of the theorem. ∎

4. Tree Networks

Previously, it was shown that the wavelength assignment problem can be solved in polynomial time for star networks. In this section, we consider arbitrary tree networks.

Theorem 3 *The wavelength assignment problem is NP-complete even if the length of any path is bounded by three.*

Proof: We provide a polynomial reduction from the *graph edge-coloring* problem.

Graph Edge-Coloring Problem:

Instance: A graph G with maximum degree Δ.

Question: Is there an assignment of colors to edges of G such that no two adjacent edges share the same color and the number of used colors is bounded by Δ ?

Let G be an instance of the graph edge-coloring problem, with $n = |V(G)|$ and maximum degree Δ. Let vertices be labeled by a function $l : V(G) \to \{1, \cdots, n\}$.

First, we construct a rooted tree T with v'_0 as the root, and v'_i, $1 \le i \le n$, as the leaves, where each v'_i corresponds to $v_i \in V(G)$. We define the directed edges (v'_i, v'_0) and (v'_0, v'_i) for all $1 \le i \le n$. Addtional vertices and edges are constructed as follows. For each $(v_i, v_j) \in E(G)$ with $l(v_i) < l(v_j)$, we add two vertices w'_{ij} and w'_{ji} to T, each connected by pairs of oppositely directed edges to v'_i. The construction of T is completed, and we now define the directed path set P in T, with $L = \Delta$.

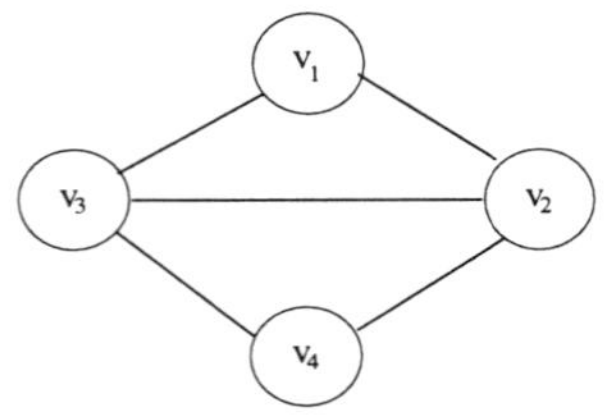

Figure 4(a): Graph G for Instance of GEC

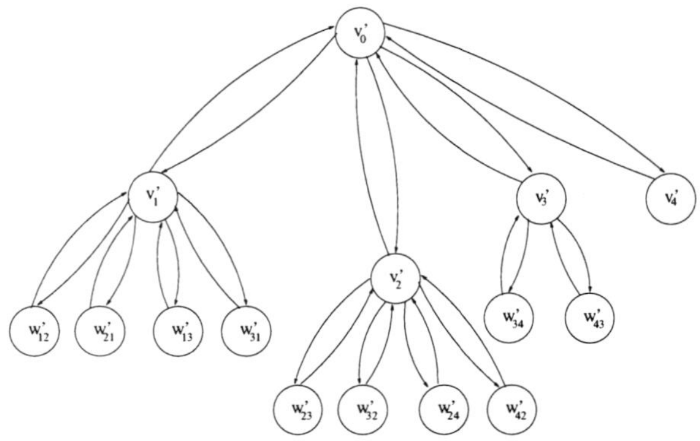

Figure 4(b): Tree Constructed from Graph G

Suppose $(v_i, v_j) \in E(G)$ and $l(v_i) < l(v_j)$. We define the following path sets:

- $p_{ij} = (w'_{ij}, v'_i, v'_0, v'_j)$,
- $p_{ji} = (v'_j, v'_0, v'_i, w'_{ji})$,
- a set of $\Delta - 1$ paths from w'_{ij} to w'_{ji}, denoted as pw_{ij}.

See Figure 4(a) for an example input graph, and Figure 4(b) for an example tree based on the graph.

Note that the set of paths pw_{ij} is required to force the the paths p_{ij} and p_{ji} to receive the same color in any proper coloring of P. This ensures that we may properly Δ-color the edges of G if and only if we may properly Δ-color the paths of P in T. The construction of T and P requires $O(n)$ time to complete, so we have a polynomial reduction if we can show the following claim:

Claim 1 *The edges of G may be properly colored with Δ colors if and only if the paths in P may be properly colored with Δ colors.*

Proof: Suppose the edges of G are properly colored with Δ colors. Let $e_{ij} = (v_i, v_j) \in E(G)$ with $l(v_i) < l(v_j)$. Let c_{ij} be the color assigned to e_{ij}. Then by the construction we may assign c_{ij} to the paths p_{ij} and p_{ji} since they do not share directed edges. All of the remaining $\Delta - 1$ colors are required to color the set pw_{ij}. This is because $|pw_{ij}| = \Delta - 1$ and the paths p_{ij} and p_{ji} each share a directed edgw with pw_{ij}. Suppose additionally that $e_{ik} = (v_i, v_k) \in E(G)$, with $l(v_i) < l(v_k)$. Denote the color assigned to e_{ik} as c_{ik}. Since G is properly edge-colored, we have $c_{ik} \neq c_{ij}$. By assigning c_{ik} to the paths p_{ik} and p_{ki} we have distinct colors assigned to paths p_{ij} and p_{ik} that share directed edges (likewise for p_{ji} and p_{ki}.). Hence we have a proper coloring of P with Δ colors.

Now suppose that the path set P in the tree T, both constructed above, is properly colored with Δ colors. For each path $p_{ij} \in P$ with color c_{ij} we color the edge $e_{ij} = (v_i, v_j) \in E(G)$ with c_{ij}, and note that if p_{ij} and p_{ik} share a directed edge for some $p_{ik} \in P$, then the color c_{ik} assigned to p_{ik} is distinct from c_{ij}, so we color $e_{ik} = (v_i, v_k) \in E(G)$ (which exists by virtue of the construction) with c_{ik}. This yields a proper edge-coloring of G with Δ colors. This completes the proof of the theorem. ∎

Theorem 4 *Let T be an arbitrary tree network, and define $\mu = \max\{\lambda(u,v) \mid (u,v) \in E(T)\}$, where $\lambda(u,v)$ denotes the sum of numbers of paths over two adjacent edges (z_i, u) and (u, v), for $z_1, \cdots, z_d$, where $(z_i, u) \in E(T)$ for $1 \leq i \leq d$. Then, there exists an algorithm that solves the wavelength assignment problem with the number of wavelengths bounded by $L + \mu$.*

When we regard a tree network as series of levels, the parameter μ may be interpreted as the load between at least two levels. This allows us to view communication requests within a level as "local requests" and requests that span levels as "global requests." The worst-case bound of this result is $2L$ as $\mu \leq L$. However, our simulation result shows that the average-case performance significantly outperforms the worst-case bound. This suggests that fewer excess wavelengths are required when most of the load is local. The detailed discussion about our heuristic algorithm can be found in the full paper.

5. Concluding Remarks

We have studied the problem of assigning wavelengths to a given set of light paths in WDM optical networks in such a way that no two paths are assigned the same wavelength if they share a directed physical link. The problem was shown to be NP-complete for arbitrary network topologies Our NP-completeness result implies that the number of required wavelengths has no relation to the value of L. Consequently, there exists no algorithm for the wavelength assignment problem which guarantees the required number of wavelengths bounded by a constant times L. For tree networks, a polynomial time algorithm was presented for star networks. For trees with path lengths larger than two, the problem was shown to be NP-complete, and a heuristic algorithm was developed.

References

[1] A. Aggarwal, A. Bar-Noy, D. Coppersmith, R. Ramaswami, B. Schieber, and M. Sudan, "Efficient Routing and Scheduling Algorithms for Optical Networks", *Proc. ACM-SIAM Symposium on Discrete Algorithms SODA 1993*, pp 412-423.

[2] R. A. Barry and P. A. Humblet, "On the Number of Wavelengths and Switches in All-Optical Networks", *IEEE Transactions on Communications*, Vol 42, No 2/3/4, 1994, pp 583-591.

[3] D. Bannerjee and B. Mukherjee, "A Practical Approach for Routing and Wavelength Assignment in Large Wavelength-Routed Optical Networks", *IEEE Journal on Selected Areas in Communications*, Vol 14, No 5, 1996, pp 903-908.

[4] B. Beauquier, J.C. Bermond, L. Gargano, P. Hell, S. Perennes, U. Vaccaro, "Graph Problems arising from Wavelength Routing in All Optical Networks," *Proc. Second Workshop in Optics and Computer Science*, Geneva, Switzerland, April 1997.

[5] C. A. Brackett, "Dense Wavelength Division Multiplexing Networks: Principle and applications," *IEEE J. Select. Areas Commun.*, vol. 8, pp. 948-964, August 1990.

[6] R. Cole and J. Hopcroft, "On Edge-Coloring Bipartite Graphs," *SIAM J.Computing*, vol. 11, no. 3, pp. 540–546, August 1982.

[7] M. R. Garey and D. S. Johnson, *Computers and Intractability: A Guide to the Theory and NP-Completeness*, W. H. Freeman and Company, 1979.

[8] K. Jansen, "Aproximation Results for Wavelength Routing in Directed Trees," *Proc. Second Workshop in Optics and Computer Science*, Geneva, Switzerland, April 1997.

[9] V. Kumar and E. J. Schwabe, "Improved Access to Optical Bandwidth in Trees," *Proc. ACM-SIAM Symposium on Discrete Algorithms SODA*, January, 1997.

[10] M. Mihail, C. Kaklamanis, and S. Rao, "Efficient Access to Optical Bandwidth," *Proc. IEEE Symposium on Foundations of Computer Science*, pp. 548 - 557, 1995.

[11] B. Mukherjee, "WDM-Based Local Lightwave Networks - Part I: Single-Hop Systems," *IEEE Network*, pp. 12 - 27, May 1992.

[12] B. Mukherjee, "WDM-Based Local Lightwave Networks - Part II: Multihop Systems," *IEEE Network*, pp. 20 - 32, July 1992.

[13] P. Raghavan and E. Upfal, "Efficient Routing in All-Optical Networks", *Proc. 26th ACM Symposium on the Theory of Computing STOC 1994*, pp 134-143.

[14] R. Ramaswami and G.H. Sasaki, "Multiwavelength Optical Networks with Limited Wavelength Conversion," *Proc. INFOCOM'97*, Kobe, Japan.

[15] R. Ramaswami and K. N. Silvarajan, "Routing and Wavelength Assignment in All-Optical Networks," *IEEE/ACM Trans. on Networking*, vol. 3, No. 5, October 1995, pp. 489 - 500.

[16] Z. Zhang and A. Acampora, "A heuristic wavelength assignment algorithm for multihop WDM networks with wavelength routing and wavelength reuse," *Proc. INFOCOM'94*, Toronto, Canada, June 1994, pp. 534 -543.

Multicasting Control and Communications on Multihop Stack-Ring OPS Networks

Afonso Ferreira and Eric Fleury
CNRS - LIP
ENS Lyon
69364 Lyon Cédex 07, France
{ferreira,fleury}@lip.ens-lyon.fr

Miltos D. Grammatikakis
Institut für Informatik
Universität Hildesheim
31141 Hildesheim, Germany
mdgramma@informatik.uni-hildesheim.de

Abstract

We propose dynamic multicasting on an $N = m \cdot n$ processor, OPS-based stack-ring topology consisting of n processor groups, with m processors each. By considering multicasting, we realize the increased network bandwidth offered by one-to-many optical communications. We assume that each processor has infinite local and network buffers and that the system performs synchronously. Assuming shortest path routing and network packet priority, we compute network throughput and latency measures as a function of the packet arrival rate. Balanced networks with $m \approx n$ offer higher throughput for uniform, multicast-free traffic. When the multicasting load and especially the locality of references increase, stack-ring systems with $n > m$ offer higher throughput and reasonable latency. A high level of locality and multicasting are necessary for achieving stack-ring network scalability.

1. Introduction

Optical technology offers a new dimension for high performance networks. Optical fiber links are relatively cheap compared to copper wires and offer high reliability (10^{-12} bit error rate), and measured bandwidth $\sim$ 10-300 Gbits/sec [12, 13]. Additional wavelength division multiplexing (WDM) may increase these rates to 75 Tbits/sec. These emerging optical technologies, such as tunable optical transmitters and receivers, and WDM allow the construction of very efficient networks. Using Optical Passive Star (OPS) couplers, one can build singlehop systems, where every processor is able to directly communicate with one another with no intermediate nodes. In order to implement such a system, at any given time, the processors' transceivers have to dynamically tune to the channels through which the communication takes place; this tuning time varies from a few milliseconds to a few microseconds over a quite broad wavelength [4], which is considered to be very slow in comparison to a typical packet transmission time. Therefore, this could represent a severe drawback when building very large networks [12].

On the other hand, the same kind of OPS couplers can be used for the construction of multihop networks, where a node is assigned to a small and static set of predefined channels, that rarely change, usually to improve network performance. Pairwise communication may then need to hop through intermediate nodes [13]. Thus, in multihop systems, communications take longer, but nodes are simpler, cheaper, and more reliable than in singlehop systems [2, 11, 15, 16]. In particular, multi-OPS topologies based on *stack-graphs* were proposed and analyzed [9], [8]. Moreover, modeling OPS networks through stack-graphs was proven very powerful. In [3] some open problems related to embeddings on partitioned OPS networks (POPS) [6] could be easily solved by using directed stack-complete graphs with loops to model POPS.

Notice that an intrinsic feature of optical communications is that the OPS couplers can span all the nodes in a group. Hence, in order to efficiently use optical technology we should study ways to implement and control multicasting communications. In this paper, we make a step in this direction by examining a centrally controlled, multihop OPS network based on the stack-ring topology (see Figure 1). The optical network is configured with $2n$ high speed OPSs (denoted B_i, $0 \leq i < 2n$) operating at the rate of several Gbits/second. Processors are divided into n *groups* composed of m processors each. Each OPS B_{2i}, $0 \leq i \leq n$, receives input from the group g_i and outputs towards the same group. Each OPS B_{2i+1}, $0 \leq i < n$, receives input from the group g_i and outputs towards the group $g_{(i+1) \bmod n}$. Hence, each group g_i is connected to OPSs B_{2i} and B_{2i+1} as input and to OPSs B_{2i} and $B_{(2(i-1)+1) \bmod n}$ as output.

0-8186-7974-3/97 $10.00 © 1997 IEEE

The OPS stack-ring network is well suited to our exploratory needs, since it allows for simple communication protocols for the network controllers, and also one-way, shortest-path routing. In our communication protocol, packet drops are not allowed but simultaneous write requests issued to the controller are executed in priority order; floating network packets are always given priority over newly generated packets to avoid system overload.

Furthermore, random polling (or round-robin) protocol can be assumed for selecting network or local packets for transmission; the average throughput and latency measures considered here are similar in both cases. Although there is a cycle in the dependency graph and multicast messages are considered, the proposed routing protocol is deadlock-free since no indefinite packet wait can occur. The protocol is also starvation-free, since floating network packets will be eventually delivered and new network packets will be able to enter the network. Notice that, if local packets were given priority, network packets could cause deadlock and starvation problems, as network demultiplexors would be held until local requests are satisfied, which may depend on other local requests being accepted by the processors.

The system operates synchronously in two distinct, repeated phases. During these phases, each OPS operates independently and implements one to many communications. In the *write (W)* phase, one of the (lower) transmitter-incident arcs in Figure 1 is activated. In the *read (R)* phase, some of the (higher) receiver-incident arcs are activated. This is in some ways similar to multi-hop store & forward packet routing. We consider this scheme to be advantageous over hot-potato (deflection) routing for stack-rings and possibly other multihop topologies due to the non-multiplicity of paths and the additional controller complexity to implement packet deflection. Furthermore, a completely asynchronous write OPS operation (without barriers) would lead to garbage on the OPSs and will not be considered.

Dynamic routing forms a reasonable network performance model [10]. In dynamic routing, each network node generates packets at a fixed rate, assigning to each packet an independently chosen random destination. All packets must then be routed in parallel to their final destinations [17]. Good approximations to empirical data have been obtained for dynamic routing on the binary hypercube, using shortest-path routing [1].

In this paper, we propose a new model for multicast communication. The term multicast refers to the transmission of data from one source to a set of destinations [5]. Both unicast, which involves a single destination node, and broadcast, in which the data is sent to all nodes in the network, are special cases of multicast. Multicast services are being increasingly demanded in many areas of communication [14]. In parallel processing, efficient multicast services can improve the performance of numerous parallel applications, are fundamental to several operations supported in data parallel languages, such as replication and barrier synchronization, and are effective in implementing shared data invalidation and updating in multiprocessors that support a distributed shared-memory paradigm.

In our multicasting model a packet is delivered from a source node to an arbitrary number of destination nodes, with limited copying. This new performance model is independent of underlying multicast addressing or queuing schemes. Generalizing previous dynamic routing methods, we propose *dynamic multicasting* as a traffic scheme for evaluating multihop networks with OPSs. We introduce the *multicasting load*, as the average number of processors that a network packet has to visit during its lifetime.

We focus on network performance measures, such as network throughput (S') and latency (L'). Network throughput corresponds to the average number of packets routed through a processor's input port per clock cycle, while the average packet delay is measured from packet generation to packet consumption at the destination processor. The throughput is sometimes normalized by the bisection bandwidth. With our single directional stack-ring architecture the bisection width is simply one; the network can be halved by removing just one edge in each direction.

We show that for similar size ($N = m \cdot n$) and hardware complexity, stack-ring systems with $m \approx n$ have higher throughput for uniform, multicast-free traffic. When locality of references and multicasting load increase, stack-ring systems with $n > m$ offer higher throughput and reasonable latency. A high level of locality and multicasting in parallel applications would be necessary for stack-ring systems to achieve network scalability.

In Section 2, we describe the system in more detail, introduce parameters for the dynamic multicasting model, and proceed with a probabilistic performance model. In Section 3, we present performance comparisons, focusing on network throughput and latency. Finally, in Section 4, we provide a summary and possible extensions to this study.

2. Models of Control and Communication

2.1. System Description

Figure 1 shows an implementation of an OPS stack-ring ($m = 3$, $n = 2$). Each processor should normally have two incoming and two outgoing queues, corresponding to writes and reads to/from the two (local and remote) OPSs. In this system simultaneous processor writes and reads could occur to/from different OPSs. Each group of processors can write to its own OPS and to the following one. It can read from its own OPS and from the previous one. This is an implementation of a directed stack-ring topology and because of limited access to multiplexers it simplifies the protocols and the resulting analysis. Further architectural details of this OPS network are shown in Figure 2.

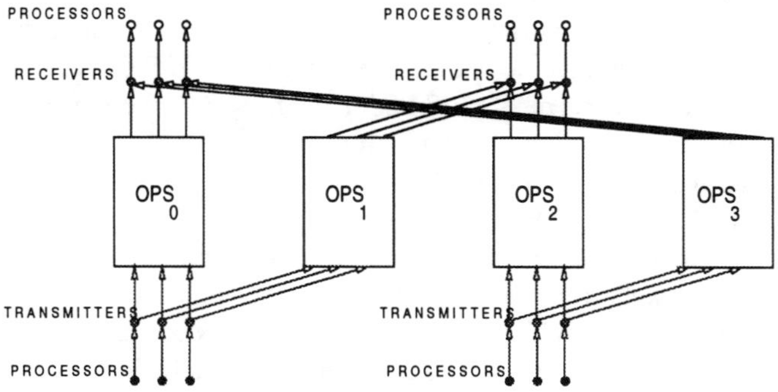

Figure 1. Network with passive optical stars ($m = 3,\ n = 2$).

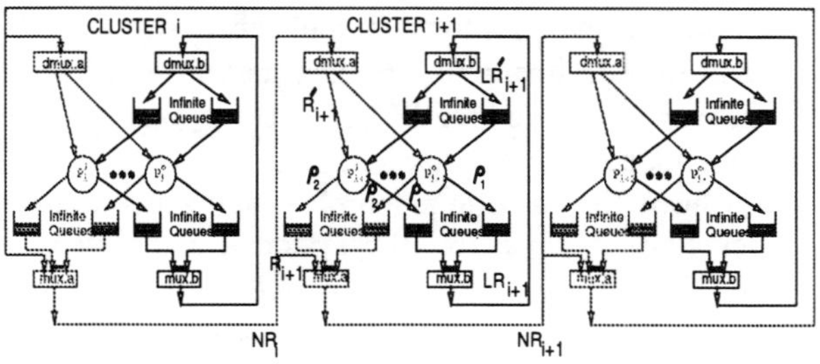

Figure 2. System diagram including accesses and control for local and network packets.

2.2. Analytical Model - Synchronous Operation

We propose a variation of *dynamic routing* incorporating multicasts. In this continuous multicast routing model, packet arrival requests are issued from processors at a constant rate. Generated packets head to identically and independently distributed (i.i.d) random output ports. Furthermore, to simplify the analysis we assume that infinite buffering is provided and that all network and local buffers are initially empty.

Notice that, because of infinite buffers, congestion tolerance schemes (either cell loss, or back-pressure) do not have to be considered. Credit-based schemes can be easily incorporated in our multicasting model, although the Markov chain analysis becomes quite involved due to existence of three different types of buffers (see Figure 2). The fourth type of buffer, corresponding to incoming network packets, can be dropped, since such packets are assumed to have (preemptive) priority over any local packets.

In our analytical model we assume a regular stack-ring topology, with all OPSs having similar speed and bandwidth specifications. Hence, all read and write accesses to buffers, and all packet processing requests take one clock cycle to complete. This poses no restrictions in modeling real systems. We only need to adjust the throughput and latency measurements using appropriate parameter constants [7].

By simple inspection of Figure 2, the overall hardware complexity (including buffers, (de)multiplexers, and links) is proportional to $N = m \cdot n$. Notice that, N represents the total number of processors.

Within the proposed framework and assuming fixed system costs (constant N), we focus on the steady-state behavior of two conventional constant rate performance metrics:

- *Network throughput S' defined as the average number of packets selected for processing by a processor's incoming link interface per clock cycle.*
- *Network latency L' defined as the average packet delay, measured from packet arrival to departure of last copy of packet from the network.* This is the sum of network latencies including processor input buffer arbitration time.

In our system, we distinguish between network and local packet latency. By our priority assumption, the processor arbitration time of network packets is zero.

Let the arrival rate from any processor to its local buffer be ρ_1, and the corresponding arrival rate to its network buffer be ρ_2. Similarly, let the *local multicasting load* μ_1, $1 \le \mu_1 \le m$ be defined as the number of processors that a local packet must access, and the corresponding *network multicasting load* be μ_2, where $1 \le \mu_2 \le (n-1)m$.

Let P_t be the termination probability of a newly received network packet; with termination we mean that the network packet is removed from the network, i.e. its last destination was on the current OPS. Let D_a be the average hops for a network packet to reach its last OPS. If $\mu_2 = 1$, then $D_a = \frac{n^2}{2 \cdot (n-1)}$ since self-addressing is not permitted for network packets. D_a increases with μ_2, approaching exponentially $\mu_2 = n - 1$. Since the graph is symmetric, and the routing algorithm does not distinguish on the paths, the network packet termination probability is

$$P_t = \frac{1}{D_a}. \tag{2.1}$$

The following parameters define how busy the network interface is, and how much of the network traffic heads to processors:

$NR_i(t)$ - probability that a network packet is arriving from group g_i to group g_{i+1}, at time t.

$R'_{i+1}(t)$ - probability that the network packet arriving from group g_i to group g_{i+1} at time t will be accessing processor P^j_{i+1}, $1 \leq j \leq m$ within group g_{i+1}, at time $t+1$.

$R_{i+1}(t)$ - probability that the network packet arriving from group g_i to group g_{i+1} at time t will continue on its way to group g_{i+2}, at time $t+1$.

Since network packets arriving at the multiplexer $mux.a$ have priority, the following equations are derived directly from the definitions and Figure 2, $(0 \leq i \leq n-1)$

$$\begin{aligned} R_{(i+1) \bmod n}(t) &= (1-P_t) \cdot NR_{i \bmod n}(t) \\ R'_{(i+1) \bmod n}(t) &= \frac{\mu_2}{(n-1)\cdot m} \cdot NR_{i \bmod n}(t) \\ NR_{(i+1) \bmod n}(t+1) &= R_{(i+1) \bmod n}(t) + \\ &[1-(1-\rho_2)^m] \cdot (1-R_{(i+1) \bmod n}(t)) \end{aligned} \quad (2.2)$$

Notice that, initially

$$NR_i(0) = 0, \; 0 \leq i \leq n-1 \quad (2.3)$$

The parameters below express how busy the local interface is, and how much of the local traffic is destined to processors:

$LR_{i+1}(t)$ - probability of packet arrival from multiplexer $mux.b$ of group g_{i+1}

$LR'_{i+1}(t)$ - probability of packet arrival from demultiplexer $dmux.b$ towards processor P^j_{i+1}, $1 \leq j \leq m$ within group g_{i+1}, at time $t+1$.

From Figure 2, it is obvious that,

$$\begin{aligned} LR_{(i+1) \bmod n}(t) &= 1-(1-\rho_1)^m \;, \; t>0 \\ LR'_{(i+1) \bmod n}(t) &= \frac{\mu_1}{m} \cdot LR_{(i+1) \bmod n}(t) \end{aligned} \quad (2.4)$$

Since infinite buffers are used, the processor throughput is easily derived.

$$\begin{aligned} S(t) &= R'_{(i+1) \bmod n}(t) + \\ &\left(1-R'_{(i+1) \bmod n}(t)\right) \cdot LR'_{(i+1) \bmod n}(t) \end{aligned} \quad (2.5)$$

The total network bandwidth is simply:

$$S'(t) = m \cdot n \cdot S(t) \quad (2.6)$$

We now consider the average latency for network (L_{net}) and local (L_{loc}) packets. In steady state, Little 's law can be applied at each incoming and outgoing buffer to obtain the number of queued packets and the corresponding delay. Hence, the average latency for local packets is,

$$L_{loc} = \left(\frac{\rho_1}{\frac{LR_i}{m}} + 1\right) + \left(\frac{LR'_{i+1}}{1-R'_i} + 1\right) \quad (2.7)$$

The average latency for network packets is,

$$L_{net} = \left(\frac{\rho_2}{\frac{1-R_i}{m}} + 1\right) + (D_a + 1) \quad (2.8)$$

3. Performance Comparisons

We first consider POS systems with m, n such that the system size $N = m \cdot n$ and overall system cost remain constant. Although the choice of m and n for OPS systems is probably $1 \leq m \leq 128$ and $1 \leq n \leq 60$, we consider all (m, n) combinations which preserve $N = 1024$. Similar results, only slightly less profound, can be observed for smaller size stack-ring systems.

Another reasonable assumption has to do with limiting the packet arrival rate combinations. We consider only high arrival rates which satisfy $\rho_1 + \rho_2 = 1$; this corresponds to one local or network packet generated at each clock cycle. In addition, for uniform traffic we take $\rho_1 = \frac{m-1}{m \cdot n - 1}$, while for communication patterns with increased locality, ρ_1 is doubled, or quadrupled over the uniform traffic rate.

A maximal condition necessary for system stability can be derived as follows. The average number of new packets entering the network each clock cycle is $N \cdot [1-(1-\rho_2)^m] \cdot (1-R_i)$. Under any routing scheme, a network packet has to cover a distance of at least D_a steps to its final destination(s). Hence, at each clock cycle there is an average demand for $N \cdot [1-(1-\rho_2)^m] \cdot (1-R_i) \cdot D_a$ network packet transmissions.

Since the maximum number of packet transmissions per clock cycle is N, the system can be stable only if $N \cdot [1-(1-\rho_2)^m] \cdot (1-R_i) \cdot D_a < N$, or $\rho_2 < 1-(1-\frac{1}{D_a \cdot (1-R_i)})^{1/m}$. Notice that, D_a depends on the network multicasting load μ_2. Bounds on R_i, which lead to ρ_2 bounds, can be readily obtained using (Eqs.) 2.2.

Finally, we take the network and local multicasting load $\mu_1 = \mu_2 = 1, 2, 4$. The larger values are possible only for certain configurations; this explains the lesser number of points in some graphs.

The overall packet latency can be obtained as a weighted average of L_{loc} and L_{net} depending on the local and network traffic rates ρ_1 and ρ_2. For uniform traffic it is simply,

$$L = \frac{(m-1) \cdot L_{loc} + (n-1) \cdot m \cdot L_{net}}{m \cdot n - 1} \quad (2.9)$$

By estimating the steady state behavior of the recurrence relations in (Eqs.) 2.1-2.9, we can compute the network throughput and average packet latency for various input parameters (m, n, μ_1, μ_2, ρ_1, and ρ_2). Our solution method is iterative until convergence of throughput and average latency measures is established. A limited number of iterations (3 or 4) are usually needed.

In Figures 3 and 4, we show the node throughput (S) and average packet latency (L') versus the logarithm of the number of groups ($log_2 n$), for $N = 1024$. The first point on the X-axis corresponds to $n = 2^0 = 1$, or a 1024-node system configured with one group of 1024 processors. The final point in Figure 3 corresponds to $n = 2^{10} = 1024$, or a

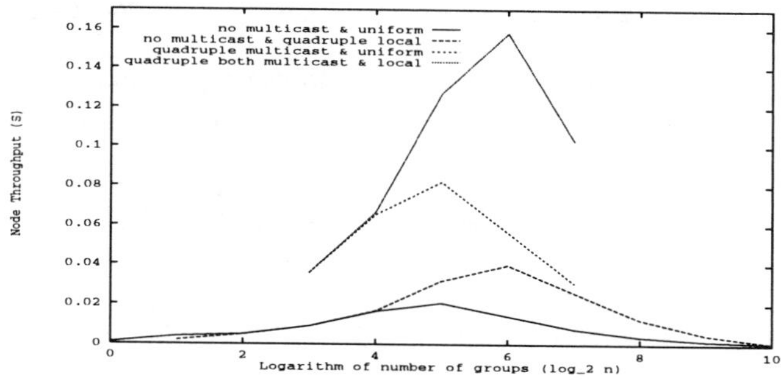

Figure 3. Node throughput (S) vs. log_2n for 1024-node stack-ring (n = number of groups).

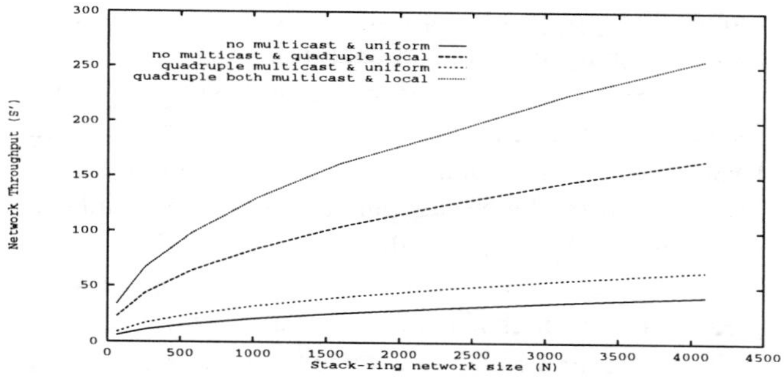

Figure 5. Network throughput (S') vs. network size (N), for balanced stack-rings.

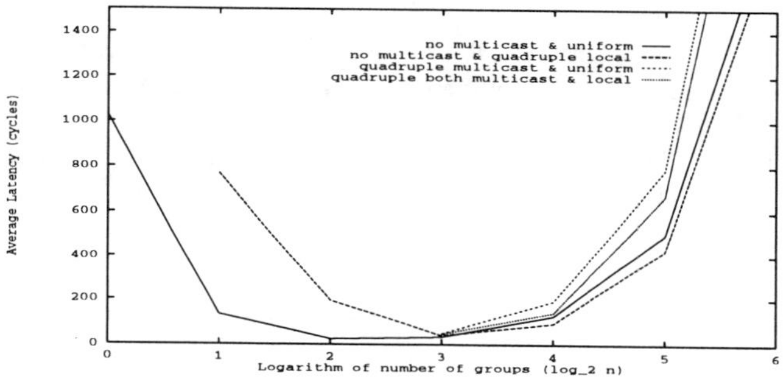

Figure 4. Average latency (L') vs. log_2n for 1024-node stack-ring (n = number of groups).

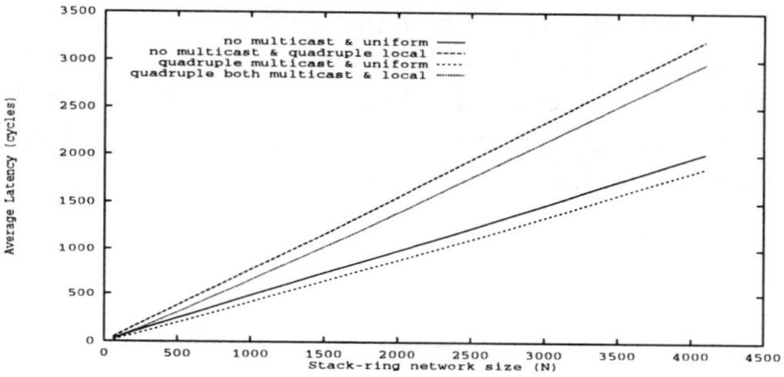

Figure 6. Average latency (L') vs. network size (N), for balanced stack-rings.

1024-node ring configured with 1024 groups, each consisting of a single processor.

From the figures, $(m,\ n) = (32,\ 32)$ appears the best configuration for uniform, multicast-free traffic. The node throughput is relatively poor; slightly less than 10 % for the parameters considered. The throughput measures increase when a higher level of multicasting load, and especially, when a higher locality of requests is assumed. When the multicasting load and locality rates are increased, $(m,\ n) = (16,\ 64)$ and possibly other configurations with $n > m$ perform better.

In Figures 5 and 6 we compare the total network throughput ($S' = m \cdot n \cdot S$) and latency (L) for various network sizes (N) of balanced stack-rings. The examined stack-ring systems are: $(m,\ n) = \{(8,\ 8),\ (16,\ 16),\ (24,\ 24),\ \ldots\ (64,\ 64)\}$.

From Figure 5, we observe that the scalability of stack-rings is limited unless the multicasting load, and especially, the locality of references increase. Empirically, the throughput increases with the locality rate in a linear way. It seems possible to verify this claim using our formulations in Section 2. Hence, parallel algorithms with a high degree of multicasting and locality are necessary for achieving high performance and network scalability on stack-ring parallel optical architectures.

4. Final Remarks

In this paper, we studied multicasting control and communications on a synchronous, multihop, OPS-based stack-ring network. The stack-ring has a cost-effective design which can exploit cost-performance improvements made possible by advancements in optical technology. In addition to examining the impact of scalability to optical network performance, we provided a model for dynamic multicast routing to help qualify network performance, for various network topologies and functionalities.

Balanced systems, with $m = n$ offer better performance for uniform, multicast-free traffic. When either a higher level of locality is exploited, or an increased multicasting load is assumed, the throughput improves dramatically and stack-ring configurations with $n > m$ perform better. Only with a high level of multicasting and locality can stack-ring systems achieve high performance and scalability.

In the future we plan to compare our models with simulations for a variety of large stack-ring systems, and empirically evaluate these systems under bursty traffic. We hope that the infinite buffer assumption used in this analysis will not cause large discrepancies from experimental results obtained from small-buffered, credit-based stack-ring systems.

The bidirectional stack-ring is more tricky to analyze. It is not clear whether its more complicated routing and control effectively improve performance over the single directional stack-ring. In the bidirectional case, other priority classes among network and local packets may be examined.

Finally, the performance evaluation of a wormhole-based, stack-ring system is an interesting open problem.

References

[1] S. Abraham and K. Padmanabhan. Performance of the direct binary n-cube network for multiprocessors. *IEEE Trans. Comp.*, 38(7):1000–1011, July 1989.

[2] A. Acampora. A multichannel multihop local lightwave network. *IEEE Conf. Global Comm. (GLOBECOM)*, pages 459–467, November 1987.

[3] P. Berthomé and A. Ferreira. Improved embeddings in pops networks through stack-graph models. 3rd *IEEE Conf. Mass. Parallel Proc. using Optic. Interc. (MPPOI)*, pages 130–136, October 1996.

[4] C. Brackett. Dense wavelength division multiplexing networks: Principles and applications. *IEEE J. Sel. Areas Comm.*, 8(6):948–964, August 1990.

[5] C.-M. Chiang and L. Ni. Multi-address encoding for multicast. *Lect. Not. Comp. Sci. (PCRCW), Springer Verlag*, 853:2–7, 1994.

[6] e. a. D.M. Chiarulli, S.P. Levitan. Multiple interconnection networks using partitioned optical passive star (POPS) topologies and distributed control. 1st *IEEE Workshop Mass. Parallel Proc. using Optic. Interc. (MPPOI)*, pages 70–80, April 1994.

[7] M. G. E. Fleury and M. Kraetzl. Performance of STC104 vs. Telegraphos (router). *Mathematical Research (PARCELLA), Akademie Verlag*, 96:29–37, September 1996.

[8] A. Ferreira and K. Marcus. Modular multihop WDM–based lightwave networks, and routing. *SPIE Eur. Symp. Adv. Net. and Serv.*, 2449:78–86, March 1995.

[9] A. F. H. Bourdin and K. Marcus. A comparative study of one-to-many WDM lightwave interconnection networks for multiprocessors. 2nd *IEEE Workshop Mass. Parallel Proc. using Optic. Interc. (MPPOI)*, pages 257–264, October 1995.

[10] F. T. Leighton. *Introduction to Parallel Algorithms and Architectures: Arrays, Trees, Hypercubes*. Morgan-Kauffman, 1992.

[11] N. Maxemchuk. Regular mesh topologies in local and metropolitan area networks. *AT&T Tech. J.*, 64(7):1659–1685, 1985.

[12] B. Mukherjee. WDM-based local lightwave networks, part i: single-hop systems. *IEEE Networks*, 6(3):12–27, May 1992.

[13] B. Mukherjee. WDM-based local lightwave networks, part ii: multi-hop systems. *IEEE Networks*, 6(4):20–32, July 1992.

[14] L. Ni. Should scalable parallel computers support efficient hardware multicast? *IEEE Conf. Parallel Proc. - Workshop Chall. Parallel Proc.*, pages 2–7, 1995.

[15] A. Sen and P. Maitra. A comparative study of shuffle-exchange, manhattan street and supercube network for lightwave applications. *Comput. Net. and ISDN Syst.*, 26:1007–1022, 1994.

[16] K. Sivarajan and R. Ramaswami. Lightwave networks based on de bruijn graphs. *IEEE/ACM Trans. Networking*, 2(1):70–79, April 1994.

[17] T. Szymanski. Hypermeshes: optical interconnection networks for parallel computin. *J. Parallel Distrib. Comput.*, 26(1):1–23, April 1995.

Inexpensive Local Interconnect Solutions Using Side-coupling Polymer Optical Fibers

Yao Li , Ting Wang, and Kenneth Fasanella

NEC Research Institute, 4 Independence Way, Princeton, NJ 08540.
yao@research.nj.nec.com

ABSTRACT

Potentially low-cost optical side-couplers embedded along a polymer optical fiber are demonstrated using etched micro-mirrors. Both serial and parallel mirror fabrication possibilities are discussed. Near uniform light distributions to as many as 256 such side-coupling ports along a single straight fiber were experimentally obtained. Various unidirectional and bi-directional all plastic array coupler concepts are presented. Some of them are experimentally demonstrated. Low-cost unidirectional and bi-directional optical data buses are proposed.

1. Introduction

Cost-effective solutions to deliver high bandwidth through optical fibers to home and to the desktop are being researched. The market pressure has let both telecom and datacom players to recognize that polymer optical fibers (POF's) could be a promising cost-effective physical layer networking solution of the future. Recent R&D indicates some large core (> 0.5 mm) POF's solutions can deliver Gbit/s optical data over 100 meter distance [1-2]. Research is also being conducted to identify methods to fabricate low-cost and low-loss POF's for long wavelengths [3]. The POF technology is expected to provide the following cost advantages over its glass optical fiber (GOF) counterparts: from raw material, to processing, and to connections. In this talk, we intend to discuss another important advantage of a POF over a conventional GOF, that is, its highly flexible mechanical processing capability.

2. Embedded Micro-mirrors

Due to a high melting temperature and rigidity, it is difficult, although possible in principle, to etch structures on glass materials. Research was performed to etch a single micro-mirror into a conventional GOF [4]. However, the corresponding low-cost volume production process is not available. In the past, optical couplers coupling light into or out of a GOF were prefabricated in a controlled environment. Methods using prisms or blazing gratings attached to fibers, using evanescent waves, and using electromagnetic mode coupling concepts are the most popular light coupling approaches. The availability of POF's makes it possible to incorporate, in addition to the above mentioned coupling approaches, a scheme to use simple optical reflection for couplings. Both the conventional reflection and the total internal reflection can easily be implemented through mirrors formed inside a POF core using mechanical or other types of low-cost etching techniques. Using a polished knife, relatively smooth surface can be etched in different shapes and angles on a POF. A mirror can be formed either by satisfying the total internal reflection condition of the etched interface or by metal deposition using a conventional metallic mirror coating process. In the later case, after a mirror is formed, it is possible to re-deposit the polymer to enclose the cut so that the mirror is physically embedded into the POF. One obvious advantage of using such mirrors to couple light into or out of a fiber is that it offers a wide range of flexible coupling directions in three-dimensional (3D) space .

3. System Modeling

Our intention is to provide coupling in and out of the fiber with embedded micro-mirrors. Owing to reversibility of a linear optical system, the coupling machanism of a sequence of uni-directional mirror-based side couplers can be modeled using the geometry of Fig.1(a). Here the two sets of parameters are: α_i $(1 \le i \le N)$ for micro-mirror reflective output coefficients, and γ_i for receiving coefficients at output. Omitting fiber's absorption and scattering for limited length of fibers and letting P_i be the output power at the ith port, it can be shown that the receiving powers N receiving ports are

$$\begin{aligned} P_1 &= \alpha_1 \gamma_1, \\ P_2 &= (1-\alpha_1)\, \alpha_2 \gamma_2, \\ &\cdots\cdots \\ P_N &= (1-\alpha_1)(1-\alpha_2) \ldots (1-\alpha_{N-1})\, \alpha_N \gamma_N \, . \end{aligned} \tag{1}$$

A uniform power distribution to N ports implies that

$$\frac{\gamma_1}{\gamma_2} \alpha_2 = \frac{\alpha_1}{1-\alpha_1} \, , \qquad \ldots\ldots \tag{2}$$

0-8186-7974-3/97 $10.00 © 1997 IEEE

$$\frac{\gamma_1}{\gamma_{N-1}} \alpha_N = \frac{\alpha_{N-1}}{1-\alpha_{N-1}}$$

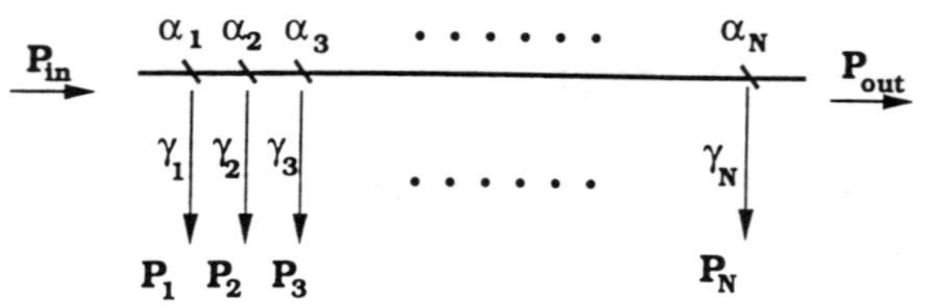

(a)

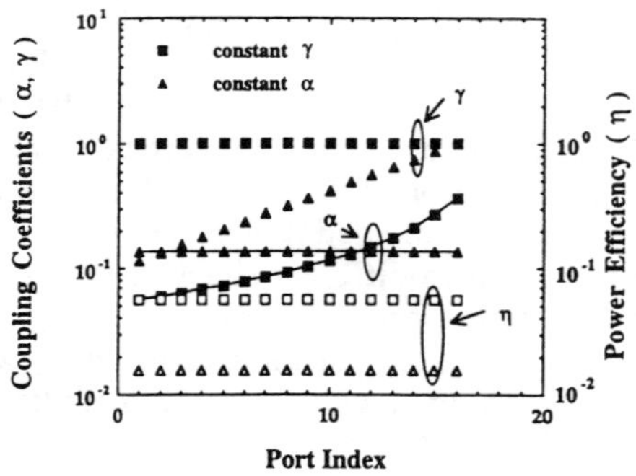

(b)

Fig.1 (a) POF side-coupling model, (b) plots of parameters.

There exist at least two ways to solve for α's and γ's. The first case is the constant γ case which requires $\gamma_1 = \gamma_2 = ... = \gamma_N = \gamma$. A simplest possible situation is that $\gamma = 1$ which corresponds to the situation of light power being coupled from the mirror-embedding fiber to free-space. The coefficients α can then be evaluated as

$$\alpha_1 = \frac{P_{in}-P_{out}}{NP_{in}},$$
$$\alpha_2 = \frac{\alpha_1}{1-\alpha_1}, \qquad (3)$$
$$......$$
$$\alpha_N = \frac{\alpha_1}{1-(N-1)\alpha_1}.$$

Correspondingly, the power outputs are

$$P_1 = P_2 = ... = P_N = \frac{P_{in}-P_{out}}{NP_{in}} \qquad (4)$$

The second case is relevant for fiber-to-fiber coupling where receiving coefficients γ's may not be identical. In this, case, by letting $\alpha_1 = \alpha_2 = ... \alpha_N = \alpha$ in the so-called constant α situation, it can be shown that

$$\alpha = 1 - [\frac{P_{out}}{P_{in}}]^{1/N} \qquad (5)$$

and

$$\frac{\gamma_2}{\gamma_1} = \frac{\gamma_3}{\gamma_2} = ... = \frac{\gamma_N}{\gamma_{N-1}} = \frac{1}{1-\alpha} \qquad (6)$$

In this case, the power outputs are

$$P_1 = P_2 = ... = P_N$$
$$= [\frac{P_{out}}{P_{in}}]^{N-1} [1 - \frac{P_{out}}{P_{in}}]^{1/N} \qquad (7)$$

The most general case is when both α and γ are not constants. Eq.(1) and Eq.(2) have to be used to calculate for each coupler. Letting $P_{out} = 0.1P_{in}$, and $N = 16$, we have calculated both cases for α, γ, and $\eta = P_i/P_{in}$. The results are plotted in Fig.1(b), where squares and triangles denote the constant α and constant γ cases, respectively.

4. Couplings between POF & Free-space

One simple but useful application of using micro-mirrors along a POF is to deliver equal intensity optical signals to N different locations along the fiber. Previous methods of delivering optical signals were reported using either holograms, stacked birefringent crystals, and integrated optical wave-guides [5-8]. The availability of a POF N-port splitter can provide a flexible yet low cost method to deliver signals to receiving terminals with larger spacing than the above mentioned situations [9].

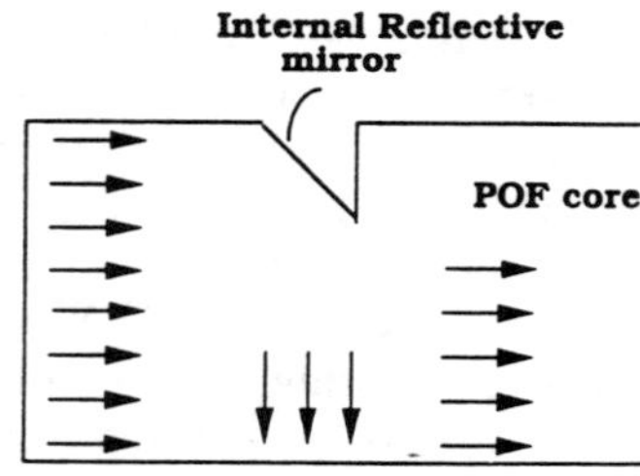

(a)

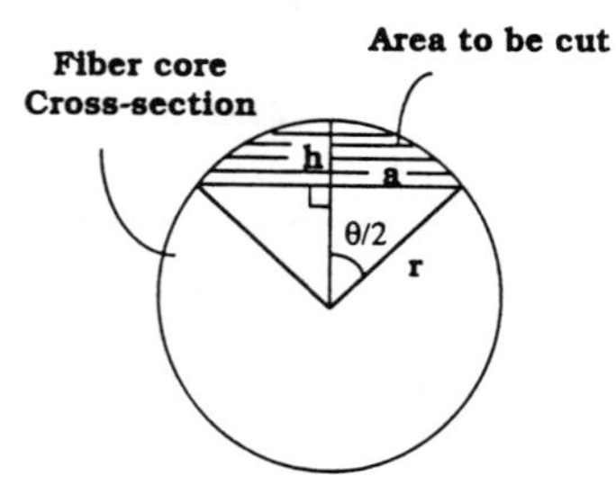

(b)

Fig.2 (a) Embedded mirror along a section of POF, (b) cross-section geometry of POF with mirror (shaded area).

In Fig.2, a section of micro-mirror embedded fiber is shown. Fig.2(a) indicates that such mirror can be formed either as a total internal reflection mirror or a metal coated mirror. While the total internal reflective mirror can be formed by cutting the fiber so that the mirror is formed between the polymer and air gap, the metal coated mirror can be formed by plating a portion of the internal reflective mirror. The shaded area indicates that in the case of forming the metal-coated mirrors, polymer can be refilled to seal the cut portion at the end. In Fig.2(b), a cross-section geometry of a fiber core is shown where the area of the simple mirror is shaded and is denoted as S. The area of the 45° cut mirror is related to the projected depth of the cut h which can easily be monitored during the cut. Using the parameters defined in Fig.2(b), it can be shown that the mirror coupling coefficient α can be defined as the ratio $\alpha = S/(\pi r^2)$. The mirror area S is

$$S = \frac{2\cos^{-1}(1-\beta)r^2}{2} - a\sqrt{r^2 - a^2} \quad (8)$$

with

$$a = r\sin(\theta/2) \quad (9)$$

where $\beta = h/r$ is the projected depth of a cut. It can then be shown that there exist the following relations between α and β:

$$\alpha = \frac{\cos^{-1}(1-\beta)}{\pi} - \frac{1}{\pi}\sqrt{\beta(2-\beta)(1-\beta)^2} \quad \text{for } 0 \le \beta < 1 \quad (10a)$$

and

$$\alpha = 1 - \frac{\cos^{-1}(\beta-1)}{\pi} + \frac{1}{\pi}\sqrt{\beta(2-\beta)(1-\beta)^2} \quad \text{for } 1 \le \beta \le 2 \quad (10b)$$

Eq(9) and Eqs.(10) can be used to determine the projected depths of all N mirror cuts along a POF.

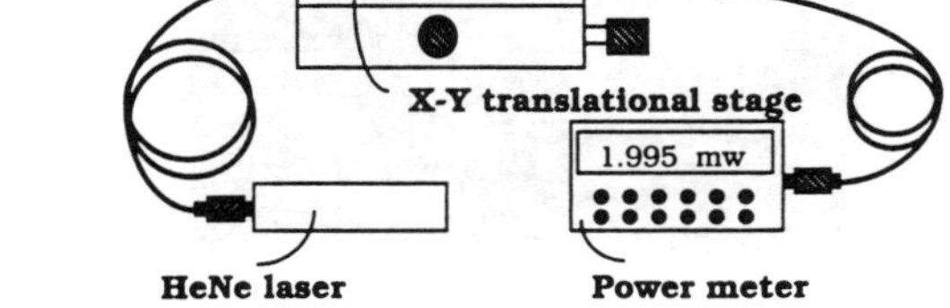

Fig.3 Mirror-etching aparatus for POF side-couplers.

Initial experiments were performed to form micro-mirrors along Polymethyl Methacryliate (PMMA) fibers (Model TB-750) obtained from Asahi Chemical, Ltd. The diameter of the fiber core is 750 μm and the material has a refractive index of $n = 1.494$ at the wavelength $\lambda = 650$ nm. The fiber was designed primarily for lighting and short distance data transmission applications and has a high numerical aperture of $NA = 0.485$ and an attenuation of 1.25 dB/m at $\lambda = 650$ nm. To ensure the quality of cutting, a system shown in Fig.3 was devised which contains a micro-meter controlled X-Y translational stage and a micro-meter controlled rotational and translational knife mount. The knife used for cutting was a polished flat razor blade connected to a thermal electric heater so that cutting temperature can be accurately selected. Although the PMMA material is sufficiently soft to be cut at room temperature, our experiment shows that a combination of using pressure and temperature ranging from 85 to 95 °F can result in a more smoothly finished

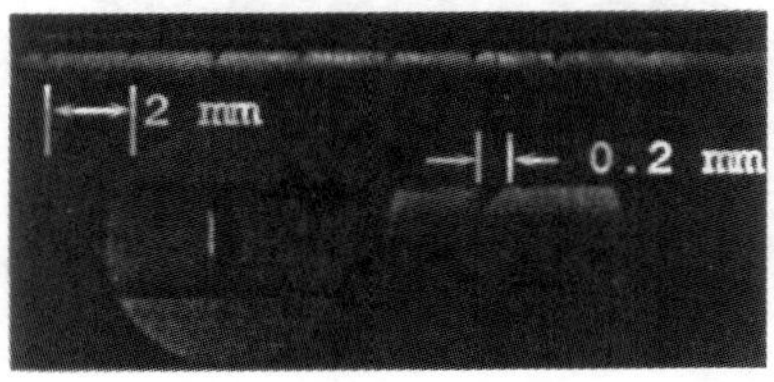

(a)

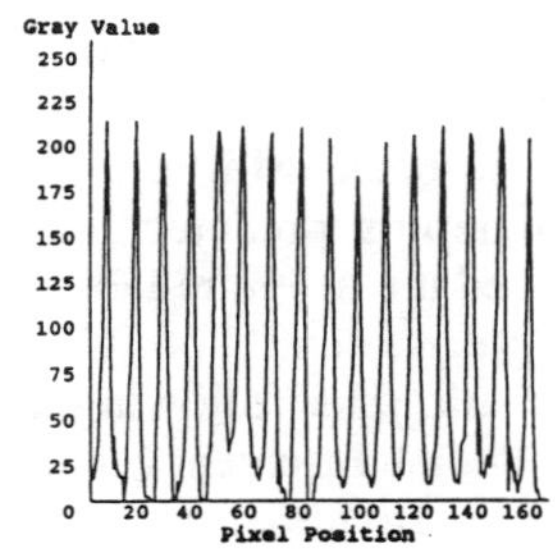

(b)

Fig.4 (a) A sequence of micro-mirrors on a POF, (b) a typical intensity profile of 16 coupling points.

surface (see Fig.4(a) for the profile of a typical cut). In our experiment, the finished surface roughness is typically between 15 - 50 μm. During the cutting process, while one end of the fiber was connected to a 2 mW HeNe laser, the other end of it was connected to a digital optical power meter which has a 4 digit measuring precision. Owing to serial processing, the intensity output of each mirror can be controlled through on-line monitoring of residue power at fiber output end. Shown in Fig.4(b) is a typical intensity profile of a series of 16 mirrors uniformed embedded along a 20 mm section of the PMMA fiber. Since for this simple case there was no metallic coating on the mirror surface, the coupling scheme is based on total internal reflection at the polymer and air interface. A good contrast ratio of better than 15:1 was observed. If instead of monitoring the residue light power at the fiber end, the output light power at individual mirrors can be directly monitored during the cuttings, we are confident that less then 5% intensity fluctuation is obtainable. Using this on-line monitoring method, PMMA fibers with one input port and as many as 200 side-emitting output ports have been made with overall port by port intensity fluctuations under 20%. Since for this fiber, the spacing between outputs was 2.0 mm, or in other words, the entire 200 port fiber has a length of 0.4 m, the absorption based attenuation was not as important as for the situations where light needs to be distributed to a longer range of distance.

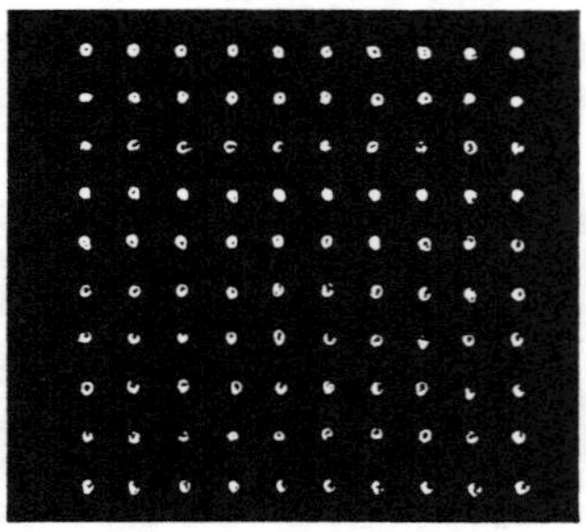

Fig. 5, 10x10 intensity output pattern from a POF embedded plate.

The above-described mirror formation method can also be modified to allow pre-specified or parallel cuttings without intensity feed-back. Multiple knifes with their cutting angles and depths predetermined can be used simultaneously to speed up the entire fabrication procedure. The trade-off is that precise control of light fluctuations will be much more difficult. The following experiment was performed. A 2 mm thick transparent Methyl Methacryliate plate was machined to provide an array of 10 parallel V-groves with a 2 mm spacing between any two consecutive grooves. A long PMMA fiber was cemented onto these groves using some transparent epoxy. The fiber columns on the fiber plate were then cut without using the on-line monitoring system previously described in an effort to study the feasibility of future parallel fabrication process. The depth of each of 100 cuts was predetermined through calculation using the above equations together with considerations of optical propagating losses in service loops between two consecutive columns of fibers. The initial result which shows a 64% light fluctuations among the 100 ports was not satisfactory. To alleviate this problem, V-groove fabrication and fiber cementing processes need to be improved on one hand. It was found, on the other hand, that a remedy procedure to correct such fluctuations to some extents is possible. The mirrors that are smaller than expected can obviously be enlarged by subjecting to additional and deeper cuts. The mirrors with larger than expected sizes can be re-processed to reduce the coupling efficiency by partial filling of the cuts with epoxy. In Fig.5, a 10x10 light spot pattern generated by the reprocessed fiber plate is shown where total fluctuation is reduced to about 19% through corrections of the 10 most fluctuated spots in the total 100 spot array. Further correction is possible but may not worth the merit as far as the total fabrication efficiency is concerned.

5. Fiber-to-fiber Couplings

Data communication and interconnection applications may require both the transmitting ports and receiving ports be connected to fibers. As an extension of the 1-to-N fiber to free-space coupling, some fiber-to-fiber POF array coupling concepts are investigated. Fig.6(a) shows a front-view of a 4x16 beam-splitting POF coupler where each of four transmitting fibers needs to couple part of its transmitting power to any or all of its four receiving fibers of the same type. The coupler proposed in the diagram uses three plastic plates which are low-cost manufactuatable using injection-molding techniques. The bottom plate is the thickest of the three because it needs to cement and hold the 16 receiving fibers using precisely located through holes. Four groves are placed on the top surface of the plate for holding the four transmitting fibers. The upper plastic plate has four groves facing downward to sandwich the four transmitting fibers. 16 larger (than the bottom plate) size through-holes are formed so that the cutting knifes which are used to form coupling mirrors can access the transmitting fibers. The cover plate is used to seal the

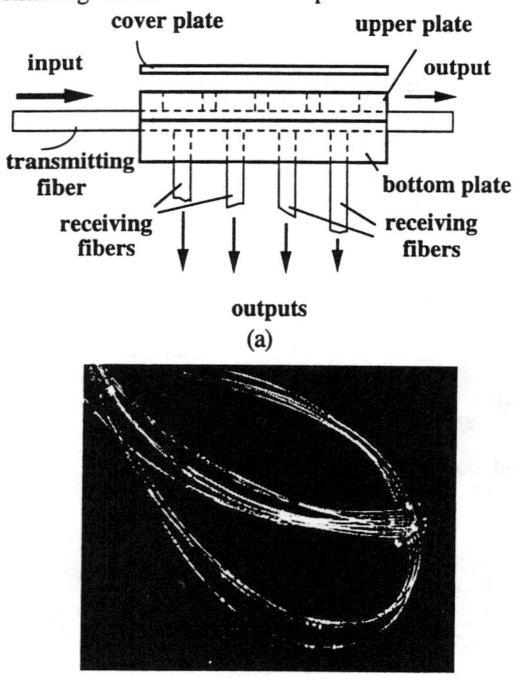

(a)

(b)

Fig.6 (a) Front view of POF side-coupling beam-splitter, (b) photo of a 4x16 beam-splitting coupler.

cutting holes once the multi-step mirror cutting process completed.

Experimental array couplers were made using Methyl Methacryliate plates. The parameters are as follows. The thickness of the cover, top, and bottom plates were 1.5 mm, 2.0 mm. and 4.0 mm, respectively. The pitch of the 16 receiving fiber through-holes was 5.0 mm in either dimension. The access hole diameter was 3 mm. Holes and grooves were fabricated using conventional milling machine. The overall plate area including the area for inserting alignment pins or screws was 35x20 mm^2. The TB-1000 PMMA fibers, of core diameters of 1,000 μm were used. All 16 receiving fibers were cemented using transparent epoxy. However, the four transmitting fibers were placed into the grooves and stabilized using screws. This procedure allows us to reuse the couplers by changing transmitting fibers for experimenting. The mirrors were cut into the transmitting fibers using a surgical blade wedged in 45° as previously described. The cutting procedure includes a pressing motion followed by a lifting motion to make sure the formed total internal reflection mirror will not be closed. For a large h/a ratio, it was difficult to obtain a flat and smooth mirror surface. Cutting with a room temperature knife usually resulted in chipped surface because of the application of excessive force. On the other hand, cutting at higher temperature sometimes also causes heat-induced surface expansion and deformation. However, when the ratio h/a is relatively small (h/a < 0.5), the quality of the mirror surface appears good. Thus, for our measurements, mirrors were prepared with either h/a = 0.1 or h/a = 0.5. A picture of an array coupler thus fabricated is shown in Fig.6(b).

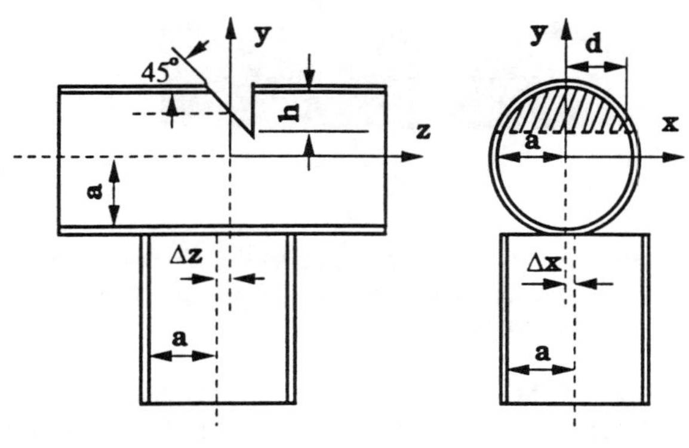

(a) (b)

Fig.7 (a) Front and (b) side views of misalignment geometry of the side-coupling.

Coupling efficiency is an important parameter of any coupler. Power loss occurs due to various intrinsic and extrinsic factors. Fig.7 is provided to help analyze and understand coupling loss of the array coupler. A schematic cut of α degree and h depth on a fiber of a diameter of $2a$ is shown in Fig.7(a). The mirror area is a section of a circular disk whose projection is the shaded area in Fig.7(b). It is appropriate to assume an uniform illumination in a step index fiber when its input beam fills up the entire numerical aperture. The coupling loss can be affected by factors such as position displacement, angular displacement and numerical aperture mismatch. In our case, the last two factors are basically similar to other multimode fiber coupling situations which have been extensively discussed [10]. The position displacements include the axial displacement Δz and the lateral displacement Δx shown in the figures. Assuming that both the transmitting and the receiving fibers are of the same type. Depending on the mirror depth h, loss occurs when the reflected beam can not be fully covered by the receiving fiber aperture.

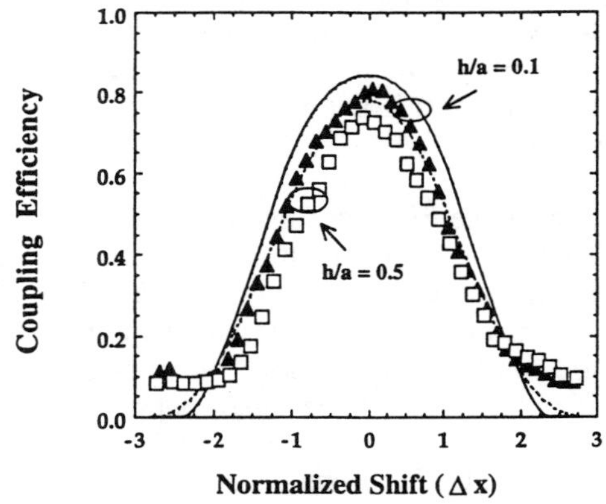

(a)

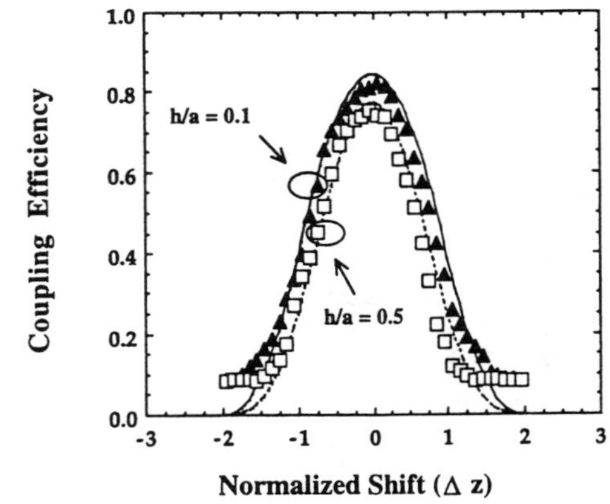

(b)

Fig.8 Coupling coefficients vs. misalignments in transversal (a) and axial (b) direstions, respectively.

Measurements of Δx and Δz were performed by scanning a receiving fiber across a transmitting fiber with an embedded mirror. Index matching liquid was used to fill out the curved gap between the fibers to minimized the one dimensional lensing effect. Both the experimentally obtained data and the calculated results are shown in Fig.8(a) and Fig.8(b). The discrete and continuous data points represent, the measured and calculated results, respectively. The following features are observed. Due to the use of large *NA* PMMA fibers, the theoretically maximum coupling efficiency is less than unity. Light reflected by a mirror will not be able to completely enter the receiving fiber aperture, especially in the direction perpendicular to the fiber axis. A smaller *h/a* ratio coupling is relatively less sensitive to the position mis-alignment than a larger *h/a* ratio coupling. The mis-alignment is relatively less sensitive along *x* than along *z* direction. In addition, the coupling loss in *z* direction is slightly asymmetric due to the mirror asymmetry along that dimension. The coupling efficiency for either case was lower than calculated efficiency. We believe that the efficiency reduction was caused by factors including power losses due to scattered light from imperfect micro-mirror surface deformation and mirror-fiber joint positions. The coupling uniformity among the 16 coupling points was 86%, can be improved if automated tool can be used to prepare the couplers.

Another possible fiber-to-fiber coupling application is a 2-way POF data bus where multiple bus ports can share a common bus line via time-division multiple access. GOF-based data bus has long been proposed where input-output couplings are implemented through directional couplers. Several other attempts have also been reported to implement optical buses using beamsplitters, holograms or waveguides [11-12]. Using side-coupling POF's, a bidirectional optical bus can also be cost-effectively implemented. Fig.9 shows the basic operational principle of such a bus where each V shape groove serves to reflect

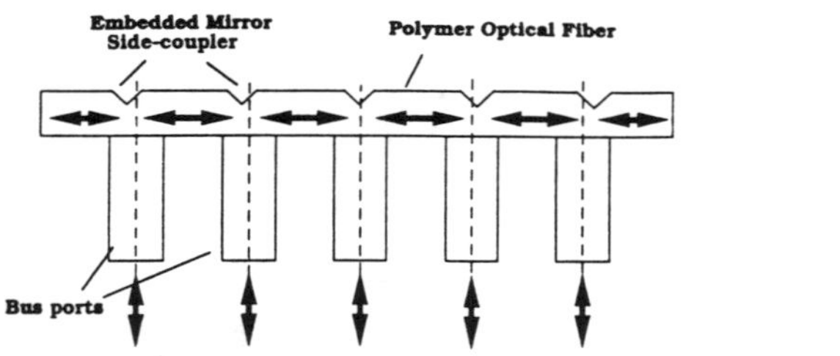

Fig.9 A schematic bidirectional POF data bus using bidirectional side-couplings.

light from a tapping fiber to two opposite directions along the bus line. It is always desirable to have uniform data distributions to all tapping ports regardless of its locations because a non-uniform distribution may demand large dynamic range detectors. To achieve tapping uniformity, the axial alignment of a tapping fiber is deliberately shifted in a way to achieve an asymmetric coupling ratio. The actual amount of shift depends on the number of bus ports and its port index. A shift in V-groove can introduce a different γ value for either directional coupling. Experiments for 4-port, 8-port, and 16-port bidirectional bus lines are being conducted. Again, plastic holding blocks which can be fabricated using low-cost injection-molding technology were used to hold both the bus line fiber and the tapping fibers. Each block typically has a longitudinal dimension of 85 mm and has a cross-sectional area of 8 x 10 mm^2. A semicircular groove was formed along the longitudinal dimension onto which the micro-mirror embeded fiber was cemented. Tapping fibers were introduced to the bus line fiber via through-holes. V-groove mirrors were formed through cuttings under a

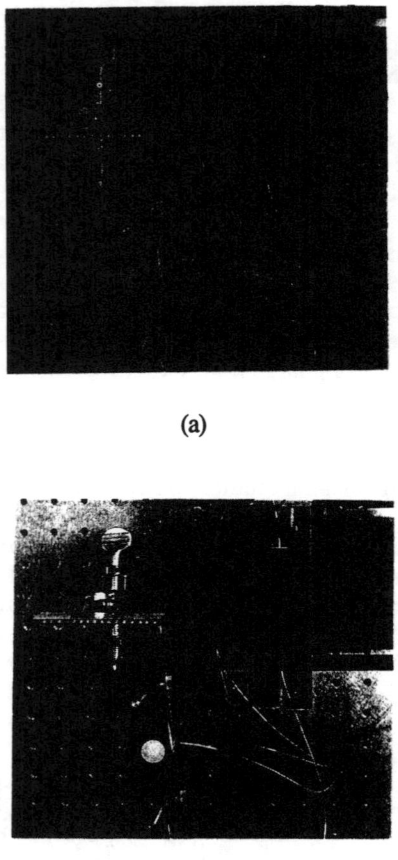

(a)

(b)

Fig.10 Photos of 16 port bidirectional coupling experimental setup. (a) and (b) Couplings from the two opposite directions.

microscope. In the extreme case of 16-port situation, we were able to obtain 80% uniformity along one direction and 50% uniformity along its opposite direction (see Fig.10 for photographs in both cases). Although in terms of distribution uniformity, our results are already much better than any reported optical bidirectional bus experiments, efforts are being made to further minimize fluctuations. The actual coupling ratios were measured to vary from 1.1% to 2.3% among all 16 ports. More measurements will be available at the conference.

6. Summary

To summarize, we have demonstrated the feasibility of making low cost plastic side couplers using embedded micro-mirrors in polymer fibers. As many as 200 coupling ports were experimentally demonstrated with an overall coupling power uniformity of better than 80%. We have also proposed a fiber-to-fiber type low-cost array coupler and demonstrated a 4x16 version of such coupler using all plastic materials. We claim that the proposed couplers can be made using low cost production process. While direct cutting can be used to form total internal reflective mirrors, metal coated mirrors are also fabricatable at additional expenses. Trade-off can be made between the ease of fabrication, coupling efficiency and sensitivity. In addition, the couplers fabricated with the direct cutting method can be potentially field-fabricatable. We have also briefly touched an important application of such side couplers: low-cost optical unidirectional buses and bidirectional buses. Using shifted V-groove mirrors, bidirectional buses of uniform tapping ratios can be implemented. Preliminary experiments have indicated the feasibility of such devices to couple up to 16 bus ports.

References

[1] Y. Koike, T. Ishigure, and E. Nihei, "High-bandwidth graded-index polymer optical fiber," *IEEE J. Lightwave Technology,* 13, pp. 1475-1489 (1995).

[2] S. Yamazaki, H. Hotta, S. Nakaya, K. Kobayashi, Y. Koike, E. Nihei, and T. Ishigure, "A 2.5 Gb/s 100 m GRIN plastic optical fiber data link at 650 nm wavelength," in *Graded Index POF,* (Information Gatekeepers, Boston, 1996), pp. 98-101.

[3] T. Ishgure, E. Nihei, Y. Koike, "Large-core high-bandwidth polymer optical fiber and its applications," *Technical Digest of CLEO/EUROPE'94*, paper CThD5.

[4] D. J. Ripin and L. Goldberg, "High efficiency side-coupling of light into optical fibers using imbedded v-grooves," *Electron. Lett.*, 31, pp.2204-2205, 1995.

[5] J. W. Goodman, F. I. Leonberger, S. Y. Kung, R. A. Athale, "Optical interconnections for VLSI systems," *Proc. IEEE,* 72, pp. 850-858 (1980).

[6] R. T. Chen, H. Lu, D. Robinson, M. Wang, G. Savant, and T. Jannson, "Guided-wave planar optical interconnects using highly multiplexed polymer waveguide holograms," *J. Lightwave Tech.*, 10, pp. 888-897 (1992).

[7] Jurgen Jahns, "Diffractive optical elements for optical computers," in *Optical Computing Hardware*, eds. J. Jahns and S. H. Lee, (Academic Press, New York, 1994), ch.6, pp.137-167.

[8] T. W. Stone and J. M. Battiato, "Optical array generation and Interconnection using birefringent slabs," *Appl. Opt.*, 33, pp. 182-191 (1994).

[9] Y. Li, and T. Wang, "Distribution of light and optical signals using embedded mirrors inside polymer optical fibers," *IEEE Photo. Tech. Lett.*, 8, pp. 1352-1354 (1996).

[10] F. C. Allard, *Fiber Optics Handbook for Engineers and Scientists,* (McGraw-Hill, New York, 1990) ch.3.

[11] A. W. Lohmann, "Optical bus networks," *Optik,* 74, pp. 30-35 (1986).

[12] C. Zhao, T. Oh, and R. T Chen, "General purpose bidirectional optical backplane: high-performance bus for multiprocessor systems," *Proc. MPPOI '95*, (IEEE Comput. Soc.) pp.188-195.

SESSION III

Free Space Optical Interconnects

Chair

Andy Walker
Heriot-Watt University

Applying Optical Interconnects to Electronic Systems Promise vs. Practicality

Julian Bristow, John Lehman, Mary Hibbs-Brenner, Yue Liu
Honeywell Technology Center
3660 Technology Drive
Minneapolis MN 55418

bristow_julian@htc.honeywell.com
612 951 7718

Abstract

Optical interconnects have long promised to solve a number of problems assumed to exist in electronic systems. A wealth of technology exists in the area, yet few electronic systems today employ optical interconnects. In many cases, it is the cost of optical interconnects which prevents their widespread adoption, as little fundamental advantage is offered by most applications of optical interconnects. The decreasing cost of optoelectronic technology and of its incorporation into electronic systems will enable further penetration of the market. Plastic fiber is likely to provide a competitive solution for intercabinet interconnects, while both high density fiber backplanes and polymer backplanes are likely to impact first high performance computer systems and eventually a broader range of systems, while free space interconnects will facilitate both advanced versions of existing architectures and the implementation of new systems. The key to practical implementation lies in providing transparency to the system integrator to minimize the departure from established practices. Significant progress is also being made in a new direction in which the inherent advantages of optics can be exploited in unique architectures, while still implementing logic functions in electronics, however such systems are unlikely to find widespread use in the near future.

1. Introduction

Since the concept was first proposed, optical interconnects have offered the possibility of eliminating packaging-related bottlenecks in electronic systems. The current focus of many workers in the field of optical interconnects can be considered an extension of the technology developed for the telecommunications industry. The same considerations of installation cost, bandwidth, cable volume, electromagnetic interference and maintenance which drove the replacement of copper with fiber are motivating the use of optical interconnects at progressively shorter distances in systems. Initial focus was on the provision of higher bandwidth than was attainable with state-of-the-art electrical interconnects for intercabinet applications, while more recent activity has extended the focus to encompass the provision of high density intracabinet interconnects following the realization that electrical interconnects are in many cases perfectly adequate on the basis of bandwidth alone.

At long distances (tens of meters or more), optics has been addressing near-term limitations in electrical interconnect bandwidth for cabinet-to-cabinet applications, and optical interconnects are already widely used in local area networks. As the interconnect distances become shorter however, electrical interconnect bandwidths are ample within a single cabinet, at least for individual interconnects, however optics offers advantages in the maximum attainable interconnect density. Electrical standards are emerging for gigabit per second interconnects over distances as great as 25 meters [1], and are targeting interconnect applications once considered likely to be the exclusive domain of optics. This belief is witnessed by the names of standards (Fiber Channel, Fiber Distributed Data Interface). Longer distances or greater bandwidths are possible if the characteristics of the copper are augmented by some form of signal processing. Individual electrical interconnects such as twisted pair are however bulky, and printed wiring boards do not offer such high bandwidth. At the backplane level, where interconnect densities are more critical than absolute bandwidth, optics does however facilitate denser packaging of electronic circuits within an enclosure. As interconnection distances are progressively decreased to the board level or individual package level, the interconnect density becomes progressively more important , and the bandwidth less critical. Since the same printed wiring board technology which is used on the backplane is also used on individual boards and in individual packages, electrical interconnects provide adequate bandwidth at these lower levels of system packaging. A jump in interconnect implementation occurs at the chip level and the RC time constant of chip-to-chip electrical interconnects is predicted to limit increases in processor speed and gatecount [2]. Free-space optical interconnects

0-8186-7974-3/97 $10.00 © 1997 IEEE

are now receiving significant attention for these short-distance applications. While within a typical electronic package, electrical interconnects are well suited to providing gigabit or greater data rates.

In addressing the difficulties of implementing electrical interconnects, optics offers advantages in bandwidth at distances over tens of meters, and immunity to EMI, reduced weight and more compact implementations for all intercabinet interconnects. Optics has also been demonstrated to offer the ability to maintain board level interconnect densities across the various levels of interface in the intracabinet signal path. In nearly every case mentioned so far, the use of optical interconnects has represented the simple removal of copper and its replacement with optics. Little advantage has been taken of the fundamental advantages of optics in developing new architectures. Free space interconnects however offer the possibility of radically new electronic system architectures since the optical interconnects now assumes a format inherently different from that of the electrical interconnects they are intended to replace.

We now describe several optical interconnects at different levels of electronic systems and summarize the issues facing those attempting to deploy optical interconnects in practical systems.

2. Intercabinet Interconnects

Some of the first demonstrations of optical interconnects involved the replacement of some form of copper interconnect with fiber in an intercabinet interconnect within a computer system [3,4]. electromagnetic interference are significant, or if the cost of the solution becomes comparable to copper. Two areas of focus are likely to reduce the cost differential for using fiber. The first is that of parallel optical links in which the packaging and connectorization costs are amortized across a number of fibers, while the second addresses lower aggregate data rates by reducing the cost of discrete fiber interconnects by using plastic optical fiber. A major advantage of plastic fiber lies in its large diameter. Bandwidth.length products of 2 - 300 MHz. km are possible with plastic fiber of 600 µm core diameter if graded-index designs are used. In glass fiber interconnects, the high cost of connectorization represents a significant fraction of the cost of an interconnect. This cost is due to the need to maintain microns of precision in the mating components. Figure 1 shows the effect of misalignment between two fibers in a connector for both standard glass and plastic fibers. The relaxed alignment tolerances on the larger plastic fiber allow the implementation of less expensive connectors. Large diameter glass fibers would allow the same reduction in alignment precision and hence reduce connector cost, but would themselves be more expensive to produce. Plastic fibers have long been available with large core diameters however only recently have the losses been sufficiently low. PMMA fibers with losses of 180 dB/km represent the current state of the art [5]. While the losses may appear high, many applications require interconnect distances of only 100 m or less. Losses of 18 dB or less may be acceptable for VCSEL-based links.

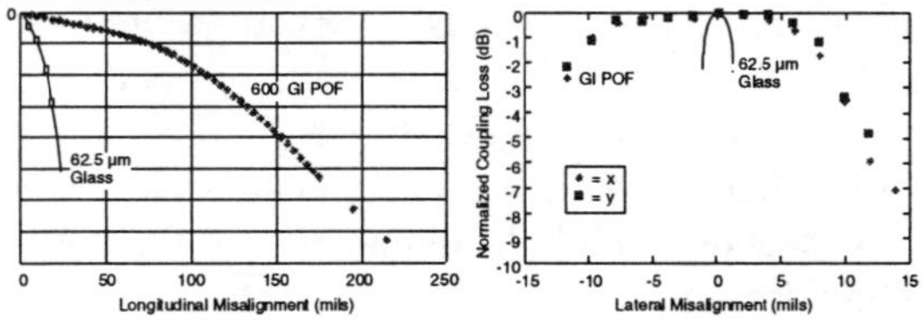

Figure 1: Effect of fiber misalignment on connector loss

Exploitation of the low losses of PMMA-based fiber requires a source with a wavelength of 650 nm which falls at attenuation minimum. LEDs offer insufficient power for most interconnect distances, and furthermore have too broad a spectral output for the narrow low-loss window in PMMA. Recent developments in red VCSELs [6] offer hope for low cost sources and hence low cost, short-distance plastic fiber interconnects. To date, reliability for red VCSELs has been poorer than that of the infra-red devices, some of which are already available as commercial products.

Most current research activities focus on evolutionary insertion of optical interconnects wherein copper is replaced by electrical interconnects at progressively shorter distances. To illustrate the tradeoffs made by a system designer, consider first the case of board-to board interconnects within a single cabinet. If electrical interconnects can provide gigahertz of bandwidth at distances of tens of meters then clearly they can provide the same bandwidth at the 1 meter distances characteristic of many intracabinet applications. At lower levels of typical systems however, the number of interconnects increases such that discrete wiring solutions become prohibitively expensive. The electronics industry solves this problem by using printed wiring boards rather than hand-wiring each interconnect in, for example, a personal computer. Considerations of interconnect density also make printed wiring boards more attractive for most systems. Electronic systems with interconnects at clock speeds of 10-100 MHz frequently use linear buses in the backplane. These are easy to implement in the physical, medium dependent layer, and give rise to an interconnect density which is independent of the number of nodes on the bus. Multidrop buses however are limited in their ability to provide high speed interconnects in simple implementations. As interconnect clock speeds increase, reflections from the impedance mismatches caused by the various drops require that greater fractions of a bit period be used for settling of the signal before a decision can be made. Based on these limitations, the optics research community targeted electronic multidrop buses for replacement with optics as projected data rates increased to several hundred megahertz and beyond, focusing on star architectures as optics is poorly equipped to implement linear bus architectures. The electrical community however continued to exploit the potential of its substantial infrastructure in copper, and started a movement towards alternative architectures. Switched interconnects in which point-to-point interconnects from each element in the system interface to a switch allow reconfiguration of the interconnects as needed for program execution. With the elimination of the impedance discontinuities of a linear bus comes the possibility of higher speed operation. Indeed, electrical backplanes may operate with interconnect clock speeds of 1 Gbps or more in point-to-point architectures. Switched architectures however impose greater requirements on the interconnect density. The number of channels required into and from a centralized switch scales with the number of processors. Both the wiring density in the backplane and the number of pins required at each board-to-backplane interface can limit both the logical and physical size of the system that can be implemented using a switched architecture, and also affects the highest degree of connectivity which can be implanted. Electronic systems today cannot always employ full connectivity, and instead rely on an interconnect fabric consisting of routers implementing limited switching [7].

Electrical technology appears well placed to provide gigabit interconnects or lower data rates at distances up to tens of centimeters or meters. Aggressive printed wiring board technologies offer linewidths of 25 um with comparable spacings, while the mainstream of the industry focuses of 100 um lines and 100 um spaces (4 mil / 4 mil). If a sufficient number of interconnect layers are integrated, this density offers adequate capability for most electronic systems. The difficulty most often encountered is in maintaining this density across the various interfaces in the system. These interfaces include those from the package to the printed wiring board, and between a line replaceable module or removable card and the backplane. The problem encountered is one of poor impedance control at the interface and of crosstalk in this ill-controlled environment. In designs in which pins mate with corresponding sockets, insertion forces of 100g per pin quickly add up to unmanageable figures for connectors incorporating hundreds of pins. Addition of more pins would require such force that removal and insertion of the board cause physical damage. Aside from the matter of insertion force, it is the crosstalk in typical connectors which limits the maximum effective pincount. As the pins are located closer together, crosstalk increases unless sufficient pins are grounded. As the data rate increases, so must more pins be assigned to ground, and so the board-edge I/O reaches an asymptotic limit. For a SEM-E connector, this figure is somewhere of the order of 1 Gbps per pin pair for a total of 700 pins, or an aggregate data rate of 350 Gbps, or one third of a terabit per second. In a chassis incorporating 16 such cards, a total of 2.8 Terabits of information per second could be transmitted per second (accounting for a path consisting of a source and a destination board). Boards with greater width at the board to backplane interface would allow proportionately greater aggregate data rate transfers, however simply using larger boards does not solve the problem as the I/O requirements for a uniformly populated board grow with the square of the board edge dimension, whereas the I/O capability grows only linearly with this dimension.

To gain near term acceptance, the minimum required of optics is that it offer a higher density than is attainable with electrical interconnects and that it affect as little of the remainder of the system as possible. Several solutions have been proposed and development of prototype systems is underway in several laboratories. The solutions include fiber, other guided wave media such as polymer waveguides, and free-space interconnects. Consider first fiber. While the core diameter of 50 or 62.5um offers compact size, the outer cladding of 125um fixes a minimum pitch of 8/mm, and the addition of the plastic buffers required to prevent long-term degradation of the fibers might increase the diameter of each line to 250um. A de facto standard for parallel fiber based interconnects is 250um pitch. In a single layer of fiber, this represents a maximum interconnect density of 4/mm, compared to a usable density in a multirow (perhaps 5 rows) electrical connector. If multiple layers of fiber were used, the density would increase in proportion. In fact, not all the board edge can be associated solely with fiber, as most fiber based board-to-backplane connectors employ some form of insert to locate the fibers within a standard connector shell. This insert occupies space that is then unavailable for interconnects. For example, an MT connector of 5 mm width supports 12 fibers in a single layer. This in a single layer gives a usable density which is comparable to the electrical case. By stacking several such inserts in a single connector, densities of 2-4x that of the electrical case can be obtained.

Fiber solutions offered little advantage over electrical technology until point-to-point architectures gained acceptance, since the bulk of fiber fan-in and fan-out circuits prevented their use in electronic systems with tight physical constraints. Even for point-to-point architectures, the minimum bend radius of typical fibers results in large areas on each board being taken up with the routing to and from the connector housing. Furthermore, the assembly time required for the backplane scales with the total number of interconnect paths. These problems can be solved in two ways. The poor scalability of the fabrication cost with interconnect count can be addressed by embedding the optical fiber with a flexible carrier to form an interconnect layer which can then be attached. Shahid [8] has developed such a technology based on telecommunications fiber. The minimum bend radius however can only be addressed by fabricating fibers with smaller cladding diameter since the minimum bend radius is dictated by the maximum tolerable stress in the surface of the fiber. High humidity contributes further to the degradation, so that deployment in military environments might require relaxing of the bend radius. It is however these very same military processors which are likely to represent the first insertions of optical interconnects.

Embedded fiber approaches offer an assembly cost which is independent of the number of interconnects, however the cost of fabrication of that layer depends on the number of interconnects being implemented. The minimum feature size is defined by the fiber drawing process. Polymer optical backplanes in contrast represent an advance towards the techniques employed to reduce cost in the electronics industry where printed wiring boards have long displaced discrete wiring schemes. Several polymer waveguide interconnect media [9,10] optical backplanes [11] have been developed. Polymer waveguides offer interconnect densities limited only by photolithographic processes. as with electrical interconnect media however, the usable density in an electronic system depends on the density at the various interfaces between the different levels of packaging in a system.

In figure 2 we show an interconnect between two multichip modules based on polymer waveguides. This interconnect, developed at Honeywell, relies on our previously reported polyetherimide/benzocyclobutene waveguide system [12]. We have developed a flexible polymer waveguide interconnect which allows fabrication of multimode polymer waveguides with dimensions limited only by the photolithographic tools used in their definition, this allowing us to produce direct analogues of electrical interconnect components. For example, we have implemented the polymer waveguides using IC and MCM fabrication tools for application within packages, and have also fabricated the flexible waveguides over larger dimensions to provide the optical equivalent of electrical flex circuits. We have also laminated the flexible circuits to rigid circuit board material to provide the optical equivalent of printed circuit boards. These components are however analogues to electrical components which themselves are perfectly adequate in many applications. It is instead the interface between a board and a backplane and a board and a multichip module which when implemented with the same density as the individual components provides a significant advantage over the electrical case. Figure 3 shows more details of the MCM-to-MCM interconnect.

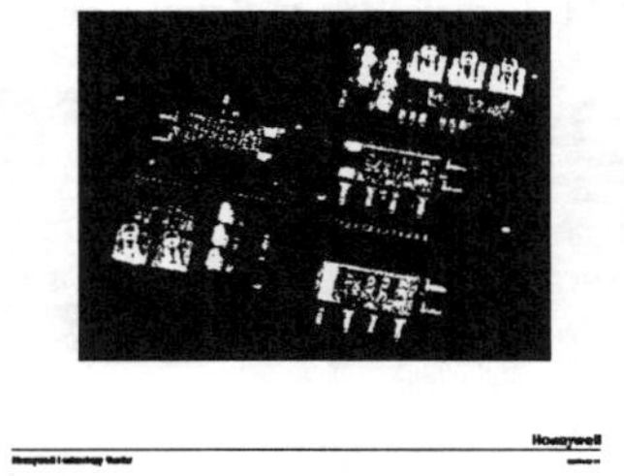

Figure 2: The first demonstration of an MCM-to-MCM interconnect using polymer waveguides.

A flexible optical waveguide element provides the interface between two rigid optical waveguide layers, one within the MCM and another on the printed wiring board. Since the flexible waveguide element is fabricated using the same techniques as the fixed components, it can be fabricated with the same density. The optical interconnects have therefore eliminated bottlenecks associated with electronic packaging in today's systems. In eliminating the bottlenecks in electronic systems, it is important that additional cost not be introduced, or at least that any additional cost be commensurate with the benefit provided. The MCM-to-board connector is integrated into the system using a passive alignment scheme. During fabrication of the waveguide layers, alignment features are defined and by virtue of the manufacturing process cannot help but be aligned to the waveguides. The features take the form of troughs immediately adjacent to the waveguide arrays. To assemble two components in the system with waveguide arrays defined, a rigid key is used. This key includes features which mate with the troughs defined on the MCM-level interconnect later and also with those on the printed wiring board level interconnect layer. By pressing the key piece into the troughs, the flexible element is brought into alignment with respect to the fixed waveguides. This clearly eliminates the need for active alignment, and furthermore offers an assembly time which is independent of the number of waveguides being connected or the dimensions of the waveguide.

One of the most critical bottlenecks in electronic systems is the board-to-backplane connector. Polymer waveguides have been demonstrated at Honeywell and AMP [11] to provide densities equivalent to a 32-to-1 pin replacement in a standard electrical shell using either expanded beam or direct contacting approaches. Direct contact offers possibly higher densities but raises some concerns over the tolerance to contamination. Manufacturable designs are under development, and have focused on providing multi-waveguide inserts. Waveguide pitches of 100 um have been demonstrated in contacting designs [13]. This allows interconnect densities of 280 per inch compared to perhaps 70 usable signal pins at 1 Ghz in a state-of-the art electrical connector.

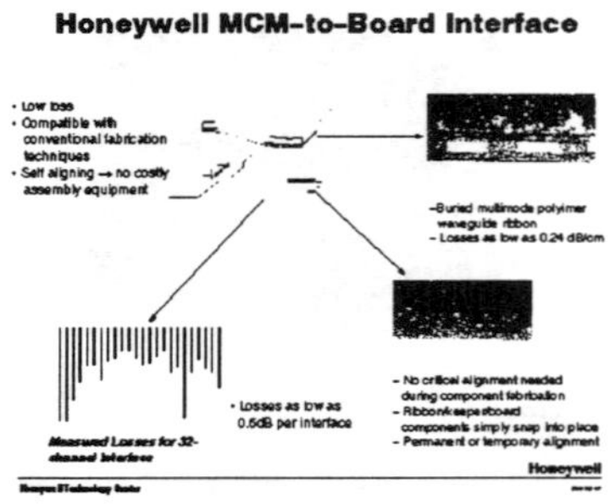

Figure 3: Details of a high-density MCM-to-board connector

3. Free-space intracabinet interconnections

If the various interfaces in an electronic system present the greatest impediment to enhancing system performance, then the greatest potential for optics to impact electronic systems may lie in eliminating those interfaces. Free space optical interconnects offer the possibility of transmission from chip-to-chip directly, without using any form of guided wave interconnect medium with its associated constraints of interconnect density. The chips may be located in the same package, on the same board, or on different boards in the same system. In most cases the adoption of free-space interconnects will cause the system to be assembled differently than is the case today, thus increasing system cost unless significant benefits accrue. One exception is a class of processor hardware in which no backplane is used today, such as the spaceborne processor shown in figure 4. It is likely that a free-space optical interconnect will perturb the system design less than the insertion of a fiber or polymer waveguide based optical backplane.

Figure 4: A spaceborne processor assembled from multiple boards without using a conventional backplane.

Free-space demonstration systems have typically relied on microoptics to provide fixed signal routing. Dense arrays of interconnect optoelectronics have been integrated with electronics using bump bonding technology [14], and total interconnect capacities of several thousand channels per cell have been demonstrated. To date, much of the work has relied on the use of modulators with limited temperature range. Modulator approaches also require external high-power laser sources and ancillary optics when used in a system.

Several major challenges remain unsolved if free space optical interconnects are to be used in electronic systems. In addition to addressing the overall cost of the system, the power dissipation for free-space interconnects must be made sufficiently small that it constitutes a negligible fraction of the total power dissipation for the system. Having reduced the power dissipation, practical, low cost alignment schemes must be developed in order that the optoelectronics may be integrated into electronic systems. Furthermore, the physical size of the optical interconnect components must be minimized if free-space interconnects are to be useful in allowing greater performance for a given size of system. The key to realizing these goals lies in improving integration technology.

We have demonstrated for the first time the integration of MSM detectors with VCSELs using a process compatible with VCSEL manufacture. Figure 5 shows the structure of the integrated detector and VCSEL. The advantages of integrating a detector and a VCSEL lie in the reduction of the component count, and hence in reduction of the packaging cost, but also in the reduction of the footprint of the optoelectronic interconnect components. Further reductions in size are possible by integrating VCSELs directly on CMOS. Bump-bonding of MQW modulators to CMOS has been demonstrated [14], while other workers have addressed the packaging of VCSELs. Figure 6 shows a VCSEL bump-bonded onto a substrate, which in this case happens to be glass. Provided the VCSEL integration does not degrade performance, the advantage of integrating directly on CMOS is that no additional area is required for the additional of optical I/O beyond that of the IC being connected. In order to use the optoelectonics in a practical free-space optical interconnect, the output from the VCSEL must be collimated and directed towards the receiver. The signal routing must be stable over time and over temperature, and would ideally require no more complex assembly techniques than are already used in the electronics industry. The routing can be performed with microoptical elements, or with diffractive optical elements. The latter offer the possibility of mass-production by exploiting established IC fabrication techniques. Figure 7 shows a photograph of a diffractive optical element integrated with a detector. Stand-offs of fixed height were used to locate the diffractive optical elements at the correct height with respect to the detector, and solder bumps used to locate the elements permanently with respect to the substrate. Since the collimation and routing are defined by the characteristics and location of the diffractive optics, the resulting module need only be aligned to the rest of the system to some fraction of the collimated beam width, rather than to the diameter of the VCSEL aperture.

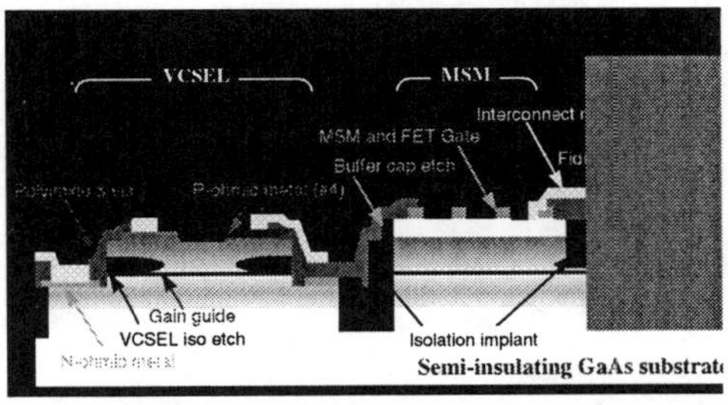

Figure 5: The structure of an integrated VCSEL with MSM detector

At the level of chip-to-chip interconnects, transparency to the integrator implies an IC level solution in which optical I/O cells can be treated as other standard cells in layout of a circuit, and also implies the ability to locate the optoelectronic modules with respect to each other with only the precision found in today's electronic systems. Ongoing developments in integration technology hold the promise for greater transparency to the system integrator.

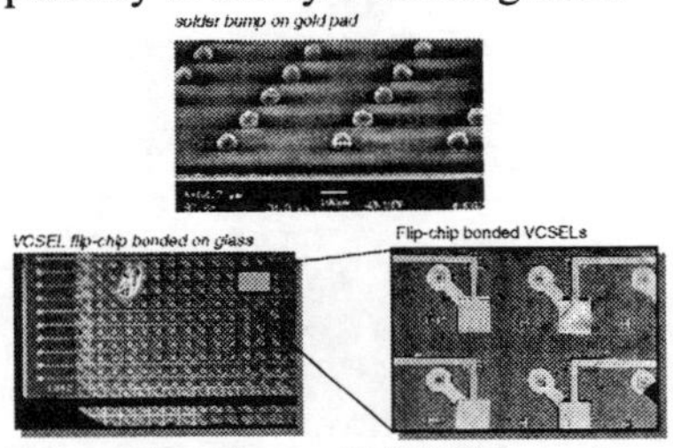

Figure 6: Bump-bonding of VCSELs onto a glass substrate

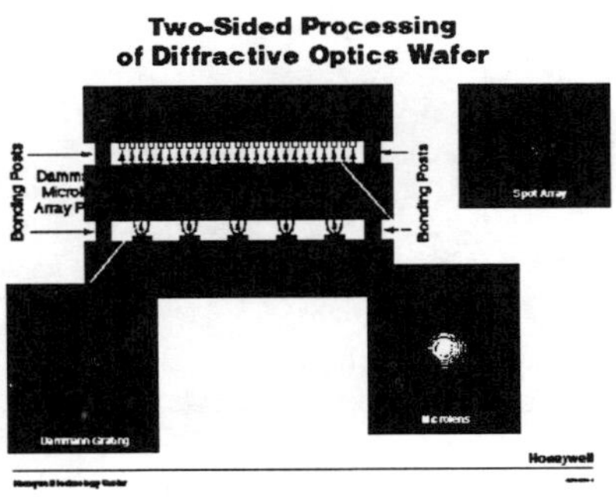

Figure 7: Integrating diffractive optics with optoelectronics

Conclusions

Optoelectronics and optical interconnects continue to hold promise for solving a number of packaging problems in electronic systems. The limited use of optical interconnects in systems today can be attributed to the inability of the optics community to predict advances in electrical packaging technology, and to the persistently high cost of adding optical interconnects to electronic systems. Most optical interconnect applications under consideration today reflect only an evolutionary advance over previous systems, and success in inserting optical interconnects will depend on providing as much transparency to the system integrator as possible. By providing direct analogues to existing component technologies, optical interconnects can be readily incorporated into systems. The keys to achieving these goals are in improved integration technology, in manufacturable intracabinet interconnects, and in low-cost plastic fiber.

References

1. See for example Foiber Channel and IEEE 1394 ("Firewire") standards
2. "Scaling Optoelectronic- VLSI Circuits into the 21st Century: A technology Roadmap", A. Krishnamoorthy, D.A.B. Miller, IEEE Journal of Selected Topics in Quantum Electronics, Vol 2, No. 1, April 1996
3. "Gigabit Optical Interconnects for Parallel Processors", T. Lane, B. Floren, J. Bristow, D. Wilson, Proceedings of the Government Microcircuit Applications Conference, November 1991, paper 16.1, pp 567-569
4. "Optical Backplanes for Massively Parallel Processors and Demonstration in the Connection Machine", A. Husain, T. Lane, C. Sullivan, J. Bristow, A. Gopinath, Proceedings of the Government Microcircuits Applications Conference, Las Vegas, November 1990
5. "High-bandwidth graded-index polymer optical fiber", Y.. Koike, T. Ishigure, and E. Nihei, IEEE J. Lightwave Technol. 13, 1475-1489 (1995).
6. "Temperature-dependent characteristics and single mode performance of AlGaInP670-690-nm vertical cavity surface-emitting lasers," M. Hagerrott Crawford, R.P. Schnieder, Jr., K.D. Choquette, and K.L. Lear, IEEE Photon. Technol. Lett., Vol. 7, pp. 724-726, 1995
7 "Flexible Optical Backplane Interconnections", M. A. Shaid, W.R Holland, Proceedings of the Third International Conference on Massively Parallel Processing Using Optical Interconnects, October 27-29, Maui, Hawaii
8. "Low-Loss High Thermal Stability Polymer Interconnects for Low Cost High Performance Massively Parallel Processing", ibid.
9 "Polymer Waveguide Applications in Multichip Modules and Board Level Optical Interconnects" , Yue Liu, Julian Bristow, Terry Marta, Sommy Bounnak, Klein Johnson, Yung Liu, Herb Cole, paper MA4, OSA Conference on Organic Thin Films for Photonics Applications, Portland, Oregon September 9-11, 1995
10. "Polymer Optical Interconnect Technology (POINT) - Optoelectronic Packaging and Interconnect for Board and Backplane Applications", Y.S.Liu, R.J.Wojnarowski, W.A.Hennessy, J.P.Bristow, Y. Liu, A.Peczalski, J.Rolwlette, A.Potts, J.Stack, M.Kadar-Kallen, J.Yardley, L.Eldada, R.M.Osgood, R.Scarmazzino, S.H.Lee, V.Ozguz, S.Patra, Proceedings of the 1996 Electronic Components and Technology Conference, Orlando, 1996, pp 308 - 315
11. "Polymer Optical Waveguide Technology", Julian Bristow, Yue Liu, David Greenlaw, Terry Marta, Klein Johnson, Brian Hanzal, Andy Peczalski, Sommy Bounnak, 1996 International Symposium on Microelectronics, ISHM, Minneaplois, October 8-10 1996, pp138-142
12. "Optoelectronic Backplane Interconnect Technology Development" Y.S Liu et al, SPIE Proceedings Volume 3005, February 1997

Two-Bounce Free-space Arbitrary Interconnection Architecture

Marc P. Christensen and Michael W. Haney
Electrical & Computer Engineering Department
George Mason University, Fairfax, VA 22203-4444

Abstract

The two bounce free-space arbitrary interconnection architecture is introduced. It is requires 3 stages of local electronic routing and 2 passes, or bounces, through a common retro-reflective optical system. The concept combines the global optical interconnection with the minimum nonblocking multistage interconnection network, the Benes network, to achieve arbitrary interconnections across a multichip backplane. The arbitrary interconnection requires only one additional pass through the optical system. The architecture is experimentally validated with a optical module and a fiber coupled LED and detector array to simulate the smart pixel I/O placement in the backplane of the module. The architecture is further evaluated using VCSEL arrays and a CCD camera for resolution and registration measurements.

1. Introduction

Free-space digital optical interconnections have been suggested to overcome interconnection limitations in large, globally interconnected multi-processor architectures [1]. Previous research in this area has focused on the mapping of multiprocessor architectural requirements onto free-space optical interconnection implementations. This has often resulted in a tradeoff between the interconnection an architecture would ideally utilize and those interconnections which the optical implementation readily provided.

The problem of mapping architectures to optical interconnections is worsened when an architecture must perform two or more differing functions. For example, two differing interconnection functions must be implemented to perform a large image 2-D FFT. First, a multi stage butterfly interconnection network must be implemented to perform row and column 1-D FFTs, secondly a corner-turn on the data set must be implemented. The interconnection requirements for these two functions are extremely different. An optical interconnection approach which is designed to perform the first function may not be capable of the second.

A physical optical interconnection approach which provides *arbitrary* interconnections is desired. As discussed in this paper, without changing lens positions or attributes, a completely different set of interconnections can be achieved – through changing local electronic interconnections. Furthermore, the optical system can be implemented with a symmetric arrangement, thereby allowing the interconnection to be folded back onto itself in a reflective architecture [2]. Section II provides background on banyan networks and the optical shuffle-connected approach, leading up to the Benes network, which is the key element of the Two-Bounce concept. The architecture is then detailed in Section III. Section IV contains the results of experiments that demonstrate the Two-Bounce's important features. Section V is a discussion of the Two-Bounce architecture. The Conclusion, contained in Section VI, summarizes the key features of the Two-Bounce architecture.

2. Background

Figure 1 depicts a shuffle based banyan network for N=16 nodes. A banyan network connects any given input/output node pair with a unique path. There are

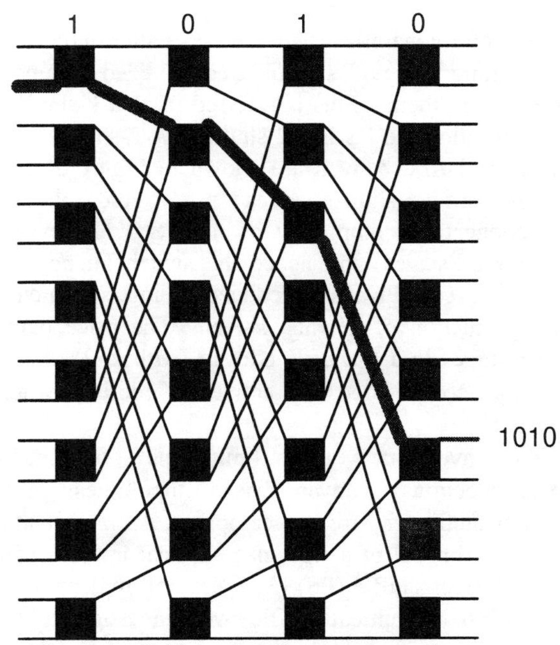

Figure 1. Self routing Banyan example.

0-8186-7974-3/97 $10.00 © 1997 IEEE

typically $\log_k N$ stages (where k is the shuffle order), with each stage consisting of a permutation link pattern, such as a shuffle, and a set of k×k crossbar switches. In many banyans, the unique path between input and output is determined by following a simple self routing algorithm. This algorithm is called a destination-tag algorithm because it has the advantage of requiring only the destination address – the routing algorithm is independent of source address. Self routing eliminates the need for external control of the switching elements and offers the means to the high throughput desired in future switching circuits. Figure 1 illustrates this approach for a banyan comprised of perfect shuffle permutations and 2×2 switches. The self routing algorithm is performed on the output address as follows: beginning with the most significant bit (MSB) of the output address, inspect one bit at each stage – if the bit is a one, exit the stage on the lower node; if its a zero, exit on the upper node. Since the perfect shuffle performs a bit rotation on the address, this algorithm will work for any destination and is independent of the source address. Figure 1 shows this algorithm for a 16 node banyan.

In a single banyan architecture, a blocking error occurs when 2 (or more if k>2) packets wish to continue to the next stage using the same connection. The connection can transmit only one of the packets, so the other(s) must be lost, or blocked. A blocked packet has no method for recovery in this single banyan architecture. The blocking probability of a banyan increases as the load (number of active inputs) increases. Therefore a single banyan has little utility for implementing arbitrary interconnection networks.

A useful generalization of the PS pattern comes from partitioning the nodes into k equal sized groups and interleaving them. This is referred to as a k-shuffle; by this definition the PS is a 2-shuffle. A 2-shuffle banyan and a 4 shuffle banyan are shown in Figure 2. . The higher order shuffle does not avoid the high interconnection complexity of the PS. However, the number of stages, and hence the switch latency, in k-shuffle based banyans is reduced to $\log_k N$, which is a strong function of k when k<<N. The price paid for fewer stages in a k-shuffle banyan (with k>2) is a need for more complicated k×k active self-routing switching elements.

To overcome the limitations of metallic interconnections, banyan based topologies can be implemented using free-space optics. An important step was the proposal of a free-space optical implementation of the perfect shuffle (PS) [3]. Several implementations of 1-D and 2-D optical shuffles were investigated [4-11]. All of these approaches use optics to effect the magnification and interleaving needed to perform the PS link pattern. Examples of 2-D shuffles are the Folded Perfect Shuffle [8], and the Separable Perfect Shuffle [4,7].

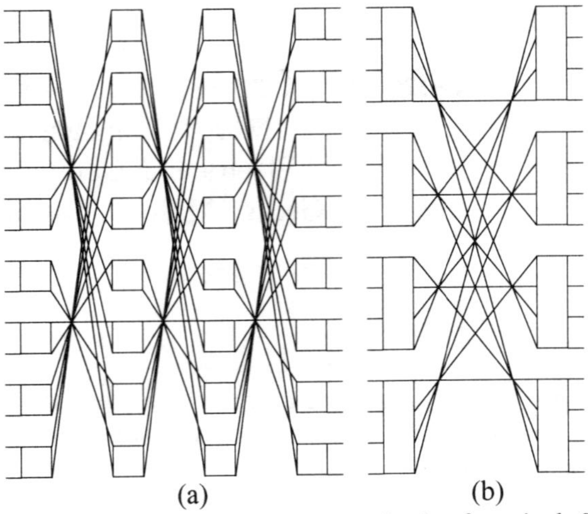

Figure 2a. A banyan comprised of optical 2-shuffles does not lend itself to a reflective architecture due to lack of symmetry. Figure 2b. A banyan of k-shuffles (case k=4) is symmetric.

One implementation of the separable k-shuffle uses two k×k lens arrays [11], a side view of which is depicted in Figure 3, for k=4 and N = 16×16 nodes. In this arrangement each pair of lenses, from the two lenslet arrays, perform a unity magnification operation that achieves the desire k-shuffle pattern as shown. Figure 2 also depicts a grouping of the 16 smart pixel nodes into 4 subgroups in which the nodes are in close proximity to each other. This subgrouping concept places the nodes on a self-similar grid [12] rather than a regular square grid. As shown in the figure, the self-similar grid concept groups the smart pixels in a manner more amenable to packaging on separate OEICs and increases the optical efficiency of the shuffling optics [12]. The symmetry of the optical k-shuffle depicted in Figure 3 is a key aspect that is exploited in the Two-Bounce implementation described below.

3. Two-Bounce Architecture

The two bounce arbitrary interconnection fabric is based on the Benes [14] multi-stage switching fabric. As discussed in the previous section if the shuffle order (k) is equal to the square root of the number of nodes the interconnection fabric is reduced to 2 switching stages interconnected by one free-space optical interconnection. Figure 2 shows banyans based on 2-shuffles and 4-shuffles for N=16 nodes. The 4-shuffle banyan requires only one interconnection stage. Furthermore, it is symmetric, and therefore readily lends itself to an interleaved reflective single plane implementation [2]. Since it is a banyan, every node has access to every other

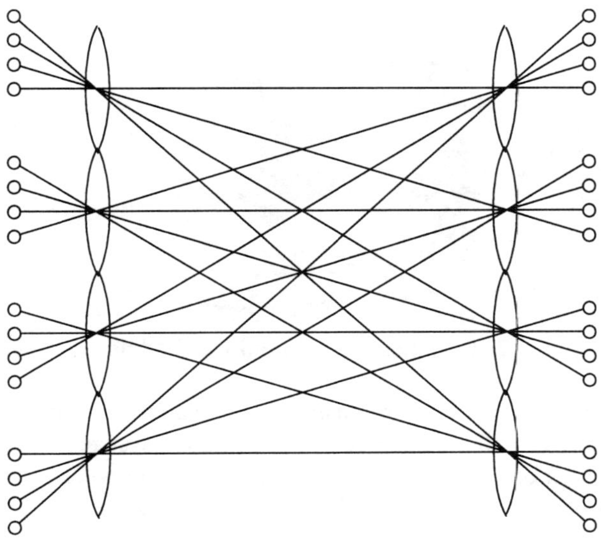

Figure 3. Optical implementation of 4 shuffle depicted in Figure 2b. Symmetry of architecture makes it amenable to reflective modules.

node in a single pass through the optical system. While many architectures may be mapped onto such an interconnection scheme, it is not general enough to provide arbitrary interconnections, or multiple differing interconnections in a single optical system.

Since the interconnection depicted in Figure 2b is a banyan, it suffers from blocking of approximately 70% on average, over all permuted interconnections [2,13]. While every node can reach every other node in the banyan, they cannot do this simultaneously. In fact, the worst case blocking occurs if all nodes on chip 1 want to communicate with all nodes on another arbitrarily selected chip. In this case, all but one of the links are blocked, resulting in a (k-1)/k blocking probability.

Banyans are, however, a useful building block for an interconnection fabric. The Benes network [14] is comprised of 2 banyans, placed end to end – one in the forward direction, and one in the reverse. This configuration has been proven to be the minimum rearrangeably nonblocking architecture. Figure 4 depicts the Benes approach when implemented with k-shuffle banyans ($N=k^2$), and 4 OEICs are utilized.

The architecture depicted in Figure 4 can be folded and pipelined, with smart pixel resources contained in a single plane in which the smart pixel I/O are interleaved [15,16]. This topological transformation places the 3 routing blocks depicted horizontally on a single OEIC. There are 4 OEICs in this example implementation. Every input node can communicate to any one output node simultaneously (assuming no two input nodes are attempting to communicate to the same output node i.e., no output contention). This arbitrary interconnection takes 2 passes through the optical system and 3 local

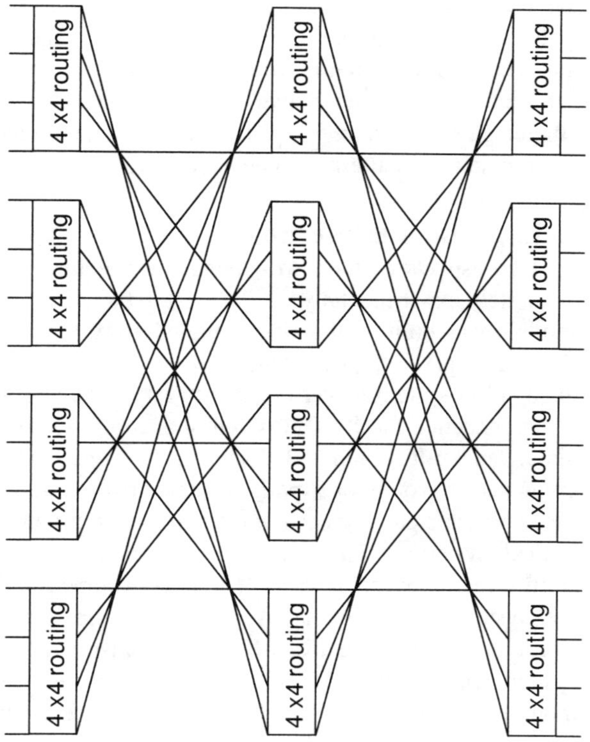

Figure 4. Interconnection fabric is comprised of 3 stages of local switching and 2 passes through a global free-space optical interconnection.

electronic routings. Figure 5 is a schematic drawing of the resulting optical module.

This arbitrary interconnection approach is not useful for direct application to packet switching since the local (on-chip) routing requires global knowledge of the interconnection. However, such a scheme can be used to implement the many fixed pattern interconnections for implementation of a packet switching architecture [13]. Furthermore, when the required interconnection pattern is known a priori (e.g., for FFTs, filtering, decoding, and related multiprocessor algorithms), the local electronic routing reduces to simple local (on chip) wiring patterns

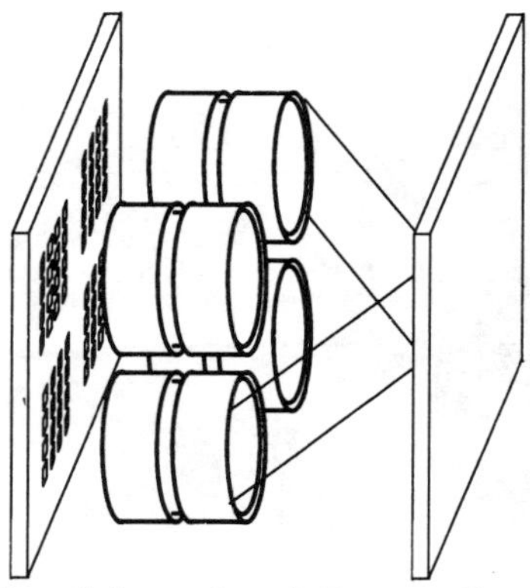

Figure 5. Schematic of Retro-reflective 4 chip optical module

on the OEICs. If multiple differing interconnection patterns are required, the local routing can be implemented as circuit switching based on look-up tables. While no "live" header decoding is implemented, many differing predetermined interconnection patterns can be paged through.

4. Experimental Results

Two aspects of the Two-Bounce architecture were separately experimentally validated. First a small scale module was built with a fiber coupled array replacing the smart pixel plane. This allowed a laptop data acquisition system to verify the arbitrary nature of the interconnection fabric. The system was comprised of 2x2 simulated OEICs with a 2x2 lens array. Each "OEIC" contained 4 groups of 2 pairs of simulated emitters and detectors (one pair for each of the two-passed through the optical system). This resulted in a module with 64 shuffle interconnected links. The overall dimensions of the system is approximately 4 cm x 4 cm x 6 cm. Secondly, a retroreflective MCM was constructed for a system with realistic VCSEL / detector pitches. This module was evaluated for resolution and registration accuracy as described in Section IV.A below.

4.1 Arbitrary Interconnection Prototype

In order to demonstrate the functionality of the Two bounce architecture, A 16 node, 4 "chip" module was designed and built. Since OEICs with the required functionality are not currently available, a fiber coupled array was utilized for optical input and output. This Two-bounce prototype has 64 fibers mounted in a faceplate. The capacity of the Two-Bounce module greatly exceeded the number of fibers utilized for the architecture verification. In order to demonstrate the extensibility of the architecture the module was also evaluated using a VCSEL array with a CCD camera as the detection device. This high resolution verification is described in Section B. Figure 6 shows the system demonstration prototype experiment. A laptop PC performs the requisite smart pixel functionality and is interfaced through a data acquisition system to a emitter/detector driver box. This box provides the electronic interface for the fiber coupled arrays in the optical prototype. If smart pixels were utilized only the small optical module would be present in this system. The rest of the hardware is used to mimic the smart pixel functionality. The optical interconnection module is shown in Figure 7. The central component of the optical interconnection module is the 2×2 lens system, designed to interconnect a 2×2 array of smart pixel ICs. We are investigating custom designed lenses for the prototype, but the initial system uses commercially available miniature projection lenses that have a wide and flat field-of-view, with high resolution. Using a VCSEL array as an input source, we characterized several low f-number lenses that are commercially available. The selected lenses are f/1.1, with useable fields of approximately .8 cm across, and with resolution spot sizes of approximately 10 μm – consistent with the anticipated parameters of smart pixel integrated circuits. The 4 lenses in the array were selected from a larger set to match their parameters to a high degree. An active alignment procedure was developed for the module that involved individual positioning of the lenses over the smart pixel backplane,. This procedure has demonstrated a registration accuracy of ~10 micrometers over the backplane, as large as 10 cm and lens arrays as large as 4x4, utilized for the optical prototype[17], which is consistent with the anticipated required smart pixel IC alignment dictated by sources such as VCSELS that will be 10-20 micrometers in diameter.

Figure 6. Demonstration Prototype Experiment.

Figure 7. Optomechanical prototype module

Figure 7 shows the optomechanical prototype module. It consists of 3 planes on a group of 4 rails. One plane holds the thin fiber I/O plane, simulating the smart pixel optical I/O. The fiber plane was precision machined to mount the 64 fibers at the desired locations across the smart pixel plane. The second plane is the lens support plane; it positions each lens over it's corresponding optical I/O and maintains the alignment between the two. The third plane holds the mirror for the retro-reflective interconnection. These three planes must be able to be adjusted so that they are perpendicular to one another within a few degrees. Since this parallelism is set *before* the lens alignment is performed, it only effects the efficiency of the interconnect, not its alignment. If the mirror were not quite perpendicular to the smart pixel plane, the lenses would be aligned with this error present and the proper interconnect would still be achieved. The parallel and symmetrical nature of the optical interconnect provides some cancellation of distortion effects, as it is a reciprocal optical system. The system has been designed to receive actual packaged smart pixel devices (in place of the fiber coupled plate), as they become available. As emitter-based smart pixel technology rapidly matures, i.e., as the pixels get "smarter" (more integrated digital logic) and have higher densities of optoelectronic I/O, the Two-Bounce prototype will be able to readily incorporate them.

The optical module was comprised of groups of I/O sites totaling 32 emitters and 32 receivers interconnected in a shuffle pattern. The overall dimensions of the system are approximately 4 cm × 4 cm × 8 cm.

A photograph of the experimental set up used to evaluate the Two-Bounce module is shown in Figure 8. The experimental system is comprised of three planes: the OE I/O plane, the lens plane and a mirror plane. The OE I/O plane holds the fiber array in place of a smart pixel OEIC. The experiments discussed in the next section replaced this plane with VCSEL arrays and a CCD imaging system. These planes are supported so that the inter-plane distance and parallelism may be adjusted. In the experiments, the backplane was used as the reference plane to which all other elements in the system were aligned. The lens array plane is comprised of a flat aluminum plate with 4 apertures, one for each lens in the lens array. A lens was precisely aligned above each group of I/O sites (OEIC) using a self-alignment procedure that is amenable to automation[17].

4.2 Preliminary Optical Experimentation

First preliminary experiments were conducted to evaluate commercially available lenses for use in the Two-Bounce architecture. Experiments used 10μm VCSELs separated by 630μm and the results were analyzed assuming 40μm detectors spaced the same. Current chip placement technology provides the ability to align chips to approximately 10μm accuracy. It is assumed that the smart pixel OEICs will have sub-micron optoelectronic registration (comparable to modern photolithographic IC technology capabilities), then the dominant source of optical misalignment and loss of efficiency will come from the lenslet array itself.

Figure 8 Experimental setup, without mirror or lenses, showing fiber coupled array

Consequently, the experiments focused on evaluating the architecture's wide field optics. The approach was to use conventional off-the-shelf refractive optical elements, leading to an eventual custom design.

The Two-Bounce concept was also evaluated for high resolution and registration accuracy. A VCSEL array (supplied by Honeywell) was used as the input source, and off-the-shelf video camera lenses were used to image the VCSELs onto a CCD detector array. The evaluation VCSEL array consisted of 4×4 individually addressable 10μm wide emitters, operating at 0.84 μm. These particular devices operated at about 10-20 mW of power consumption. Figure 9 shows the results of a resolution and registration experiment in which 3 collinear VCSEL elements, spaced by 630 μm, were imaged onto a CCD array with a lens array system consisting of 25 mm focal length miniature video camera lenses. The white outline squares indicate the locations and size of evenly spaced 40 μm detectors that would be part of the smart pixel. As shown in the figure, the off-the-shelf video lens performs fairly well in this off-axis imaging system. The inherent distortion of the imaging system (primarily due to vignetting of the narrow VCSEL beam by the barrel of the lens mount) begins to become apparent for total fields of view greater than about 20 degrees. In addition to the broadening of the focused VCSEL imaged spots, at the widest angles the array's images are beginning to misalign with the target detector array patterns. The widest angle data for the imaged VCSEL array correspond to a back-plane of size of about 4 inches and a total system length of about 12 inches due to the video lenses field of view limitations. To achieve the desired length-to-width ratio of ~1 in the optical system requires flat field imaging optics with a total field of view of approximately 56 degrees. Although this is not a trivial design, our preliminary studies indicate that a detailed optical design, which meets the distortion and off-axis imaging criteria is not overly difficult.

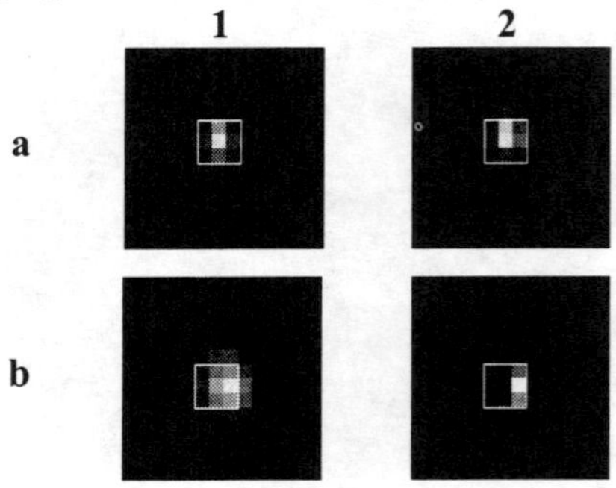

Figure 9. Data for 2 VCSELs separated by 630μm. a: on-axis, b: 10° FOV.

The experimental results yielded ~10 μm resolution and registration accuracy for all possible interconnections across a 10 cm x 10 cm simulated OE backplane when lenses that were carefully chosen to be nearly optically and optomechanically identical were used in the macro-lens array. This is on the order that is needed for this architecture since 10 μm emitters and 30 μm detectors are envisioned as smart pixel technology evolves. If the emitters are mapped to within 10 μm of their prescribed locations with minimal blurring then a large fraction of the transmitted energy from each emitter will be captured by the corresponding detector and the interconnection will be completed. As expected, the experiments showed that the registration accuracy for a given interconnection depends strongly on the lenses used to make that particular interconnect. Small differences in the optical or optomechanical parameters (i.e., effective focal length, position of focus relative to lens mounting barrel, etc.) of the lenses in the lens array leads to larger registration errors. Therefore, in order to implement a FSOI module the lenses that make up the lens array must be very well matched. In the future this will be accomplished by using custom lenses that have very tight optical specifications and optomechanical tolerances.

5. Discussion

The two bounce interconnection architecture requires simply one extra pass through the optical system to achieve any *arbitrary* point-to-point interconnectivity among a multiprocessor system. This is the first proposed arbitrary non blocking interconnection architecture based on scaleable macro-optics [16]. This arbitrary interconnection comes at the price of a fixed 1 stage latency. The penalty of this extra bounce is significant only when the processor throughput is so high that processors will be waiting for data from the interconnection fabric. Most multiprocessor architectures will require multiple clock cycles for the actual processing of the data. When this is the case, the extra bounce of the optical interconnection is insignificant.

The two bounce arbitrary interconnection architecture relies on symmetric k-shuffle optics and local electronic routing. A multi-chip module (MCM) based retroreflective macro-optical architecture which can implement this has been demonstrated [17] to readily implement the required global k-shuffle interconnection pattern. Such an approach is depicted in Figure 3 for a 4x4 OEIC array with a k=16 shuffle. This interconnection module approach has been shown to scale well for large globally interconnected architectures [16].

The retro-reflective FSOI architecture is shown to have several important advantages over multi-plane FSOI architectures in both optomechanical packaging, and performance [16,17]. Only a single OE backplane, a single macro-lens array, a planar mirror, and a relatively simple optomechanical package are required to implement the arbitrary Two-Bounce architecture. The optomechanical alignment of the system is easily automatable since at most two variables need to be adjusted at one time. This is facilitated by the simple lens self-alignment technique that has been developed to align the lenses within the lens array. Once all the lenses are individually self-aligned all of the lenses in the array are automatically aligned. By locating all of the optical I/O on one backplane all and employing this alignment technique, all rotational alignment and lens to lens alignment issues are eliminated. Finally, since each lens in the system acts as both a receiving and transmitting lens there is a natural symmetry in the optical system that can be exploited to minimize aberrations in the macro-lens array.

The FSOI approach used in the Two-Bounce architecture has been experimentally evaluated. The experimental results yielded ~10 μm resolution and registration accuracy for all possible interconnections across a 10 cm x 10 cm simulated OE backplane when lenses that were carefully chosen to be nearly optically and optomechanically identical were used in the macro-lens array. This is on the order that is needed for this architecture since 10 μm emitters and 30 μm detectors are envisioned as smart pixel technology evolves. If the emitters are mapped to within 10 μm of their prescribed locations with minimal blurring then a large fraction of the transmitted energy from each emitter will be captured by the corresponding detector and the interconnection will be completed. As expected, the experiments showed that the registration accuracy for a given interconnection depends strongly on the lenses used to make that particular interconnect. Small differences in the optical or optomechanical parameters (i.e., effective focal length, position of focus relative to lens mounting barrel, etc.) of the lenses in the lens array leads to larger registration errors. Therefore, in order to implement a Two-Bounce FSOI module the lenses that make up the lens array must be very well matched. In the future this will be accomplished by using custom lenses that have very tight optical specifications and optomechanical tolerances.

6. Conclusion

Through simply adding a single pass through the optical system, a banyan interconnection scheme can be converted into a generalized or higher order Benes – the proven minimum rearrageably nonblocking interconnection fabric. Through applications of topological transformations, this architecture is implemented in a single coplanar MCM stage with the scalability of macro-optical refractive lens elements. This arbitrary interconnection can be fixed upon integration (routing wires) or circuit switched for added flexibility.

Aspects of this work have funded through contracts with DARPA and BMDO that are monitored by AFOSR.

References

[1] DARPA/ETO Workshop on Optoelectronic Processing (OEP), May 29, 1996.

[2] M. W. Haney & M. P. Christensen, "Optical freespace sliding tandem banyan architecture for self-routing switching networks," *Digest Int. Conf. Optic. Computing*,. August, 1994.

[3] A. W. Lohmann, et al., in Digest of the Conference on Optical Computing, (Optical Society of America), Washington, D. C., paper WA3, 1985.

[4] A. W. Lohmann, "What classical Optics Can Do for the Digital Optical Computer," Applied Optics, Vol. 25, pp. 1543-1549, 1986.

[5] G. Eichmann, and Y. Li, "Compact Optical Generalized Perfect Shuffle," Applied Optics, Vol. 26, pp. 1167-1169, April 1987.

[6] S.-H. Lin, T. F. Krile and J. F. Walkup, "2-D Optical Multistage Interconnection Networks," Proc. SPIE, vol. 752, pp.209-216, 1987.

[7] K.-H. Brenner and A. Huang, "Optical Implementations of the Perfect Shuffle Interconnection," Applied Optics, vol. 27, pp. 135-137, Jan. 1988.

[8] C. W. Stirk, R. A. Athale, and M. W. Haney, "Folded Perfect Shuffle Optical Processor," Applied Optics, Vol. 27, pp. 202-203, 1988.

[9] A. A. Sawchuk and I. Glaser, "Geometries for Optical Implementations of the Perfect Shuffle," Proc. SPIE, Vol. 963, p. 270, 1988.

[10] M. W. Haney and J. J. Levy, "Optically Efficient Free-space Folded Perfect Shuffle Network," Applied Optics, Vol. 30, No. 20, pp. 2833-2840, July, 1991.

[11] G. C. Marsden, P. J. Marchand, P. Harvey, and S. C. Esener, "Optical Transpose Interconnection System Architecture," Optics Letters, Vol. 18. No. 13, pp. 1083-1085, July 1, 1993.

[12] M. W. Haney, "Pipelined Optoelectronic Free-Space Permutation Network," Optics Letters, Vol. 17, No. 4, pp. 283-285, February, 1992.

[13] M. W. Haney & M. P. Christensen, " Sliding Banyan Network,", *Journal of Lightwave Technology*, May, 1996.

[14] F. T. Leighton, *Introduction to Parallel Algorithms and Architectures: Arrays, Trees, Hypercubes,* 1992.

[15] M. W. Haney, "Pipelined optoelectronic free-space permutation network," *Optics Letters*, February, 1992.

[16] M. W. Haney & M. P. Christensen, "Fundamental Geometric Advantages of Free-space Optical Interconnections," *MPPOI*, October, 1996.

[17] R. R. Michael, M.W. Haney, & M. P. Christensen, "Experimental Evaluation of the 3-D Optical Shuffle Interconnection Module of the Sliding Banyan Architecture," September, 1996.

Design of a Compact Alignment Tolerant Optical Interconnect for Photonic Backplane Applications

B. Robertson

McGill University, Department of Electrical Engineering, Montréal, Québec, Canada H3A 2A7

Abstract

This paper describes a compact alignment tolerant interconnect designed for use within a prototype modulator based photonic backplane. To simplify the optical design, the optical input and output of each smart pixel array are clustered separately, thereby allowing a Fourier-plane patterned mirror array to be used in the beam-routing optics. The primary advantages of this scheme are the simplicity of the optical design and the alignability associated with clustered window microchannel relay systems making it ideally suited for high density interconnection applications.

1. Introduction

Over the past few years, a number of prototype free-space photonic backplanes have been developed by both industry and academia[1-4]. Interest in this field has been primarily motivated by the difficulties that conventional electronic backplane technology faces in meeting the projected throughputs required by future switching and computer systems [5]. In addition, there has been a number of key technological advances in the fields of optoelectronics and optics which have made the construction of these systems feasible. These include the introduction of low cost, efficient diffractive optics technology, the availability of large 2-D arrays of optoelectronic devices such as MQW modulators and vertical cavity surface emitting lasers (VCSELs), the ability to integrate optoelectronic device arrays with conventional electronic processing technology such as CMOS, and the introduction of computing and switching architectures which take advantage of the ability of optics to provide high density parallel communication data links.

The development of compact, alignment tolerant interconnection systems is vital if this technology is ever to compete with conventional electronic backplane technology. Figure 1 shows the functional layout of a free-space backplane based on smart pixel modulator arrays. Such a system could, for example, be used to implement the Hyperplane architecture [6]. Electronic data from the processing layer is sent in parallel to the photonic backplane where it is converted into an optical data stream. Each data packet has a specific address header added to it as it passes through the message processor. The smart pixels have three possible states; transmit, receive and relay. The address header is read each time it reaches a new smart pixel array. If the data packet is addressed to a particular processor node, the information is dropped, otherwise it is relayed onto the next stage.

In order to implement this scheme optically, three arrays of optical beams must be routed at each interconnect stage; the "optical power supply" beams to stage p which read the state of the modulators, the modulated signal beams from stage p to stage p+1, and the signal beams from stage p-1 to stage p. Thus, in the case of a 16x16 array of smart pixels in which the data is encoded using dual rail logic, a total of 1536 optical beams must be simultaneously relayed by each interconnection stage. This places stringent demands on the interconnect design.

A number of beam combination techniques based on polarization optics, aperture division, and patterned mirror arrays have been previously demonstrated [7-9]. The simplest approach involves using a 50/50 beamsplitter to route the beams. However, this method results in a 75% system loss which is unacceptable as optical power requirements dominate the system cost. Aperture division, although lossless, requires low f/number optics which introduces problems related to scaleability. A commonly used technique is based on a combination of polarization optics and patterned mirror arrays. An example of a typical system is shown in figure 2. As the patterned mirror is situated in an image plane, precise alignment tolerances must be met to ensure that the beams are correctly routed.

This paper introduces a novel compact microchannel interconnect designed for use with such a photonic backplane. To simplify the optical design, the optical input and output of each smart pixel array are clustered separately. This allows a Fourier-plane patterned mirror array to be used in the beam-routing optics, thereby removing two passes through the microlens arrays and increasing the alignment tolerances of the system. The discussion will detail the optical design and discuss the trade off between such parameters as smart pixel window layout, channel density, window size and field of view. Finally an analysis of the optical power budget and image rotation properties of the interconnect will be presented.

0-8186-7974-3/97 $10.00 © 1997 IEEE

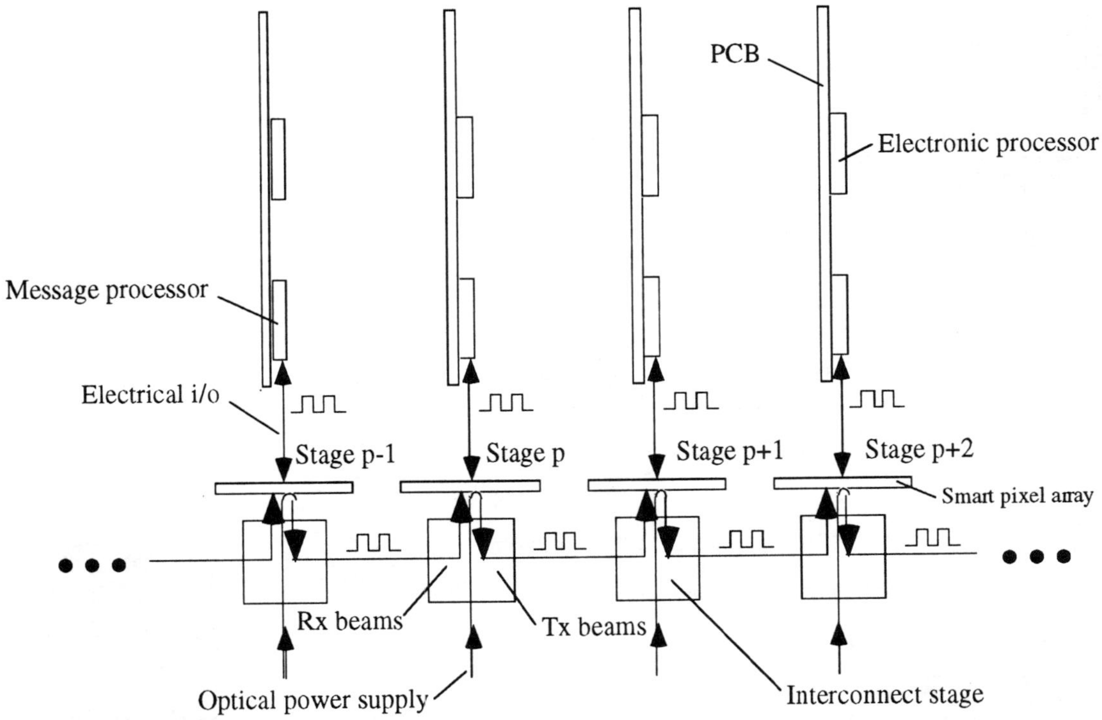

Figure 1 - Functional outline of modulator based backplane.

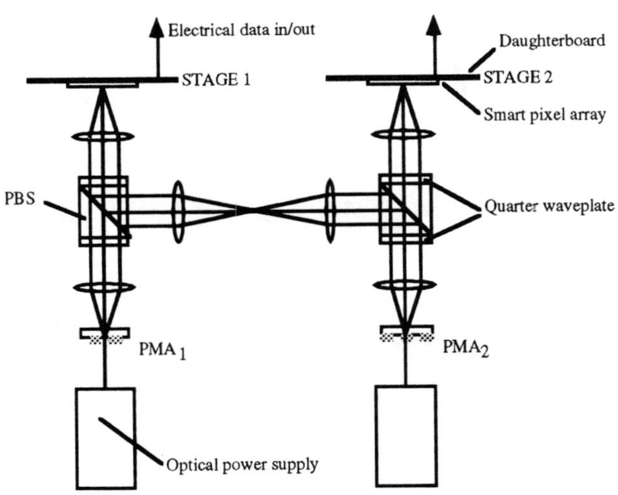

Figure 2 - Example of interconnect which uses polarization optics and patterned mirror arrays (PMA_1 and PMA_2) to route the optical beams.

2. Optical Design

Figure 3 shows the basic conceptual design of the interconnection system. Each interconnection stage contains an NxN microlens array, a quarter-waveplate/polarizing beam splitter assembly (comprised of a polarizing beam splitter and two quarter-waveplates), and a combined fan-out element/patterned mirror array element (PMG). In addition, a relay system is required to route the signal beams from device array 1 to device array 2. Although several possible variations of this design are possible, a microchannel based relay system is considered in this analysis. Such an approach has several advantages over a conventional or hybrid optics implementation including compactness, low component count, minimal latency, low cost, and scaleability [10]. In addition, it does not suffer from field dependent aberrations inherent in a system using single relay lenses.

An array generation system produces an NxN/2 array of small diameter (<1mm) circularly polarized collimated Gaussian beams as shown in figure 3. Each of these are then fanned-out by the grating, G_1, to produce an MxM array of beams in each microchannel. These beams are focused down by the microlens array, L_1, onto the modulators on the first device array. The reflected signal beams are subsequently routed to the next stage of the system via the relay optics, where they reflect from the patterned mirrors and are focused by the second microlens array, L_2, onto the detectors of the second stage. Optimum optical performance is obtained since the Gaussian beam waists are located at the fan-out grating plane to ensure the system operates in a telecentric configuration.

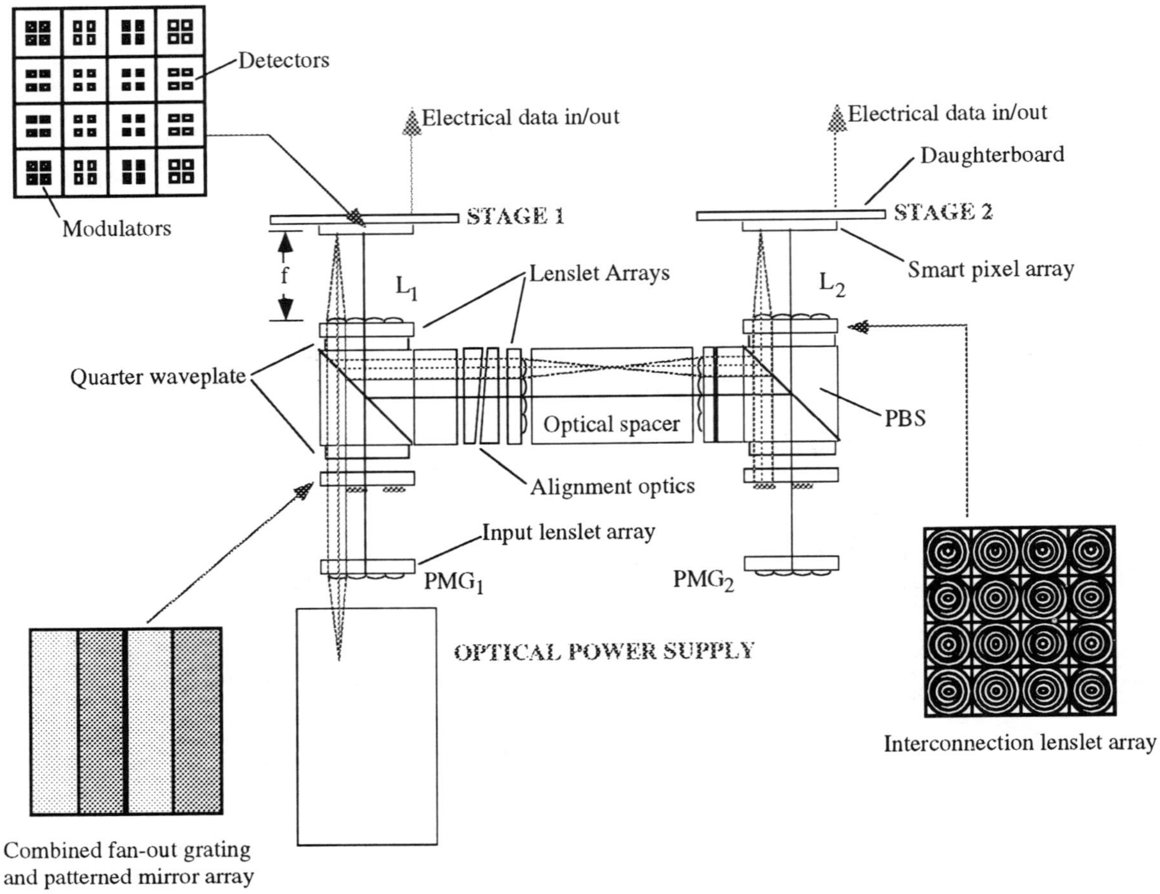

Figure 3 - Design of optical interconnect.

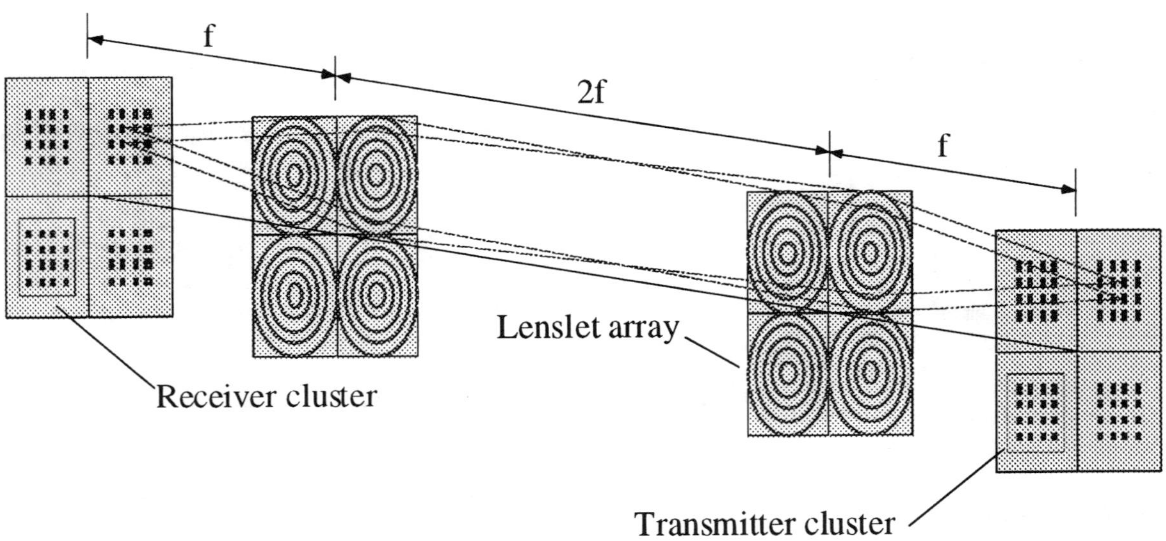

Figure 4 - Clustered window interconnect geometry.

It should be noted that the patterned mirror array and grating need not necessarily be combined. However, by fabricating the patterned mirror and grating on the same substrate we remove two optical surfaces from the system, thereby simplifying the overall optomechanical design. Furthermore, the design has been initially restricted to the case where the patterned metal mirror array is used in an internal reflection mode. This makes fabrication easier as high surface quality of the patterned mirror arrays is more easily obtained.

3. Design Analysis

The following section presents a design analysis of the clustered microchannel optical interconnect described in figure 3. The aim of this analysis is to outline the optimum smart pixel detector and modulator layout design space. This involves simultaneously maximizing the channel density and interconnect alignment tolerances whilst minimizing the modulator size and required die area.

Figure 4 illustrates the basic layout of a clustered window microchannel interconnect. Rather than interconnecting a single optical beam though each microchannel, MxM signal beams are transmitted simultaneously through each of the NxN array of symmetric telecentric relays. This approach has a number of advantages from the point of view of system scaleabiltity and alignment tolerances [11].

The following boundary conditions will be used in the analysis. The interconnect is comprised of an array of 16x16 smart pixels, where each smart pixel contains two modulator windows and two detector windows (dual rail logic). The analysis will concentrate primarily on a cluster arrangement with 4x4 optical i/o per cluster. A parameter defining the area devoted to the optical i/o, D_{die}, will be used to determine the real estate required by a specific design. For this particular application, the restriction that 6mm > D_{die} was applied. In addition, it will be assumed that the interconnect is based on an array of symmetric ($f_1 = f_2 = f$) telecentric microchannel relays operating at a wavelength of 852nm. Finally, the spacing between optoelectronic device windows, d_s, is taken to be fixed at 90μm in both the x and y directions (figure 5). The windows are arranged in 8x8 separate clusters of 4x4 modulators and detectors as described in section 2. An upper limit on the spot size (3w definition) at the modulator windows of 40μm will be assumed. Above this value, the compression ratio (defined as the spot separation divided by the 3w spot size) of the optical power supply beams will become too low for conventional Fourier-plane array generation techniques to be reliable [12].

Gaussian beam propagation theory will be used initially to analyze the interconnect, where the effects of clipping, non-uniform lenslet diffraction efficiency, non-ideal power supply beams, aberrations, and misalignments are ignored. Thus, if w_o is the ($1/e^2$) beam radius at the modulator window and w_L the radius at the first lenslet,

$$w_L = w_o\,[1 + (f\,\lambda/\,\pi w_o^{\,2})^{\,2}]^{\,1/2} \qquad (1)$$

and r_b , the beam radius at the lenslet facet, equals $\alpha\ w_L$, where α is the clipping ratio of the beam at the lenslet. Similarly, the modulator window size, d_m, is related to the input beam radius by $d_m = \beta_m\, w_o$, where β_m is the clipping ratio of the optical beam at the modulator, and the detector window size, d_r, is given by $d_r = \beta_r\, w_{rec}$, where β_r is the clipping ratio of the optical beam at the detector window. In previous systems a ratio of three has been used to minimize the effects of clipping on beam propagation, although the greater the clipping ratio, the better the alignment tolerances of the interconnect. For the purposes of this analysis, a clipping ratio of $\alpha = 3/2$, $\beta_m = 3$ and $\beta_r = 3$ is used. Thus, if there is no clipping and aberrations are negligible, the spot radius at the detector windows, w_{rec}, will be the same as that at the modulators, i.e. $w_{rec} = w_o$.

In each of the cases studied, the field of view of the relay system is given by the equation F_{ov} = ArcTan[h/f], where h is the distance from the optic axis to the furthest away modulator window. Figure 6 gives the dependence of F_{ov} on focal length.

From these curves it can be seen that the choice of focal length will be determined by the acceptable field of view of any specific relay system. If the field of view is too large we will end up with excessive aberrations which will lead to a lower system throughput and, potentially, to higher levels of optical crosstalk. For example, if it is assumed that the field of view has to be kept below ±2 degrees, the focal length for a 4x4 cluster system having a 90μm window separation must meet the criteria $f \geq 5.47$mm.

In the case of diffractive lenslets, we must also consider limits associated with f/number. For any given number of phase levels there will exist a lower limit on f/number below which manufacturing problems - including initial mask production faults, mask alignment errors, over etching, non-rectangular features, etc. - lead to inaccurate fabrication of the fine features at the edge of each facet. In addition, when the feature size is of the same order as the wavelength, scalar diffraction theory will no longer be adequate to predict the local diffraction efficiency and a rigorous diffraction analysis must be adopted. For the purposes of this analysis, a limit on the f/number of diffractive lenslets of f/# ≥ 8 will be imposed. This assumes the lenslets to be fabricated with eight phase levels [11,13].

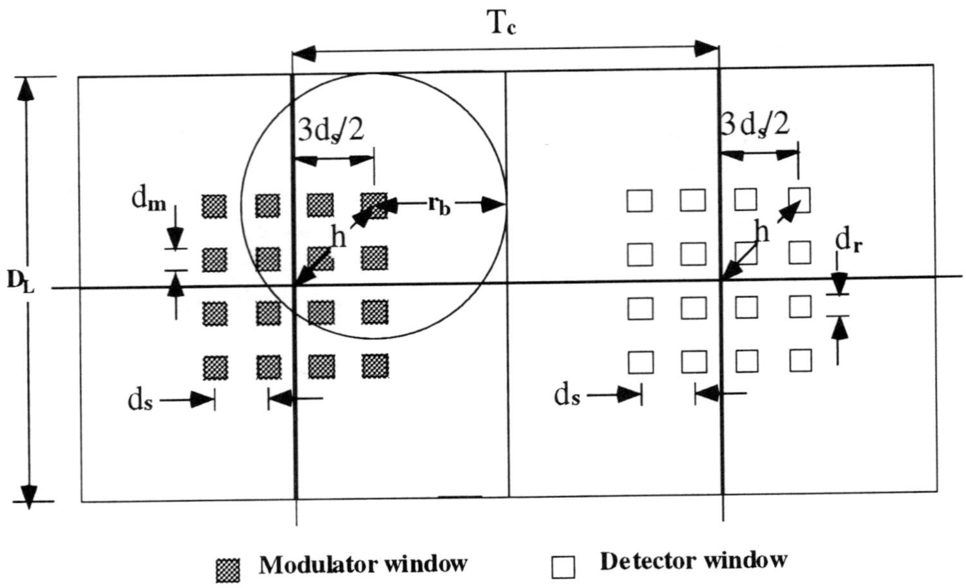

Figure 5 - Layout of 4x4 clustered window geometry. D_L - dimensions of lenslets, d_s - pitch between device windows, d_m - dimensions of modulator windows, d_r - dimensions of detector windows, T_c = pitch between window clusters.

4. Square Diffractive Lenslets - 4x4 Cluster Geometry

The device window layout of a 4x4 cluster of optical i/o is shown in figure 5. Note that it has been assumed that the dimensions of each lenslet facet is the same as the pitch between window clusters. Using the model developed in the previous section, it can be shown that $h = (3/\sqrt{2})\, d_s$, and

$$D_L = 2[(3/2)\, d_s + \alpha\, w_o\, [1 + (f\,\lambda/\,\pi\, w_o^2)^2]^{1/2}] \quad (2)$$

where $w_o = d_m/\beta_m$. Thus, for any given combination of d_m, d_s, α, β_m, w_o, f and λ it is possible to calculate the corresponding lenslet dimensions. From this equation, the field of view, F_{ov}, the cluster pitch, T_c, and the window density, W_D may be calculated. In addition, equation 2 can be used to determine

(1) Size of optoelectronic die, D_{die}. In the case of an NxN array of clusters (each cluster containing MxM windows)

$$D_{die} = (N\text{-}1)\, D_L + (M\text{-}1)\, d_s + d_m/2 + d_r/2 \quad (3)$$

where $d_r = \beta_r\, w_o$. This is the die area which is devoted to optical i/o, defined from the edges of the extreme modulator and detector windows in the array. The actual size of the die will also be governed by the processing electronics and bond pad space requirements.

(2) Lenslet f/number. It is important to note that the Gaussian beams do not completely fill the entire area of each lenslet. Thus, from the point of view of fabrication limits, we may define an effective f/number, $f/(h + r_b)$, which determines the area of the lenslet which must be manufactured correctly. In the case of a 4x4 cluster, this is given by

$$ef/\# = f\,/\,(2\,[(3/\sqrt{2})\, d_s + \alpha\, w_o\, [1 + (f\,\lambda/\,\pi\, w_o^2)^2]^{1/2}]) \quad (4)$$

Using the above expressions, the dependence of lenslet dimensions (and thus cluster pitch), window density, size of optoelectronic die, and effective f/number have been plotted against modulator window size for a range of focal lengths (f = 6, 7, 8, 9, and 10mm). To relate the above equations to modulator window size, the relation $d_r = \beta_r\, w_o$ has been used, where β_r is the clipping ratio, defined for the purposes of this analysis as $\beta_r = 3$. The results of these calculations are shown in figure 7(a) - (d).

The trends displayed in figures 7(a) - (d) are typical for all the cases studied. Probably the most important point to note is that there is an inherent trade off between modulator window size (which dominate capacitance and therefore the electrical and optical power consumption) and die dimensions. Using the restrictions that $D_{die} < 6$mm,

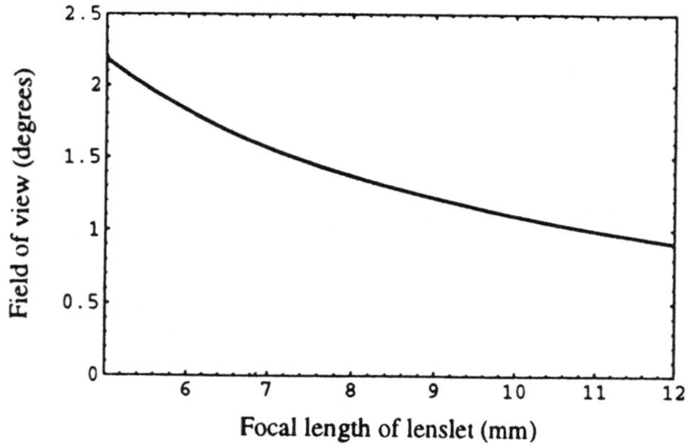

Figure 6 - Field of view versus focal length for a 4x4 cluster on a 90μm pitch.

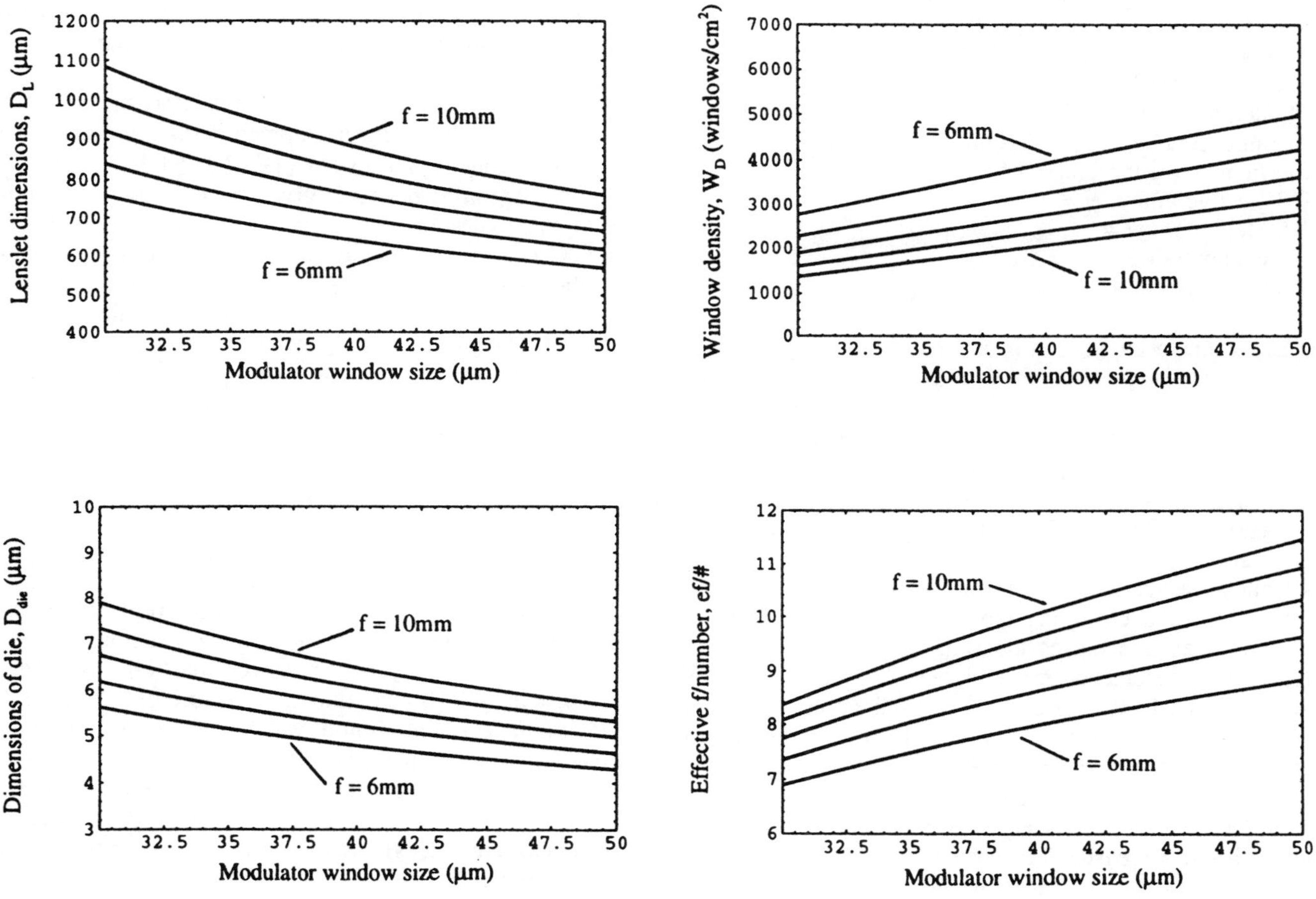

Figure 7(a) - (d) - Lenslet size, window density, die dimensions and effective f/number versus modulator window size for a range of focal lengths (f = 6, 7, 8, 9, and 10mm).

$d_m \leq 40\mu m$, and ef/# ≥ 8, it is clear that the design space allows for quite a variation in acceptable solutions. From figure 7(c) it follows that if $d_m \leq 40\mu m$, the focal length must be kept just below 9mm. A second limit on the focal length can be derived by considering the effective f/number; if the ef/# $\geq$ 8, then f > approximately 6mm. Thus, we have a range for focal length of 6mm < f < 9mm which gives us our design space.

5. Microchannel Relay Design

5.1. Outline of Design

Based on the results presented in figure 6 and 7(a)-(d), it was decided to perform a more detailed simulation of an interconnect having the following design parameters

1) Focal length of lenslets = 8.5mm.
2) Dimensions of lenslets = 800μmx800μm.
3) Spot size at optoelectronic device windows ($1/e^2$ radius) = 13.1μm.
4) Modulator window size = 40μm.
5) Detector window size = 40μm.
6) Pitch between optoelectronic device windows = 90μm.
7) Dimensions of die = 5.910mmx5.910mm.
8) F/number of lenslets = 7.51.
9) Effective f/number = 9.38.
10) Field of view = ±1.29°.
11) Compression ratio = 2.29.
12) Window density = 2500 windows/cm^2.

These values were chosen in order to maximize the stage separation (maximize the focal length) whilst ensuring that the conditions D_{die} < 6mm, ef/# $\geq$ 8, and $d_m \leq 40\mu m$ were met. The power of optical interconnection technology is highlighted by the large connection density possible with this technique - 2500 windows/cm^2. By comparison, in the case of 0.8μm ECL technology, off-chip electrical connections require an area of 930 by 150μm. The novel scheme presented here for the first time is superior to the interlaced Tx/Rx clustering approach discussed by Rolston et al [11] as it achieves the same window density with fewer optical elements and a higher alignment tolerance. An interlaced Tx/Rx system would require a configuration similar to that shown in figure 2, thereby requiring an extra lenslet array and a patterned mirror positioned in the corresponding image plane. This would introduce additional loss (appoximately 20% in the case of an eight level diffractive lenslet A.R. coated only on one side). In addition, the patterned mirror would have to be precisely positioned with respect to the focused spots in the image plane resulting in tighter alignment tolerances. Fewer passes through lenslet arrays will also reduce the overall aberations introduced by the optical train. These attributes result in separate clustered i/o having a significant advantage over an interlaced approach.

5.2. Patterned Mirror/Grating Parameters

Assuming a spot radius ($1/e^2$) at the modulator window of 13.1μm, the beam radius, w_g, at the patterned mirror/grating element (given by $w_g = f\lambda/\pi w_o$) will equal 176μm, and the full beam diameter (99% points) will be 528μm. Obviously, the alignment tolerances for PMG_1 and PMG_2 are quite large, as both the grating and mirror strips are equal to the lenslet width, D_L = 800μm. Translational alignment tolerances will therefore be in the range of ±100μm, and the required rotational tolerances will be primarily governed by the necessity of aligning the optical beams with the device arrays. However, it should be noted that the modulated signal beams must be reflected at the correct angle from the patterned mirrors to be incident on the detectors. This can be achieved using a set of Risley beam steerers within the microchannel relay. In addition, in order for the optical interconnect to operate optimally, the collimating microlenses of the optical power supply should be placed exactly one focal length from the PMG elements and illuminated by an array of Gaussian sources positioned in their front focal planes.

In order to generate the required spot array pattern at the modulator windows, the grating period (assuming an even-orders missing design) must equal, $P = 2f\lambda/d_s$. As d_s = 90μm, the grating period is given by P = 161μm. Thus, each beam generated by the power supply will illuminate 3.3 periods of G_1. Ideally, to minimize the field of view of the relay, we want the windows to be positioned as close together as possible. However, from the point of view of the initial array generation we want the power supply beams as far apart as possible to improve uniformity. The optimum compromise between these two factors needs to be determined [14].

5.3. Optical Power Budget

Previous analyses of modulator based interconnects have shown that even small nonuniformities in the optical power supply beams and modulator reflectivity can dramatically increase the input power requirements to the system [11]. In practice, however, the various system parameters will be continuously distributed between a maximum and a minimum value. Thus, as the input power is reduced, channels will begin to fail depending on how close to the edge of the operating window they are. In the following section, a statistical analysis is used to more accurately determine the optimum power required to operate the interconnect. The model assumes a normal distribution of operating parameters randomly spread across the smart pixel arrays in order to calculate the minimum power below which channels will probably begin to fail. By using this approach it is possible to determine the probability of the system operating successfully for any given optical input power.

Consider an interconnect with the following component losses

1)	Diffraction efficiency of power supply lenslet = 0.94 (8 phase levels).
2)	Reflection loss from power supply lenslet = 0.95 (one side A.R. coated).
3)	Diffraction efficiency of fan-out grating = 0.86.
4)	Number of beams generated = 16 (4x4)
5)	Reflection loss from fan-out grating = 0.96 (not A.R. coated).
6)	Reflectivity of patterned mirror = 0.98 (normal reflection).
7)	Reflection loss at back of PMG element = 0.99.
8)	Efficiency of PBS/QWP assembly = 0.96 (perfect input polarization state).
9)	Diffraction efficiency of interconnection lenslet array = 0.94.
10)	Reflection loss from interconnection lenslet = 0.95 (one side A.R. coated).
11)	Reflectivity of modulator (High = 40% and Low = 10%).
12)	Throughput of Risley beam steerers = 0.98. (Four surfaces with 0.5% reflection loss per surface).
13)	Polarization loss = 15%
14)	Alignment loss = 25%

Table 1 - First pass interconnect parameters

1)	Non-uniformity of power supply fan-out grating	±5.0%
2)	Non-uniformity of PMG fan-out	±7.5%
3)	Non-uniformity of modulator reflectivity (high)	±5.0%
4)	Non-uniformity of modulator reflectivity (low)	±5.0%
5)	Minimum differential power at detector windows	10μW

Table 2 - Interconnect nonuniformities

These parameters result in the following expected performance values

a) Throughput of interconnection lenslets = 89.34%
b) Throughput from input to PMG to modulator = 3.91%
b) Efficiency of interconnect from modulator to detector window = 53.05%
c) Throughput to detector: High = 0.53%, Low = 0.13%

If we require a differential switching power of 10μW, the resulting input power to the system (at the power supply lenslet array) will be ideally 81mW per stage. This power could be obtained from a single diode laser. However, to be more the effects of power supply beam uniformity and component uniformity should be included. Assuming the following system parameters the worst case input power required is 107mW, an increase of 32% compared to the ideal operating power. This is the power required to ensure that all the channels will operate assuming absolute worst case conditions. A more realistic approach to determining the required optical power involves calculating the probability of channel failure for a specific power assuming a statistical distribution in system parameters. We can then design a system around a lower input power as long as the probable channel failure rate per smart pixel is acceptable.

For the purposes of this analysis it will be assumed that the power spectrum associated with the optical power supply grating, the power spectrum associated with the PMG fan-out element, and the performance of the MQW modulators in both the high and low reflectivity states each follow a normal distribution which has a probability density function given by

$$F(x) = \frac{1}{\sqrt{2\pi}\sigma} \exp[-(x-\mu)^2/2\sigma^2] \quad (5)$$

where μ is the mean value and σ is the standard deviation. The resulting spread in performance values will be calculated using the corresponding cumulative distribution function

$$F(z) = \frac{1}{\sqrt{2\pi}} \int_{-\infty}^{z} \exp[-z^2/2]\,dz \quad (6)$$

where z = (x - μ)/σ. A typical calculation of channel failure rate versus optical input power is shown in figure 8 for a random distribution of optical power supply beams and modulator reflectivity's. This analysis was repeated 30 times for different random distributions of system parameters across the smart pixel array. In all cases, channel failure did not occur until the optical power fell below 100mW. From the calculated data it was concluded that if the input power is 97mW, the probability of only one channel failing in the entire smart pixel array due to insufficient optical power is 6.7%. If the power is kept at 98mW, the probability of successful operation is 96.7%. Thus, the ideal optical power per stage is 81mW, the power required to ensure that absolutely no channels will fail under any conditions is 107mW. However, in reality, a power of 98mW will be sufficient to ensure that only one smart pixel *array* in every 30 suffers a channel failure, a significant reduction in operating power.

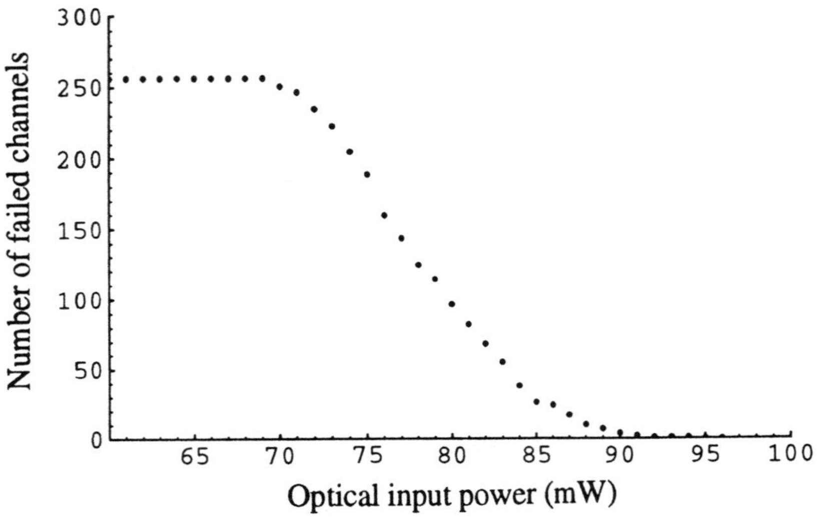

Figure 8 - Number of failed channels versus optical input power.

5.4. Image Mapping

One of the most influential design parameters for any interconnect is its image mapping as this effects the layout and architecture of the smart pixel array. A matrix approach may be used to analyze the effect that image rotation (how the beams are spatially permuted as they pass between device planes) has on the design of the system [11]. Designate each 4x4 cluster as C_{ij}, where i refers to the row and j refers to the column. After passing through the microchannel relay based interconnect, cluster C_{ij} on device plane 1 is mapped to cluster C_{ij} on device plane 2. That is, the clusters are directly mapped. Thus, if we arrange the smart pixel array into alternating columns of modulators and detectors, modulated signal beams will be directly mapped onto modulator windows rather than onto the detectors as is required. There are a number of possible techniques for avoiding this problem including rotating successive device arrays (although this will lead to complexity with respect to the smart pixel layout as data will end up inverted), and introducing an extra reflection with a 45° prism to reflect the beams such that C_{ij} maps to cluster $C_{(i)(N+1-j)}$. Modulated beams will therefore map directly onto detector windows.

If we treat the mapping of windows within a specific cluster in the same manner, it can be shown that, the windows are also mapped directly. Thus, representing each window within a cluster with the term W_{pq}, we end up with the mapping W_{pq} -> W_{pq}, i.e., the signal beam in the top left hand corner of a cluster maps to the detector window in the top left hand corner. This is due to two inversions, three reflections and one implicit reflection (turning device plane 2 around to face the beams) which occur as the beams propagate through the interconnect. However, if we introduce an extra reflection with a 45° prism, the beams will be reflected within each cluster, i.e., W_{pq} -> $W_{(p)(M+1-q)}$. This again will introduce a degree of complexity into the smart pixel design.

6. Conclusions

The design of a compact free-space interconnect developed for use within a photonic backplane was presented. From the results of the Gaussian beam analysis it can be seen that there exists a trade off between modulator window size, focal length, and area covered by the optical i/o. However, by using this design it is possible to simultaneously achieve a high window density (2500 windows/cm^2) with a moderate window size (40μm) and a stage-to-stage separation suitable for photonic backplane applications. Using a statistical analysis the optimum operating power requirements of the system was determined to be 98mW per stage assuming a differential switching power of 10μw. Future work will concentrate on the development of a more rigorous tolerancing model where the various parameters are weighted according to their overall importance to the systems performance (minimum energy requirements, maximum alignment tolerances, minimum crosstalk, etc.).

7. Acknowledgments

The author would like to acknowledge F. A. P. Tooley for his many suggestions regarding this work. This work was funded by the Nortel/NSERC Chair in Photonic Systems.

8. References

1) D. V. Plant, B. Robertson, H. S. Hinton, W. M. Robertson, G. C. Boisset, N. H. Kim, Y. S. Liu, M. R. Otazo, D. R. Rolston, and A. Z. Shang, "An optical backplane demonstrator system based on FET-SEED smart pixel arrays and diffractive lenslet arrays", IEEE Photon Tech. Lett. **7**, pp. 1057-1059 (1995).

2) T. Sanko, T. Matsumoto, and K. Noguchi, "Three-dimensional board-to-board free-space optical interconnects and their application to the prototype multiprocessor system - COSINE-III", Appl. Opt. **34**, pp. 1815-1822 (1995).

3) D. Z. Tsang and T. J. Goblick, "Free-space optical interconnection technology in parallel processing systems", Opt. Eng. **33**, pp. 1524-1531 (1994).

4) S. Araki, M. Kajita, K. Kasahara, K. Kubota, K. Kurihara, I. Redmond, E. Schenfeld, and T. Suzaki, "Experimental free-space optical network for massively parallel computers:, Appl. Opt. **35**, pp. 1269-1281 (1996).

5) R. A. Nordin, A. F. J. Levi, R. N. Nottenburg, J. O'Gorman, T. Tanbun-Ek, and R. A. Logan, "A systems perspective on digital interconnection technology", J. Lightwave Tech. **10** pp. 811-827 (1992).

6) T. H. Szymanski and H. S. Hinton, "A reconfigurable intelligent optical backplane for parallel computing and communications", Appl. Opt. **35**, pp. 1253-1268. (1996).

7) M. E. Prise, N. C. Craft, R. E. LaMarche, M. M. Downs, S. J. Walker, L. A. D'Asaro, and L. M. F. Chirovsky, "Module for optical logic circuits using symmetric self-electrooptic devices", Appl. Opt. **29** pp. 2164-2170 (1990).

8) S. M. Prince, F. A. P. Tooley, S. Wakelin, and M. R. Taghizadeh, "Implementation of an optical perfect shuffle module", Appl. Opt. **34**, pp. 1775-1782 (1995).

9) H. S. Hinton in "An introduction to photonic switching fabrics", Applications of Communications Theory Series, Plenum Press (1993).

10) F. A. P. Tooley, "Challenges in optically interconnecting electronics", J. Quantum Electron. **2**, pp. 3-13 (1996).

11) D. R. Rolston, B. Robertson, H. S. Hinton, and D. V. Plant, "Analysis of a microchannel interconnect based on the clustering of smart-pixel device windows", Appl. Opt. **35**, pp. 1220-1233 (1996).

12) Y. S. Liu, B. Robertson, D. V. Plant, H. S. Hinton, W. M. Robertson, "Design and characterization of a microchannel optical interconnect for optical backplanes", accepted at Appl. Opt. (1996).

13) J. Jahns and S. J. Walker, "Two dimensional array of diffractive microlenses fabricated by thin film deposition", Appl. Opt. **29**, pp. 931-936 (1990).

14) A. L. Lentine and F. A. P. Tooley, "The relationship between speed and tolerances for self electro-optic effect devices", Appl. Opt. **33**, pp. 1354-1375 (1994).

HADLOP – A Hardware Description Language for the Design of digital 3-D optoelectronic circuits

Guido Grimm, Marko Degenkolb and Dietmar Fey
Friedrich Schiller Universtität Jena, Institut für Informatik
Ernst-Abbe-Platz 1–4, 07743 Jena, Germany

Abstract

A tool for computer-aided design and simulation of digital 3-D optoelectronic computing systems is presented. The program especially considers the features offered by the optics. The usefulness and the large flexibility of the tool was demonstrated exemplary for both architecture proposals published in literature and own proposals. The simulation system is freeware and is available via the Internet http://www2.informatik.uni-jena.de/pope/HADLOP/hadlop.html.

1 Introduction: The necessity of design tools in optoelectronic computing

Recent advances in the development of active and passive devices for optoelectronic computing [1, 2, 3] make the use of high dense optical interconnections in the chip-to-chip area more and more likely. The increasing availability of fine-grain optoelectronic integrated circuits (OEIC) - with a high number of parallel optical input/output (I/O) channels - promises to overcome one of the major problems in today's very large scale integrated circuit (VLSI) technology: limited I/O bandwidth because of too few and comparatively slow pins. One possible solution for this problem is the use of optical transmitters and receivers, which send and detect light vertical to the circuit's surface. Besides this technological aspect, the use of three-dimensional (3-D) interconnection schemes between electronic circuits is also very attractive for computer architects. For the first time the computer architect has the chance to develop 3-D processing units. This does not only allow quantitative improvements which are based on a higher pin number compared to planar processing structures. Also qualitative improvements are possible if the additional degree of freedom, the third dimension offers [4, 5], is adequately exploited. Further progress in optoelectronic VLSI technology will allow the design of complex 3-D circuits very soon. These systems consist of cascaded optoelectronic fine-grain processing planes. In order to manage the complexity of such 3-D circuits as well as to support the design of low level algorithms - well adapted to the optical interconnect technology - computer aided design tools are indispensable.

The design of fine-grain 3-D OEIC's is more complicated compared to the design of VLSI circuits because both, optical and electronic components, have to be considered as well as the optoelectronic interface and the optical interconnection system. There are a lot of design tools for analogue and digital electronic circuit design, e.g. VHDL for the digital system view and SPICE for the analogue view on device level. Hence, the question arises, what is the reason for developing a new hardware description language? The answer is that most design tools used for electronic circuits do not adequately consider the nature of light and its interaction to the optoelectronic circuit.

The following features are very important for the computer-aided design of computing structures based on optoelectronics. These mechanisms are not supported well in standard design tools for electronic circuits:

- Parallel computing of 2-dimensional (2-D) binary matrices with processing layers consisting of identical groups of gates (as for example in smart pixel systems).
- Simple modeling of parallel regular interconnections like perfect shuffle, butterfly, crossover, etc., whose efficient realization by optical means was often shown in the past.
- Output of data layers as simulation results and not an event trace of a collection of signals like in electronic design systems.
- Simultaneous simulation of pipelining of processing layers which are optically connected in the third dimension as well as field processing within processing layers.
- An input stimuli consisting of subsequent 2-D data layers which are brought step by step into the 3-D system under investigation.
- Synthesis of layouts (being appropriate for the manufacturing process of micro-optic devices and OEIC's) from the designs of 3-D optoelectronic computing structures.

Most of the points listed above could also be realized by ex-

0-8186-7974-3/97 $10.00 © 1997 IEEE

panding existing design systems for electronic circuits with a kind of macro programming such tools sometimes offer. But this is often very difficult to achieve and unpragmatic. For example, if we think of a data layer with 32x32 pixels. Apparently it is inconvenient to see 1024 digital event traces one above the other. What we need are design tools that well support the thinking in 3-D systems, operating on 2-D data layers. This is not foreseen in current design systems so far. Hence, we decided to develop an own system called HADLOP (HArdware Description Language for Optical Processing). This new simulation system adequately allows to consider the third dimension and the mutual influence between optical interconnection modules (OIM's) and OEIC's. The necessity of new design tools and models explicitly regarding optics was also realized by other research groups [6, 7]. In [8] the physical behavior of devices is focused. In a system called OptiCAD [9] digital optical systems are modeled on a more abstract level with data flow graphs. In the system Optism [10] OEIC's are modeled on gate level – also supported in HADLOP. In addition to that, HADLOP maintains OEIC's and the corresponding OIM's. HADLOP is equipped with a modern graphical user interface (GUI). Furthermore, a concept for the next step, the automatic synthesis of layouts for OIM's and OEIC's that can be passed directly to manufacturers is presented in this paper. In section 2 we explain the system HADLOP and its working "philosophy" in more detail. The simulation system is introduced in section 3. Section 4 shows the developed concept for the automatic synthesis. A summary and conclusion constitutes section 5.

2 What is HADLOP ?

The digital design process is a complicated task containing different design steps. In order to manage this complexity and to simplify the mapping of an algorithm onto a specific hardware, so-called abstraction levels are created. Abstraction is a method to rule the complexity by hiding details [11]. In each abstraction level one step in the design process is carried out (see Fig. 1). For example in a top-down design of a VLSI circuit you start in the most abstract layer, the *architecture layer*, specifying the main components of a processor and the data paths between them. A representation of an architecture in the *logic* (*gate*) *level* can be achieved via transformations from previous levels (*algorithm level* and *register transfer level*, respectively). The *algorithm level* considers the corresponding low-level algorithms which are represented as set of registers and Boolean expressions in the *register transfer level*. In the *logic level* a system is specified as a combinatorial connection of logical gates and flip-flops. This is exactly the layer HADLOP belongs to. In addition to the modeling of digital circuits HADLOP provides permutation elements in order to consider the needs of optics explicitly. The levels

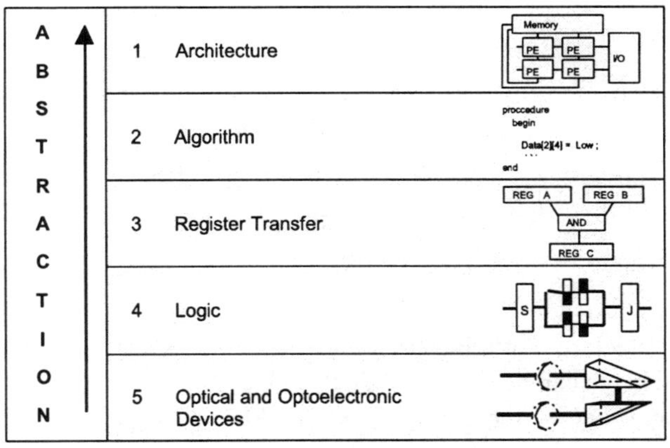

Figure 1. Abstraction layers for hierarchical design of digital systems

1 to 4 all consider the digital behavior of a design. The last level, the level of the devices, concerns the analogue values that are important for the hardware setup, i.e. the necessary light power or the deflection angles of gratings or a symbolic layout for an OEIC and an OIM. A specification on device level for a 3-D OEIC could end up with a description of a set-up consisting of devices like lenses, holograms, fibers, light emitters, photoreceivers and a symbolic layout for the OEIC. The beginning of the development of HADLOP in 1987 was determined by the need for a simulator tool for symbolic substitution logic (SSL) [12]. This early simulator program was expanded step by step towards optoelectronic smart pixel systems. Now it is object-orientated programmed and equipped with a modern graphical user interface using OSF/MOTIF to offer a user friendly and easy to learn design environment. The current version 2.2.1, which this paper is related to, is available via the Internet (http://www2.informatik.uni-jena.de/pope/HADLOP/hadlop.html) for everyone who would like to work with it.

3 Principles of HADLOP

HADLOP is a simulation system for 3-D optical and optoelectronic circuits on the logical level. The information is carried by spatially distributed light beams. Physical existing devices can be emulated using the HADLOP primitives. A two-dimensional binary optical data matrix passes through the HADLOP primitives while performing a single simulation step. In this way a HADLOP architecture processes these optical data matrices. Doing this, HADLOP just considers whether light occurs on a particular position (pixel) of the optical data plane – or not. This emphasizes the logical character of the simulation system.

Some HADLOP primitives are controlled by a clock signal. This allows transient simulations of a HADLOP ar-

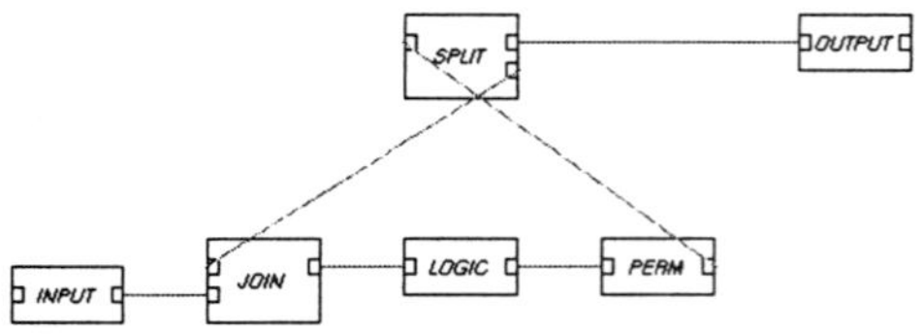

Figure 2. Ripple Carry Adder in the HADLOP simulation system [13]

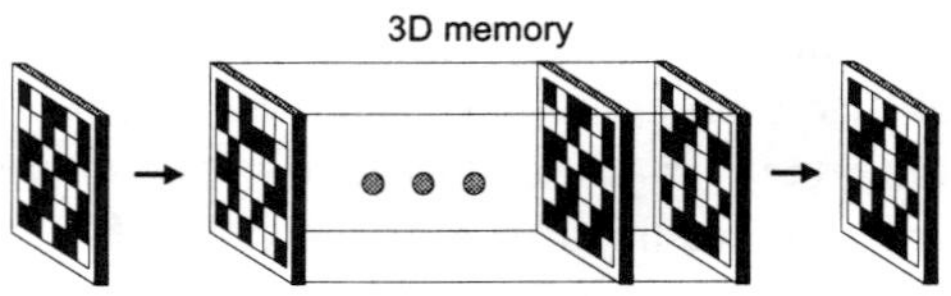

Figure 3. Modeling a 3-D memory as an input stimuli with the architecture primitive INPUT

chitecture. An arbitrary number of any desired clock pulse scheme can be specified. Such a clock type and delay times may be set for every clocked HADLOP primitive. The functional and physical behavior of a HADLOP primitive can be set very easily. Each primitive has powerful mechanisms making it possible to specify a desired characteristic. The following section describes some important HADLOP primitives.

Fig. 2 shows a HADLOP architecture in the main working window of the simulation system. While creating a HADLOP architecture it is often necessary to verify the correctness of certain primitives or parts of the architecture. Then it is helpful to carry out the simulation step by step. All HADLOP primitives offer a "Show Data window" in order to check the optical information (output planes) of the selected primitive. While debugging an HADLOP architecture the use of this feature is indispensable.

There are many HADLOP architectures available [14, 13] which were designed by ourselves and taken also from the literature. Unfortunately, an investigation of a HADLOP architecture would be out of the scope of this paper.

3.1 The INPUT and OUTPUT primitives

It is necessary to test systems modeled with HADLOP using different input data. The input data of a simulation arrangement are stored in a special 3-D HADLOP primitive named INPUT (see Fig. 3). This element can be considered as a shifter for optical data planes. While performing a simulation step the first data plane, a 2-D data matrix, leaves the INPUT at a certain time. This corresponds to a laser array, for example, having the same dimension like this optical data matrix. The INPUT allows various possibilities to look at the optical data stored inside. For example, bit vectors can be entered at an arbitrary position of any plane of the 3-D "data block". This can be done using the features provided by the "Modify" window of the INPUT primitive. The bits which are set inside a highlighted part of a manipulation matrix in the "Modify" window are interpreted as a decimal number. The contents of the matrix (binary data words) can be changed by clicking on an arbitrary bit position using the mouse. It is more comfortable to select the desired line number (via the item "Line Number") and to enter the value in the edit subwindow called "Value". Furthermore, the values represented by the stored numbers (binary data words) can be read out by choosing the correct line number.

The output data planes of a simulation can be caught using the OUTPUT primitive. This architecture element corresponds to the INPUT primitive with the exception that the data stored inside can not be modified. It is convenient to analyze the output data using the mechanisms provided by that HADLOP primitive. This primitive automatically carries out a conversion from a binary pixel presentation of the data into a decimal number, for example.

3.2 The PERM primitive

Normally we assume parallel and straight beams of light between the HADLOP primitives. However, the PERM primitive allows to realize arbitrary point to point connections between an incoming bit position of the optical plane and any outgoing bit position. It is possible to connect incoming light beams to any bit position of the outgoing data plane. This models the functionality of an optical permutation element (OIM), as realized with a diffractive holographic optical element, for example. The functional behavior can be specified as a set of point-to-point interconnections between rays of light of the optical input plane and rays of light of the optical output plane. So the input plane is to be considered as the place of the "transmitter" pixels and the output plane serves as the place for all "receiver" pixels. These locations are specified in discrete coordinates. HADLOP also directly supports regular interconnection patterns such as perfect shuffle or butterfly, for example, which were demonstrated by the device community very often. Moreover, rows and columns of the incoming data plane can be shifted to any desired direction.

3.3 The LOGIC primitive

The LOGIC primitive corresponds to the smart pixel concept (OEIC's). Single processor elements or digital electronic circuits are distributed over the whole optical plane. Every processor element carries out its Boolean function on the incoming local beams of light which are related to the position of the processor element in the optical data plane (see Fig. 4). Each cell performs the same function on different data, so we have a real SIMD structure. In a processor element the number of optical inputs equals

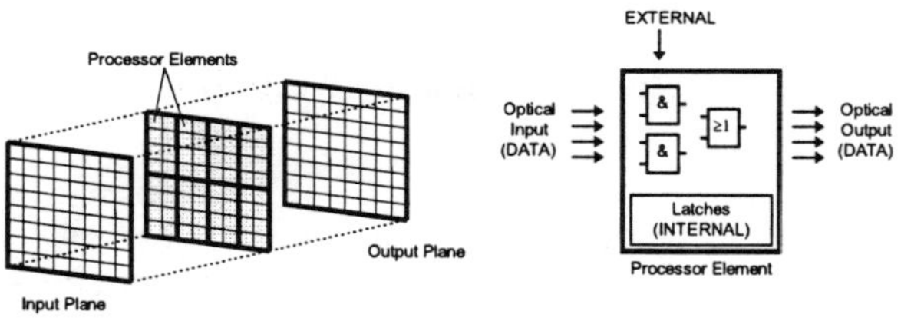

Figure 4. Setup of the LOGIC primitive. *Left:* processor elements are distributed over the optical data plane, *right:* local I/O data flow and global control signals of a processor element.

the number of optical outputs. We distinguish three different classes of bit signals which can be found in the LOGIC primitive. One class is called *external signals*. These are global control flags valid for all processor elements. Furthermore, every processor cell may have local memory (flip flops) in order to store current states. This can be done using the *internal signals*. In contrast to the *external signals* these flip flop cells are locally assigned to every processor element. The optical inputs and outputs of a processor element can be addressed by the *data signals*. The logical behavior of the electronic circuit can be specified with Boolean functions. The equations combine identifiers of signals belonging to one of the three data classes mentioned above. The results of the equations are assigned to the optical outputs and to the *internal signals*.

3.4 SPLIT and JOIN

These elements allow to multiply (SPLIT) and to combine (JOIN) optical data planes of a HADLOP architecture. The SPLIT primitive corresponds to a beam splitter in order to duplicate the incoming two-dimensional data plane in different paths. Each optical output plane is equal to the incoming matrix of light beams. The JOIN models an optical device combining different incoming data planes to a single optical output plane.

3.5 The MACRO primitive

Large architectures are sometimes difficult to manage. The MACRO primitive serves as a container element for other HADLOP primitives. Parts of an architecture can be stored inside the MACRO. A copy of any MACRO - performing a particular functionality – may be used on different places of any architecture. This allows to keep the arrangement of the whole architecture clear and makes it easy to handle parts of the architecture in a library.

4 Future plans - a roadmap for an optoelectronic "silicon compiler"

"Silicon-compiler" are one of the best known approaches to develop automatic transformations from one abstraction layer to the next one. A functional description of an electronic circuit is automatically transformed into a geometrical layout ready for the manufacturing process. Up to now similar design tools for 3-D OEIC's do not exist. We developed a concept to expand HADLOP in the future towards an optoelectronic "silicon compiler". This tool considers both the OEIC VLSI circuits (5.1) and the corresponding OIM's (5.1).

4.1 OEIC Technology Mapping

We intend to support the following promising OEIC technologies for the mapping of an OEIC specified in HADLOP syntax onto a real hardware device:

- Massively parallel OEIC's based on hybrid SEED technology for fine-grain architectures,
- OEIC's with lower I/O channel number but fast switching speeds based on monolithic GaAs technologies for coarsely grained architectures and
- Monolithically integrated smart detectors based on BiCMOS technologies [15].

The corresponding cell libraries and design rules for the mentioned technologies have to be provided. We will adapt them to our design environment HADLOP in order to make the different technologies conveniently available for the circuit designer. The main differences between the design of a pure electronic VLSI circuit and an OEIC are determined by the following constraints given by the optics:

- A fixed raster of the optical I/O pads distributed over the whole chip area,
- Segmentation of the chip in rectangular partitions containing autonomous processing elements, e.g. in smart pixel systems. A group of locally neighbored optical I/O pads is related to each partition (processor element).

An automatic synthesis of a symbolic layout has to respect these circumstances.

We intend to use different techniques for the generation of the symbolic layouts from a HADLOP architecture in order to offer sufficient flexibility for the users. This can be fulfilled by building an interface between HADLOP and commercial as well as public domain VLSI design tools.

Using a powerful design tool like CADENCE shall be one approach. The CADENCE feature of block designs offers, for example, an efficient handling of the constraints in the design of an OEIC mentioned above. By means of so-called *areas* it is possible to assign fixed points in the chip core to optical I/O pads. The connections of the input and output cells will be routed to these I/O pads. Furthermore, it is possible to define a region within the chip area in which the layout of a smart pixel processing element has to be routed. There is no need to be familiar with the internal wiring in advance. The advantages of tools like CADENCE for optoelectronic chip design are determined by the synthesis performance such tools offer.

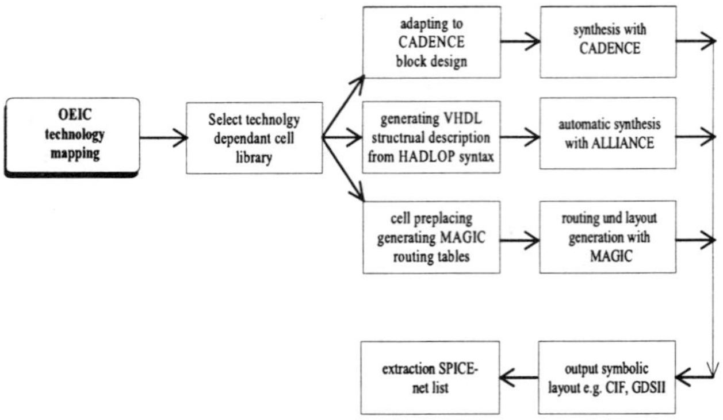

Figure 5. OEIC Technology Mapping

We also plan to offer a cheaper and easier alternative being very interesting for research purposes. This can be achieved by using the design tool ALLIANCE from the University of Paris. Since ALLIANCE is freeware, the VHDL simulator tool of ALLIANCE is comparatively easy to integrate into HADLOP as well as the automatic mapping capabilities onto symbolic layouts. A netlist compatible to ALLIANCE can be generated directly from a HADLOP description of an OEIC given as a gate netlist. This is the starting point for the automatic layout generation carried out by ALLIANCE. All the necessary steps – including a SPICE netlist extraction – will be controlled by our HADLOP environment using the ALLIANCE package. Thus a transparent design system is directly offered to the user. Of course, the synthesis features of ALLIANCE can not be compared to that of CADENCE. But we expect to realize a solution very quickly. Furthermore, this solution will be available for everyone and saves costs and time.

A similar situation is given for our last approach of the OEIC technology mapping. Here we intend to realize a link from HADLOP to the layout tool MAGIC from the University of Berkeley. MAGIC was also recommended for the design of H-SEED circuits. We derive the necessary standard cells from the Boolean equations specifying an OEIC in HADLOP. Using these standard cells HADLOP will generate a MAGIC compatible file. This file includes standard cells placed in an area determined by the number and the pitch of the optical I/O pads. The required optical I/O pads are arranged in a fixed raster directly above the layout of the standard cells. Polygons corresponding to the inputs/outputs of the standard cells and the I/O pads are named with labels. Afterwards MAGIC compatible routing tables will be produced by HADLOP specifying the necessary connections between the labels. The wiring itself will be carried out by MAGIC. This happens very efficiently as we can confirm due to own gained expectations.

Finally the main tasks for the OEIC technology mapping are summarized in Fig. 5.

4.2 Mapping onto Optical Interconnection Modules – Optical Technology Mapping

The consideration of the mutual interference between OEIC's and OIM's is absolutely necessary for an efficient technology mapping of a 3-D OEIC. The performance and the features of the OIM's are determined by the logic which is implemented in the circuits. Vice versa, the arrangement of transistors, optical I/O pads, transmitter and receiver circuits is determined by the OIM. For example, the required minimum area for a diffractive element, which shall operate as a deflection element, may exceed the area of the corresponding part of the OEIC. Then a larger distance between the different circuits on the chip (belonging to the diffractive element) is forced. This reduces the degree of parallelism. This may force a redesign of the basic concept of the OEIC. Normally the design of a 3-D OEIC starts with the development of the optoelectronic circuits. Then the suitable OIM's have to be found. This probably causes feedback to the OEIC. Analogous to electronic circuit design we denote this feedback as "optical backannotation". The optical backannotation has to supply significant information about important physical units, e.g. the expected optical path length, the possible pixel density and the light efficiency. This is important for transient analysis of the 3-D OEIC as well as for the final layout considering OEIC's and OIM's together.

But before the optical backannotation can take place we have to found a suitable OIM for two neighbored OEIC's that are to be linked to each other. The selection of the desired OIM shall result from an access to a database containing components whose feasibility and functionality was proved by prototypes and demonstrators in the past. Here we think of beam splitters, 1-to-1 imaging elements, permutation elements like butterflies and perfect shuffles. For the setup as well as for the enlargement of the database we aspire close cooperation with the device community. The database shall contain paramaterized descriptions of the stored elements. This allows to support both manufacturing and optical backannotation. In case a necessary OIM is not found in the database, it has to be checked, if it can be generated as a computer-generated hologram for example. Here we plan to set up an interface between HADLOP and a CAD design tool for planar optics [16] that is planned at the Fernuniversität Hagen (University of Hagen, Germany). For example, the pixel coordinates given by the HADLOP architecture primitive PERM (s. above) are the starting point to calculate deflection angles and corresponding diffractive optical elements. The achieved information is helpful for the design, simulations and evaluations which can be done using the CAD tool for the planar optics. Fig. 6 gives an impression of the mapping process of a HADLOP architecture onto an optical 3-D system using planar optics.

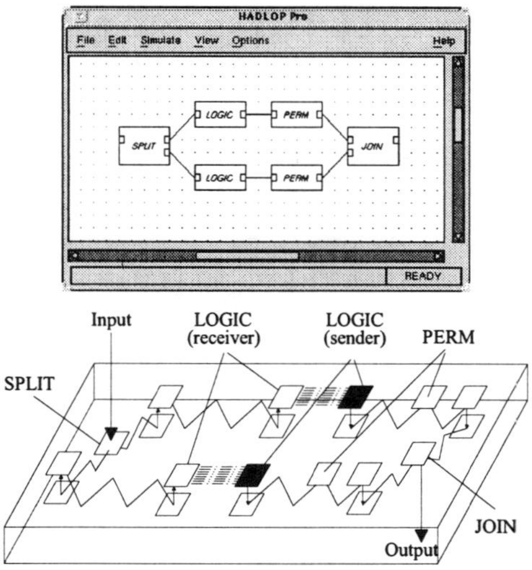

Figure 6. Scheme of the mapping of a HADLOP architecture onto an planar optical 3-D system

5 Summary and conclusion

HADLOP is a user friendly simulation tool for 3-D optoelectronic digital systems running on many UNIX workstations. It allows to carry out architecture and algorithm studies, especially considering the nature of optics. HADLOP works on the gate level, i.e. OEIC's and OIM's are specified by Boolean expressions and by a set of point-to-point interconnections, respectively. We see HADLOP as a tool which offers a contribution to close the gap between the architecture and the device community. A roadmap for an optoelectronic "silicon compiler" was presented to support this "device-architecture-interaction" more efficiently in the future. This will be achieved by an automatic synthesis of a symbolic layout description for OEIC's and OIM's from a HADLOP architecture.

References

[1] F.E. Kiamilev, J.S. Lambirth, R.G. Rozier, and A.V. Krishnamoorthy. Design of 64-Bit, 100 MIPS Microprocessor Core IC for Hybrid CMOS-SEED Technolgoy. In *Proceedings 3rd Int. Conf. on Massively Parallel Processing Using Optical Interconnects*, pages 53–60. IEEE Computer Society Press, Los Alamitos, October 1996.

[2] A.V. Krishnamoorthy, A.L. Lentine, and et. al. 3-D integration of MQW modulators over active submicron CMOS circuits: 375Mb/s transimpedance receiver-transmitter circuit. In *IEEE Photonics Tecgnology Letters*, volume 7 11, pages 1288–1290, November 1995.

[3] T. Kurokawa and T. Ikegami. Optical Interconnection Technologies Based on Vertical-Cavity Surface-Emitting Lasers and Smart Pixels. In *Proceedings 3rd Int. Conf. on Massively Parallel Processing Using Optical Interconnects*, pages 300–305. October 1996.

[4] D. Fey. Transformation of a 2-D VLSI systolic adder circuit in 3-D circuits using optical interconnections. In *L. Bouge et. al. (Eds.) EURO-PAR'96 Parallel Processing*, volume II, pages 478–485. 2nd Int. Euro-Par conference, Lyon, France, August 1996.

[5] D. Fey. A Comparison Study between 2D VLSI Circuits and 3-D Circuits based on Multifunctional Smart Pixels. In *Proc. of Int. Conf. on Applications of Photonic Technology*. Int. Conf. on Applications of Photonic Technology, Montreal, eds.: R.A. Lessard, Applications of Photonics Technology, Plenum Publishing 1997, August 1996.

[6] A. Louri and M.C. Major. A Generalized Methodology for Modeling and Simulating Optical Interconnection Networks Using Diffraction Analysis. *Applied Optics*, 34(20):4052–4065, July 1995.

[7] A. Louri and J. Na. A Modeling and Simulation Methodology for Digital Optical Computing Systems. *Applied Optics*, 33(10):1549–1559, March 1994.

[8] S.P. Levithan, P.J. Marchand, M.A. Rempel, D.M. Chiarulli, and F.B. McCormick. Computer-Aided Design of Free-space Optoelectronic Interconnection (FSOI) Systems. In *Proceedings on 2nd Int. Conf. on Massively Parallel Processing Using Optical Interconnections*, pages 239–245. IEEE Computer Society Press, Los Alamitos, 1995.

[9] M.A. Memon. OptiCAD - A System for Prototyping Optical Architectures. Thesis University Dharan, Saudi-Arabia, 1996.

[10] N. Langloh, S. van Langendonck, H. Sabli, V. Christopoulos, and J. Cornelis. Optism: A tool for the design of optical parallel computer architectures. In *Proc. Int. Conf. on Applications of Photonics Technology (ICAPT96)*. Montreal, August 1996.

[11] T.F. Melham. *Abstraction Mechanism for Hardware Verification, in: G.Birtwistle, P.A.Subrahmanyam, VLSI Specification*. Kluwer Academic Publishers, Boston, 1988.

[12] K.H. Brenner, A. Huang, and N. Streibl. Digital Optical Computing with Symbolic Substitution. *Applied Optics*, 25:3054–3006, 1986.

[13] D. Fey and G. Grimm. *The HADLOP Quick Tutorial 1.0*. Parallel Optoelectronic Processing Group, Friedrich Schiller University Jena, Department of Computer Architecture and Communication, 1996. http://www2.informatik.uni-jena.de/pope/HADLOP/hadlop.html.

[14] M. Degenkolb and G. Grimm. Homepage of the HADLOP simulation system: http://www2.informatik.uni-jena.de/pope/HADLOP/hadlop.html.

[15] H. Berger, J. Sturm, F. Estafahni, and et. al. Contactless Function Test of Integrated Circuits on The Wafer - General Survey. Proceedings Microsystems, Berlin, 1995.

[16] S. Sinzinger and J. Jahns. Planar Optics for Optical Interconnections in Computers. In *Proc. Topical Meeting on Optical Computing*. Topical Meeting on Optical Computing, Sendai, Japan, 1996.

CONFERENCE PANEL

Moderator: Frank Tooley, *McGill University*
Julian Bristow, *Honeywell*

Panelists: R. Wickman, *Cray*
C. DeCusatis, *IBM*
C. Lund, *Mercury*
R. Wallace, *Nortel*
H. Hesselbom, *Ericsson*

The evolution of optical interconnects: capabilities, limitations, and markets

Moderators: F. Tooley & J. Bristow

McGill University and Honeywell

Panelists

C. DeCusatis - IBM
H. Hesselbom - Ericcson
C. Lund - Mercury
R. Wallace - Nortel
R. Wickman - Cray

Topics for discussion

The use of optical interconnects to provide high-performance links over increasingly short distances is currently of interest. Several aspects of optical interconnects make their use potentially advantageous, yet electrical interconnect technology continues to make advances, albeit at the expense of increasing complexity. Electrical interconnects are currently used to implement two standards (FDDI and Fiber Channel) once considered obvious candidates for optics. Developers of optical interconnects are once again proposing their technology for a new set of interconnect applications. The panelists are asked to highlight any recent progress in electrical and optical interconnect technology they may be aware of and its proposed and currently used applications.

Comment on why optical interconnects have been introduced? What aspects of the performance of optical interconnects is it that is of importance? What problems are they currently capable of solving that electrical interconnects are less suited to? Speculate on what performance future electrical and optical technology will be capable of achieving. Will there be a requirement to have the increased performance of which optical interconnects is capable? Are optical interconnects likely to displace otherwise acceptable electrical interconnects on the basis of cost? What limits the use of electrical interconnects? What are the barriers that need to be overcome in the more widespread use of optical interconnects? Is there a market for optical interconnects and how will this market change in the next few years?

Position statements were unavailable at time of press

0-8186-7974-3/97 $10.00 © 1997 IEEE

Tutorial Session II

Switching Techniques, Adaptive Routing and Deadlock Handling in Interconnection Networks

Jose Duato
Facultad de Informatica
Universidad Politecnica de Valencia
Camino de Vera, 14 46071 - Valencia, SPAIN
E-mail: jduato@gap.upv.es

Abstract:

This tutorial surveys three key issues in the design of interconnection networks: switching techniques, mechanisms for deadlock handling, and routing algorithms. These three issues are closely related to each other. Switching techniques have a major impact on performance. Several switching techniques will be described, including some recent hybrid techniques, and highlighting the relationship between switching technique and network technology.

Routing algorithms determine the path followed by messages from source to destination. Adaptive routing algorithms have the potential to increase link utilization and throughput by avoiding congested regions in the network. However, adaptive routing algorithms are prone to deadlock. The tutorial will present several techniques for deadlock handling in interconnection networks, and their application to the design of adaptive routing algorithms. The talk will describe techniques for deadlock avoidance and recovery, mainly focusing on proposals that allow cyclic dependencies between network resources. Progressive deadlock recovery is emerging as an alternative to deadlock avoidance. In order to make it viable, it is necessary to reduce the frequency of deadlock and to implement an efficient deadlock detection mechanism. Deadlocks will be characterized, presenting mechanisms to reduce the frequency of deadlock, and describing efficient mechanisms for distributed deadlock detection.

Several methodologies for the design of adaptive routing algorithms will be described, as well as their application to multicomputer networks and networks of workstations with irregular topologies. Networks of workstations may require long links to connect different nodes and switches. The effect of wire length on performance, and the relationship with flow control mechanisms will be analyzed. Finally, some evaluation results will show the impact of different design parameters on performance.

0-8186-7974-3/97 $10.00 © 1997 IEEE

SESSION IV

Massively Parallel Processor Interconnects

Chair

Ted Szymanski
McGill University

Commercial MPP Networks: Time for Optics?

Craig B. Stunkel
IBM T. J. Watson Research Center
P.O. Box 218
Yorktown Heights, NY 10598
stunkel@watson.ibm.com

Abstract

Today's commercial MPP machines do not employ optics within their interconnection networks. In this paper we identify several recent trends in MPP networks and attempt to predict how these trends will affect the incorporation of optical interconnect technologies in the near future. We also recognize that successful commercial systems tend to change in an evolutionary fashion, and some possible evolutionary scenarios are discussed.

1 Introduction

Today's commercial massively parallel processor (MPP) machines do not employ any form of optics within their interconnection networks. Optical interconnects potentially provide much higher bandwidth capability and advantages such as low skew and absence of DC coupling. Despite these optical advantages, electronics have been used in increasingly sophisticated fashion to reach the bandwidth targets of current machines while adequately satisfying other constraints such as electromagnetic emissions limits.

Commercial MPP machines have succeeded in winning a growing set of customers who are betting their future computing plans on MPP technology. To minimize the risk towards this customer base, the movement toward optical technologies will likely be evolutionary rather than revolutionary. Thus it is likely that optics will initially be introduced as a replacement for copper, rather than as a replacement for the entire network. This paper focuses on recent trends in MPP networks that will affect the introduction of optics. Most of the trends cited are applicable to both copper replacement and all-optical networks.

In §2 we examine a few of the recent trends in MPP machines and attempt to extrapolate them into the near future. In §3 we relate these trends to the eventual use of optics in MPPs.

2 MPP trends

MPP systems have existed through sufficient generations that we can categorize trends in their architecture and in their marketplace. Some of these trends include:

- The economic reality that successful MPP vendors will survive by selling mostly small machines containing only a few nodes.
- The movement toward distributed shared memory (DSM) architectures.
- The use of SMP (symmetric multiprocessor) nodes.
- The inclusion of the attributes of networks of workstations (NOWs) into MPPs.
- The increasing complexity of the crossbar switches that are the interconnected building blocks of the network.
- The use of cut-through switching techniques for low latency.
- The embedding of collective communication support into the network.

In this section we examine these trends and briefly examine how each trend may affect the introduction of optics into MPPs.

2.1 Successful MPP vendors will sell mostly small machines

Government purchases of large ($\geq$ 100 processors) MPP machines generate exciting headlines and help provide bragging rights for MPP vendors. Nevertheless, these same vendors can no longer survive while selling large machines exclusively. Today, all leading MPP players are either large companies that were already selling workstations, PCs, and

0-8186-7974-3/97 $10.00 © 1997 IEEE

servers (e.g., IBM), or are MPP/Supercomputing companies that have been bought by workstation vendors (e.g., Cray, Convex). In fact, it may not currently make business sense to design MPP machines unless these machines themselves can be effectively "scaled down" to systems containing a few nodes. In another example, although Intel has large revenues from the manufacture of microprocessors and mother-boards, they have ceased to market MPPs.

The IBM RS/6000 SP [1] series provides one example of how the balance of MPP purchases has changed. When the machines were introduced in 1992, they were sold mostly to technical customers, with most of the nodes sold going into relatively large machines. In 1996, more than half of the nodes were sold to commercial customers, and more than half of the systems sold had 16 nodes or less. These smaller commercial purchases have allowed the SP series to remain a growing and profitable business.

This economic reality—that MPP machines must also be downwardly scalable—has an effect on many of the trends that will be discussed in the rest of this paper.

2.2 The movement toward distributed shared memory architectures

Until recently, MPP machines were—almost by definition—message-passing machines. The IBM SP is a current example of this architecture [1, 21] and has enjoyed much success in the MPP marketplace. It has generally been accepted that very large machines could not efficiently support the shared memory programming model. However, customers are increasingly interested in solutions which provide the abstraction of shared memory. Customers perceive that it is easier to port their applications to this model. Which architecture provides acceptable performance for various applications is far beyond the scope of this paper.

However, the last decade of research into distributed shared memory architectures has helped to position DSM as a viable option in the marketplace, as evidenced by recent offerings from SGI/Cray, HP/Convex, Sequent, and others. It is probable that DSM will continue be designed into larger and larger systems, although message-passing architectures will also remain important in the near future.

The primary implication of DSM is the need for dynamic, very low latency routing of packets. In comparison, the network latencies for message-passing are currently small compared to the software overhead for message transmission and reception. Thus, routing solutions which depend upon circuit switching, or routing decisions via off-line scheduling, or other high-latency or static routing techniques will severely impact the performance of DSM systems. Figure 1 shows approximate latency and bandwidth ranges for current types of interconnects, including LAN, MPP, DSM, and SMP interconnects. As interconnects progress from LAN to MPP to DSM, performance requirements force vendors to provide higher link bandwidth and lower latency. For example, the recently announced SGI Origin 2000 and the HAL Mercury interconnect contain switches with pin-to-pin latencies of 40ns and 42 ns respectively, and are targeted for DSM machines. Other MPP machines shown are the Cray T3E [18], the IBM SP, and Meiko CS-2 [3], and the Thinking Machines CM-5 [11]. The bandwidth and latency requirements for LAN-connected machines is not as severe, due to high TCP/IP software overheads and due to connection though commodity I/O busses.

Looking at bandwidth requirements is relatively meaningless, though, without considering the associated link length requirements. Table 1 lists the bandwidth and link length characteristics for many of the interconnects shown in Figure 1 and includes some other LAN and SAN (system area network) technologies. Two trends are evident. The first trend is that the implementations that currently push bandwidth most aggressively have higher per-wire transfer rates, wider data paths, and shorter maximum link lengths. The second trend is technologies which allow attachment of devices up to 25 meters or so. These technologies each have a 1-byte link width and lower link transfer rates. The 1-byte link width is a consequence both of cable diameter considerations for long links and of switch chip pin count.

The IBM SP and Myrinet technologies in particular attack a difficult bandwidth versus link-length region for copper. With 25 meter copper links and 150 Mb/s per signal, skew between different signals on the parallel link can conceivably arrive in different clock cycles. It is no coincidence that, of the listed technologies, only the SP and Myrinet implementations perform de-skewing among the bits on the link. As copper implementations become more aggressive, this bit de-skewing will become common. The smaller skew of optics will be advantageous here.

2.3 The use of SMP nodes

Regardless of the eventual outcome between message-passing and distributed shared memory architectures, a related trend is the use of SMP nodes within a larger MPP or DSM system. An example of this is one of the winning bids for the government's ASCI (Advanced Scientific Computing Initiative) competition. IBM's "ASCI Blue" SP machine planned for late 1998 will contain 512 nodes, each of which is an 8-way SMP, for a total of 4K processors.

Hence, not only must interconnects track the exponentially increasing improvement in microprocessor power, but they must also support multiple processors per link. While this is an impact on required link bandwidth, the optimal size of an SMP might not grow. For example, the Cray T3D [8] contained two-processor SMP nodes, while the successor T3E [18] nodes contain a single processor. It is likely that

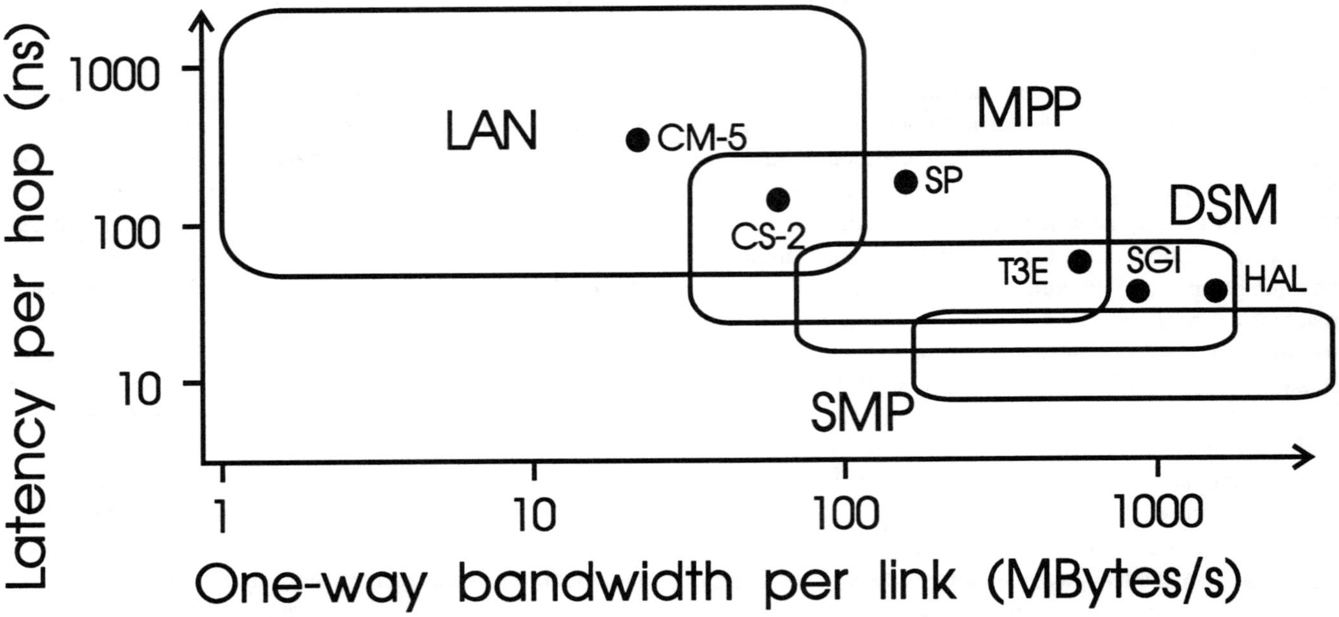

Figure 1. Link speeds and feeds

Table 1. Link speeds and feeds

Interconnect	Per signal (Mb/s)	Link width (Bytes)	Bandwidth (MB/s)	Distance (meters)
Tandem ServerNet [6]	50	1	50	30
IBM SP	150	1	150	25
Myricom Myrinet [19]	160	1	160	10–25
Cray T3E [18]	375	2	600	1
SGI Origin2000 [5]	400	2	800	5
HAL Mercury [26]	400	4	1600	2

Intel's choice of 4 processors per SMP motherboard for PC servers will have a impact on other vendors' choices of an optimal node size.

2.4 The trend toward networks of workstations attributes

While some argue that NOWs will largely replace MPP machines [2], another scenario is more likely: many of the advantages and attributes of NOWs will increasingly be incorporated into MPPs. Programmers and users of MPPs typically do most of their work on workstations, and they rely heavily on the functionality of that environment, including the multitasking operating system, complete with virtual addressing, paging, and local disk storage. Full workstation node functionality has been a major selling point of IBM's RS/6000 SP from its introduction. Programmers can immediately see their workstation program running on a single node, unchanged, and executed from a familiar operating system and environment, giving them immediate positive feedback.

Each vendor's attention is focused on converting the latest processor technology into workstations or PCs as quickly as possible. The volumes demand and reward this effort. The relatively small volumes of MPPs make it more difficult to "ride the workstation performance curve" unless each MPP node is simply a workstation.

Workstation owners also appreciate the ability to add communication enhancements or other functionality to arbitrary nodes simply by adding adaptor cards. MPPs are often far more limited in this respect. For example, some tightly-packed 2-dimensional meshes only allow I/O along the "sides" of the mesh.

There are disadvantages to NOWs as well. Geographically dispersed networks cannot communicate with the enormous bandwidth of typical MPP network links. System management of hordes of stand-alone workstations can be a nightmare. When workstations are "owned" by individuals, they are naturally possessive of their CPU and I/O resources, even though these resources remain idle much of the time.

MPP machines that cluster large numbers of workstation system boxes together into a single managed cluster with centralized control of power, clocking, initialization and boot, etc. attack these weaknesses of NOWs while incorporating most of their desirable attributes. Clustering workstations together potentially results in higher bandwidth links for higher bandwidth communication. These are strategies used in IBM SP machines, which are often described as NOWs with switching networks. We predict that most future successful MPPs will be workstation-based.

But how does the incorporation of NOW attributes into MPPs affect their interconnect? Off-the-shelf workstations capable of housing a variety of adaptor cards occupy significant real estate. Thus, the space required for communication links within the MPP is likely to be a small fraction of the overall volume of the system. Hence, any assumption of a constrained bisection area [4] that favors 2-dimensional meshes is not applicable, and therefore optimal topologies are more complex and more richly connected.

Topologies which scale bandwidth well and accommodate NOWs tend to contain at least some long links. Less scalable topologies can often be constructed solely with short links. Even though it is common to pipeline bits on long wires in these systems [17, 24], this only superficially equalizes the bandwidth possible across varying lengths of wire. Short wires can be driven at higher bandwidths. This is of no concern when the bandwidth is limited by the internals of the switch, but as CMOS performance improves, this is becoming the exception.

A second effect of NOWs concerns their availability. Nodes are more likely to be added, removed, power cycled, or crashed than in the more controlled environments of MPPs. Thus any network that connects distributed NOWs must handle node state changes gracefully without affecting the connectivity of the remaining nodes in the system. Indirect networks accomplish this; for example fat-trees (a type of bidirectional multistage interconnection network) have recently been suggested for connecting NOWs [12]. Hence it is no accident that networks of workstations are typically connected in a hierarchical fashion, and are beginning to employ switches even at the lowest level in the hierarchy. An example of this is the rapid movement toward switched ethernet and ATM LAN technologies.

2.5 The increasing complexity of switches

MPP networks are constructed by interconnecting numerous crossbar switches in a pattern, or topology. With each new generation of MPP networks, the complexity and buffering capability of these crossbar switches has increased. While chip pin count is still the primary determiner of switch chip size, switch designers usually fill any remaining chip space with buffers for improving throughput. For example, the Vulcan switch chip [23] used in the IBM SP1 [25] and SP2 [24] contained a 1 KB central buffer for storing blocked packet bytes. The current SP switch contains a 4 KB central buffer.

In current MPPs these switch chips are almost always designed in CMOS standard cell or gate array technologies. Switch designers will resist abandoning CMOS for less dense technologies such as GaAs, despite the optical advantages. Bandwidth and throughput requirements will require the larger and more complex buffers that CMOS can offer.

2.6 Cut-through switching techniques

The first generation of microprocessor-based MPPs used the store-and-forward switching technique (e.g., the Intel iPSC). The second generation used circuit-switching (e.g., the Intel iPSC/2). Since then, however, to minimize packet for dynamic traffic patterns, cut-through techniques [4, 7] have been used almost exclusively in MPP networks.

Cut-through switches examine the first few bits of an arriving packet (the header) to determine the packet route, and then immediately attempt to route the packet through the desired output port before the entire packet has been received. Any optical technology that is substituted for electronics must be able to achieve similar low latencies for the dynamic traffic patterns of MPP machines, particularly with the increasing influence of shared memory designs.

2.7 The embedding of collective communication support

Architects have long argued about whether or not to embed collective communication support into hardware [14]. The T3E [18], CS2 [3], and CM5 [11] are examples of MPP systems that support different types of collective functions directly in the hardware. If optical technologies are inherently more suited for multicasting, then these advantages could be exploited.

3 Solving MPP problems with optics

In this section we examine implications of the trends identified in §2 and relate these implications to the introduction of optical technology into today's electronic MPP networks.

The fact that MPP vendors must sell machines that are downwardly scalable affects optical interconnect design choices. For instance, switch crossbars with 32 ports or more will be largely wasted for many customer purchases. MPP vendors tend to build networks out of multiple small crossbars, typically containing from 5 to 8 input and output ports. Bidirectional multistage networks [16] and k-ary n-cubes [4] are two current topology choices, and should remain popular [20, 22]. Similarly, any optical technology employed must remain cost-effective for very small systems.

Optical fiber interconnect potentially equalizes the bandwidth of short and long links up to a much greater distance than copper. Optics also addresses other copper problems such as coupling, electromagnetic noise, inter-signal skew and heavy link cables. We believe that optics will become mandatory for driving links longer than 5–10 meters for the $\geq$Gb/s signaling that will become commonplace in MPP networks.

Unfortunately, adding optical transceivers on both ends of a communication link—outside of CMOS switch ASICs—is relatively expensive compared to CMOS on-chip drivers and copper links. However, the cost of optical transmitters and receivers has been decreasing, and the cost of multimode optical fiber is less than copper wires, making "cheap" optics competitive already for high-bandwidth links longer than 10–15 meters.

MPP network latencies must continue to be driven downward, particularly because of the growing emphasis on providing the abstraction of shared memory. Therefore optical technologies must be able to dynamically route packets in a cut-through fashion.

Integration of optical and electronic technologies

As hypothesized earlier, the incorporation of optics into MPP networks is likely to occur in an evolutionary fashion, with optical technologies replacing copper in some manner. Even in large MPP systems there are many short links for which copper technology will likely suffice in the near term. For these short links, engineers will, by nature, propose copper solutions over optical answers because of CMOS's familiarity, transistor density, and low cost. However, longer links will soon be difficult to build with copper. To solve this dilemma, engineers will likely rely on off-chip optoelectronic transceivers to interface with the CMOS ASICs of the switches and network interfaces.

However, a preferable solution would be to directly integrate optical I/O with a CMOS core [13, 9, 15, 27]. This would maintain today's chip area for the complex switching and buffering functions of today's MPP switches while relieving the myriad of problems caused by electronic I/O. The ability to attach fiber [10] to such a hybrid package may have the most chance of winning over engineers; they might view the change as very evolutionary: the substitution of fiber for copper. This would also negate the arguments for using copper for short links. Hopefully hybrid chip technologies will also prove much cheaper than traversing separate optoelectronic transceiver chips, and would provide a one-chip solution that permits longer links without optical redrive.

4 Conclusion

Fully electronic interconnect is confronted with major challenges in providing sufficiently high bandwidth for MPP systems. Optical interconnect can certainly solve many of these challenges. In replacing electronics, optics must maintain the low latencies achieved by electronic solutions. MPPs that resemble networks of workstations will require optical solutions to connect devices separated by several meters.

MPP design engineers are not generally familiar with the choices in optical technologies, and design changes will tend to be evolutionary rather than revolutionary. Therefore we predict that optics will first appear in MPP systems as a copper replacement well before any migration to free-space switches. The hybrid CMOS-optical I/O technologies may be promising possibilities in this regard.

Acknowledgements

A special thanks to Prof. Timothy Pinkston of USC for several insightful discussions and for helping me to understand some of the current developments in optoelectronic technology.

References

[1] T. Agerwala, J. L. Martin, J. H. Mirza, D. C. Sadler, D. M. Dias, and M. Snir. SP2 system architecture. *IBM System Journal*, 34(2):152–184, 1995.

[2] T. E. Anderson, D. E. Culler, and D. A. Patterson. A case for NOW (Networks of Workstations). *IEEE Micro*, 15(1):54–64, Feb. 1995.

[3] J. Beecroft, M. Homewood, and M. McLaren. Meiko CS-2 interconnect Elan-Elite design. *Parallel Computing*, 20:1627–1638, Nov. 1994.

[4] W. J. Dally. Performance analysis of k-ary n-cube interconnection networks. *IEEE Trans. on Computers*, 39(6):775–785, June 1990.

[5] M. Galles. Spider: A high-speed network interconnect. *IEEE Micro*, 17(1):34–39, Jan./Feb. 1997.

[6] R. W. Horst. TNet: A reliable system area network. *IEEE Micro*, 15(1):37–45, Feb. 1995.

[7] P. Kermani and L. Kleinrock. Virtual cut-through: A new computer communications switching technique. *Computer Networks*, 3(4):267–286, Sept. 1979.

[8] R. E. Kessler and J. L. Schwarzmeier. Cray T3D: A new dimension for Cray Research. In *Proc. 38th IEEE Int. Computer Conf.*, pages 176–182, Spring 1993.

[9] F. E. Kiamilev, J. S. Lambirth, R. G. Rozier, and A. V. Krishnamoorthy. Design of a 64-bit, 100 MIPS microprocessor core IC for hybrid CMOS-SEED technology. In *Proc. Massively Parallel Processing Using Optical Interconnections*, pages 53–60, Oct. 1996.

[10] A. V. Krishnamoorthy et al. The AMOEBA chip: An optoelectronic switch for multiprocessor networking using dense-WDM. In *Proc. Massively Parallel Processing Using Optical Interconnections*, pages 94–100, Oct. 1996.

[11] C. E. Leiserson, Z. S. Abuhamdeh, D. C. Douglas, C. R. Feynman, M. N. Ganmukhi, J. V. Hill, W. D. Hillis, B. C. Kuszmaul, M. A. St. Pierre, D. S. Wells, M. C. Wong, S.-W. Yang, and R. Zak. The network architecture of the Connection Machine CM-5. In *Proc. 1992 Symp. Parallel Algorithms and Architectures*, pages 272–285. ACM, 1992.

[12] Q. Li and D. Gustavson. Fat-tree for local area multiprocessors. In *Proc. 9th Int. Parallel Processing Symp.*, pages 32–36, April 1995.

[13] D. A. B. Miller. Hybrid SEED – massively parallel optical interconnections for silicon ics. In *Proc. Massively Parallel Processing Using Optical Interconnections*, pages 2–7, Oct. 1995.

[14] L. M. Ni. Should scalable parallel computers support efficient hardware multicast? In *Proc. ICPP Workshop on Challenges for Parallel Processing*, pages 2–7, Aug. 1995.

[15] T. M. Pinkston and C. Kuznia. A smart pixel-based optical multichannel network interface asic. *Applied Optics Journal*, to appear in 1997.

[16] I. D. Scherson and C.-H. Chien. Least common ancestor networks. In *Proc. 7th Int. Parallel Processing Symp.*, pages 507–513, 1993.

[17] S. L. Scott and J. R. Goodman. The impact of pipelined channels on k-ary n-cube networks. *IEEE Trans. on Parallel and Distributed Systems*, 5(1):2–16, Jan. 1994.

[18] S. L. Scott and G. M. Thorson. The Cray T3E network: Adptive routing in a high performance 3D torus. In *Hot Interconnects IV*, Aug. 1996.

[19] C. Seitz. Myrinet—a gigabit-per-second local-area network. In *Hot Interconnects II*, Aug. 1994. Current information on link bandwidth found at http://www.myri.com/.

[20] H. J. Siegel and C. B. Stunkel. Inside parallel computers: Trends in interconnection networks. *IEEE Computational Science and Engineering*, 3(3):69–71, Fall 1996.

[21] M. Snir, P. Hochschild, D. D. Frye, and K. J. Gildea. The communication software and parallel environment of the IBM SP2. *IBM System Journal*, 34(2):205–221, 1995.

[22] C. B. Stunkel. Commercially viable MPP networks. In *Proc. ICPP Workshop on Challenges for Parallel Processing*, pages 52–63, Aug. 1996.

[23] C. B. Stunkel, D. G. Shea, B. Abali, M. M. Denneau, P. H. Hochschild, D. J. Joseph, B. J. Nathanson, M. Tsao, and P. R. Varker. Architecture and implementation of Vulcan. In *Proc. 8th Int. Parallel Processing Symp.*, pages 268–274, April 1994. (An extended version of this paper is also available as Research Report RC19492 from the IBM T. J. Watson Research Center, Sept. 1993.).

[24] C. B. Stunkel, D. G. Shea, B. Abali, et al. The SP2 high-performance switch. *IBM System Journal*, 34(2):185–204, 1995.

[25] C. B. Stunkel, D. G. Shea, D. G. Grice, P. H. Hochschild, and M. Tsao. The SP1 high-performance switch. In *Proc. 1994 Scalable High-Performance Computing Conference*, pages 150–157, May 1994.

[26] W.-D. Weber, S. Gold, P. Helland, T. Shimizu, T. Wicki, and W. Wilcke. The mercury interconnect architecture: A cost-effective infrastructure for high-performance servers. In *Proc. 24th Ann. Int. Symp. on Computer Architecture*, June 1997.

[27] T. K. Woodward, A. V. Krishnamoorthy, A. L. Lentine, and L. M. F. Chirovsky. Performance of the direct binary n-cube network for multiprocessors. *IEEE J. of Selected Topics in Quantum Electronics*, 2(1):106–116, April 1996.

Application of Massively Parallel Processors to Real Time Processing of High Speed Images

YoungJoong Joo, Suzanne Fike, Kee Shik Chung
Martin Brooke, Nan Marie Jokerst, D. Scott Wills

School of Electrical and Computer Engineering
Georgia Institute of Technology
Atlanta, Georgia 30332

Abstract

This paper demonstrates that the real-time utilization of image sequences, at frame rates far above what is currently possible, can now be achieved with an optically interconnected massively parallel processor. A focal plane processing chip with an on-chip array of sigma-delta analog to digital converter front ends under each pixel is presented. This two layer chip is a scaleable high frame rate image capture building block, however it requires a third layer of data processing to filter the sigma-delta front end data to obtain images. The use of an array of optically connected processors beneath the chip proves to be the best solution to this challenging data processing task.

1. Introduction

To achieve image processing systems that operate, in real time, on large images with frame rates in the high kHz or MHz is beyond the capability of today's imaging systems. For example, a sigma-delta analog to digital converter (ADC) generating a sequence of 256x256 8 bit images at a frame rate of 400 kHz must be clocked at more than 1.7 THz. Even when parallel ADCs are placed along the edge of the imaging array the problem is only partially mitigated because the speed at which the ADCs must operate still increases with image size. To generate 256x256 8 bit images at a frame rate of 400 kHz 256 ADCs need to be clocked at more than 6.6 GHz.

In this paper we will describe a chip that implements a fully parallel front end with one ADC per pixel. This provides a scaleable solution to the real time high frame rate image capture problem when coupled to a massively parallel optically interconnected processor. We show that to generate a sequence of 256x256 8 bit images at a frame rate of 400 kHz a 8x8 array of 102 MHz pipelined processors (each operating at 435 MIPS) is required. To keep the design scaleable the processors must reside beneath the imaging chip, which uses 3-D electrical interconnect for parallel connection to the detector plane. To connect to subsequent layers of processing, a through-substrate parallel optical data link is used.

2. Architecture of focal plane readout systems

In conventional focal-plane readout systems, a single ADC performs data conversion for the entire array. In this case, noise can be introduced in the long analog shift register chains that cannot be removed and will cause a reduction of dynamic range. In addition, the analog circuits in a serial ADC are required to operate with the highest bandwidth of all focal-plane components, since the conversion rate is the same as the pixel data rate. For the example of sigma-delta conversion of a 400 kHz frame rate 256x256 8 bit image sequence, if we assume an oversampling ratio of 32 then the sampling rate of the ADC front end must be more than 1.7 THz, so clearly a single ADC based architecture is not a good choice for a high frame rate image readout system.

2.1 On-focal-plane readout

To improve the signal-to-noise ratio (SNR), serial on-focal-plane readout systems have been proposed as shown in Figure 1(a).

This architecture removes pick-up and vibration sensitivity since no off-chip analog cabling is required [1]. However, the data rate required is not changed and noise can still be introduced in the analog shift registers between the focal plane and ADC.

0-8186-7974-3/97 $10.00 © 1997 IEEE

Semi-parallel architectures have been proposed [1], [2], [3] to overcome these problems as shown in Figure 1(b). The ADC conversion rate of this circuit is the much lower row read out rate. For our example of the sigma-delta conversion of a 400 kHz frame rate 256x256 8 bit image sequence, if we assume all 256 rows have an ADC attached in parallel as in Figure 1 (b), then the clock rate of the ADC front end drops by 256 to slightly more than 6.6 GHz. This is at least a feasible clock speed, although only heterojunction bipolar transistor (HBT) technology has demonstrated the capability to realize near commercial ADCs at these speeds, although not an array of 256 of them. Thus this is not currently a feasible architecture and still does not solve the problem of noise being introduced through the long analog lines between the pixels and the ADCs.

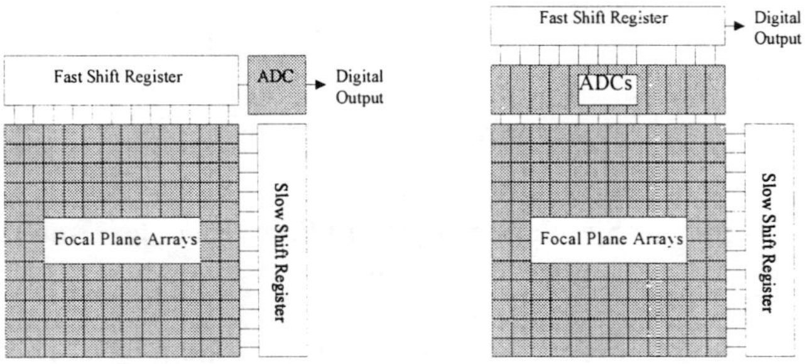

(a) (b)

Figure 1. Architecture of on-focal-plane readout system

2.2 Fully parallel on-focal-plane readout

To overcome the limitations of serial and semi-parallel readout, we have implemented a focal plane array (FPA) using a fully parallel readout architecture. Figure 2 shows the basic concept of this architecture. Each pixel has its own ADC. To keep the area of the ADC circuitry small only the front end of the sigma-delta converter is implemented on a per pixel basis. Since sigma-delta converters process only digital data after the front end, further noise cannot be introduced to the signal by shifting the row digital data. A digital signal processor is now needed to complete the ADC process.

We propose that the pixels be grouped into subarrays each served by one digital signal processing (DSP) unit to perform the conversion. An integrated optoelectronic emitter on each sub array allows through-silicon wafer output of digital image data from the focal plane to the processor stacked below each subarray. This vertical coupling to the image plane allows the detector and processor arrays to be scaled while maintaining a fixed level of processing per pixel. The number of pixels included in the subarray is depend on the bandwidth of DSP circuits.

An example of the type of processor proposed is the SIMPil processor as mentioned in [5], [6]. If an 8x8 subarray is used, the size of the processor and focal plane subarray seem to match reasonably well so that by tiling an 8x8 array of processor chips each containing 16 nodes, a 256×256 pixel resolution focal plane could be achieved.

2.3 Massively parallel processor performance

To achieve a 400 kHz frame rate each processor would need to process data at more than 820 Mbps (for an 8x8 subimage image oversampled by 32 at 400 kHz).

If we assume a fully pipelined 8 bit processor clocked at 102 MHz (achieving more than 410 MIPS) a frame rate of only about 50 kHz is possible. To achieve a 400 kHz frame rate we need to assume that the first comb filter stage of the sigma-delta converter is also under each pixel.

For our example, if we assume that an 4 tap comb filter (which is no more than a 2 bit counter) is added to each pixel, then the 435 MIPs processors need only implement the remaining 4 tap low pass filter to produce the 8 bit image output. This filter can be implemented by the proposed processor to achieve the required 400 kHz frame rate.

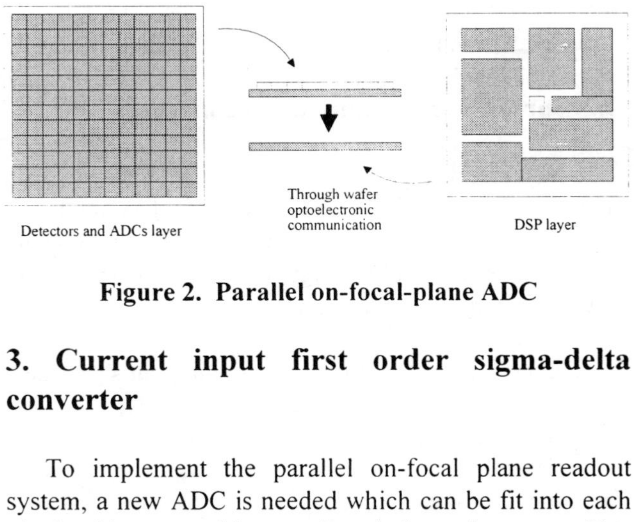

Figure 2. Parallel on-focal-plane ADC

3. Current input first order sigma-delta converter

To implement the parallel on-focal plane readout system, a new ADC is needed which can be fit into each pixel with reasonable speed and dynamic range. This section presents the current input first order sigma-delta converter that satisfies this requirement.

3.1 Sigma-delta converter

ADCs can be divided into two classes. One is the converters limited by component matching and the other is based on counting algorithms. Flash converters, pipeline converters, recursive converters and successive approximation converters are included in this first class. The accuracy of these converters is ultimately limited by the component matching. A solution to overcome this limit is to use ADCs based on counting algorithms. One of these converters is the dual slope converter. This converter can be very accurate but the conversion rate is too slow. For instance, to obtain 8 bit accuracy, the converter needs a clock 256 times faster than the sample rate. This implies that the conversion rate is 256 times slower than the internal clock frequency. Sigma-delta converters are another data converter based on a counting algorithm [7], [8].

For a given accuracy, the internal clock frequency of an sigma-delta converter can be much smaller than that of a dual slope ADC. For example while a dual slope ADC requires an internal clock frequency of 256 times the sampling rate to obtain 8 bit accuracy, an oversampling ratio of 32 [7] or more is sufficient for a first order sigma-delta converter to achieve 8 bit accuracy. Because of its efficient counting algorithm, the trade-off between speed and accuracy is more advantageous for an sigma-delta converter.

In addition, the sigma-delta converter front end or modulator is small and low power. Only the modulator needs to be on the focal plane since its output is digital. Approximately 90% of the sigma-delta ADC circuitry is digital and can be located off the focal plane. This eases the problem of fitting the modulator into the allocated space under each pixel.

3.2 Current input sigma-delta converter

The current input sigma-delta ADC consists of a modulator and a digital filter section. The modulator samples the analog input and develops a corresponding digital bit stream, and the digital filter compresses the bit stream into the Nyquist rate multibit codes and performs noise filtering.

Figure 3 shows the proposed current input sigma-delta modulator. It is composed of four parts. The first is a current buffer which controls the bias voltage of the photodetector. The second is a current integrator which is implemented with a capacitor. The capacitor size is as large as possible for low 1/f noise. The third is a current D/A converter which provides a reference current to the input depending on the sign of output. The last stage is a comparator.

Figure 4 shows the PSPICE simulation of this converter with a sinusoidal input. The digital output contains the analog input and must be filtered digitally to get a digital representation of the signal.

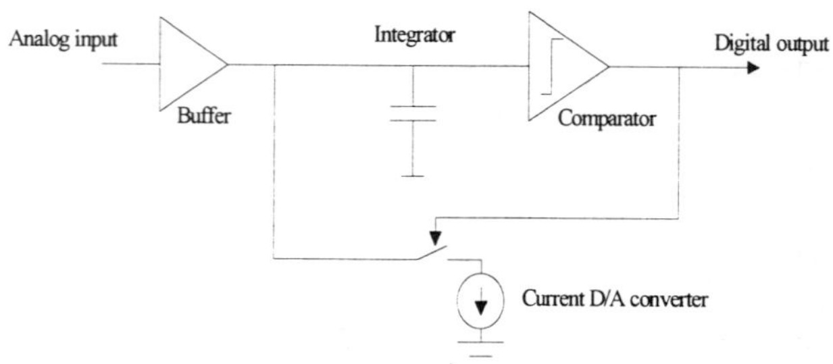

Figure 3. First order sigma-delta modulator

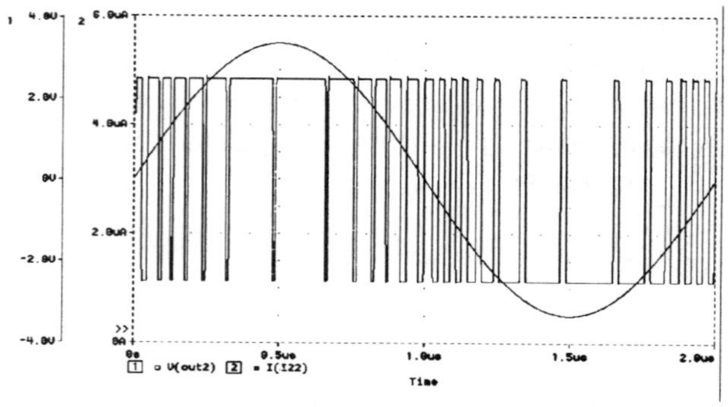

Figure 4. Simulation results of first order sigma-delta modulator

3.3 8x8 array of sigma-delta converters with through wafer emitter driver

Figure 5 shows a fabricated chip with an 8×8 array of ADCs, associated readout shift registers, and emitter driver. This chip sits above the DSP node that processes its data. Figure 6 (a) and (b) show the test results of this chip when electrical DC inputs are provided. The chip is functional and that with the addition of an array of detectors on top of each ADC and a DSP below, one tile of a scaleable high frame rate imaging system can be realized.

Figure 5. Chip with 8×8 ADCs, shift registers, and emitter driver

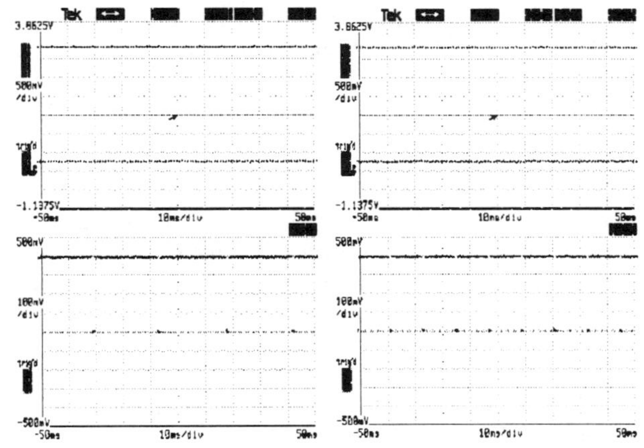

(a) $I_{in} = 0.03\mu$ (b) $I_{in} = 0.06\mu$

Figure 6. 8x8 ADC per pixel test results.

4. Thin film detector integration

To integrate the detector imaging array onto the silicon circuitry there are several options which can be explored. The detectors can be fabricated using monomaterial (single material) integration in the silicon CMOS, however, to achieve high fill factors and scaleable arrays the processing circuitry associated with each pixel must be minimized. An additional drawback to silicon detectors realized on a CMOS circuit process is the low absorption coefficient. The low absorption coefficient translates to low responsivity since the absorption length achievable in CMOS processes is small.

Hybrid integration, or the bonding of a separately grown detector array on top of the silicon circuitry, is an attractive option for the integration of the detector array. These integration techniques include the bump bonding of arrays of detectors onto pads on the silicon circuit, which is currently a commonly used technique for fabricating infrared focal plane arrays [9], and, alternatively, thin film integration can be utilized, which is similar to bump bonding, save that the detector devices and bonds are very thin in comparison to bump bonds [10].

Hybrid integration is an attractive alternative to monomaterial integration for two reasons. First, the material which comprises the detector array is fabricated separately from the electronics. Because of this fact, the detectors need not be the same material as the electronics (Si), which enables the use of higher responsivity materials such as direct gap compound semiconductors. This also implies that the detector materials do not have to be lattice matched to the circuitry materials (for example, direct growth onto the silicon circuitry). The second advantage of hybrid integration is that the detectors are integrated directly on top of the silicon circuitry, which enables scalability with high fill factors and the direct interconnection of every detector to circuitry which lies beneath it. One disadvantage of using flip chip bonding for hybrid integration of detector arrays is that the substrate must be transparent. Thin film bonded detector arrays do not suffer from this limitation since the substrate is removed from the devices.

There are two basic types of detectors which can be integrated with the silicon circuits: P-i-N and MSM (metal-semiconductor-metal) detectors. While MSM detectors are a viable option for integration since they are high speed, low capacitance detectors [11], they have a lower responsivity than the P-i-N detector and their geometry does not lend itself as well as the P-i-N to array integration. The MSM is a planar device which has two bonding pads in the same plane (the interdigitated fingers of the MSM). To achieve individually addressable pixels using MSMs, the spacing of the devices has to be large enough to allow space for the contact pads, thus decreasing the fill factor.

The integration method used with the P-i-N results in a higher fill factor than that of the MSM. This increased fill factor comes from exploiting the non-planarity of the P-i-N structure. The P-i-N device contacts are on the top and bottom of the structure; this is useful in terms of the integration because the pixels can be individually addressed through the device side bonded to the silicon circuit and share a common top contact, eliminating the pad space between detectors. For example, to electrically connect an NxN array of P-i-N detectors only N^2+1 dedicated pads on the silicon circuit are necessary, with N^2 pads located underneath the detector array.

Examples of hybrid integration of compound semiconductor detectors onto silicon circuits include GaAs MSMs [10], which detect at 850nm, and InP/InGaAs/InAlAs MSMs [10], which detect at 1.3 and 1.55 micron wavelengths. Arrays of GaAs/AlGaAs double heterostructure P-i-N detectors [12] have also been integrated directly on top of silicon circuits, as shown in the photomicrographs in Figure 7.

(a) (b) (c)

Figure 7. Photomicrographs: (a) the unintegrated circuit as received from MOSIS, (b) the silicon circuit with a bonded thin-film array, (c) the integrated OEIC with a common top contact.

Figure 7(a) is a photomicrograph of the unbonded silicon circuit as received from the MOSIS foundry. Figure 7(b) is a photomicrograph of the GaAs thin film detector array bonded onto the top of the circuitry, and Figure 7(c) shows the final integrated optoelectronic circuit, with the common top contact deposited onto the detector array, connecting the array to the silicon circuit. Each detector is individually interconnected to the silicon circuitry which lies beneath it through a metallized overglass cut on the circuit.

5. Conclusion

We have shown that a massively parallel focal plane data processing architecture with sigma-delta modulators in each pixel, and massively parallel processing optically interconnected below the focal plane which can achieve high frame rate imaging for large images. The parallel processing image capture method described is scaleable which means it can be used to achieve arbitrarily high resolution without a degradation in frame rate. In addition, more optically connected parallel processor layers could be added to perform real time processing of the high frame rate images generated by the system.

6. Acknowledgment

This work is supported by a grant from the AFOSR (F49620-95-1-0246).

7. References

[1] Bedabrata Pain, Eric R. Fossum, "Approaches and analysis for on-focal-plane analog-to-digital conversion," Proceedings of SPIE - The International Society for Optical Engineering, v 2226, pp. 208-218, 1994.

[2] Ulf Ringh, Christer Jansson, Kevin Liddiard, " Readout concept employing a novel on chip 16bit ADC for smart IR focal plane arrays," Proceedings of SPIE - The International Society for Optical Engineering, v 2745, pp.99-110, 1996.

[3] Zhimin Zhou, Bedabrata Panicacci Pain, Barmak Nakamura Roger Mansoorian, Eric R. Junichi Fossum, "On-focal-plane ADC: recent progress at JPL," Proceedings of SPIE - The International Society for Optical Engineering, v 2745, pp. 111-122, 1996.

[4] William J. Mandl, Carl Rutschow, "All-digital monolithic scanning readout based on sigma-delta analog-to-digital conversion," Proceedings of SPIE - The International Society for Optical Engineering, v 1684, pp. 233-246, 1992.

[5] H. H. Cat., J. C. Eble, D. S. Wills, V. K. De, M. Brooke, N. M. Jokerst, Low Power Opportunities for a SIMD VLSI Architecture Incorporating Integrated Optoelectronic Devices, GOMAC'96 Digest of Papers, pages 59-62, Orlando, FL, March 1996.

[6] Huy H. Cat, D. Scott Wills, Nan Marie Jokerst, Martin A. Brooke, April S. Brown, "Three-dimensional, massively parallel, optically interconnected silicon computational hardware and architectures for high-speed IR scene generation," Proceedings of SPIE - The International Society for Optical Engineering, v 2469, pp. 141-145, 1995.

[7] J. C. Candy, G. C. Temes, "Oversampling methods for data conversion," Proc 91 IEEE Pacific Rim Conf Commun Comput Signal Process, pp. 498-502, 1991.

[8] J. C. Candy, G. C. Temes, "A tutorial discussion of the oversampling method for A/D and D/A conversion," Proceedings - IEEE International Symposium on Circuits and Systems, v 2. pp. 910-913, 1990.

[9] "Special issue on solid state image sensors," *IEEE Trans. on Elec. Dev..*, vol. 38, 1991.

[10] C. Camperi-Ginestet, Y.W. Kim, N.M. Jokerst, M.G. Allen, M.A. Brooke, "Vertical Electrical Interconnection of Compound Semiconductor Thin-Film Devices to Underlying Silicon Circuitry," *IEEE Photonics Technology Letters*, vol. 4, no. 9, pp 1003-1006, September 1992.

[11] Olivier Vendier, Nan Marie Jokerst, Richard P. Leavitt, "Thin Film Inverted MSM Photodetectors," *IEEE Photonics Technology Letters*, vol. 8, no. 2, pp 266-268, February 1996.

[12] S.M. Fike, B. Buchanan, N.M. Jokerst, M.A. Brooke, T.G. Morris, S.P. DeWeerth, "8x8 Array of Thin-Film Photodetectors Vertically Electrically Interconnected to Silicon Circuitry," *IEEE Photonics Technology Letters*, vol. 7, no. 10, pp 1168-1170, October 1995.

SESSION V

Guided and Free-Space Optical Systems

Chair

Louis Lome
BMDO

Wavelength Recognizing Switches: Architectures and System Applications

Bogdan Hoanca and Alexander A. Sawchuk
University of Southern California
Signal and Image Processing Institute, MC 2564
Los Angeles, CA 90089-2564
Tel. (213) 740-4652
Fax (213) 740- 4651
e-mail: hoanca@usc.edu

Abstract

We present and model possible system applications of a recently demonstrated wavelength recognizing switch (WRS). The switch allows all-optical self routing in very wide bandwidth networks. In this work, we discuss architectures using multiwavelength all-optical WRS devices, we analyze possible network access strategies and we assess the feasibility of cascading WRS devices. We conclude with a novel view of a higher level of data aggregation, where the basic switching unit is a wavelength packet (multiple modulated wavelengths switched as a single entity).

1. Introduction

The term "all-optical networks" [1, 2] generally refers to networks in which the *data paths* are all-optical, that is, no optical-to-electronic conversions are performed on the data itself, although the control and routing may be in general electronic. As rates increase, it is clear that all-optical *control* and *routing* will be needed to reduce network delay and eliminate bottlenecks.

Recently, a class of wideband wavelength recognizing switch (WRS) devices having all-optical routing, control and data paths have been devised and experimentally demonstrated [3]. In this paper we show how the WRS can be combined into various multiwavelength switches, which can further be connected to form self routing networks, with data format transparency and distributed routing control. These networks route wavelength packets which we envision as a novel and higher level of data aggregation. With the understanding that many practical issues will still need to be solved, we present estimates of network performance, including contention, crosstalk and noise, based on WRS measured device parameters.

2. WRS description and operation

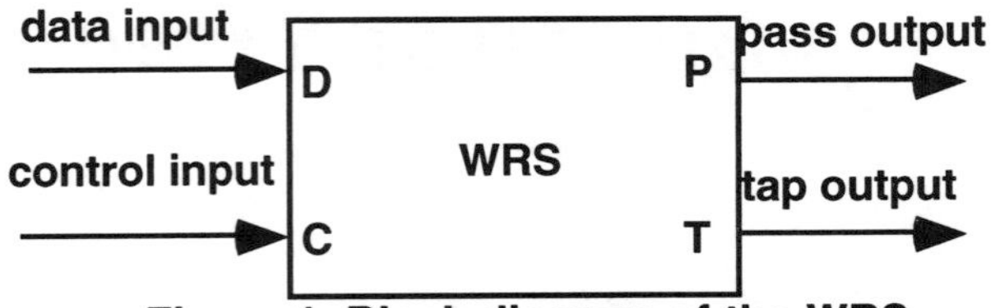

Figure 1. Block diagram of the WRS

Several different implementations of a WRS have been proposed [4]. A recently reported implementation [3] is based on a compressively strained InGaAsP quantum well semiconductor amplifier. Optical fibers are used to couple light into the input facet, and then out of the output facet of the device. The device is intended for the 1.3 μm optical fiber communications window.

The device operation is based on the non-collinear nearly degenerate four wave mixing (FWM) interaction of the optical fields applied at the inputs. Conceptually, the device (Fig. 1) has two inputs (D-data, C-control) and two optical outputs (P-pass, T-tap). A set of wavelengths is applied at the D input, simultaneously with a single *control wavelength* applied to the C input. If *any one* of the wavelengths at the D input is within the recognition bandwidth (RB) of the WRS (centered on the control wavelength), the two electromagnetic fields are phase matched. Then, the beat frequency between the control wavelength and the matching wavelength within the RB (the *address wavelength*) is low enough and can be followed by the carrier dynamics in the gain medium. This way, the carrier distribution writes a refractive index grating in the nonlinear material of the switch. In turn, this grating switches the whole packet of wavelengths present at the D input (Fig. 2.a). The recognition bandwidth for a 3 dB drop in the switching efficiency is 0.57 GHz. The switching bandwidth (SB) is defined as the wavelength range at input D within which the

0-8186-7974-3/97 $10.00 © 1997 IEEE

switching efficiency decreases by no more than 3 dB. The reported SB is 42 nm, and the switching speed (the time required to build up the index grating) is 0.6 ns.

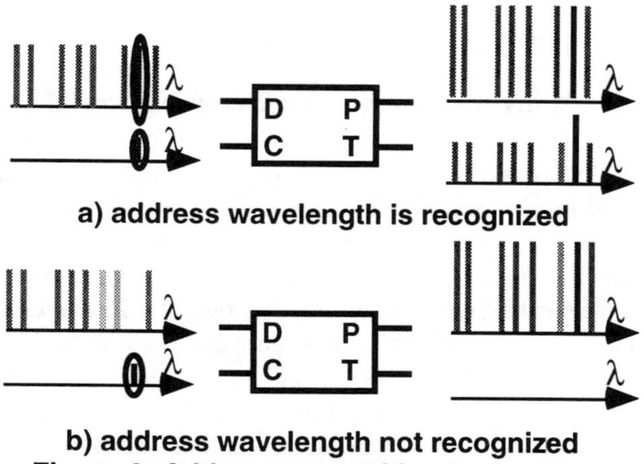

Figure 2. Address recognition in the WRS

Conversely, if none of the D input wavelengths are within the RB, the grating is not written because the device material cannot respond to the fast changes in the optical fields. Ideally, with no grating present, the power applied at the D input is passed to the P output (Fig 2.b) and no power is switched to the T output.

In practice, the WRS functions more like a tap, rather than a switch. Most of the power at the D input is still passed to the P output, whether the address wavelength at the D input is recognized or not. In turn, this may be an advantage in cascading WRS by daisy-chaining the P output of one device to the D input of another. Due to the built-in gain of the device, the output power at the P port is actually larger than the input power. This excess power at the P input can be used in conjunction with an acousto-optic tunable filter (AOTF) to equalize the output signal powers. We will show shortly that the WRS though acting as a tap, can be used to build true switches.

The self routing feature of the WRS is now apparent. The device can route incoming packets *without the need of any external logic*, based solely on the nonlinear interaction between the address wavelength and the control wavelength. In a network where both the address and control wavelengths can only have discrete values on a preassigned grid, recognition and routing occur transparently for both the packet and the routing node.

For the ease of fabrication, a broad area architecture [3] was chosen among possible WRS implementations. For this device geometry, the separation of the switched and non-switched data is done on the basis of the angular position of the output beams, which allows a tradeoff between a good switching efficiency (at nearly collinear interaction) and good crosstalk performance (for wide angular separation of the beams). The current WRS implementation was optimized for crosstalk performance. The peak switching efficiency reported was 8.2 dB, while the crosstalk was as low as -28.7 dB. Crosstalk-tolerant network topologies (using dilation [5, 6]) would allow a design with higher device crosstalk, which in turn would allow higher efficiency. A disadvantage of the broad area geometry is that devices are more difficult to package.

3. Wavelength packets

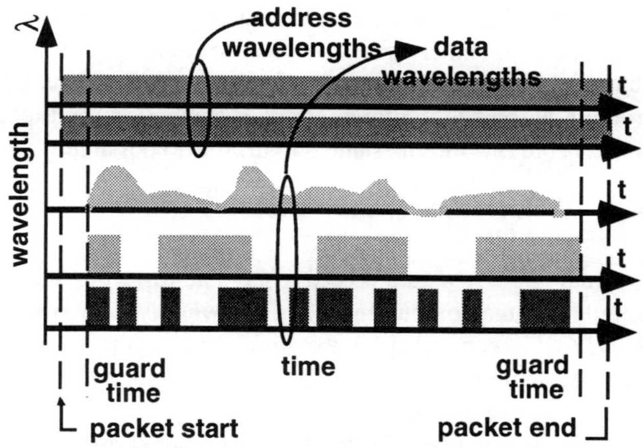

Figure 3. Structure of a wavelength packet

Based on the device functionality described above, we propose the wavelength packet as a new level of data aggregation. A wavelength packet (WP) is a set of wavelengths within the SB of the WRS that can be switched together as a single entity. Figure 3 depicts a set of five such wavelengths, arranged vertically. We designate some of the available wavelengths to be continuous wave (CW), unmodulated address wavelengths. The rest of the wavelength space is used for data. Depending on the device structure, the data and address wavelength spaces may or may not be interleaved with each other, but they must consist of distinct wavelengths.

The data formats and data rates of the various channels in a WP are completely independent. The only requirements are for sufficient guard spacing between different wavelength channels. This is similar to Wavelength Division Multiplexing (WDM), but here the whole set of data and address wavelengths is switched together as a single entity. The destination of the packet is encoded by the CW address wavelengths. The address wavelengths could in principle be separated by only a few GHz, for maximum density, and to allow most of the available bandwidth for the data.

WPs can also be used in multihop networks, where the encoding of the new destination is considerably simplified if the data and address wavelength spaces are not interleaved. When setting up the packet address for the next hop, the old address wavelengths can be filtered out (with a relatively wide band filter) and the new address can then be inserted. At the same time, the data wavelengths can be passed to the output unchanged, allowing for full data format and data rate transparency.

4. Basic switch architectures using WRS

In this section we demonstrate some of the possible implementations of low level building blocks using the WRS. The simplest network building block is the 2 x 2 crossbar switch which can independently switch either of its inputs to either of its outputs without any internal blocking. While this switch can accommodate broadcast (one input sent to multiple outputs), contention (multiple inputs addressed to the same output) is also possible.

4.1 Architecture of the switch

Four WRS taps are needed to be able to switch either input to either output in a 2 x 2 switch. The switch (Fig. 4) is controlled by the two wavelengths: λ_{up} and λ_{dn}. An input packet that contains λ_{up} is routed to Out_{up}. An input containing λ_{dn} is routed to Out_{dn}. Signals containing both control wavelengths are broadcast to both outputs, while signals that do not contain any of the two control wavelengths are simply blocked by the switch. This ensures a certain degree of redundancy that protects against inaccurate address wavelengths; if the drift of the address wavelengths brings them outside the RB of the WRS, the packet is blocked, rather than misrouted.

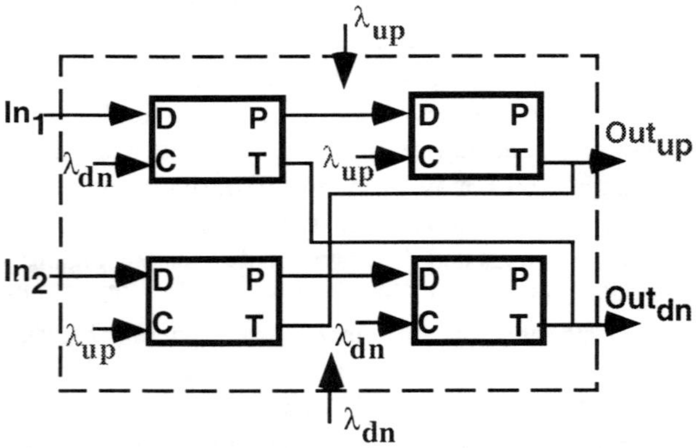

Figure 4. Architecture of the basic 2 x 2 switch

To extend this architecture for multistage networks, a new set of λ_{up} and λ_{dn} needs to be used at each stage. Overall, for an n stage network, a total of $2n$ address wavelengths $\{\lambda_{up_1}, \lambda_{dn_1}, \ldots, \lambda_{up_n}, \lambda_{dn_n}\}$ are required. At each stage in the network the WRS tests for the presence of either or both of the wavelengths that perform the routing at that particular stage. Global broadcasting is then achieved if all the wavelengths are present in the address of a packet: the packet will be routed to all the outputs in each of the stages. Partial broadcasting can be made if for some of the stages both of the address wavelengths λ_{up} and λ_{dn} are present. The packet will then be routed to all the outputs of those stages, and subsequently routed to multiple destinations.

4.2 Many wavelengths 2 x 2 crossbar switch

For some applications, multiple wavelengths may need to be routed through a 2 x 2 switch. In general, out of the set of recognized input wavelengths, some wavelengths may be routed to one of the outputs, while the rest of the wavelengths are routed to the other output. In particular, a useful switch recognizes a given wavelength at the input and routes it to one port, while routing the rest of k-1 wavelengths to the other port. We show in Fig. 5 a 1 x 2 switch which can recognize four wavelengths λ_1 through λ_4. Wavelengths λ_1 and λ_2 are routed to Out_{up}, λ_3 and λ_4 are routed to Out_{dn}. A 2 x 2 switch would have two such channels, with outputs connected in parallel.

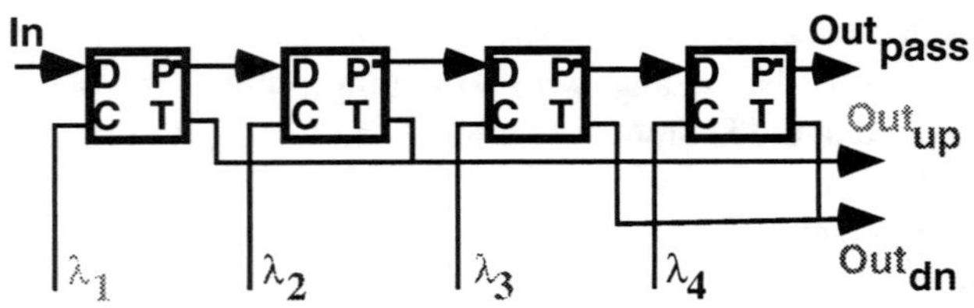

Figure 5. Multiwavelength switch: λ_1 and λ_2 are routed to the upper output, while λ_3 and λ_4 are routed to the lower output.

4.3 Extended *n* x *n* crossbar switch

An immediate extension of the 2 x 2 switch is the n x n switch, requiring an array of n x n WRS. For such an architecture, if an input contains wavelength k it is routed to the k output. A total of n wavelengths is needed for the control of the switch. This switch is rather inefficient in terms of the number of devices required (n^2), compared to a multistage network based on the 2 x 2 switch (which would require only $2n\log(n)$ WRS). On the other hand, the n x n switch would require only n address wavelengths, compared to $2\log(n)$ address wavelengths for the multistage network. In addition, the main advantage of the n x n switch over the multistage network are its non-blocking properties.

5. System issues and performance

5.1 Provisions for contention resolution

Contention is the situation that arises when two or more packets are simultaneously present at the inputs of a switch, share the same wavelength space and are addressed to the same output. Contention resolution requires that:

- if two packets arrive simultaneously, only one gets routed to the desired output; the other one is blocked;
- no packet is blocked once it has successfully entered the switch;
- if a packet is blocked, either save it to retransmit later, or ask the sender to retransmit the packet.

There is no natural way of resolving contention using the WRS, due to the optical transparency and due to the passive routing nature of the device. External logic is needed to resolve contention, either locally, in a random access network, or globally, by synchronizing packets at the source such that contention will not occur. Both schemes have disadvantages. Local contention detection requires optical-to-electronic conversion, which defeats the advantage of all-optical transparency. Global control on the other hand is less desirable and harder to implement than local, distributed control as with the native WRS.

5.2 Parasitic broadcasting

A particular phenomenon in the operation of the WRS is responsible for an avalanche increase in the contention probability for high system loads (when a large number of the network nodes attempt to transmit at the same time) in random access multistage networks. We call this phenomenon "parasitic broadcast," because a packet with a single destination may be in fact broadcast to multiple destinations following a collision with another packet.

For the WRS, the switch is transparent for incoming signals, due to its self-routing properties. Two packets destined for the same output will be routed together to the desired output and their signals will merge and propagate together. We call such a situation a collision between two packets. In case of collision, the payloads of the two packets become scrambled with each other, and also the address wavelengths overlap. While the overlapping of the data payloads is deleterious only for the packets involved in the collision, the overlapping of the addresses has much more devastating effects.

To understand the reasons for the parasitic broadcasting, assume the encoding scheme suggested above, where a set of wavelengths λ_{up} and a λ_{dn} is required to specify a packet output destination at each stage. If at the first stage two packets collide, their address wavelength sets are combined. Assume an example in which one packet has all the wavelengths after the first stage set to the corresponding λ_{up}, while the second packet has all its wavelengths set to λ_{dn}. After the collision, the resulting set of wavelengths is broadcast to all the outputs, since it contains all the possible address wavelength combinations. Even though this is a worst case scenario, it is illustrative of the possible effects of the avalanche multiplication of collisions.

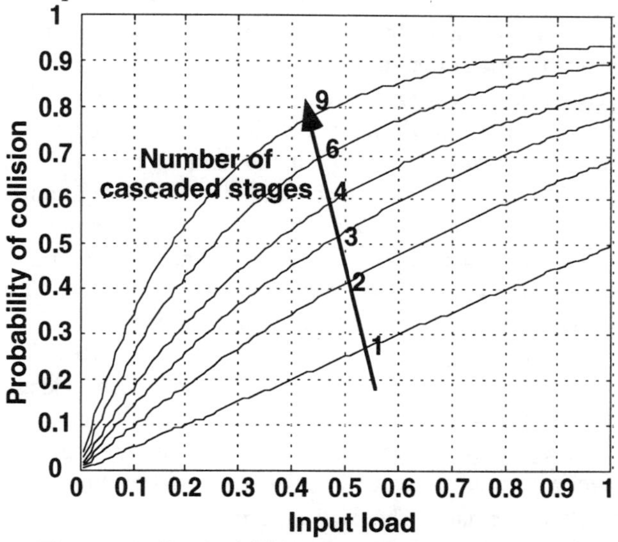

Figure 6. Probability of collision vs. load in a multistage random access WRS network

A plot of the collision probability versus system load is shown in Fig. 6 for a multistage random access network plagued by parasitic broadcast. Although this network is transparent to data rate and format and the packets self route, the probability of collision makes the network unusable with more than a few stages and with even minimal load. The only way to eliminate the parasitic broadcast is to resolve and eliminate contention.

5.3 Crosstalk

The size of practical communications systems is essentially limited by the accumulated crosstalk, rather than by optical path loss [5, 7]. For the WRS routing, crosstalk can be inter-WP and intra-WP crosstalk. Intra-WP crosstalk results from the mixing product of data wavelengths within a wavelength packet. Due to the low power and large wavelength separation (making phase matching for data streams impossible), the efficiency of any FWM mixing on the data streams is extremely low. This makes the intra-WP crosstalk most likely negligible. No experimental data is available on intra-WP crosstalk.

The second type of crosstalk, inter-WP, occurs due to optical power leaking through a supposedly off tap (when the input wavelength is not recognized) into a correctly routed packet. Practically, the inter-WP crosstalk for a 2 x 2 crossbar switch is equal to the device crosstalk (the reported value is -28.7 dB). For a network with cascaded stages, the crosstalk figure can rapidly deteriorate due to accumulation of crosstalk at each stage. Dilated networks can be used to reduce the crosstalk to values even below the single-device crosstalk [8].

5.4 Switching speed

The switching of the WRS is limited by the setup time needed for the grating to build up from the beating of the address and control wavelengths (about 0.6 ns [3]). This does not impose a limit on the data rate, but requires a minimum guard time between the address bits and the data. The address bits must be turned on 0.6 ns before the data can be switched, to allow for the grating to build up. Similarly, at the end of the packet a guard time must ensure that the address bit stays on sufficiently long after the last data bit, to avoid any undesirable transients.

In a multistage network, guard times will need to be compounded, to ensure transmission of each address wavelength through previous routing stages. Overall, in an n stage network, the address wavelengths for the k-th stage will need a guard time of $(n-k+1)\cdot 0.6\text{ns}$ with respect to the data. This will ensure guard times between any two consecutive address wavelengths, which in turn will allow the address wavelengths to propagate with their intended duration. Guard times are needed at both the beginning and the end of a WP, which makes the total guard time in an n stage network $2\cdot n\cdot 0.6\text{ns}$. Clearly, guard times may become appreciable for a large number of stages, but they are only needed at the beginning and the end of the packet, rather than for every bit in the payload. If the WP is relatively long as compared to the guard times, the overhead is relatively low.

5.5 Wavelength inaccuracies

For good recognition, the address wavelengths must be stable within the RB of the device. A larger RB would trade off wavelength stability to drift for wavelength spacing. On the other hand, as shown earlier, if the wavelength drift makes the address wavelength unrecognizable, packets are blocked, rather than misrouted.

5.6 Noise

The WRS switch is a gain medium in which the fields of the two input optical fields interact. Because of the signal gain, amplified spontaneous emission (ASE) will be generated in the WRS. ASE noise may accumulate over cascaded WRS stages, especially given the very large bandwidth of the WRS. While no experimental data is available on the noise performance of the WRS, ASE will limit the maximum number of stages that can be cascaded [9], thus limiting the size of the network. If the ASE figure is prohibitively large, data may need to be regenerated, and data transparency may be lost.

5.7 Other system limitations

As previously shown, noise or crosstalk may limit the maximum number of stages that can be cascaded. In addition, the maximum number of inputs and outputs per switch may be limited either by interconnection complexity or by the number of address wavelengths available in the system. Multistage networks built with 2 x 2 switches would be the most efficient in terms of both interconnection complexity and wavelength usage.

6. All-optical Self-Routing Networks

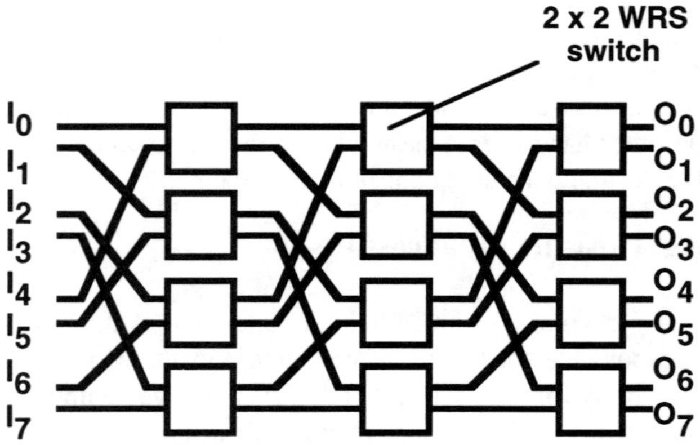

Figure 7. WRS based Omega Shuffle network

Based on the 2 x 2 WRS crossbar switches described above, we envision very high throughput, all-optical networks, which do not require any external logic for routing WPs. A self-routing Omega-Shuffle topology can be used to build multistage networks in which WP self-route (Fig. 7). The routing logic is embedded in the WRS switch, hence is distributed and local. A fast mechanism for contention resolution is still needed at the periphery of the network. Also, noise and crosstalk issues have to be addressed, both limiting the maximum number of cascaded stages, and hence the size of the network.

Because of its very high throughput, such a network would serve as a hub in a broadband communications network. We can envision such a WP network as the next highest level of data aggregation. Multiple low-bandwidth channels are currently time division multiplexed (TDM) onto a single wavelength carrier. Multiple TDM channels are sent in the same fiber to form a WDM stream, but each channels is actually switched and routed independently. We envision the WP as the next level of aggregation (Fig. 8). Multiple wavelengths can be routed together as a single switching entity in a WRS network. This higher level of aggregation would simplify the routing protocols, since a smaller number of data entities would need to be routed for a given total bandwidth.

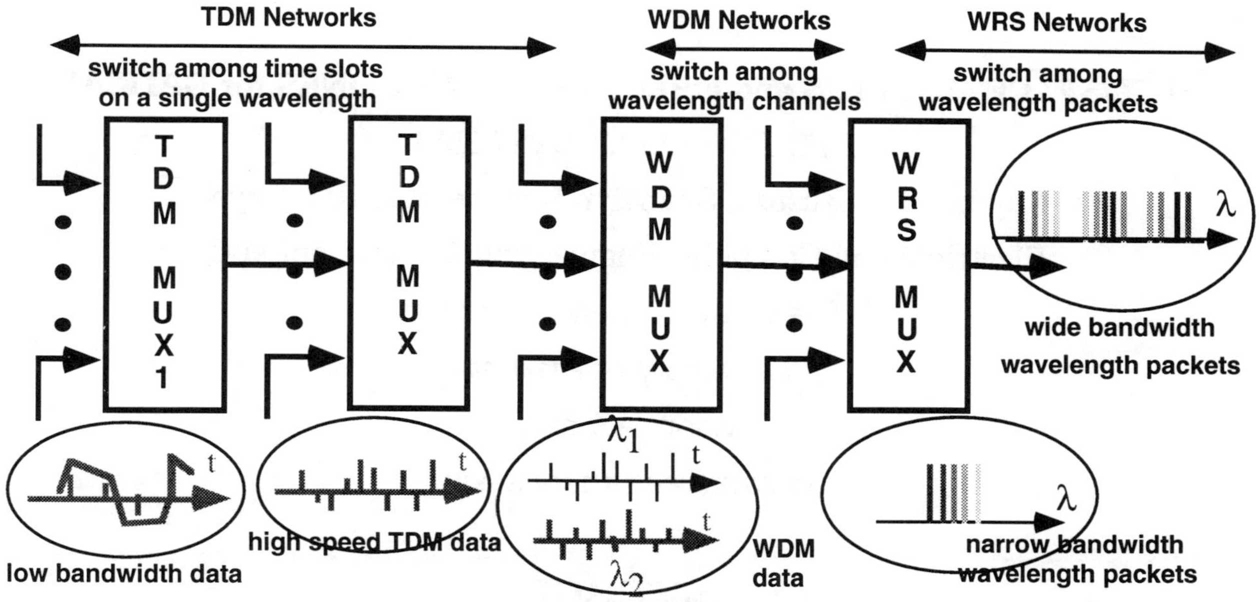

Fig. 8 New level of data aggregation using wavelength packets

7. Summary and conclusions

The wavelength recognizing switch presented in this paper allows truly all-optical routing of multiwavelength signals, that is, routing in which not even the control signals need to be converted to electronic form. At the same time, WRSs allow full data rate and data format transparency. While such a transparent network has already been demonstrated [10], it was implemented using classical WDM building blocks, and needs external logic and circuitry for routing. The WRS on the other hand is naturally suited to route wavelength packets (a group of data-modulated wavelengths encapsulated together and routed as a single entity). In a WRS network, wavelength packets are self-routed, with no external logic. All the routing decisions are incorporated in the functionality of the device itself. We presented architectures for the basic building blocks and then more complex topologies for very high throughput all-optical networks that can be built with WRS. We also proposed a higher level of data aggregation, where wavelength packets would be routed as encapsulated data entities through WRS.

Acknowledgment This research was supported in part by DARPA through the Army Research Laboratory under Contract No. DAAL01-94-K-3429 and by the Joint Services Electronics Program (JSEP) through the Air Force Office of Scientific Research under Contract No. AFOSR 749620-94-C-0022.

8. References

[1] L. Buckman, M.S. Wu, , G. Giaretta,, G. S. Li, P. K. Pepeljugoski, J.W. Goodman, A. Varma, K.Y. Lau, and C.J. Chang-Hasnain, "A novel all-optical self-routed wavelength-addressable network (SWANET)," *IEEE Photon. Technol. Lett.*, vol. **7**(9), pp.1066-1068, 1995.

[2] C.A. Brackett, A.S. Acampora, J. Sweitzer, G. Tangonan, T. Smith, W. Lennon, K.-C. Wang, and R.H. Hobbs, "A scalable multiwavelength multihop optical network: a proposal for research on all-optical networks," *IEEE J. Lightwave Technol.*, **11**(5/6), pp. 736-753, 1993.

[3] D. X. Zhu, S. Dubovitsky, W. H. Steier, K. Uppal, D. Tishinin, J. Burger, and P. D. Dapkus, "A novel all-optical self-routing switch: the wavelength recognizing switch," submitted to *IEEE Photon. Technol. Lett.*

[4] S. Dubovitsky and W. H. Steier, "Tunable wavelength filters based on nonlinear optical interactions in semiconductor amplifiers," *IEEE J. Lightwave Technol.*, vol. **14**(6), pp. 1020-1026, 1996.

[5] J. Sharony, K.W. Cheung, and T.E. Stern, "The Wavelength Dilation Concept in Lightwave Networks - Implementation and System Considerations," *IEEE J. Lightwave Technol.*, vol. **11** (5/6), pp. 900-907, 1993.

[6] T. T. Lee and S. C. Liew, "Broadband Packet Switches Based on Dilated Interconnection Networks," *IEEE Trans. Comm.*, vol. **42** (2-4), pp. 732-744, 1994.

[7] E. L. Goldstein, L. Eskildsen, "Scaling Limitations in Transparent Optical Networks Due to Low Level Crosstalk," *IEEE Photon. Technol. Lett.*, vol. **7**(1), pp. 93-94, 1995.

[8] R. A. Spanke, "Architectures for Large Nonblocking Optical Space Switches," *IEEE J. Quant. Electron.*, vol. **QE-22**(6), pp. 964-967, 1986.

[9] R.F. Kalman, L.G. Kazovsky, and J.W. Goodman, "Space Division Switches Based on Semiconductor Optical Amplifiers," *IEEE Photon. Technol. Lett.*, vol. **4**(9), pp. 1048-1051, 1992.

[10] T. E. Stern, K. Bala, S. Jiang, and J. Sharony, " Linear lightwave networks: performance issues," *IEEE J. Lightwave Technol.*, vol. **11** (5/6), pp. 937-950, 1993.

FREE-SPACE MODULES and FIBER ARRAY DATA LINKS for OPTICAL INTERCONNECT SYSTEMS

Raymond K. Kostuk, Shanalyn Kemme, and Rob Boye
Electrical and Computer Engineering Department and
The Optical Sciences Center
University of Arizona
Tucson, AZ 85721
kostuk@ece.arizona.edu

ABSTRACT

It is generally agreed that optics is advantageous for interconnect applications requiring high speed signal propagation over distances greater than several centimeters. This is especially true when signals must be transferred between substrates. Evidence of this exists in the development of high speed VCSEL based parallel data links. One approach to increasing the capacity of these systems is to use free-space optics to provide fanout, and fiber optic arrays to transfer signals over long connection distances. In this paper we summarize the transfer and interconnect properties of free-space optical systems used in conjunction with multi mode parallel fiber arrays, and then discuss two designs for accomplishing fanout and fiber coupling functions.

Fiber Optic Interconnect Systems

A number of VCSEL based fiber optic links have been developed to fill the need for high bandwidth connections over appreciable distances between electronic processing systems[1]. However, these are primarily arrays of point-to-point links without fanout. In order to provide signal splitting, multiple star couplers are required which can significantly increase system cost. Since a great deal of effort has been invested into developing these links it would seem advantageous to increase the capability of these systems. One approach to accomplish this is to use free-space optics to realize signal fanout and spatial routing. Cost reduction can be achieved using binary optic and replication methods which allow fabrication of multiple elements in parallel.

Two approaches to implementing free-space optics for signal broadcasting operations in fiber optic networks are 1) cascade beamsplitting components in sequence, and 2) use single beam fanout coupled to multiple fibers. The effects of power loss in cascaded optical systems, and problems associated with imaging between multimode waveguides will be addressed in this presentation.

0-8186-7974-3/97 $10.00 © 1997 IEEE

Cascaded Optical Systems

A number of interconnect systems have been proposed in which cascade multiple elements tap signals from a transmitted beam [2-4]. These systems operate in a manner similar to an electrical backplane. The fanout capability of these systems is determined by the minimum detectable power required at the receiver for a desired bit error rate (BER), the optical power from the source, and the losses incurred per stage.

The minimum detectable power (MDP) can be determined by first calculating the thermal and shot noise currents for a specific receiver type and then adding a factor to allow for parasitic electrical noise effects [5]. The thermal and shot noise limits for different bipolar and FET type receivers can be found in the literature [6]. The resulting MDP is given by

$$P_{MIN} = \frac{Q\, F_p \langle i_{ckt}^2 \rangle^{1/2}}{R_d} ,$$

where Q is the parameter corresponding to the required BER (i.e. BER(Q) = exp(- $(Q^2/2)/[(2\pi)^{1/2}Q]$, ,$\langle i_{ckt}{}^2 \rangle^{1/2}$ is the bandwidth dependent current noise, and R_d is the detector responsivity in A/W. Figure X shows the MDP for a FET type receiver with values given in [5] and three values of parasitic noise. At 500 MHz and a BER of 10^{-16} the MDP is about 50 μW.

One arrangement for coupling fiber ribbon arrays through a free-space optical distribution system is illustrated in Figure 2. This configuration was previously used to connect four laser transmitters and receivers for simultaneous signal broadcasting [4]. For this application it can be modified for interfacing four MT fiber array connectors which have a pitch of 2.5 mm and an array of 10 multi mode fibers with a 250 μm center spacing. A beam from a fiber passes through two beamsplitting gratings and two microlenses. If the efficiency of the beamsplitter is η_B, and that of the microlens is η_L, then the power reaching a receiver after passing through M modules is

$$P_R = \frac{1}{M-1} [\eta_L\, \eta_B]^{2(M-1)}\, P_S ,$$

where P_S is the source power. Using 81% and 95% for the efficiencies of the beamsplitters and microlenses respectively (corresponding to 4 and 8 phase level binary elements [7]) and an incident source power of 4 mW (Optobus I VCSEL array [8]), then 6 modules can be cascaded and connect 14 processing boards.

Single Stage Fanout System

An alternative approach to implementing a fiber to free-space optical system is to minimize the number of beam tapping devices in the system. Figure 4 shows an arrangement of this type in which only one fanout element is used. A 1 X N VCSEL array provides a parallel optical data set which is then collimated by a matching microlens array. The beams then pass through a 1:M one-dimensional fanout grating and is partially collimated through a cylindrical lens, and then focused into an N X M array of microlenses. An array of fiber ribbons are coupled to either a single receiver array to form a single bus, or to multiple receiver arrays to form a multiple bus. The multiple bus arrangement reduces contention for an connection path in the system [9]. The power transferred to an individual receiver in this arrangement is

$$P_{RX} = \frac{1}{M-1} \eta_L^3 \eta_{BS} \eta_C P_S ,$$

where η_L is the efficiency of a microlens, η_{BS} is the efficiency of the beam splitter, and η_C is the efficiency of the cylindrical lens. A plot of P_{RX} is illustrated in Figure 3 and shows a significant improvement over the cascaded arrangement. In this case, with a fanout grating efficiency of 75%, and micro lens efficiencies of 81%, less than 2 mW of optical source power is required to connect 14 processing elements with half the power required for the cascaded case.

The geometrical limit on fanout fanout with this arrangement can be determined by computing the maximum diffraction angle for the grating and the minimum separation angle between linear fiber arrays. The maximum diffraction angle is fixed by the minimum grating period that can be reliably manufactured and the minimum width of the fiber connectors. If the fabrication resolution (Λ) is 1 μm, and the wavelength (λ) is 0.85 μm, then for a normally incident beam the diffraction angle is $\theta = \sin^{-1} (\lambda/\Lambda) = 58.2°$. The width of typical MT fiber array connectors is on the order of 2.5 mm [10]. If the separation between the fanout grating and the cylindrical lens is 20 mm, then approximately 25 beam arrays can be defined with this system. This provides nearly a factor 2 improvement in connectivity over the cascaded design. From the previous power analysis this would require approximately 4 mW of laser output power with the lower efficiency microlenses and fanout grating, but is still consistent with commercially available VCSEL array powers.

Imaging Systems with Multi-Mode Fiber Arrays

The above analysis assumed that the input and output beams are Gaussian with well behaved transfer characteristics [11]. However for low cost packaging considerations, most VCSEL array data links are being developed with multi mode fibers. These fibers typically have core diameters ranging from 50 -100 μm and numerical apertures (NAs) from 0.20 to 0.30. The large effective NA of these fibers results from geometrical total internal reflection properties and therefore must be considered as an extended optical source. For many common fiber array connectors (such as the MT) fiber separation is 250 μm. Therefore, in order to prevent overfilling of collimation lenses, the lens focal lengths must be less than $fl < (d_{FA}/2 - a)/\tan\alpha$, where d_{FA} is the separation between fiber centers in the array, a is the fiber radius, and α is the angle corresponding to the NA. Even after satisfying this condition, the core appears as an extended set of point sources, and the beam is not collimated after passsing through the lens. One way to accomodate this condition is to use a dilute array imaging system which does not require beam collimation [12]. A second less elegant approach is to allow the beams to overlap and to suffer a loss in signal-to-noise ratio.

Another problem associated with using multi mode fibers as sources for free-space optical systems is the field speckle caused by mode interference. With an NA of 0.3, λ = 850 nm, and a fiber diameter of 62.5 μm the corresponding fiber V# is 69. Since the number of modes can be approximated as $V^2/2$, a high level of mode interference is possible at the output face of the fiber and can give rise to spatial filtering of the intensity. This results in modal noise and increases the system BER.

Simulation and experimental results on fiber-to-free-space optical systems will be presented during the discussion.

Acknowledgements
The authors wish to acknowledge the National Science Foundation and the Semiconductor Research Corporation for supporting this work.

References:
1. F. A. P. Tooley, ``Optically interconnected electronic - challenges and choices," IEEE Proceeding of MPPOI'96, Maui, HI, 138-145 (1996).
2. C. Zhao, J. Liu, and R.T. Chen, ``Hybrid optoelectronic backplane bus for multiprocessor-based computing systems," IEEE Proceeding of MPPOI'96, Maui, HI, 313-320 (1996).
3. S. Araki, M. Kajita, K. Kasahara, K. Kubota, K. Kurihara, I. edmond, E. Schenfeld, and T. Suzuki, ``Experimental free-space optical network for massively parallel computers,;; Appl. Opt., Vol. 35, 1269-1281 (1996).
4. R. K. Kostuk, T. J. Kim, D. Ramsey, T-h> Oh, and R. Boye, `` Connection cube and interleaved optical backplane for a multprocessor data bus," IEEE Proceeding of MPPOI'95, San Antonio, TX, 144-151 (1995).
5. C. Fan, B. Mansoorian, D. A> Van Blerkom, M. W. Hansen, V. H. Ozguz, S. C. Esner, and G. C. Marsden, `` Digital free-space optical interconnections: a comparison of transmitter technologies," Appl. Opt., Vol. 34, 3103-3115 (1995).
6. MOSIS FET paramters for the 0.8 μm CMOS process.
7. J. Jahns and S. H. Lee, *Optical Computing Hardware*, Academic Press, Boston, MA, Chap. 6, pp. 148-150.
8. D. B. Schwartz, C.K.Y. Chun, N. Choi, D. Diaz, S. Planer, G. Raskin, and S. G. Shook, ``OPTOBUS I: Performance of a 4 Gb/s optical interconnect," IEEE Proceeding of MPPOI'96, Maui, HI, 256-263 (1996).
9. T. N. Mudge, J. P. Hayes, G. D. Buzzard, and D. C. Winsor, `` Analysis of Multiple Bus Interconnection Networks," J. Parallel and Distributed Computing, Vol. 3, 328-343 (1986).
10. See for example USCONEC specification sheet for fiber array MTA connectors (MTA-002, 004, and 014).
11. F. B. McCormick, F. A. P. Tooley, T. J. Cloonan, J. M. Sasain, H. S. Hinton, K. O. Mersereau, and A. Y. Feldblum, ``Optical interconnections using

microlens arrays," Opt. Quant. Electr., Vol. 24, S465-S477 (1992).
12. A. W. Lohmann, `` Image formation of dilute arrays for optical information processing," Opt. Comm., Vol. 86, 365-370 (1991).

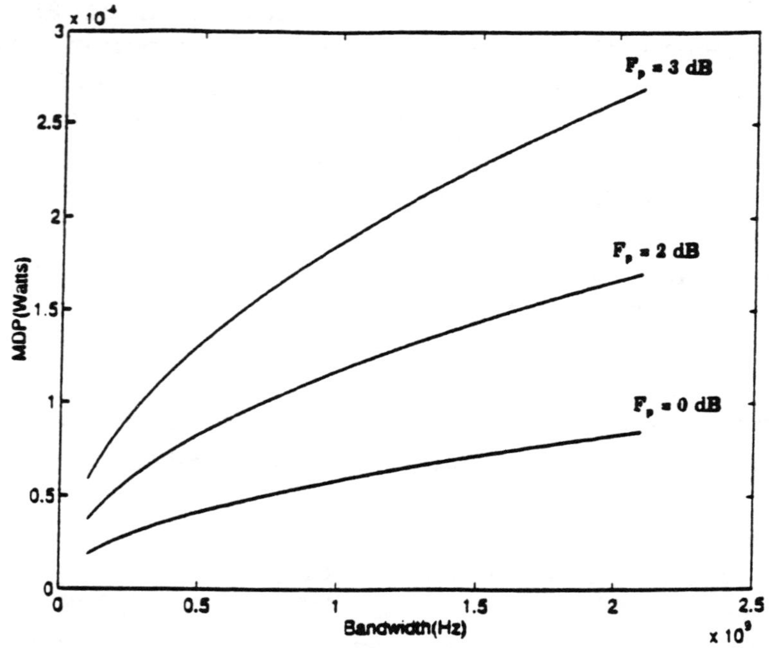

Figure 1. Plot of minimum detectable power as a function of bandwidth for a typical FET type receiver and different amounts of parasitic noise (F_p).

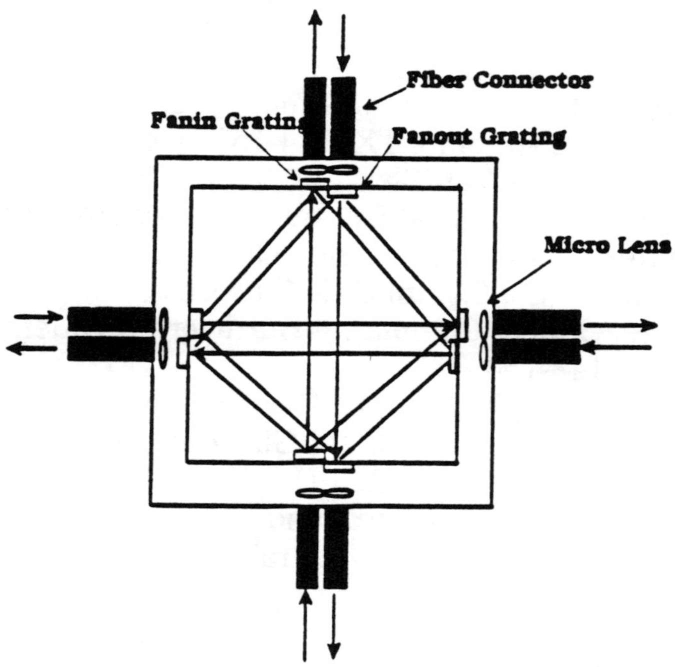

Figure 2. A module for connecting four transmitting and receiving arrays of fibers. This basic arrangement can be cascaded to link additional processing nodes.

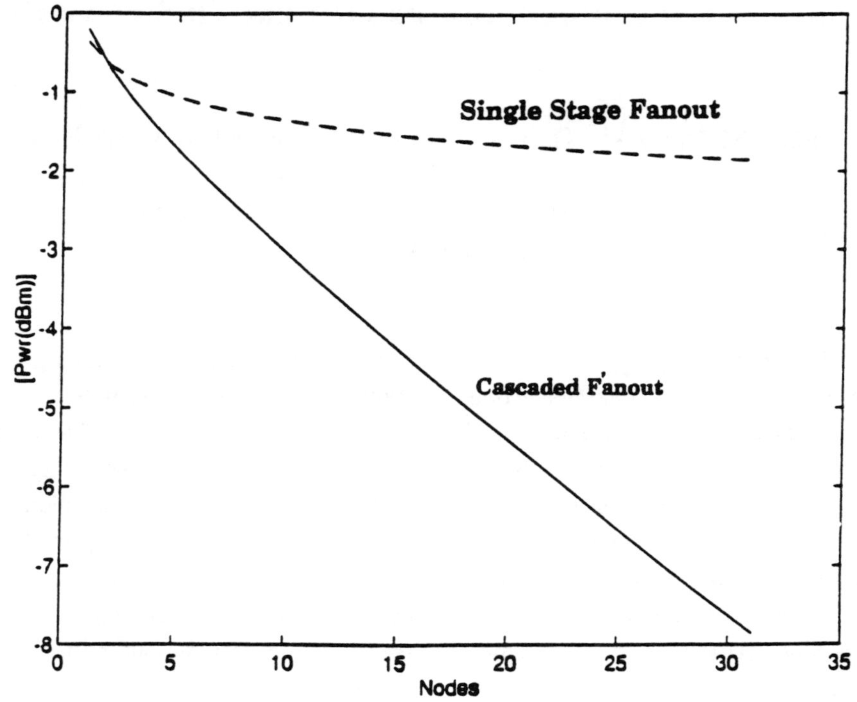

Figure 3. Losses as a function of increasing number of nodes in an interconnect system for cascaded modules shown in Figure 2 and for the single fanout system shown in Figure 4.

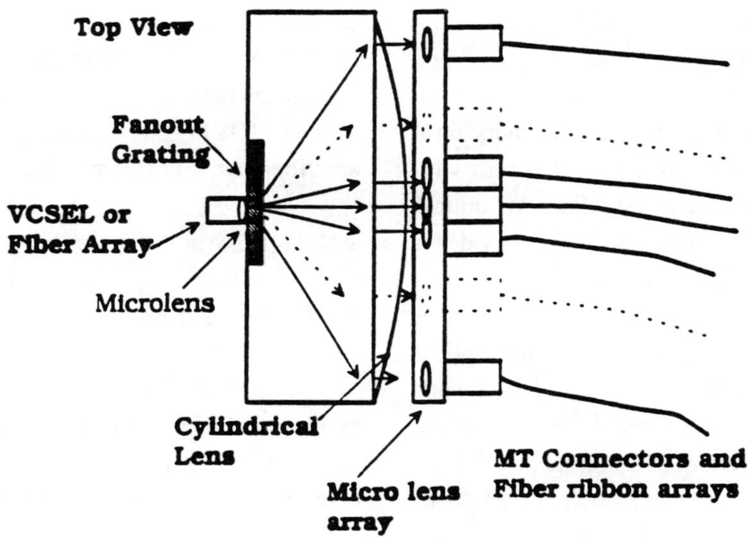

Figure 4. Free-space optical system with a single fanout stage. Losses are computed by assuming that an additional microlens is used at the receiver.

8.5 Gbit/s/port Synchronous Optical Packet-switch

Yoshiharu Maeno, Akio Tajima, Yoshihiko Suemura and Naoya Henmi
NEC Opto-electronics Research Laboratories
4-1-1 Miyazaki, Miyamae-ku, Kawasaki 216 Japan
email: maeno@optsys.cl.nec.co.jp

Abstract

A synchronous optical network interconnecting processors effectively reduces network latency and enhances bandwidth. If, however, synchronization is not accurate and stable, skew and jitter in received packets may cause transmission errors. Timing margin design must consider the tolerance of the receiver to the skew and jitter. A theoretical analysis shows that the tolerance is ±12% of a bit period. Synchronization by clock distribution is achieved on an 8.5 Gbit/s/port packet-switch testbed utilizing semiconductor optical amplifier gates. An experiment shows that the sensitivity penalty induced by removing the preamble from the packet header and suppressing guard time is less than 0.5 dB.

1 Introduction

The interconnection network (INW) is a critical element determining the performance of multiprocessors. Ensuring small network latency[1],[2] as well as large bandwidth and scaleability is a major issue in its design. To implement a physically uniform shared memory on a multiprocessor supercomputer, fast memory access with network latency below 100 ns is essential. An optical INW based on optical links[3] and a switch[4] provides a bandwidth of more than 1 Gbyte/s/port.[5] It has never, however, been recognized that there are three redundant fields in the packet header on the conventional optical INW, which result in an overhead that degrades network latency. The redundant fields are guard time, preamble and word synchronization pattern. During the guard time, the switch connects an input port to an output port. With the preamble, a receiver in a network interface recovers a bit clock and a digital bit stream from a received signal.[6] With the word synchronization pattern, the receiver aligns S-P (serial-to-parallel *or* bit-to-word) converted parallel bits into their original position in the extracted word-frame. The three fields are timing margin for switching and receiving packets transmitted asynchronously.

A synchronous INW that suppresses the timing margin as shortly as possible is therefore attractive. It has been a simple and reliable technique for synchronization in an intra-cabinet INW to provide an external timing reference by a clock distribution. A clock distribution by optical couplers[7] is advantageous in that it is free from skew of electrical fan-out buffers. On the other hand, significant transmission errors may occur unless the synchronization is highly accurate and stable. A relative bit phase deviation (BPD), which may exist among packets received from different transmitters, must be carefully taken into account in designing timing margin.

In this paper we demonstrate the feasibility of a synchronous intra-cabinet INW operating at the bit rate of 8.5 Gbit/s/port with clock distribution and accurate design of signal line length. We report (1) a theoretical analysis on a tolerance of an optical receiver to an instantaneous BPD among received packets and (2) a synchronization experiment with an 8.5 Gbit/s/port optical packet-switch testbed (OST) incorporating semiconductor optical amplifier gate (SOAG) switches.

2 Design issue

2.1 Configuration

Figure 1[A] shows a system configuration for a multiprocessor interconnected with an intra-cabinet INW based on an optical switch. The transmission distance between optical components on the printed circuit boards is less than 1 m. Figure 1[B] shows a 4×4 gated-divider-and-passive-combiner (GDPC) optical switch.[8],[9] It consists of splitters, SOAGs[10] and combiners.[11] The SOAG is ideal for a fast packet-switch, as it has a short switching time of 1 ns with a small driving current of 10

0-8186-7974-3/97 $10.00 © 1997 IEEE

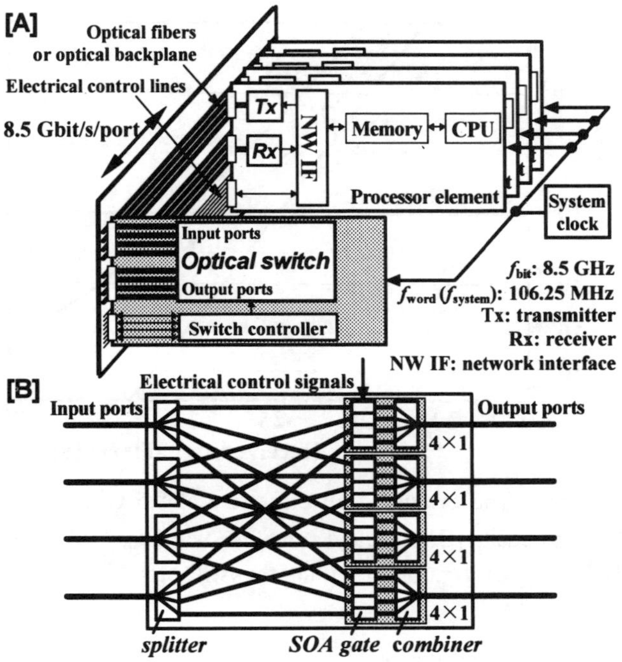

Figure 1 [A]: a multiprocessor incorporating 4 processor element boards and an optical switch board. [B]: a 4×4 gated-divider-and-passive-combiner optical switch.

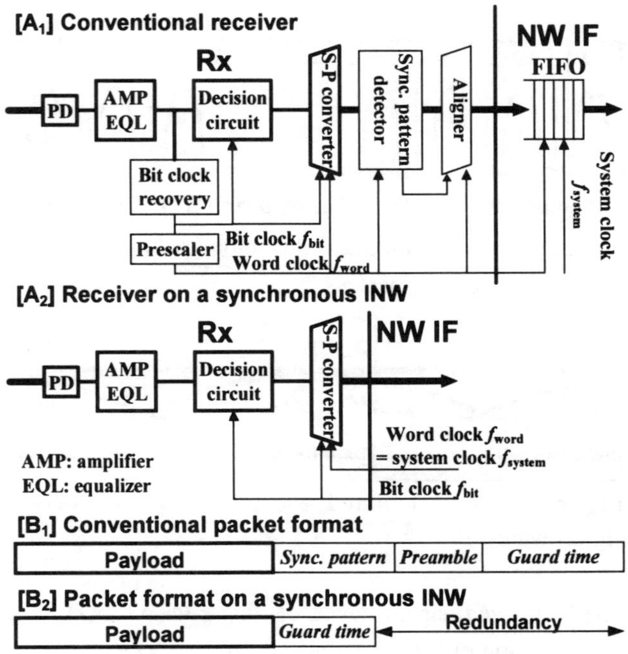

Figure 2 [A]: a configuration for an optical receiver and [B]: a packet format on the optical INW.

mA. It is driven by electrical circuits, including an arbiter. Both bit and word clock are distributed to transmitters (Tx), receivers (Rx) and the optical switch.

Figure 2 shows a configuration for a receiver and a packet format. The decision circuit recovers the original bit stream from a received signal with the distributed bit clock. It eliminates the clock recovery circuit and the preamble. The distributed word clock externally provides a word-frame used by an S-P converter. It eliminates the word synchronization pattern detector for finding a word-frame in the recovered bit stream and the aligner for rotating the S-P converted bits into the proper order. Referring to the word clock, the optical switch switches connections during short guard time. It removes the redundant timing margin within the guard time.

2.2 Synchronization

Figure 3 shows a case where succeeding packets have a significant BPD. The skew in distributed bit and word clock must be minimized. The signal line length must be accurately designed and fabricated to ensure that *the largest BPD is within the tolerance of the receiver.* A quantitative analysis on the tolerance is given in section 3. Synchronization is categorized into two classes.

□ **Bit synchronization**

To minimize the BPD at the receiver the signal line length from transmitters to the receiver must be equal. The transmitters must lock the bit phase of outgoing packets relative to the bit clock.

□ **Word synchronization**

To minimize a word-frame phase deviation among packets at the optical switch and the receiver the signal line length from transmitters to the optical switch and from the transmitters to the receiver must be equal. The transmitters must lock the word-frame phase of outgoing packets relative to the word clock. An optical switch must switch connections during the guard time by referring to the word clock.

3 Theoretical analysis

3.1 Theoretical model and assumptions

We evaluate, theoretically, the bit error rate (BER) of received packets and the tolerance of an optical receiver to the instantaneous BPD. The decision timing D_t is locked to the distributed bit clock, regardless of the optimum value D_{to}. The BPD is defined as $\Delta D_t \equiv D_t - D_{to}$.

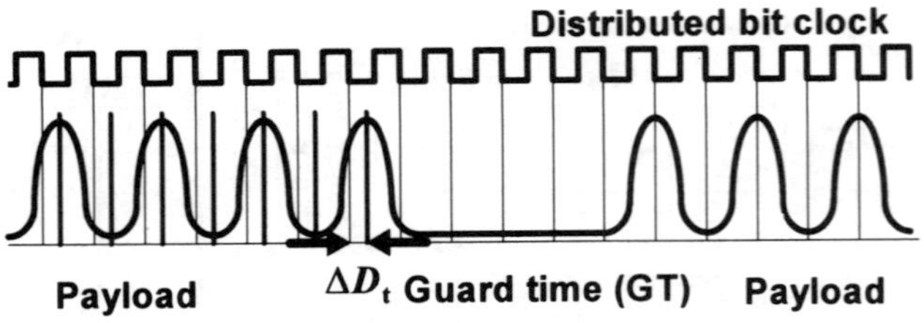

Figure 3 A relative bit phase deviation ($\Delta D_t \neq 0$) between succeeding received packets.

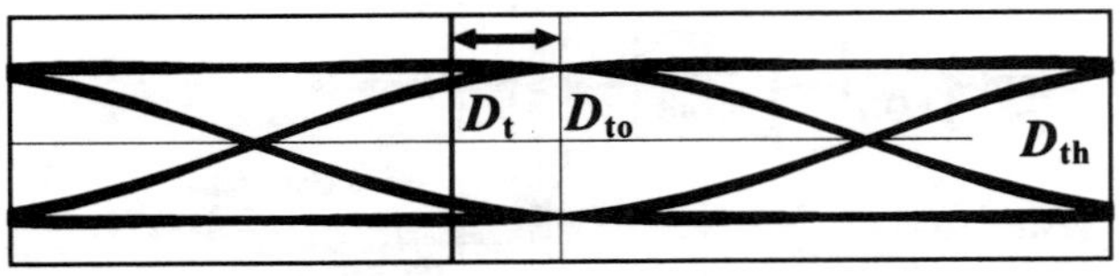

Figure 4 The calculated eye pattern of a received signal when $\beta = 0.9$.

The equalized signal level of the k-th bit $S(k)$ is a superposition of the normalized bit pulse $p(t)$ which has a raised cosine profile[12]. They are given by

$$\begin{aligned} S(k,\Delta D_t) &= s(b_k)\cdot p(\Delta D_t) + \sum_{l\neq k} s(b_l)\cdot p(\Delta D_t - (k-l)T) \\ p(t) &= \sin(\frac{\pi\cdot t}{T})\cdot\cos(\frac{\pi\beta\cdot t}{T}) / [\frac{\pi\cdot t}{T}\{1-(\frac{2\beta\cdot t}{T})^2\}] \end{aligned} \quad ,(1)$$

where b_k, $s(b_k)$ and T are a bit sequence, its signal level and a bit period. The summation stands for an interference from other bits. The parameter β describes the flatness of the equalization and the transfer function of the receiver. Figure 4 shows the eye pattern when $\beta = 0.9$.

The BER depends on the noise level (σ), which results from amplified spontaneous emission (ASE) noise of the SOAG (σ_{SOAG}) and thermal noise of the receiver (σ_{R}). Both are Gaussian noise, *i.e.* $\sigma^2 \approx \sigma_{\mathrm{SOAG}}^2 + \sigma_{\mathrm{R}}^2$. Details of σ_{SOAG} are given by[13]

$$\begin{aligned} \sigma_{\mathrm{SOAG}}^2 = 2e^2BM^2\,[\,&F\{\Gamma G\frac{P_{\mathrm{SOAG}}}{h\nu} + 2\Gamma(G-1)n_{\mathrm{sp}}\Delta f\} \\ &+ \{2\Gamma^2 G(G-1)\frac{P_{\mathrm{SOAG}}}{h\nu}n_{\mathrm{sp}} + 2\Gamma^2(G-1)^2 n_{\mathrm{sp}}^2\Delta f\}\,] \end{aligned} \quad .(2)$$

$B \approx 1/T$ is the bandwidth of the receiver. Γ is a span loss that includes the coupling loss of an SOAG module and the quantum efficiency of a photodiode (PD). M and F are multiplication and excess noise factor of the PD. G, n_{sp}, Δf and $P_{\mathrm{SOAG}}/h\nu$ are chip gain, spontaneous emission coefficient, spectral width of the ASE and photon number flux (incident on the chip) of the SOAG. The four terms in equation (2) are signal shot noise, ASE shot noise, signal-ASE beat noise and ASE-ASE beat noise. As a function of

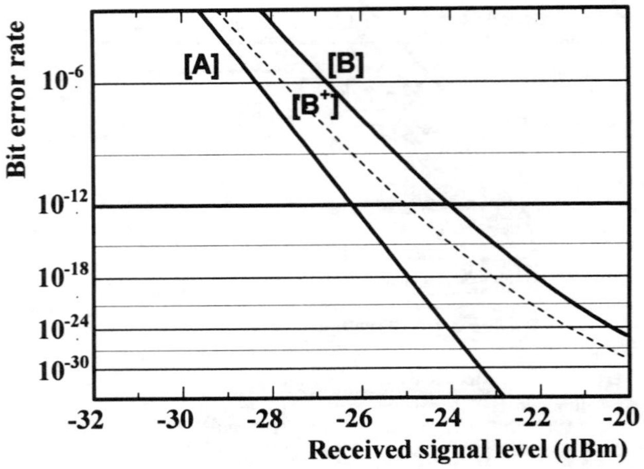

Figure 5 The evaluated bit error rate at 8.5 Gbit/s. [A]: back-to-back, [B]: through an SOA with n_{sp} = 2.2 and [B$^+$]: with calibration excluding the ASE offset level.

ΔD_t the BER R_{err} is given by

$$\begin{aligned} R_{\mathrm{err}}(\Delta D_t) = &\sum_{b_m=\text{"1"}} \frac{1}{2}\mathrm{erfc}(\frac{S(m,\Delta D_t) - D_{\mathrm{th}}}{\sqrt{2}\,\sigma_1}) \\ &+ \sum_{b_n=\text{"0"}} \frac{1}{2}\mathrm{erfc}(\frac{D_{\mathrm{th}} - S(n,\Delta D_t)}{\sqrt{2}\,\sigma_0}) \end{aligned} \quad , \quad (3)$$

where D_{th} is a decision threshold. It is fixed to be the optimum value when ΔD_t = 0. The noise level when receiving "1" is larger than that when receiving "0" ($\sigma_1 > \sigma_0$). Both are assumed to be constants, regardless of the bit sequence.

3.2 Parameters for analysis

We derived the parameters which appeared in equations (1), (2) and (3) from experiments.

□ **Semiconductor optical amplifier gate**

When the injection current to the SOAG module is set to 50 mA, the observed fiber-to-fiber gain is 10 dB. The chip gain G is 20 dB. Noise figure, including the coupling loss of the module of 5 dB/facet, is 12 dB. They give the value of $n_{\mathrm{sp}} \approx 2.2$. The spectral width of the ASE of the SOAG is $\Delta f \approx$ 6.2 THz ($\Delta\lambda \approx$ 50 nm).

□ **Optical receiver incorporating an APD**

Multiplication, excess noise factor and a quantum efficiency of the avalanche photodiode (APD) are M = 15,

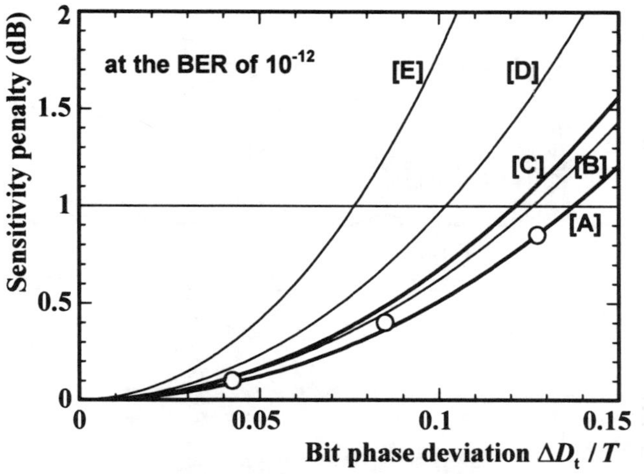

Figure 6 The evaluated sensitivity penalty when $\beta = 0.9$. [A]: back-to-back (*circle*: observation at 8.5 Gbit/s). [B] through an SOA with n_{sp} (NF) = 1.0 (8.3 dB), [C]: 2.2 (12.1 dB), [D]: 6.0 (17.4 dB) and [E]: 10.0 (20.5 dB).

F = 5 and 0.6. For an 8.5 Gbit/s signal, the observed minimum sensitivity at the BER of 10^{-12} is -26.2 dBm. It gives an equivalent noise level of the receiver of $\sigma_R/\sqrt{B} \approx 25$ pA $/\sqrt{\text{Hz}}$. An analysis of the eye pattern and the spectrum of the equalized signal gives the bandwidth of the receiver $B \approx 10$ GHz and the parameter $\beta \approx 0.9$.

3.3 Evaluated sensitivity penalty

Figure 5 shows the evaluated BER when the input signal level into the SOAG is P_{SOAG} = -20 dBm. The sensitivity penalty at the BER of 10^{-12} is about 2 dB. The degradation results mainly from the signal shot noise and the signal-ASE beat noise. The span loss Γ is larger than 20 dB, which suppresses the beat noise ($\propto \Gamma^2$) to the same order as the shot noise ($\propto \Gamma$). The ASE added to the signal is estimated to give an offset level of about 1 dB. When it is excluded, the sensitivity penalty is about 1 dB. The BER of 10^{-18} is achieved above the received signal level of -22 dBm in spite of the existence of a slight floor below the BER of 10^{-12}.

Figure 6 shows the evaluated sensitivity penalty at the BER of 10^{-12} relative to the sensitivity at $\Delta D_t = 0$ as a function of ΔD_t. As the ASE (n_{sp} and σ_{SOAG}) gets larger, the tolerance decreases. *For n_{sp} = 2.2, the tolerance within which the sensitivity penalty is less than 1 dB is ± 12% of a bit period, which corresponds to the skew of ± 15 ps (or signal line length of ± 3 mm) at 8.5 Gbit/s.*

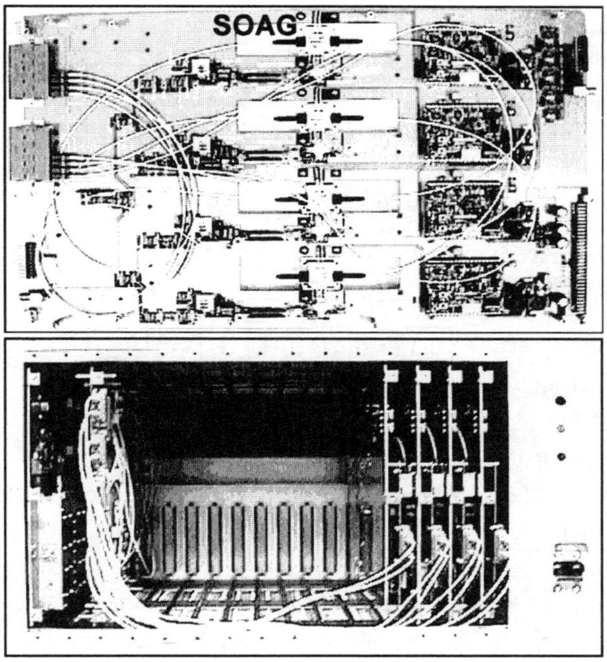

Figure 7 UPPER: the developed optical packet-switch testbed board (23 cm×36 cm) and LOWER: the testbed mounted in a rack with clock and four transceiver boards.

3.4 Discussion

As seen above, an optical receiver operating at 8.5 Gbit/s possesses a tolerance to the instantaneous BPD as large as ± 15 ps. For fibers as long as 1 m used in an intra-cabinet INW, it has been common to control their length to an accuracy within 1 mm (*or* skew of 5 ps) with a state-of-the-art connecterization technique. The tolerance and the connecterization technique ensure sufficient timing margin against the BPD. The accurate signal line length and timing margin can be designed without applying tunable delay lines. For waveguides fabricated on a printed circuit board, more accurate computer-aided-design[14] of their length is available. It should be noted that the tolerance depends on n_{sp}. An SOAG with a small noise figure and a small coupling loss improves the tolerance as well as the minimum sensitivity.

Both the signal line length and signal velocity depend on temperature. A thermal expansion coefficient of a fiber is about 10^{-5} /K. For fibers of 1 m, a temperature variation of ± 20 K induces skew of ± 1 ps. The temperature coefficient of the refractive index is also about 10^{-5} /K. The overall temperature variation in an air-cooled cabinet is much smaller than ± 20 K. The

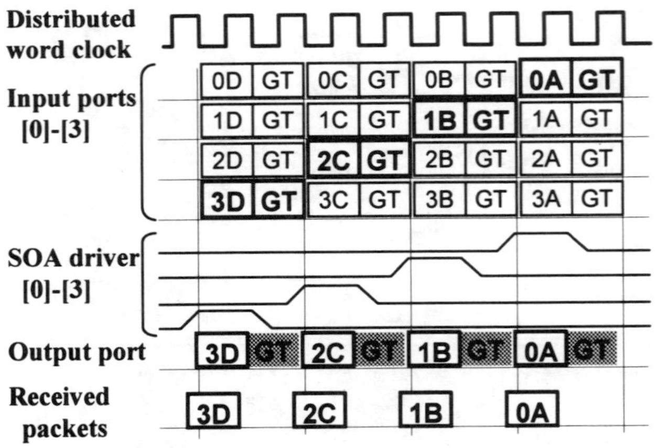

Figure 8 Operations of the testbed as a 4×1 packet-switch. The connection is switched every packet (two words).

thermally induced skew is within the tolerance of the receiver at the bit rate of 8.5 Gbit/s. The synchronization is therefore thermally stable without temperature control.

4 Experimental results

4.1 Optical switch testbed

Figure 7 (UPPER) shows a photograph of a developed 8.5 Gbit/s/port synchronous optical packet-switch testbed (OST) board. It incorporates four SOAG modules and their driver circuits. The driver circuit includes a duty-cycle controller which compensates a turn-on delay of the SOAG as long as 2 ns. The testbed can be configured as either a 4×1 or a 2×2 switch. The 4×1 switch is a building block of the 4×4 GDPC switch shown in figure 1[B]. Figure 7 (LOWER) shows a photograph of the OST board mounted in a rack with four transceiver boards and a system clock board.

4.2 Synchronization experiment

An 8.5 Gbit/s bit stream defined in the Fibre Channel (FC) standards was transmitted through the OST configured to function as a 4×1 packet-switch. An 8.5 GHz bit clock and a 106.25 MHz prescaled (one eightieth) word clock were distributed over the INW. The skew of the distributed clocks and transmitted packets were minimized by controlling the signal line length to an accuracy within 1 mm. The word length was 80 bits, which corresponds to 8 bytes in the 8B-10B code. The

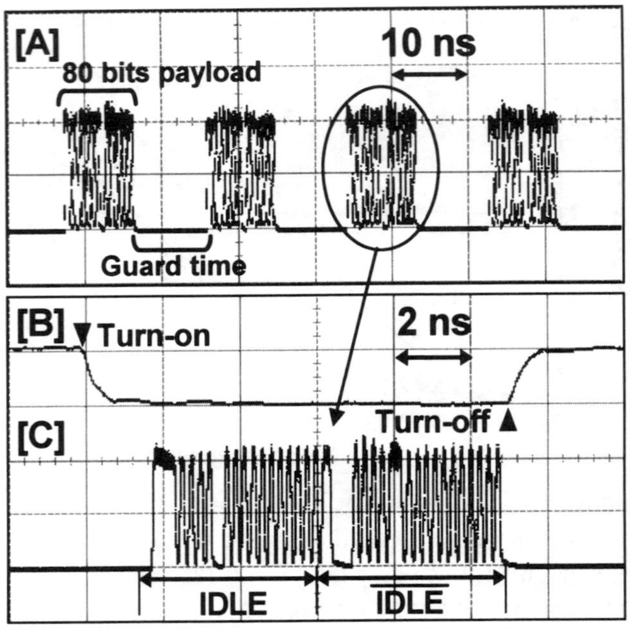

Figure 9 The observed waveform of [A], [C]: packets from the switching testbed and [B]: the control signal driving an SOAG. The IDLE pattern is a combination of K28.5 ("0011111010"), D21.4 ("1010100010") and two D21.5 ("1010101010").

payload in the experiment was 1 word. It was a fixed combination of the 40 bits IDLE pattern (one of the control sequences defined in the FC standards) and its inversion. The guard time (GT) was suppressed to 1 word, 9.4 ns, by taking advantage of the short switching time of the SOAG. It was an 80 bit "0" pattern. The preamble for clock recovery in the packet header was eliminated. The connection from four input ports to the output port of the OST was switched every 2 words. Figure 8 shows a timing chart of the operations.

Figure 9 shows the observed waveform of packets received from the OST. The transceiver incorporates a 1550 nm DFB-LD/an $LiNbO_3$ intensity modulator and an APD[15]/an SiGe preamplifier.[16] The OST switches the connection during the guard time accurately because the jitter of the distributed word clock was small. Figure 10 shows the BER observed through the OST. No BER floor was observed down to the BER of 10^{-12}. The sensitivity penalty due to the ASE of the SOAG was about 2 dB, which is in good agreement with the evaluated BER shown in figure 5. *The excess sensitivity penalty caused by synchronous switching of the OST was estimated to be less than 0.5 dB.* That results from eliminating the preamble and suppressing the guard time. The skew of the

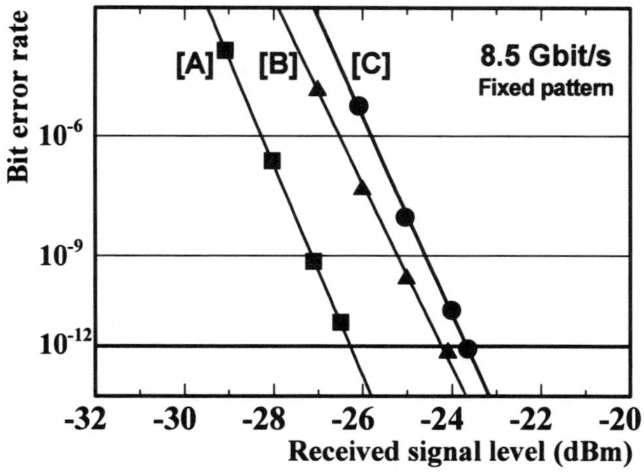

Figure 10 The observed bit error rate. [A]: back-to-back, [B]: through a single SOAG and [C]: through the testbed.

distributed bit clock and the BPD among received packets were sufficiently small. *We verified error free operation for more than 1 hour (BER of 10^{-14}).*

5 Conclusion

We have demonstrated the feasibility of an 8.5 Gbit/s/port synchronous optical INW from the theoretical analysis and the experiment. The theoretical analysis shows that the optical receiver possesses a tolerance to an instantaneous bit phase deviation as large as ±12% of a bit period. It can be increased by improving the noise figure and the coupling loss of an semiconductor optical amplifier switch gate module. The tolerance and the state-of-the-art connecterization technique used for controlling the signal line length ensure sufficient timing margin against the bit phase deviation. An 8.5 Gbit/s/port synchronous optical packet-switch testbed has been developed. The preamble for clock recovery and the redundant guard time for switching are eliminated from the packet header to reduce network latency. The observed excess sensitivity penalty due to the elimination is less than 0.5 dB. Stability of synchronization is verified by error free operation for more than 1 hour. The combination of clock distribution and accurate design of the signal line length is a simple and reliable technique for synchronizing a Gbyte/s/port intra-cabinet interconnection network.

---

[1] A. Nowatzyk *et al.*, "The S3.mp scaleable shared memory multiprocessor," Proceedings of the ICPP, I10 (1995)

[2] M. Galles *et al.*, "Scaleable pipelined interconnect for distributed endpoint routing," Proceedings of the Hot Interconnects IV, 141 (1996)

[3] Y. Suemura *et al.*, "1 Gbyte/s error-free optical interconnection using a forward error-correcting code," Technical Digest of the OFC'96, WH7 (1996)

[4] Y. Maeno *et al.*, "A novel interconnection network using semiconductor optical amplifier gate switches for shared memory multiprocessors," Proceedings of the MPPOI'96, 239 (1996)

[5] Y. Maeno *et al.*, "10 Gbit/s/port and 256 ports optical crossbar switch with reduced hardware and improved modularity," submitted to the 23rd ECOC (1997)

[6] S. Nakamura *et al.*, "A 4.25 GHz BiCMOS clock recovery circuit with an AV-DSPD architecture for NRZ data stream," Technical Digest of the ISSCC, 248 (1997)

[7] S. Tang *et al.*, "1-GHz clock distribution for multi-processor super computers," Proceedings of the MPPOI'96, 186 (1996)

[8] S. Takahashi *et al.*, "10 Gbps/ch space-division optical cell switching with 8×8 gate type switch matrix employing gate turn-on-delay compensator," Technical Digest of the Photonics in Switching, PThC1 (1995)

[9] G. Soulage *et al.*, "4×4 space-switch based on clamped-gain semiconductor optical amplifiers in a 16×10 Gbit/s WDM experiment," Proceedings of the 22nd ECOC, ThD.2.1 (1996)

[10] K. Hamamoto *et al.*, "Insertion-loss-free 1×4 optical switch fabricated using bandgap-energy-controlled selective MOVPE," Proceedings of the 22nd ECOC, ThD.2.3 (1996)

[11] A. Tajima *et al.*, "10 Gbit/s/port gated divider passive combiner optical switch with single-mode to multi-mode combiner," Technical Digest of the OFC, WL59 (1997)

[12] H. Kressel *eds.*, "Semiconductor devices for optical communication," chapter 4, Spriger-Verlag (1980)

[13] T. Okoshi *et al.*, "Coherent optical fiber communications," KTK/Kluwer, Tokyo/Dordrecht (1988)

[14] M. A. Shahid *et al.*, "Flexible optical backplane interconnect," Proceedings of the MPPOI'96, 178 (1996)

[15] I. Watanabe *et al.*, "Large gain-bandwidth-product, low dark-current InAlAs/InAlGaAs quaternary-well superlattice avalanche photodiodes," Technical Digest of the OFC'93, ThG1 (1993)

[16] M. Soda *et al.*, "Si-analog ICs for 20 Gb/s optical receiver," Technical Digest of the ISSCC, 170 (1994)

SESSION VI

Switches and Topological Embedding

Chair

Afonso Ferreira
CNRS-LIP

Switches and Switch Interconnects *

Lionel M. Ni , *Wenjian Qiao* and *Mingyao Yang*

Department of Computer Science
Michigan State University
East Lansing, MI 48824-1027
{ni,qiaow,yangming}@cps.msu.edu

Abstract

Switched networks are receiving much attention and supplying a major class of interconnect networks. This paper discusses major issues in switch design and switch interconnects. Due to the importance of high-speed switches in building switched LANs, major design issues are studied and several commercial switches are reviewed. Among different techniques used in switch design, cut-through switching promises short latency delivery and thus is well suited to distributed/parallel applications. The back pressure flow control of cut-through switching also prevents packet loss due to buffer overflow. For economical and practical reasons, switch interconnects should support irregular topologies, which makes deadlock-free routing more difficult. To provide good network performance, a key point is to develop a traffic-balanced network with minimum diameter and average path length. It is important to understand the issues and solutions in these areas in order to meet the increasing performance demand.

Keywords: Cut-through switching, Deadlock-free routing, Switch architecture, Switch interconnects, Network planning, Performance metrics

1 Introduction

Switch-based networks are becoming popular to meet the increasing demand for higher network performance. Traditional shared-medium Local Area Networks (LANs) do not provide satisfactory throughput and latency for some communication intensive applications, especially those emerging multimedia applications. A fast workstation can easily choke a 10Mbps Ethernet. On a shared-medium network only one host can be a sender and other hosts can only be receivers at one moment. Switch-based networks make such applications possible by providing virtual point-to-point communication. Therefore, higher bandwidth and lower latency can be achieved. Security is improved than that of share-medium networks because data on the physical link is no longer always available to every host on the subnet. Switched LANs are also an incremental approach to upgrade LAN performance since the investment in existing adapters, cables, and drivers are preserved and switched LANs still conform to widely accepted network standards. Many problems existing in shared-medium networks also occur in the switches. Therefore, good switch design and interconnection of switches play significant roles in improving LAN performance to better support distributed multimedia applications or high performance computing based on networks of workstations.

Various switching hubs are getting applied in switched LANs. Commercial products have been developed for Ethernet, Fast Ethernet, FDDI, FCS (Fiber Channel Standard), Myrinet, and ATM. The data unit to be switched in ATM networks is a fixed-size cell of 53 bytes. The data unit to be switched in traditional networks is usually a frame, which tends to be much larger than a cell. For example, the MTU (maximum transmission unit) for Ethernet and FDDI is 1500 bytes and 4352 bytes, respectively, not including the link layer header and trailer. A Myrinet [1] data packet can be an arbitrary-length byte stream constrained by the memory capacity on the host interface card.

There are two common switching techniques used in building LAN switches: store-and-forward and cut-through. Store-and-forward must keep a whole frame of data buffered before forwarding the data. The disadvantages of this approach include increased latency and buffer space, especially for frame-switching networks. Cut-through switching can forward partially received data as long as the packet header is received and decoded, thus promises low-latency delivery and relieves the burden on buffer space. Packets are sent in a pipeline fashion with cut-through switching. Furthermore, cut-through switching can provide primitive link-to-link flow control capability due to the back pressure mechanism in each link. Store-and-forward can make better decisions for corrupted or truncated frames by receiving a whole packet. Cut-through switching just

* This work was supported in part by NSF grants MIP-9204066 and MIP-9528903, DOE grant DE-FG02-93ER25167 and a grant from Hewlett-Packard Co..

0-8186-7974-3/97 $10.00 © 1997 IEEE

propagates a frame all the way to its destination. If a frame is corrupted or truncated, it may not be able to be fully removed from the network until it reaches the destination, thus wasting network bandwidth. However, in a local network environment the error rate for a data frame is generally very low. Therefore, latency-sensitive real-time applications and high performance computing will greatly benefit from cut-through switching because of its shorter latency. Cell-switching networks such as ATM also pipeline data due to small fixed cell size. However, there is more overhead involved in transmitting a packet since each cell carries a fixed-size header besides payload data. In contrast, frame-switching networks allow variable packet size and have relatively less overhead incurred by headers if the frame size is large. Many new generation switches support cut-through switching, such as the DEC GIGAswitch [2] for FDDI networks, the Ancor FCS 266/1062 [3] switches for FCS networks, the Myricom Myrinet [1], and many new generation Switched Ethernet [4]. Note that cut-through switching is different from virtual cut-through switching, where a large buffer will hold the entire packet when the outgoing channel is in use.

Switch interconnects, i.e. switched networks, are supplying a major class of interconnect networks. In a switched network, each host computer has a network adapter connecting to a switch. When the scale of the network increases due to the increasing number of host computers and the increasing demand of aggregate network bandwidth, more switches can be added to the network. To design a economical and practical switched network, irregular interconnection of switches should be supported. A key issue to solve in cut-through switching is deadlock resulted from circular blocking of a number of packets. The design of an appropriate network topology is also a complex undertaking.

The objective of this paper is to identify those issues in the design of switches and switch interconnects. The paper is organized as follows. The design issues of switches, especially cut-through switches are discussed in Section 2. Section 3 reviews the technical properties of some commercial switches. In Section 4, we discuss the major issues in switched networks and present some existing solutions to them. Finally, Section 5 concludes the paper.

2 Switch Design Considerations

A high-level view of a cut-through switch architecture is shown in Figure 1. Its function is to switch packets from input ports to output ports. The switch fabric is based on many small switching elements. Switch modules are built from switching elements, where a switch module is usually a physical chip. A switch board is built from a number of interconnected switch modules. A switch consists of many stacked switch boards, where the number of switch boards is determined by the switch capacity, i.e., the number of ports.

When a MAC-layer frame arrives, a routing tag is added to the front of the frame immediately after destination MAC address is available for its routing decision. Then the frame is routed through the switch to the output port using the routing tag. The routing tag is stripped at the output port and the frame is delivered to a destination host or another switch. An internal packet includes a routing tag, MAC-layer header and trailer, and payload data.

There are some input FIFO buffers for packets which cannot be delivered immediately because of port/channel contention in the switch. Some output FIFO buffers are available to accommodate network links of different speed. Cut-through switching pipelines a packet through a sequence of switches without fully buffering the packet at each switch.

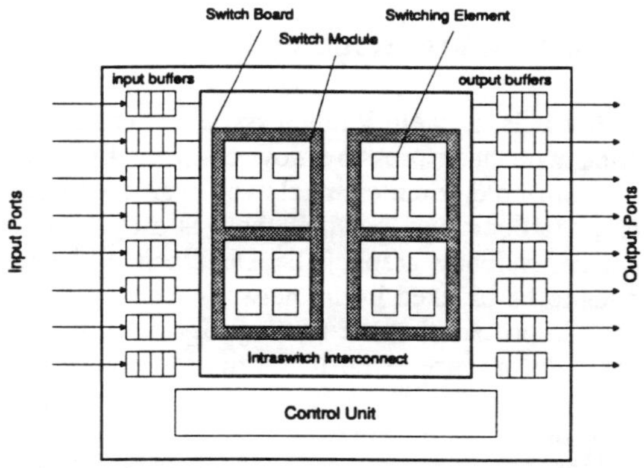

Figure 1. A high-level view of a cut-through switch.

2.1 Link-level Back Pressure Flow Control

When the input or output buffers in a switch are nearly full, back pressure is generated. This back pressure can be propagated to the sending source to throttle it from sending more data when a packet is blocked. Thus, there is less packet loss caused by buffer overflow if this mechanism is utilized. In a local environment, most packet loss is due to buffer overflow instead of transmission error. Packet loss is generally handled by high-level network protocols which involve timeout and other overhead. Therefore, both network throughput and latency will benefit from less packet loss due to cut-through switching with link-level flow control.

2.2 Scalability and Incremental Expandability

A scalable switch means that the same switch architecture can be applied when higher performance is demanded from the switch. Therefore, bottlenecks existing in the switch architecture will severely degrade its scalability. For example, design based on a high-speed bus is not scalable. The bandwidth of a bus is constrained by some physical limits. The bus becomes a bottleneck when the bandwidth for each port needs to be increased beyond some point. Design based on shared memory is not scalable either because the memory latency and bandwidth of dual-ported memory module limits the performance of the switch.

The scale of a switch tends to grow with the increasing number of hosts connected to it. To achieve good expandability in switches, modular design is usually followed. A switch is constructed from switch boards which are also built from some building modules. Ideally the minimum requirement to expand a switch to the next allowed configuration is a single switch board. For example, if a switch board has four input and output ports, it is more economic to expand the switch by adding four ports, that is one switch board at a time rather than having to add at least eight or even more extra ports.

2.3 Deadlock-Free Routing

Deadlock is a well known issue in cut-through switching with back pressure flow control. Because a message can hold some channels and wait for another channel, deadlock may occur if there is a cycle in the channel dependency graph [5]. Deadlock will cause messages to be blocked in the network forever. Therefore, it is important that the routing algorithm is deadlock free. In practice, even if the routing algorithm is deadlock free, deadlock may still occur due to some hardware or software errors, such as a lost trailer signal. A long-period timeout to force a packet out of the network can be used to avoid deadlocks completely for such rare cases [6].

There are two levels of deadlock freedom in a switch-based network. One guarantees that within a switch the routing is deadlock free, i.e., if the whole network is connected to a single switch, deadlock never happens. This may be referred to as *intra-switch deadlock freedom*. The other guarantees that the switching in a network which is interconnected by more than one switch is deadlock free. This may also be referred to as *inter-switch deadlock freedom*. To achieve inter-switch deadlock freedom, careful considerations need to be made on switch design, network topology and routing algorithm.

2.4 Nonblocking vs. Blocking

Nonblocking switch guarantees that any routing request to any free output port can be supported without interference with other packets being routed. Nonblocking switches have dedicated bandwidth for each port and is helpful to guarantee the quality of service for some applications.

Nonblocking switch is also important to inter-switch deadlock freedom when transmitting data through several interconnected cut-through switches without buffering messages between switches [7]. For a network environment which only requires intra-switch deadlock freedom, blocking switches may well meet the performance requirement. Nonblocking switches help in an environment which requires inter-switch deadlock freedom.

2.5 Packaging and Layout Issues

For ease of maintenance and expandability, the switch design must follow a modular approach. There may be many hierarchies of modules, from chips to switch boards. How to efficiently design 2D layout on a board and stack switch boards in 3D is a critical engineering issue. When a switch is expanded or reconfigured due to fault, it is desirable that minimum number of rewiring is required. Packaging of a switch decides the physical space consumed, wiring complexity, wire length, whether a switch is stackable, easy to configure and maintain, and ready for expansion [7].

2.6 Hardware Multicast

Multicast communications are critical in teleconferencing, video-on-demand, distributed computing, and so forth. Conventional shared-medium networks have a very natural way to support multicast/broadcast communications. In a switch-based network, however, each switch must possess multicast capability. Hardware multicast in networks based on cut-through switching with back pressure flow control is not a trivial task because it is very difficult to prevent deadlock. A multicast capable cut-through switch design was proposed in [7].

2.7 Fault Tolerance

It is likely that one or more of the building modules of a switch are faulty sometime. A fault tolerant switch either can continue to function well regardless of the faulty module(s), or is able to function well by making minimal reconfiguration to the existing boards, without adding new good boards. We call the former on-line fault tolerance and the latter board-level fault tolerance. On-line fault tolerance can afford faulty boards without loss of service. Board-level fault tolerance may lose some service upon failure but allows quick and easy recovery.

3 Switch Examples

3.1 Myrinet

Myrinet [1] supports cut-through switching in arbitrary local network topologies. It was developed from two research projects: Caltech Mosaic [8] which was a multicomputer and USC/ISI ATOMIC [9] which was a high-speed local area network built using Mosaic components.

A Myrinet network consists of a number of Myrinet switches and host interfaces. Myrinet can be both a LAN of relatively small physical diameter and a System Area Network (SAN) that clusters computer components. A Myrinet link has a full-duplex pair of Myrinet channels. Each channel carries a sequence of 9-bit characters. A SAN channel operate at 1.28 Gb/s up to 3 meters. A

LAN channel operate at 1.28 Gb/s up to 10 meters or at half this speed up to 25 meters. The core of a Myrinet switch is a pipelined crossbar for cut-through switching. A custom VLSI CMOS chip that implements link level protocol and flow control have SAN ports. Another custom VLSI COMS chip can translate SAN ports to LAN ports. Flow control is done on each physical channel with STOP and GO control characters and "slack buffer" at the receiver. A slack buffer has 80 bytes. A STOP control character is sent to the sender when the slack buffer begins to be filled with more than 48 bytes and a GO control character is sent to the sender when data in the slack buffer drops to less than 32 bytes. An 8-bit CRC character is computed on each packet. Low-latency and low-error-rate communication is achieved in Myrinet with its cut-through switching, flow control and error control.

A Myrinet Control Program (MCP) is running on each host interface. MCP interacts with host to send packets from the host to the network or deliver incoming packets to the host. MCP also maps network addresses to routes. The routing algorithm is designed to be deadlock free. Up/down routing [10] is currently being used. Deadlock due to hardware failure is guarded against with a long timeout of 50ms.

3.2 ServerNet

ServerNet [11] is a SAN which integrates I/O transfers and inter-processor communication within the same network. Scalable I/O is achieved by decoupling processor buses from I/O buses with an interconnection network between processors and I/O components. The basic components of ServeNet include six-way crossbar routers, dual-ported processor interfaces on a PCI card and low-cost peripheral-device interfaces. The addressing and routing provided by ServerNet can support communications between CPUs, from CPUs to I/O devices, or between I/O devices. ServerNet allows reliable, scalable and powerful computing systems to be built using clustered commodity components.

A ServerNet router has FIFO buffers on the inputs, logic for arbitration and flow control, a routing table and a crossbar switch. Cut-through switching is implemented by the routers to provide low latency communication. Link-level flow control prevents packet loss during network congestion. Six-port switches allow various network topologies such as hypercube, mesh, and tree. Routing is based on table lookup. The 1024 entry routing table maps the destination address in the packet header to the output port. Deadlock freedom is achieved by routing table entry design. Configurations with circular dependencies are disallowed. New topologies called "fractahedrons" [12] were proposed for ServerNet deadlock avoidance.

3.3 Ethernet Switches

Ethernet has been the most popular local area network for more than a decade. As more and more communication intensive applications appear, tradition shared-medium Ethernet is approaching bottle status. To achieve higher bandwidth, Ethernet switching hubs are being deployed to replace traditional shared-medium Ethernet.

There are generally three switching modes in an Ethernet switch: fast-forward (cut-through), fragment-free, and store-and-forward. Store-and-forward buffers a whole frame, makes an error check, and forwards the frame. Invalid frames are filtered out. To cut switching latency, a packet can be partially received before it begins to be forwarded. In fast-forward, a frame is switched as soon as the destination address or a few more following bytes are received. Corrupted packets may be propagated through the network since they are forwarded before frame errors can be detected. Fragment-free switching buffers at least 64 bytes of data before switching is made. Buffering 64 bytes of data allows Ethernet collision fragments to be filtered out. Collision may happen often in a heavily loaded network, such as when a port is shared by many host interfaces. A good Ethernet switch design should be able to select the switching mode adaptively based on the network traffic conditions.

In a client/server computing environment, a server is shared by many clients and requires higher network bandwidth than a client. This can be achieved by using switches which support both Ethernet and Fast Ethernet ports. A server can be connected to a Fast Ethernet port for higher bandwidth. When switching a frame from an Ethernet port (10Mb/s) to a Fast Ethernet port (100Mb/s), store-and-forward is necessary to adjust the speed difference of input and output ports. When switching a frame from a Fast Ethernet port to an Ethernet port, a frame can be partially received before being switched.

Back pressure mechanism can also be applied in Ethernet switches to keep the sending source from delivering more frames to an overloaded port. A congested port can fake collision-detection frames which let the sending source think that collision is occurring and back off its attempt to send a frame according to CSMA/CD protocol [4].

Each Ethernet port can support multiple MAC addresses which may correspond to individual workstations, repeaters, or switches. Address learning can be done by automatically learn the source address of frames received on each port. Address table can also be manually maintained. Old addresses not in use are aged out from the address table. Spanning-Tree protocol (part of IEEE 802.1d standard) is generally used to interoperate between compliant bridges and switches. Spanning tree allows networks to dynamically maintain a loop-free topology and establish redundant paths in event of lost connections.

Some Ethernet switches allow virtual LANs to be built. Ports on the switch are grouped into separate logical networks. Virtual LAN limits broadcast traffic and offers higher security.

4 Switch Interconnects

The interconnection of those switches defines various network topologies. Regular network topologies do not have good incremental scalability due to the stringent interconnection constraints and may not be able to use the original routing schemes with faulty nodes. Therefore, a natural approach is to allow irregular switch interconnects like Autonet [13], Myrinet, and ServerNet. Irregular switched networks are truly incrementally scalable and have potential to be reconfigured to adapt to the dynamics of network traffic. Many challenging issues need to be studied in a switched network. Some major tasks include routing and flow control, topology design and incremental reconfiguration, traffic pattern, performance evaluation, reliability, scalability, and fault tolerance.

4.1 Routing Algorithms

Routing plays an important role in a switched network. Routing decision is usually implemented based on table lookup or on a finite state machine. An important engineering issue is to make the routing decision as fast as possible. A major difficulty in constructing a large-scale network with cut-through switches is to avoid deadlock among simultaneously transmitting frames. Irregular switch interconnects make the problem even harder. Three philosophies have been used to develop deadlock-free routing algorithms. One is based on deadlock prevention which never allows the formation of a cycle and is quite conservative. Another approach allows the existence of cycles [14, 15], but does provide a path to escape from the cycle. The third and more aggressive approach is based on deadlock detection [16]. Practical, convincing, and meaningful quantitative evidence is needed to demonstrate the superiority of one approach over other approaches.

For regular topologies like k-ary n-cube, many deadlock-free routing algorithms have been proposed in literature. For irregular switched networks, the first known deadlock-free routing algorithm is probably the up*/down* routing used in the DEC AN1 system [13]. A similar approach is used in the Myrinet. In the up*/down* algorithm, a breadth-first spanning tree is constructed from a selected root. Based on the direction to the root node, the network is divided into two acyclic subnetworks (up and down). When a packet enters the down subnetwork, it will never enter the up subnetwork to ensure cycle free. The algorithm is simple and easy to understand, but it may introduce severe traffic congestion near the root and allow a routing path as twice long as a shortest path.

Some other routing algorithms have been proposed as well. Adaptive-trail routing (ATR) was proposed in [17] to allow deadlock-free adaptive routing in irregular switched networks. The basic idea of ATR is using an Eulerian trail as a 'base line' to maintain channel dependency order and allow reasonable routing. To minimize the path length, shortcuts are added to the Eulerian trail. The smart routing (SR) [18] created a channel dependency graph from the network topology and broke dependency cycles one by one, which minimized a heuristic cost function based on average path length. The routing is represented by the final non-cyclic channel dependency graph. The traffic balancing, which assumed uniform traffic, depends on a linear programming solver and is the most time consuming part.

Graph partitioning is applied in [19] to avoid deadlock. To evaluate it in irregular networks, a simple and efficient implementation has to be enforced, which may not be intuitive. A recent research [20] proposed a general methodology for the design of adaptive routing algorithms in irregular topologies. In this method, all physical channels are split into two virtual channels: 'original channels' and 'new channels'. For 'original channels', a deadlock-free routing algorithm like up*/down* is defined. A message can only leave source from 'new channels', but it can use 'original channels' at intermediate switches if none of 'new channels' is available. Once a message is transmitted on any 'original channel', it cannot go back to 'new channels' any more.

Extensive simulation experiments have been conducted to evaluate the performance of up*/down*, ATR, and SR under different topologies and workloads [21]. It is observed in the simulations that a premature bottleneck channel is one main reason to cause poor network performance. The SR is the only algorithm putting significant effort and computation time to balance channel traffic. Note that traffic balancing should be guided by real traffic pattern in the network. The SR assumes a unrealistic traffic pattern, uniform traffic, so it may not provide better performance in non-uniform (e.g., client/server) traffic. A good heuristic routing algorithm may have good network performance under many network conditions. For example, a much more simple algorithm ATR can offer as good performance as SR in most cases [21]. However, to achieve near optimal performance, traffic balancing should be considered if routing table computation time is not very critical.

4.2 Topology Design and Reconfiguration

The design of an appropriate network topology can be a complex undertaking and the configuration of a traffic-balanced network is not an easy task. A systematic method should be applied in topology design, which concerns some basic parameters. The key parameters are the number of switches, the number of ports per switch and the bandwidth of each port, the required number of host computers, the estimated traffic distribution, and the average path length.

When designing a network topology, a primary consideration should be minimizing diameter and the average path length. Longer paths mean more network resources are consumed per packet sent. Although it is a difficult problem to find a network with a minimal average path length, there are still some basic ideas that can make it easier. In general, each channel should run between a unique pair of switches; extra channels between a particular pair of switches does not decrease the path length, and almost always more performance can be gained by connecting two otherwise unconnected switches. If a significant fraction of traffic flows among a set of end computers (i.e., a workgroup), we should consider to place them on the same switch if possible, or on two switches connected by at most one hop.

In addition to minimizing average path length, there should be no obvious bottleneck. Such a bottleneck might be a single switch connected with only one or two channels. It is also important to ensure that the bisection is not too small, because such a 'channel cut' is usually a performance bottleneck.

Network planners need to be responsive to the demands of client/server traffic. A server contention may become a main bottleneck because many clients communicate with the server. A key part of scaling network performance is to eliminate bottlenecks to servers. Based on the server's throughput capacity, dedicated bandwidth is needed to release server bottleneck.

To provide good network performance, a key point is to balance traffic flow among channels. It is important to know the real or estimated traffic distribution. For a particular topology, given routing algorithm and estimated traffic distribution, traffic flow on each channel and the maximum attainable aggregate flow can be calculated with a multi-commodity flow solver. This solution will also identify bottleneck channels.

After a network is operational, it may need to be reconfigured because more network resources are available, the traffic pattern may change, or the network performance is under desire. Therefore, one practical question is how to make a minor change to a network to obtain a significant improvement in performance.

The first step is to diagnose what causes the problem. If the real traffic distribution is much different from the estimated traffic distribution, the topology and routing algorithm may need to be redesigned. If the average path length of routing is much longer than the average path length of the base topology, chances are that experimenting with some additional routing strategies might improve the performance significantly. If neither the routing nor the base topology is the problem, additional resources may need to be added. If there are spare ports on any switches, additional channels might be added to yield a performance increase. In general, additional channels should be added between switches that are a maximum distance apart (taking some long paths and making them shorter), or between switches that have few channels attached already.

If adding one or more channels is not possible or does not provide adequate performance improvement, one or more switches can be added. To add a switch to an existing network, it may be necessary to connect a number of channels to switches that are as widely spaced (with respect to path length) as possible. We may consider to redistribute some end nodes to the new switch. When adding channels or switches, the routing should be recalculated from scratch. Such a change has a profound impact on the path length and potential deadlock in the system. Since most of these switches have configurable routing tables, this yields a practical solution.

4.3 Traffic Characteristics and Measurement

Some common characteristics of LAN traffic have been observed in previous work. It is found that both transmitted and received traffic patterns are highly asymmetric, which can be explained as the consideration of client/server traffic model. Another observation is the existence of workgroups, which means that a large portion of traffic is localized among relative small workgroups of host computers. 'Bursty traffic' is also an important traffic activity of local area networks. This burstiness causes congestion within the network which reduces the overall network performance.

To manage network performance and reconfigure a network, it is important to measure network usage and traffic flow. Many LAN switches support standard-based simple network management protocol (SNMP) management, which can be used to collect information about network traffic passing through each port of a switch.

4.4 Performance Metrics and Evaluation

From an application program's point of view, the most important performance metric of a network is *communication latency*, which is the time interval between the instant that a send command is issued until the instant that the message is completely received by the recipient. The metric communication latency consists of network latency (including the blocking time due to unavailable output channels) and software latency, which is software overhead introduced by the sender and receiver.

From the network point of view, an important metric is *network throughput* which is defined as the total amount of traffic transmitted in the network per unit of time. The *sustained network throughput* is dependent on the communication pattern, message size distribution, and the rate at which each node is able to inject messages into the network. Due to the limitation of network contention and output contention, the maximum sustained network throughput is usually much smaller than the maximum theoretical network throughput.

Once the network load exceeds some limit (where some queues are filling up and become bottlenecks), fairness may become a major concern; some ports will essentially starve while others will inject more traffic. In such a case, the aggregate throughput may not be enough to indicate the actual network performance. Thus, *fairness ratio* is introduced as the ratio of the maximum traffic generated in a node over the minimum traffic generated in a node.

For a given network workload, the performance of a switched network is best represented by its latency-throughput curve as shown in Fig. 2. This figure shows that the network throughput can reach up to 19% of the network's maximum throughput. The average network latency increases when the throughput increases. However, when more messages are injected into the network after the network has reached its maximum sustainable throughput, the network throughput will decrease while the average network latency will continuously increase, creating the so-called over-saturated or unstable region. In such a situation, unfairness may be caused among end nodes and the unfair cases are marked with a shaded rectangle in Fig. 2.

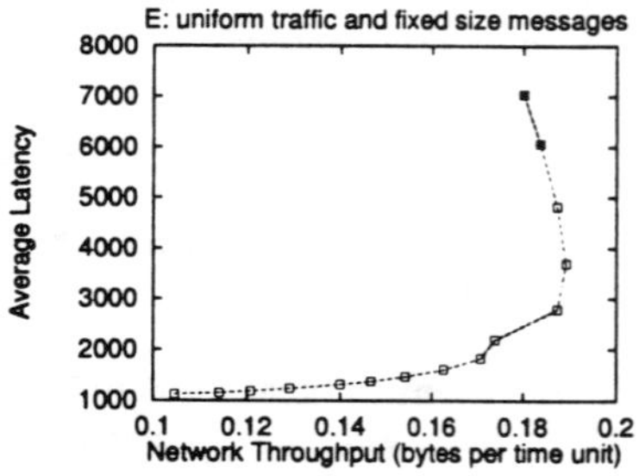

Figure 2. An example of an irregular switched network

Both analytic models and simulation results can be used to evaluate network performance. By assuming the knowledge of network workload and applying multicommodity flow model and queuing theory, a good analytic model may indicate message latency and bottleneck channel and obtain optimal or sub-optimal solutions for network design. However, due to the dynamic nature of networking environments, analytic modeling is unlikely to give practical insight to the network behavior and performance. Simulation experiments can be conducted to show the performance. But we can hardly trust the simulation results as well. For example, most of the network simulation studies do not consider software latency and assume an infinite input source. This may lead researchers to investigate something that may never (or very rarely) occur in an actual network. Even worse, most of the models used to characterize the network workload are far from realistic. Trace-driven or execution-driven simulation based on real applications should be considered.

4.5 Other Issues

Topology design will be further complicated by topological constraints (such as reliability or physical layout constraints) upon the network. To consider reliability, a traditional method is to make more than one switch-disjointed path available between each pair of sources and destinations.

It is clear that efficient multicast communication support is critical to the performance of many applications. A recent paper [22] proposed heuristic multicast algorithms in switched networks, which assumed the underlying routing algorithm is up*/down* routing. While efficient multicast communication is becoming very important and obtaining much attention, multiple multicasts and the effect of background traffic should be considered as well. Since the performance of multicast algorithms are various on different platforms, a practical approach is to consider some critical machine-specific parameters in the design of platform-independent algorithms as proposed in [23].

In large scale networks, the probability of having a faulty channel or switch is relatively high. An intuitive solution is to simply shutdown the system and replace the faulty elements. In addition to some simple solutions like redundancy, a practical and useful scheme is demanded to automatically detect faulty elements, handle dynamic faults, properly deal with transmitting messages, isolate faulty elements for live replacement, and avoid routing deadlock [24].

Flow control determines the amount of packets that can be injected into the network in order to avoid congestion. As indicated in Fig. 2, without proper flow control, the network throughput will decrease after reaching its maximal. In addition to local flow control like link-level back-pressure in cut-through switching, there also needs global flow control (e.g., end-to-end flow control) to limit the total number of packets that can be handled by network simultaneously. If flow control mechanism works properly, further input to network should be stopped well before the network is over-saturated.

5 Conclusions

This paper studied the major issues in the design of switches and switched networks. A good switch design is important to improve the performance of a switched network. To design a scalable and expandable switch, switch architecture should avoid any bottleneck and adopt proper modular design. To guarantee a deadlock-free inter-switch routing scheme, nonblocking switches are usually assumed. For practical and economical reasons, switched networks should support irregular topologies. It is challenging to develop an efficient deadlock-free routing algorithm under irregular topologies using cut-through switches. To achieve good performance, a key point is to design a traffic-balanced network and avoid bottleneck. A practical method is to make a minor change of a network to obtain a significant improvement in performance. This should be guided by monitoring network behavior and diagnosing traffic bottleneck.

Switches and switched networks are receiving much attention and becoming the trend to support the increasing demand of higher network performance. New technologies continue to be proposed in these areas. For many issues discussed in this paper, further study is demanded to propose new and practical solutions to support the changing environment.

References

[1] N. J. Boden and et al, "Myrinet – a Gigabit-per-second local area network," *IEEE Micro*, vol. 15, pp. 29 – 36, Feb. 1995.

[2] R. J. Souza and et al, "The GIGAswitch system: A high-performance packet switching platform," *Digital Technical Journal*, vol. 6, Jan. 1994.

[3] Ancor Communications Inc. *http://www.ancor.com/cxt.html.*

[4] T. W. Giorgis, "29 switching hubs save the bandwidth," *BYTE*, pp. 162 – 169, July 1995.

[5] L. M. Ni and P. K. McKinley, "A survey of wormhole routing techniques in direct networks," *IEEE Computer*, vol. 26, pp. 62 – 76, Feb. 1993.

[6] Myricom, "Myrinet link specification," *http://www.myri.com/products/documentation/link/.*

[7] M. Yang and L. M. Ni, "Design of scalable and multicast capable cut-through switches for high-speed lans," *accepted to appear in the Proceedings of the 1997 International Conference on Parallel Processing*, Aug. 1997.

[8] C. Seitz and et al, "The design of the Caltech Mosaic C multicomputer," *Proceedings of the University of Washington Symposium on Integrated Systems*, 1993.

[9] D. Cohen and G. Finn, "ATOMIC: A low-cost, very-high-speed, local communication architecture," in *Proceedings of the 1993 International Conference on Parallel Processing*, vol. I, pp. 39 – 46, Aug. 1993.

[10] M. Schroeder and et al., "Autonet: a high-speed, self-configuring, local area network using point-to-point links," *IEEE Journal on Selected Areas in Communications*, vol. 9, Oct. 1991.

[11] R. Horst, "TNet: A reliable system area network," *IEEE Micro*, pp. 36 – 44, Feb. 1995.

[12] R. Horst, "ServerNet deadlock avoidance and fractahefral topologies," *Proceedings of the International Parallel Processing Symposium*, pp. 274 – 280, Apr. 1996.

[13] S. S. Owicki and A. R. Karlin, "Factors in the performance of the AN1 computer network," *Performance Evaluation Review*, vol. 20, pp. 167 – 180, June 1992.

[14] J. Duato, "Deadlock-free message routing in multiprocessor interconnection networks," *IEEE Transactions on Parallel and Distributed System*, vol. 4, Nov. 1993.

[15] X. Lin, P. McKinley, and L. Ni, "The message flow model for routing in wormhole-routed networks," *IEEE Transactions on Parallel and Distributed Systems*, pp. 755 – 760, July 1995.

[16] A. K. VenKatramani and T. M. Pinkston, "An efficient fully adaptive deadlock recovery scheme: DISHA," *Proceedings of the 22nd International Symposium on Computer Architecture*, pp. 201 – 210, June 1995.

[17] W. Qiao and L. M. Ni, "Adaptive routing in irregular networks using cut-throughput switches," *Proceedings of the 1996 International Conference on Parallel Processing*, vol. 1, pp. 52 – 60, Aug. 1996.

[18] L. Cherkasova, V. Kotov, and T. Rokicki, "Fibre channel fabrics: Evaluation and design," *29th Hawaii International Conference on System Sciences*, Feb. 1995.

[19] B. Abali, "A deadlock avoidance method for computer networks," *Proceedings of the First International Workshop on Communication and Architectural Support for Network-based Parallel Computing*, pp. 61 – 72, Feb. 1997.

[20] F. Silla, M. Malumbres, A. Robles, P. Lopez, and J. Duato, "Efficient adaptive routing in networks of workstations with irregular topology," *Proceedings of the First International Workshop on Communication and Architectural Support for Network-based Parallel Computing*, pp. 46 – 60, Feb. 1997.

[21] W. Qiao and L. M. Ni, "Evaluate routing algorithms in cut-through switched networks," Tech. Rep. MSU-CPS-ACS-96-07, Michigan State Univ., Dept. of Computer Science, June 1996.

[22] R. Kevavan, K. Bondalapati, and D. Panda, "Multicast on irregular switch-based networks with wormhole routing," *Third International Symposium on High Performance Computer Architecture (HPCA-3)*, pp. 48 – 57, Feb. 1997.

[23] J. L. Park, H. Choi, N. Nupairoj, and L. M. Ni, "Construction of optimal multicast trees based on the parameterized communication model," *Proceedings of International Conference on Parallel Processing*, vol. 1, pp. 180 – 187, Aug. 1996.

[24] L. M. Ni, "Issues in designing truly scalable interconnection networks," *Proc. of the 1996 ICPP Workshop on Challenges for Parallel Processing*, pp. 74 – 83, Aug. 1996.

BPC Permutations On The OTIS-Mesh Optoelectronic Computer*

Sartaj Sahni and Chih-fang Wang
Department of Computer and Information Science and Engineering
University of Florida
Gainesville, FL 32611
{sahni,wang}@cise.ufl.edu

Abstract

We show that the diameter of an N^2 processor OTIS-Mesh is $4\sqrt{N} - 3$. Two possible embeddings of an $N \times N$ mesh onto an OTIS-Mesh are evaluated. OTIS-Mesh algorithms for some commonly performed permutations – transpose, bit reversal, vector reversal, perfect shuffle, unshuffle, shuffled row-major, and bit shuffle – are developed. We also propose an algorithm for general BPC permutations.

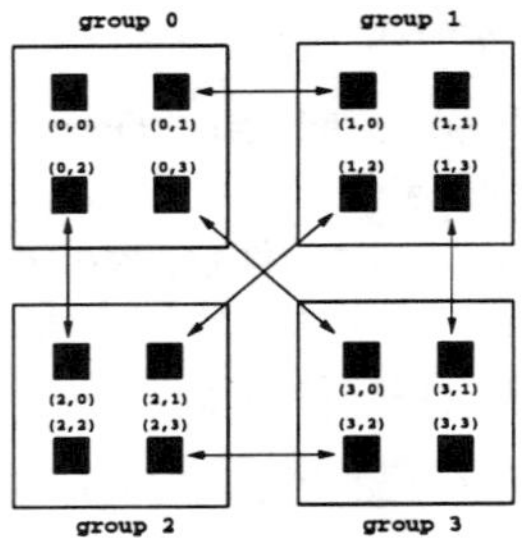

Figure 1. Example of OTIS connections with 16 processors

1. Introduction

Marsden *et al.* [6], Hendrick *et al.* [2], and Zane *et al.* [9] have proposed large scale parallel computer architectures in which the processors are divided into groups. Each group of processors is realized using one or more high density chips or modules with electronic interprocessor connections. Interconnections between processors in different groups are realized via free space optics. These optoelectronic architectures use electronic interconnects over short distances (i.e., for the local intra group interconnects) and free space optics for the longer inter group interconnects. This is so as it is known [1] [3] that free space optical connects provide power, speed, and crosstalk advantages over electronic interconnects when the connect distance is more than a few millimeters. Further, when optical interconnects are used, the per group I/O bandwidth increases in proportion to the group's layout area while when electronic interconnects are used, this bandwidth grows in proportion to the layout perimeter.

Krishnamoorthy *et al.* [4] have shown that the bandwidth and power consumption are minimized when the number of processors in a group equal the number of groups. That is when an N^2 processor system is partitioned into N groups each containing N processors. As a result, we limit our study of optoelectronic architectures to those partitioned in this manner. The specific optoelectronic architecture proposed by Marsden *et al.* [6] employs the optical transpose interconnection system (OTIS). In this, processor i of group j is connected to processor j of group i via an optical link. Figure 1 shows a 16 processor OTIS architecture. The processor indices are represented as pairs of the form (G, P) where G is the group index and P the processor index (within the group).

Some of the suggested topologies for the intra group electronic connections are mesh, hypercube, and mesh of trees [6]. These, respectively, result in the OTIS-Mesh, OTIS-Hypercube, and OTIS-MT optoelectronic architectures. Figure 2 shows a 16 processor OTIS-Mesh computer. The processors of groups 0 and 2 are labeled using two dimensional local mesh coordinates while the processors in groups 1 and 3 are labeled in row major fashion.

Zane *et al.* [9] have shown that the OTIS-Mesh can simulate each move of an $\sqrt{N} \times \sqrt{N} \times \sqrt{N} \times \sqrt{N}$ four dimensional mesh by using either an electronic move local to a group or one local electronic move and two inter group moves using the OTIS (or optical) interconnection. We shall refer to the latter as OTIS moves.

In this paper, we study the OTIS-Mesh architecture and obtain properties and basic permutation routing algorithms.

*This work was supported, in part, by the Army Research Office under grant DAA H04-95-1-0111.

0-8186-7974-3/97 $10.00 © 1997 IEEE

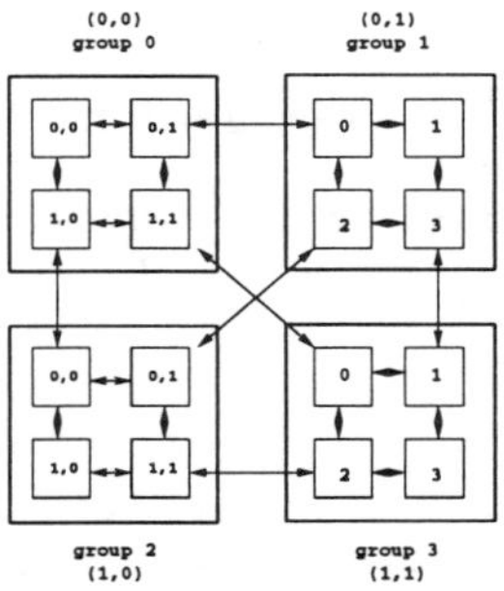

Figure 2. 16 processor OTIS-Mesh

These algorithms can in turn be used in the development of efficient application codes. We begin, in Section 2, by deriving the diameter (i.e., maximum distance between any two processors) of the OTIS-Mesh. In Section 3, we consider the problem of embedding a two dimensional $N \times N$ mesh into an N^2 processor OTIS-Mesh. Algorithms to perform popular data rearrangements such as transpose, reversal, and shuffle are developed in Section 4. An algorithm for general BPC (bit permute complement) permutations is presented in Section 5.

2. OTIS-Mesh Diameter

Let (G_1, P_1) and (G_2, P_2) be two OTIS-Mesh processors. The shortest path between these two processors is of one of the forms:

(a) The path involves only electronic moves. This is possible only when $G_1 = G_2$.

(b) The path involves an even number of optical (i.e., OTIS) moves. If the number of OTIS moves is more than two, we may compress paths of this form into the shorter path $(G_1, P_1) \xrightarrow{E} (G_1, P_2) \xrightarrow{O} (P_2, G_1) \xrightarrow{E} (P_2, G_2) \xrightarrow{O} (G_2, P_2)$. Here E denotes a sequence (possibly empty) of electronic moves and O denotes a single OTIS move.

So, we may assume that the path is of the above form with exactly two OTIS moves.

(c) The path involves an odd number of OTIS moves. In this case, it must involve exactly one OTIS move (as otherwise it may be compressed into a shorter path with just one OTIS move as in (b)) and may be assumed to be of the form $(G_1, P_1) \xrightarrow{E} (G_1, G_2) \xrightarrow{O} (G_2, G_1) \xrightarrow{E} (G_2, P_2)$.

Let $d(i, j)$ be the shortest distance between processors i and j of a group using a path comprised solely of electronic moves. So, $d(i, j)$ is the Manhattan distance between the two processors of the local mesh group. Shortest paths of type (a) have length $d(P_1, P_2)$ while those of types (b) and (c) have length $d(P_1, P_2) + d(G_1, G_2) + 2$ and $d(P_1, G_2) + d(P_2, G_1) + 1$, respectively.

The preceding development results in

Theorem 1 *The length of the shortest path between processors (G_1, P_1) and (G_2, P_2) is $d(P_1, P_2)$ when $G_1 = G_2$ and $\min\{d(P_1, P_2) + d(G_1, G_2) + 2, d(P_1, G_2) + d(P_2, G_1) + 1\}$ when $G_1 \neq G_2$.*

Theorem 2 *The diameter of the OTIS-Mesh is $4\sqrt{N} - 3$.*

Proof See [8]. □

3. Embedding Of An $N \times N$ Mesh

Zane *et al.* [9] have shown that a $\sqrt{N} \times \sqrt{N} \times \sqrt{N} \times \sqrt{N}$ mesh may be embedded into an N^2 processor OTIS-Mesh so that each mesh move may be performed by either one electronic OTIS-Mesh move or one electronic and two optical OTIS-Mesh moves. The embedding is rather straightforward with processor (i, j, k, l) of the mesh being identified with processor (G, P), $G = i\sqrt{N} + j$, $P = k\sqrt{N} + l$ of the OTIS-Mesh. The mesh moves $(i, j, k \pm 1, l)$ and $(i, j, k, l \pm 1)$ can be performed with one electronic move of the OTIS-Mesh while the moves $(i, j \pm 1, k, l)$ and $(i \pm 1, j, k, l)$ require one electronic and two optical moves. For example, the move $(i, j + 1, k, l)$ may be done by the sequence $(i, j, k, l) \xrightarrow{O} (k, l, i, j) \xrightarrow{E} (k, l, i, j + 1) \xrightarrow{O} (i, j + 1, k, l)$.

The above efficient embedding of a 4D mesh implies that 4D mesh algorithms can be run on the OTIS-Mesh with a constant factor (at most 3) slowdown [9]. Unfortunately, the body of known 4D mesh algorithms is very small compared to that of 2D mesh algorithms. So, it is desirable to consider a 2D mesh embedding. Such an embedding will enable one to run 2D mesh algorithms on the OTIS-Mesh. Naturally, one would do this only for problems for which no 4D algorithm is known or for which the known 4D mesh algorithms are not faster than the 2D algorithms.

There are at least two intuitively appealing ways to embed an $N \times N$ mesh into the OTIS-Mesh. One is the *group row mapping* (GRM) in which each group of the OTIS-Mesh represents a row of the 2D mesh. The mapping of the mesh row onto a group of OTIS processors is done in a snake-like fashion as in Figure 3(a). The pair of numbers in each processor of Figure 3(a) gives the (row,column) index of the mapped 2D mesh processor. The thick edges show the electronic connections used to obtain the 2D mesh row. Notice that the assignment of rows to groups is also done in a snake-like manner. Let (i, j) denote a processor of a 2D mesh. The move to $(i, j + 1)$ (or $(i, j - 1)$) can be done with one electronic move as (i, j) and $(i, j + 1)$ are neighbors in a processor group. If all elements of row i are

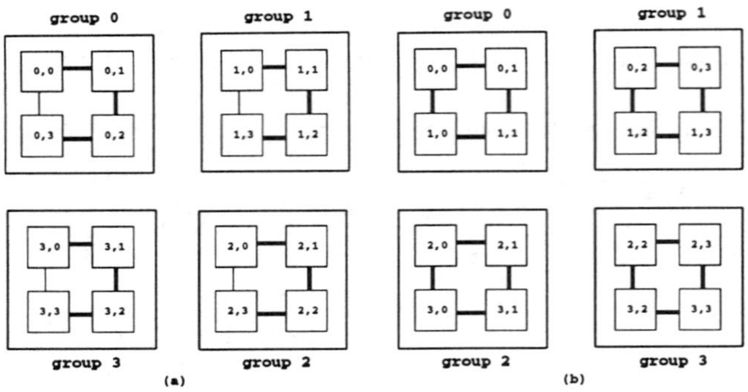

Figure 3. Mapping a 4×4 mesh onto a 16 processor OTIS-Mesh: (a) GRM; (b) GSM

to be moved over one column, then the OTIS-Mesh would need one electronic move in case of a MIMD mesh and 3 in case of a SIMD mesh as the row move would involve a shift by one left, right, and down within a group. A column shift can be done with 2 additional OTIS moves as in the case of a 4D mesh embedding. GRM is particularly nice for the matrix transpose operation. Data from processor (i, j) can be moved to processor (j, i) with one OTIS and zero electronic moves.

The second way to embed an $N \times N$ mesh is to use the *group submesh mapping* (GSM). In this, the $N \times N$ mesh is partitioned into N $\sqrt{N} \times \sqrt{N}$ submeshes. Each of these is mapped in the natural way onto a group of OTIS-Mesh processors. Figure 3(b) shows GSM of a 4×4 mesh. Moving all elements of row or column i over by one is now considerably more expensive. For example, a row shift by $+1$ would be accomplished by the following data movements (a boundary processor is one on the right boundary of a group):

Step 1: Shift data in non-boundary processors right by one using an electronic move.

Step 2: Perform an OTIS move on boundary processor data. So, data from (G, P) moves to (P, G).

Step 3: Shift the data moved in Step 2 right by one using an electronic move. Now, data from (G, P) is in $(P, G + 1)$.

Step 4: Perform an OTIS move on this data. Now data originally in (G, P) is in $(G + 1, P)$.

Step 5: Shift this data left by $\sqrt{N} - 1$ using $\sqrt{N} - 1$ electronic moves. Now, the boundary data originally in (G, P) is in the processor to its right but in the next group.

The above five step process takes $\sqrt{N}$ electronic and two OTIS moves.

GSM is also inferior on the transpose operation which now requires $8(\sqrt{N} - 1)$ electronic and 2 OTIS moves.

Theorem 3 *The transpose operation of an $N \times N$ mesh requires $8(\sqrt{N} - 1)$ electronic and 2 OTIS moves when the GSM is used.*

Proof See [8]. □

Based on the relative performance of GRM and GSM with respect to the common mesh operations of shift by row or column and transpose, we recommend the use of GRM.

4. Common Data Rearrangements

Since an N^2 input three stage OTIS multistage interconnection network (MIN) composed of N N-input–N-output switches in each stage is rearrangeable [6] and since the N processor mesh in each group of an N^2 processor OTIS-Mesh is able to realize every permutation of N elements, an N^2 processor OTIS-Mesh can realize any permutation of N^2 data (one to each processor) using at most two OTIS moves. However, additional OTIS moves are needed to determine the local group data rearrangements that must be made. Another way to accomplish arbitrary data permutations is to use sorting. The optimal 4D mesh sorting algorithm of [5] may be run on an OTIS-Mesh using the simulation described in [9]. This yields an OTIS-Mesh sorting algorithm that takes $12\sqrt{N}$ OTIS and $14\sqrt{N}$ electronic moves.

Nassimi and Sahni [7] have developed optimal 4D mesh algorithms for several frequently arising permutations. These may be simulated using the method of [9] to obtain algorithms for the OTIS-Mesh. Table 1 gives the number of 4D mesh moves used by the optimal 4D mesh algorithms, a break down of the number of moves in the first two and last two dimensions, and the number of electronic and OTIS moves required by the simulation.

Assume that the N^2 OTIS-Mesh processors are numbered/indexed 0 through $N^2 - 1$ such that in the binary representation of a processor index the left half bits give the group number and the right half give the processor number local to a group. So, a processor index I is of the form $I = GP$ where I, G and P are represented in binary and G and P have the same number of bits. G and P may be decomposed into halves to get $G = G_x G_y$ and $P = P_x P_y$ such that G_x and G_y give the group location by row and column in an array layout of groups (as in Figure 1) and P_x and P_y locate processor P of a group by its row and column coordinates.

The permutations of Table 1 are members of the BPC (bit permute complement) class of permutations defined in [7]. In a BPC permutation, the destination processor of each data is given by a rearrangement of the bits in the source processor index. For the case of our N^2 processor

Permutation	4D mesh			OTIS-Mesh Simulation	
	total	dimension $1+2$	dimension $3+4$	OTIS	electronic
Transpose	$8(\sqrt{N}-1)$	$4(\sqrt{N}-1)$	$4(\sqrt{N}-1)$	$8(\sqrt{N}-1)$	$8(\sqrt{N}-1)$
Perfect Shuffle	$4\sqrt{N}$	$2\sqrt{N}$	$2\sqrt{N}$	$4\sqrt{N}$	$4\sqrt{N}$
Unshuffle	$4\sqrt{N}$	$2\sqrt{N}$	$2\sqrt{N}$	$4\sqrt{N}$	$4\sqrt{N}$
Bit Reversal	$8(\sqrt{N}-1)$	$4(\sqrt{N}-1)$	$4(\sqrt{N}-1)$	$8(\sqrt{N}-1)$	$8(\sqrt{N}-1)$
Vector Reversal	$8(\sqrt{N}-1)$	$4(\sqrt{N}-1)$	$4(\sqrt{N}-1)$	$8(\sqrt{N}-1)$	$8(\sqrt{N}-1)$
Bit Shuffle	$\frac{20}{3}\sqrt{N}-4$	$\frac{8}{3}\sqrt{N}-2$	$4\sqrt{N}-2$	$\frac{16}{3}\sqrt{N}-4$	$\frac{28}{3}\sqrt{N}-4$
Shuffled Row-major	$\frac{20}{3}\sqrt{N}-4$	$\frac{8}{3}\sqrt{N}-2$	$4\sqrt{N}-2$	$\frac{16}{3}\sqrt{N}-4$	$\frac{28}{3}\sqrt{N}-4$
G_yP_x Swap	$4(\sqrt{N}-1)$	$2(\sqrt{N}-1)$	$2(\sqrt{N}-1)$	$4(\sqrt{N}-1)$	$4(\sqrt{N}-1)$

Table 1. Optimal moves for 4D mesh and respective OTIS-Mesh simulations

OTIS-Mesh we assume that N is a power of two and so the number of bits needed to represent a processor index is $p = \log_2 N^2 = 2\log N$. A BPC permutation [7] is specified by a vector $A = [A_{p-1}, A_{p-2}, \ldots, A_0]$ where

(a) $A_i \in \{\pm 0, \pm 1, \ldots, \pm(p-1)\}, 0 \le i < p$ and

(b) $[|A_{p-1}|, |A_{p-2}|, \ldots, |A_0|]$ is a permutation of $[0, 1, \ldots, p-1]$.

The destination for the data in any processor may be computed in the following manner. Let $m_{p-1}m_{p-2}\ldots m_0$ be the binary representation of the processor's index. Let $d_{p-1}d_{p-2}\ldots d_0$ be that of the destination processor's index. Then,

$$d_{|A_i|} = \begin{cases} m_i & if \quad A_i \ge 0, \\ 1 - m_i & if \quad A_i < 0. \end{cases}$$

In this definition, -0 is to be regarded as < 0, while $+0$ is ≥ 0.

The permutation vector A for each of the permutations of Table 1 is provided after each subsection title.

4.1. Transpose $[p/2-1, \ldots, 0, p-1, \ldots, p/2]$

The transpose operation may be accomplished via a single OTIS move and zero electronic moves.

4.2. Perfect Shuffle $[0, p-1, p-2, \ldots, 1]$

Let $b_{G(i)}$ and $b_{P(i)}$, respectively, denote the bits in position $G(i)$ and $P(i)$ of G and P. So $b_{G(p/2-1)}$ and $b_{P(p/2-1)}$ are the most significant bits of G and P while $b_{G(0)}$ and $b_{P(0)}$ are the least. Let $G = b_{G(p/2-1)}G'$ and $P = b_{P(p/2-1)}P'$. A perfect shuffle may be performed as below:

Step 1: Perform a local perfect shuffle in each group.

Step 2: This step involves processors in groups G such that $b_{G(p/2-1)} = 0$ only. In these groups, odd processors exchange data with corresponding even processors (note that the processors exchanging data differ only in bit zero).

Step 3: Perform an OTIS move on all processors.

Step 4: Perform a local shuffle in each group.

Step 5: This step involves only processors in even groups. In these groups, odd processors exchange their data with the corresponding even processors.

Step 6: Perform an OTIS move on all processors.

Step 7: Same as Step 5.

Steps 1 and 4 perform perfect shuffles in $\sqrt{N} \times \sqrt{N}$ meshes. Each of these can be done optimally in $2\sqrt{N}$ electronic moves using the algorithm of [7]. Steps 2, 5, and 7 requires exchanging data between mesh neighbors. Each exchange moves data in opposite directions on the same link and takes two electronic moves. Steps 3 and 6 take one OTIS move each. So, the total number of moves is $4\sqrt{N}+6$ electronic and 2 OTIS only.

4.3. Unshuffle $[p-2, p-3, \ldots, 0, p-1]$

This is the inverse of a perfect shuffle and may be done by running the seven step shuffle algorithm backwards (i.e., beginning with Step 7) and replacing the local shuffles of Steps 1 and 4 by local unshuffles. The number of data moves is the same as for a perfect shuffle.

4.4. Bit Reversal $[0, 1, \ldots, p-1]$

A bit reversal can be done using one OTIS and $8(\sqrt{N} - 1)$ electronic moves as below.

Step 1: Do a local bit reversal in each group.

Step 2: Perform an OTIS move of all data.

Step 3: Do a local bit reversal in each group.

Steps 1 and 3 are done optimally in $4(\sqrt{N}-1)$ electronic moves each using the optimal 2D mesh bit reversal algorithm of [7].

4.5. Vector Reversal $[-(p-1), -(p-2), \ldots, 0]$

A vector reversal can be done using $8(\sqrt{N}-1)$ electronic and two OTIS moves. The steps are:

Step 1: Perform a local vector reversal in each group.

Step 2: Do an OTIS move of all data.

Step 3: Perform a local vector reversal in each group.

Step 4: Do an OTIS move of all data.

Note that Step 1 moves data from GP to $G\overline{P}$ (where $\overline{P}$ is the complement of P). Step 2 moves this data from $G\overline{P}$ to $\overline{P}G$. Next, Step 3 sends that data to $\overline{PG}$ and finally Step 4 sends it to $\overline{GP}$ completing the vector reversal. The number of data moves is easily obtained by noting that the optimal way to perform the local vector reversals takes $4(\sqrt{N}-1)$ electronic moves [7].

4.6. Bit Shuffle $[p-1, p-3, \ldots, 1, p-2, p-4, \ldots, 0]$

Our algorithm to perform this permutation employs a G_yP_x Swap permutation in which data from processor $G_xG_yP_xP_y$ is routed to processor $G_xP_xG_yP_y$. So, let us first see how to perform this permutation.

4.6.1 G_yP_x Swap $[p-1, \ldots, 3p/4, p/2-1, \ldots, p/4, 3p/4-1, \ldots, p/2, p/4-1, \ldots, 0]$

We have two algorithms for this. The first uses $2(\sqrt{N}-1)$ electronic and $\log_2 N$ OTIS moves. The second uses $6(\sqrt{N}-1)$ electronic and 2 OTIS moves. While the second algorithm uses a larger number of moves, it is to be preferred when the cost of an OTIS move is considerably larger than that of an electronic move. Details of the first algorithms are provided below. The second is given in [8].

The first algorithm performs a series of bit exchange permutations of the form $B(i) = [B_{p-1}, \ldots, B_0]$, $0 \leq i < p/4$, where

$$B_j = \begin{cases} p/2+i, & j = p/4+i \\ p/4+i, & j = p/2+i \\ j & otherwise \end{cases}$$

The permutaion $B(i)$ may be realized as below:

Step 1: Processors GP with $b_{G(i)} \neq b_{P(p/4+i)}$ route their data to corresponding processors that differ only in bit $b_{P(p/4+i)}$. This requires moving data left and right on rows of $\sqrt{N} \times \sqrt{N}$ meshes by 2^i positions (in each direction).

Step 2: Perform an OTIS move.

Step 3: The data moved in Step 1 is routed from their current processors to corresponding processors that differ only in bit i. This requires data moves left and right along rows of $\sqrt{N} \times \sqrt{N}$ meshes. The distance is 2^i in each direction.

Step 4: Perform an OTIS move.

The total number of moves is 2^{i+2} electronic and two OTIS.

To perform a G_yP_x Swap permutation, we simply perform $B(i)$ permutations for $0 \leq i < p/4$. This takes $p/2 = \log_2 N$ OTIS moves and $\sum_{i=0}^{p/4-1} 2^{i+2} = 4(2^{p/4}-1) = 4(\sqrt{N}-1)$ electronic moves.

4.6.2 Bit Shuffle

A bit shuffle may be performed following these steps:

Step 1: Perform a G_yP_x swap.

Step 2: Do a local bit shuffle in each group.

Step 3: Do an OTIS move.

Step 4: Do a local bit shuffle in each group.

Step 5: Do an OTIS move.

Using the $4(\sqrt{N}-1)$ electronic and $\log_2 N$ OTIS move algorithm for the G_yP_x Swap and the optimal mesh bit shuffle algorithm of [7], the number of moves becomes (approximately) $\frac{28}{3}\sqrt{N}-4$ electronic and $\log_2 N+2$ OTIS.

4.7. Shuffled Row-major $[p-1, p/2-1, p-2, p/2-2, \ldots, p/2, 0]$

This is the inverse of a bit shuffle and may be done in the same number of moves by running the bit shuffle algorithm backwards. Of course, Steps 2 and 4 are to be changed to shuffled row-major operations.

5. BPC Permutations

Every BPC permutation, A, may be realized by a sequence of bit exchange permutations of the form $B(i,j) = [B_{p-1}, \ldots, B_0]$, $p/2 \leq i < p$, $0 \leq j < p/2$, and

$$B_q = \begin{cases} j, & q = i \\ i, & q = j \\ q, & otherwise, \end{cases}$$

and a BPC permutation $C = [C_{p-1}, \ldots, C_0] = \Pi_G \Pi_P$ where $|C_q| < p/2$, $0 \leq q < p/2$, Π_G and Π_P involve $p/2$ bits each. Let Π'_G be the permutation obtained from Π_G by subtracting $p/2$ from each entry whose absolute value exceeds $p/2 - 1$. For example, if $\Pi_G = [-3, 5, 4]$, then $p = 6$ and $\Pi'_G = [-0, 2, 1]$.

The transpose permutation may be realized by the sequence $B(p/2 + j, j)$, $0 \leq j < p/2$; bit reversal is equivalent to the sequence $B(p - 1 - j, j)$, $0 \leq j < p/2$; vector reversal can be realized by performing no bit exchanges and using $C = [-(p-1), -(p-2), \ldots, -0]$; perfect shuffle may be decomposed into $B(p/2, 0)$ and $C = [p-2, p-3, \ldots, p/2, p-1, p/2-2, \ldots, 1, 0, p/2-1]$ ($\Pi_G = [p-2, p-3, \ldots, p/2, p-1]$, $\Pi_P = [p/2-2, \ldots, 1, 0, p/2-1]$).

A bit exchange permutation $B(i, j)$ may be performed in $2^{i'} + 2^{j'}$ electronic, where

$$i' = \begin{cases} i - p/2, & i < 3p/4 \\ i - 3p/4, & i \geq 3p/4; \end{cases}$$

$$j' = \begin{cases} j, & j < p/4 \\ j - p/4, & j \geq p/4 \end{cases}$$

and 2 OTIS moves following a process silimar to that used for $B(i)$ in Section 4.6.1.

Our algorithm for general BPC permutations is:

Step 1: Decompose the BPC permutation A into the bit exchange permutations $B_1(i_1, j_1)$, $B_2(i_2, j_2)$,..., $B_k(i_k, j_k)$ and the BPC permutation $C = \Pi_G \Pi_P$ as above. Do this such that $i_1 > i_2 > \cdots > i_k$, and $j_1 > j_2 > \cdots > j_k$.

Step 2: If $k = 0$, do the following:

Step 2.1: Do the BPC permutation Π_P in each group using the optimal algorithm of [7].

Step 2.2: Do an OTIS move.

Step 2.3: Do the BPC permutation Π'_G in each group using the algorithm of [7].

Step 2.4: Do an OTIS move.

Step 3: If $k = p/2$, do the following:

Step 3.1: Do the BPC permutation Π'_G in each group.

Step 3.2: Do an OTIS move.

Step 3.3: Do the BPC permutation Π_P in each group.

Step 4: If $k < p/4$, do the following:

Step 4.1: Perform the bit exchange permutation $B_1, \ldots, B_k$.

Step 4.2: Do Steps 2.1 through 2.4.

Step 5: If $k \geq p/4$, do the following:

Step 5.1: Perform a sequence of $p/2-k$ bit exchanges involving bits other than those in $B_1, \ldots, B_k$ in the same orderly fashion described in Step 1. Recompute Π_G and Π_P. Swap Π_G and Π_P.

Step 5.2: Do Steps 3.1 through 3.3.

The local BPC permutations determined by Π_G and Π_P take at most $4(\sqrt{N} - 1)$ electronic moves each [7]; the bit exchanges cumulatively take at most $4(\sqrt{N} - 1)$ electronic and $\log_2 N$ OTIS moves. So, the total number of moves is at most $12(\sqrt{N} - 1)$ electronic and $\log_2 N + 2$ OTIS.

References

[1] M. Feldman, S. Esener, C. Guest, and S. Lee. Comparison between electrical and free-space optical interconnects based on power and speed considerations. *Applied Optics*, 27(9), May 1988.

[2] W. Hendrick, O. Kibar, P. Marchand, C. Fan, D. V. Blerkom, F. McCormick, I. Cokgor, M. Hansen, and S. Esener. Modeling and optimization of the optical transpose interconnection system. in Optoelectronic Technology Center, Program Review, Cornell University, Sept. 1995.

[3] F. Kiamilev, P. Marchand, A. Krishnamoorthy, S. Esener, and S. Lee. Performance comparison between optoelectronic and vlsi multistage interconnection networks. *Journal of Lightwave Technology*, 9(12), Dec. 1991.

[4] A. Krishnamoorthy, P. Marchand, F. Kiamilev, and S. Esener. Grain-size considerations for optoelectronic multistage interconnection networks. *Applied Optics*, 31(26), Sept. 1992.

[5] M. Kunde. Routing and sorting on mesh-connected arrays. In *Proceedings of the 3rd Agean Workshop on Computing: VLSI Algorithms and Architectures, Lecture Notes on Computer Science*, volume 319, pages 423–433. Springer Verlag, 1988.

[6] G. C. Marsden, P. J. Marchand, P. Harvey, and S. C. Esener. Optical transpose interconnection system architectures. *Optics Letters*, 18(13):1083–1085, July 1 1993.

[7] D. Nassimi and S. Sahni. An optimal routing algorithm for mesh-connected parallel computers. *Journal of the Association for Computing Machinery*, 27(1):6–29, Jan. 1980.

[8] S. Sahni and C.-F. Wang. Bpc permutations on the OTIS-Mesh optoelectronic computer. Technical Report 97-008, CISE department, University of Florida, 1997. Available by anonymous ftp login from ftp.cise.ufl.edu under directory tech-report/tr97/tr97-008.ps.gz.

[9] F. Zane, P. Marchand, R. Paturi, and S. Esener. Scalable network architectures using the optical transpose interconnection system (OTIS). In *Proceedings of the second International Conference on Massively Parallel Processing Using Optical Interconnections (MPPOI'96)*, pages 114–121, 1996.

Embedding Binary Trees in Arrays with Optical Buses*

Yousong Mei and Chunming Qiao
Department of ECE
SUNY at Buffalo
Buffalo, NY 14260
{ymei,qiao}@eng.buffalo.edu

Abstract

Optical bus based architectures have received much attention lately, and how to take advantage of the unique communication capabilities of such architectures in application development needs to be demonstrated. In this paper, we first describe an embedding of a binary tree into a Reconfigurable Array with Spanning Optical Buses (or RASOB), which achieves a near minimal expansion cost. We then describe an embedding of a large binary tree into a small RASOB, which achieves a near optimal load balance. In both embeddings, all packet transfers between parents and children in the binary trees can be accomplished in one bus cycle, which implies that the embeddings achieve an optimum dilation cost of 1.

1 Introduction

Since optical interconnects can offer many advantages over their electronic counterparts including high connection density and relaxed bandwidth-distance product, multiprocessor systems based on optical buses have received an enormous amount of attention recently in terms of technologies [3, 9, 18], architectures [4, 5, 10, 11, 12, 14], and algorithm development [6, 13, 15]. In this paper, we describe optimal embeddings of binary trees into the Reconfigurable Array with Spanning Optical Buses (RASOB) [13, 14].

The RASOB possesses many desirable features which include rich connectivities and low hardware and control complexities. It adopts a two dimensional structure with row and column buses in order to maintain a reasonable optical path length even when its size is scaled to hundreds of nodes. However, unlike ordinary two-dimensional structures with row and column buses such as the one based on optical buses [5], the RASOB can establish an *all-optical* path between any two nodes just as in a one-dimensional structure [10, 11], even though the two nodes are *neither* at the same row *nor* at the same column. The RASOB is also unique in that it uses only one 2×2 optical switch (e.g. a Lithium Niobate directional coupler [1]) at each intersection of a row bus and a column bus, resulting in a much lower hardware complexity than other reconfigurable arrays based on optical buses and optical switches [4, 12].

Another important feature of the RASOB is that all its switches are set to the same state at the same time, and hence switch control is extremely simple compared to that in [4, 12]. This, however, limits the communication capability of the RASOB as follows: a conflict occurs when two (or more) packets need to be transferred from a row to the same column, unless the sources and destinations of these two (or more) packets are all at the same row. Accordingly, it is interesting yet challenging to develop efficient algorithms that can take advantage of the unique characteristics of the RASOB. An early work on using the RASOB architecture in conjunction with an all-optical addressing technique called coincidental pulse [3] for supporting MIMD-type communications was described in [14]. In [13], efficient algorithms for matrix operations were developed on the RASOB as a proof-of-principle for supporting SIMD-type communications.

A binary tree is an important communication structure in multiprocessor systems, on which many fundamental algorithms have been developed. Efficient embeddings of binary trees into other common topologies including meshes have been studied extensively in the past (see [8] and additional references therein). Of particular relevance to this study is the embedding of binary trees of (almost) equal size in arrays with optical buses described in [4, 5]. This study will serve as an example of how to take advantage of the unique characteristics of the RASOB in developing efficient embedding algorithms. We will consider embedding both a binary tree of (almost) equal size and a larger binary tree in a RASOB. In the former case, we achieve a minimal expansion ratio (almost 1), and in the latter case, we achieve an optimal load balance. In both cases, we can accomplish all packet transfers among parents and children in a binary tree

*This research is supported in part by a grant from NSF under contract number MIP-9409864

0-8186-7974-3/97 $10.00 © 1997 IEEE

in one bus cycle (to be defined later) in the RASOB. This, in a sense, achieves a minimum dilation cost of 1.

The rest of the paper is organized as follows. Section 2 contains a brief review of the RASOB architecture, and in particular, includes the definition of a bus cycle and a description of how the nodes in the RASOB communicate with each other. Section 3 contains the basic embedding results, in which a binary tree of $N^2 - 1$ nodes is embedded into a $(N + 1) \times N$ RASOB. Section 4 extends the basic results by embedding a larger binary tree into the RASOB. Section 5 concludes the paper.

2 The RASOB Architecture

Figure 1 illustrates the architecture of an $N \times N$ $RASOB$, which consists of N folded row buses and N folded column buses. Each processor transmits to the upper segment of a row bus (only), and receives from the lower segment of the row bus and the right segment of a column bus. There is a 2×2 switch at the intersection of each row bus (to be more precise, the lower segment) and each column bus (the left segment) so that a packet transmitted to a row bus may continue to propagate on the row bus, or be *switched* to a column bus. Once a packet is switched, the switches are kept in straight long enough so that it continues to propagate on the column bus without being switched back to a row bus.

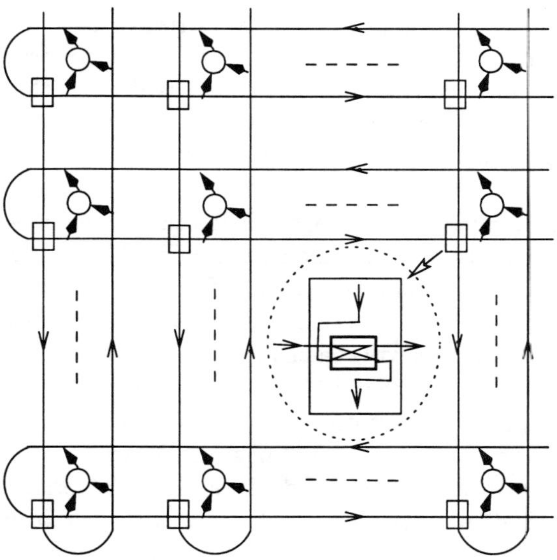

Figure 1. An $N \times N$ RASOB

In the RASOB, the processors communicate with each other by letting a source send a packet at a specific point in time and by letting its destination receive the packet at another specific point in time later. In particular, the RASOB may alternate between two phases, namely, a row phase and a column phase. In a row phase, all the switches stay at *straight* to allow each processor to communicate with others at the same row. In a column phase, all the switches will be set simultaneously to *cross* at a certain point in time to allow each processor to communicate with others at different rows, which may or may not be at the same column. If needed, a processor may also communicate with others at the same row in a column phase. Due to the high switching speed (tens to hundreds of picoseconds) of the Lithium Niobate switches [1], the switch control overhead is almost negligible.

Like in other optical bus based architectures employing Time Division Multiplexing (TDM) communications, synchronization is a crucial issue. Such an issue, however, is beyond the scope of this paper. Suffice it to say that the larger fan-out, less power loss, better noise immunity and other desirable features of optics make it possible to distribute a high-frequency global clock to hundreds of receiver modules with little clock skew [7, 17]. Additionally, the jitters that optical data signals encounter in single-mode fibers of a length less than one kilometer is small and can be tolerated by using narrow (e.g. 10 bits) guard bands at each end of a time slot (up to a few hundreds of bits) [2, 16].

A bus cycle in the RASOB, or simply *cycle* hereafter, is defined to be $4N$ units, where a unit (on the order of nanoseconds) is the propagation delay between two adjacent nodes (or their transmitting/receiving interfaces) at a row or column bus. Since optical signals propagate unidirectionally, it will take a signal at most $2N$ units to traverse a row bus (first the upper segment and then the lower segment), and at most another $2N$ units to traverse a column bus (first the left segment and then the right segment). Note that, alternatively, one may use two buses per row (or per column), one for downstream and another for upstream transmissions in order to reduce the propagation time on each row or column bus to N, and the cycle to $2N$ as in [4, 5]. However, each node will have to have four transmitters and receivers instead of one transmitters and two receivers, which is an expensive proposition.

As described in [13, 14], each row or column phase in the RASOB takes at most $4N$ units and thus can be completed in one cycle. In the following, we concentrate on a row bus and use the train loading/unloading model to illustrate how row and column phases can be *pipelined* in the RASOB so that a throughput of four phases per cycle can be achieved, but will omit the detailed descriptions of how the timings for transmitting and receiving packets can be derived.

As shown in Figure 2 (a), let us imagine that two trains are formed on the upper segment of a row bus at the beginning of a cycle, $t = 0$. The first train is called a "row" train, and the second a "column" train. In either train, the cars are numbered 0 through $N - 1$ from left to right, and each car can be regarded as an empty packet slot with a duration of a unit time. At 2.5 Gb/s, for example, a 32-bit packet can easily fit into a car with a duration of $20ns$.

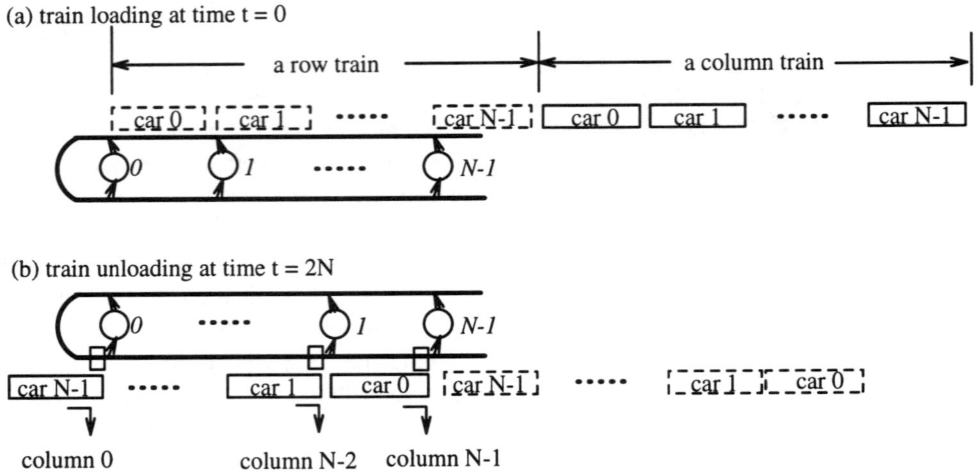

Figure 2. An illustration of pipelined packet transfers and phases in a RASOB

Row Phase: There are two methods of allocating the cars in a train, namely *Time Division Source-oriented Multiplexing* (TDSM) and *Time Division Destination-oriented Multiplexing* (TDDM) [14]. In TDSM, processor i loads a packet to car i; whereas in TDDM, it receives a packet from car $(N - 1) - i$ of a row train, where $0 \leq i \leq N - 1$. They allow processors to transmit and receive, respectively, a packet simultaneously. In either case, the loaded row train then continues on the lower segment of the row bus, enabling each packet to be unloaded (or copied) by one or more destination processors at that row. The row train will leave the row bus at $t = 2N$ units (see Figure 2 (b)).

Note that with TDSM, any one-to-one, one-to-many (multicasting), and many-to-one communication patterns among the processors at the same row may be accomplished in a row phase. With TDDM, on the other hand, any simulcasting pattern among the processors at the same row, in which no two (or more) processors try to send to the same processor, can be accomplished in one row phase.

Column Phase: Communications in a column phase is slightly more complicated since cars (or packets) are to turn (or be switched) from a row bus to column buses. In particular, the simple switch control in the RASOB dictates that all the cars in a column train will turn onto different column buses at the *same* time since all the switches will be set to cross at the same time. Specifically, as shown in Figure 2 (b), car 0 of the column train will turn onto column bus $N - 1$, car 1 onto column bus $N - 2$ and so on, and car $N - 1$ will turn onto column bus 0. Assume that the switches are placed at (or closely to) the receiving interfaces on the lower segment of each row bus, every car of a column train will arrive at its turning point at $t = 2N$ units, as illustrated in Figure 2(b). Note that at this moment, a third and a fourth trains, which can be either row or column trains, may form on the upper segment of the row bus as in Figure 2(a) in a pipelined fashion. In this way, four trains are loaded in $4N$ units, achieving a pipelined throughput of 4 phases in one cycle.

Note that once the cars of the above column train finish the turning (at $t = 2N + 1$ units), all the switches are *reset* to straight. Each column bus now looks quite similar to a row bus at the start of a row phase, which is rotated 90° degree counter-clockwise. More specifically, a train of N cars, one from each row bus, is formed on the left segment of each column bus, and the train will continue onto the right segment, enabling each packet carried in a car to be unloaded (or copied) by one or more destination processors at that column. We also note that a processor may send to, in addition to receiving from, processors at different columns by loading multiple cars of a column train as long as there is no conflicts. Specifically, we have

Condition for Conflict: A conflict occurs if and only if two or more packets from the same row need to be transferred to the same processor at a different row, or to two or more processors at the same column in a column phase (since these packets will contend for the same car).

Obviously, there is also a limitation imposed by the bandwidth, which requires that no more than N packets be transmitted in one (row or column) phases. A key to the development of efficient embedding (and other algorithms) in a RASOB is to be able to fully take advantage of the RASOB's strong ability to support many other conflict-free one-to-one, one-to-many and many-to-one communication patterns so as a minimal number of phases will be needed for the embedding (and execution of the algorithms).

3 Basic Embedding Results

In this section, we first discuss general issues related to embedding a binary tree into a RASOB. To facilitate our discussions, we consider a binary tree of $N^2 - 1$ nodes, where $N = 2^l$ for some l. Such a tree thus has $2l$ levels, and we number them from 0 to $2l - 1$ starting at the root. The nodes in the tree are numbered in a breadth-first fashion, starting at 1 as shown in an example given in Figure 3. This way, give a tree node X, its left-child and right-child (for $X < 2^{2l-1}$) are $2X$ and $2X + 1$, respectively, and its parent (for $X > 1$) is $\lfloor \frac{X}{2} \rfloor$.

The two basic packet transfer patterns in a binary tree that we will embed in a RASOB are *parent-to-children* (P-to-C) and *children-to-parent* (C-to-P). In P-to-C communications, every node (except the leaves) sends a packet to both its left child and right child. We will assume that a parent may perform a *multicasting* operation in which two identical copies are sent to its children although, alternatively, it may also perform a *simulcasting* operation in which two different copies are sent. In C-to-P communications, every node (except the root) sends a packet to its parent. The two packets from the two children of a parent are usually different. Note that in order for a tree node to be able to send (and receive) a packet to (and from) its parent and one packet to (from) each of its children all in one step, it must have three transmitters (and receivers).

Our goal is to embed *both* patterns in a RASOB in one cycle so that any communication operation requiring one step in a tree can be emulated in one cycle in the RASOB. Specifically, let $R()$ be the mapping function used in the embedding. Then, every RASOB node emulating a tree node X, denoted by $R(X)$, will be able to send a packet to $R(2X)$ and $R(2X + 1)$ (except if X is a leaf), and send a packet to $R(\lfloor \frac{X}{2} \rfloor)$ (except if X is the root) within a cycle time *concurrently* with all other RASOB nodes. This will be accomplished by pipelining four phases as to be described in details later.

In the remaining of this section, we describe how to embed a $2l$-level binary tree (of $N^2 - 1$ nodes) into a $(N + 1) \times N$ RASOB.

3.1 Embed a $2l$-level Binary Tree

To obtain a simple yet efficient embedding, we first cut the $2l$-level tree between levels $l - 1$ and l, and thereby partitioning it into several l-level *subtrees*. An example in which $l = 2$ is shown in Figure 3 (a). The top l levels of the tree becomes what we call the *top subtree*. This top subtree has 2^{l-1} leaves, whose 2^l children in the original tree now become the roots of additional subtrees, which we call *bottom subtrees*. The bottom subtrees will be assigned indices 0 to $2^l - 1$ from left to right.

As a result of the above partition, we obtain a total of $N + 1$ subtrees, each having $N - 1$ nodes. Accordingly, a straight-forward observation is to embed one subtree at each row in the $(N + 1) \times N$ RASOB. Such an embedding can easily support any *intra*-subtree communications since they are among the processors at the same row, and can be accomplished in a row phase in the RASOB.

Let the leaves of the top subtree be denoted by set $\mathcal{P}_t$, and the roots of the bottom subtrees (as their children) be denoted by set $\mathcal{C}_b$. Clearly, every node in $\mathcal{P}_t$ may need to send two packets, one to each of its children in $\mathcal{C}_b$ for the inter-subtree P-to-C communications. Such packet transfers have to be accomplished in column phases since the nodes in $\mathcal{P}_t$ are at the same row, and the nodes in $\mathcal{C}_b$ are at N different rows. Moreover, in order to accomplish them in *one* column phase, it is required that all the N nodes in $\mathcal{C}_b$ be at *distinct* columns to avoid any conflicts. Note that this requirement also explains why the RASOB has to have N columns, instead of $N - 1$, even though the embedding results in one idle RASOB node at each row.

An example of the proposed embedding of a 4-level tree is illustrated in Figure 3 (b). A general description is as follows:

1. The top subtree is placed at row N with node X in the top subtree at column X, where $1 \leq X \leq N - 1$. This may be viewed as a breadth-first embedding of the top subtree starting at column 1.

2. The bottom subtree having index s is placed at row s, where $0 \leq s \leq N - 1$. Its nodes are also embedded breadth-first but with a different starting column and a possible wrap-around (from column $N - 1$ to column 0). Specifically, the root of the bottom subtree is placed at column $N - 1 - \frac{s}{2}$ if s is even, and at column $\frac{N}{2} - 1 - \frac{s-1}{2}$ if s is odd.

As can be seen from Figure 3 (b), one of the effects of such an embedding is that the nodes in $\mathcal{P}_t$ (e.g. 2 and 3) are at columns $\frac{N}{2}$ to $N - 1$ (at row N). Meanwhile, their left children in $\mathcal{C}_b$ (e.g. 5 and 7) are at columns $N - 1$ down to $\frac{N}{2}$, and their right children (e.g. 4 and 6) are at columns $\frac{N}{2} - 1$ down to 0, respectively. In addition, two siblings in $\mathcal{C}_b$ are always $N/2$ columns (and one row) apart. Such a regular, *skewed* pattern makes inter-subtree communications between $\mathcal{P}_t$ and $\mathcal{C}_b$ easy to be accomplished in a column phase. More specifically, all the nodes in $\mathcal{P}_t$ can send to their left children at the same time, and after $N/2$ units, send to their right children at the same time. These packets will then be received by all the nodes in $\mathcal{C}_b$ at the same time.

In summary, we can use a row phase to transfer packets for intra-subtree P-to-C communications and a column phase to transfer packets for inter-subtree P-to-C communications. These two phases are pipelined as described in Figure 2. Similarly, we can transfer packets for the intra-subtree and inter-subtree C-to-P communications using an additional row and an additional column phases, respectively. Such an embedding allows any communication operation requiring T steps in the tree to be finished in T cycles

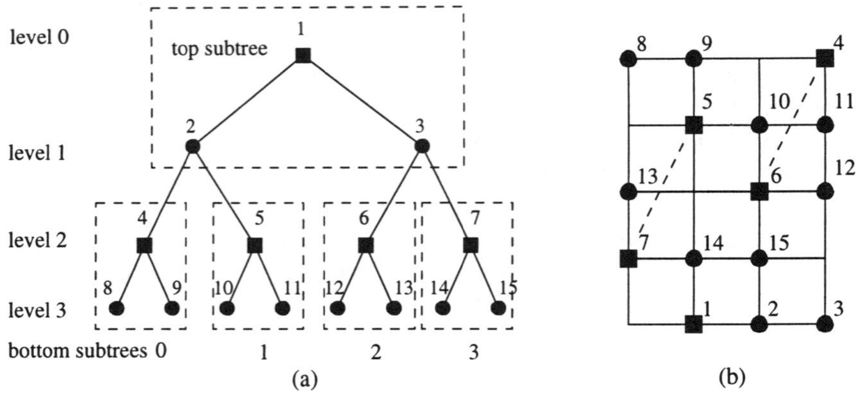

Figure 3. Examples (a). A 4-level binary tree. (b). Its embedding in a 5×4 RASOB.

in the RASOB. Moreover, we note that the root of the tree can now broadcast to all the leaves (in fact, to all the tree nodes) in just one cycle in the RASOB, whereas such an operation would take $O(l)$ steps in the tree.

4 Embed a $(2l + k)$-level Binary Tree

In this section, we extend the above embedding to make the results more useful. Specifically, since it is often necessary to emulate a larger binary tree by a smaller RASOB, we will describe an embedding of a binary tree having $(2l + k)$ levels and $2^k N^2 - 1$ nodes (for any $k > 0$) into the $(N + 1) \times N$ RASOB. Such an embedding requires that a RASOB node emulate more than one tree nodes by, for example, multiprogramming. The number of tree nodes emulated by a RASOB node will be called the *load* of the RASOB node. The proposed embedding will accomplish all packet transfers for P-to-C and C-to-P communications in the binary tree in one cycle while balancing the load of each RASOB node (at about 2^k tree nodes).

The first step in the embedding is similar to that taken when embedding a $2l$-level tree. More specifically, we cut the $(2l + k)$-level tree between levels $l - 1$ and l as before, and in addition, between levels $2l - 1$ and $2l$ (see Figure 4 (a)). This partitions the top $2l$ levels of the tree into $N + 1$ subtrees, each of which has l levels and is embedded into the RASOB in the same way as it is embedded before. However, the bottom k-level of the tree become what we call *minitrees*, which need to be embedded as well.

Let the $\frac{N}{2}$ leaves of bottom subtree s be denoted by $\mathcal{P}_b^s$, where $0 \leq s \leq N - 1$. Since each leaf has two children that are the roots of two minitrees underneath, the number of minitrees under each bottom subtree is N (and the total number of minitrees is N^2). These minitrees are embedded at the *same row*, s, as the bottom subtree, one minitree per RASOB node, as illustrated in Figure 4 (b). There are two advantages, one is that intra-minitree P-to-C and C-to-P communications do not require any packets be sent between RASOB nodes. And the other is that at each row s, all but one node have a load of 2^k (and the node which is left idle when embedding the bottom subtree has a load of $2^k - 1$). This results in a good load balance except at row N, where all but one node have a load of 1 since no minitrees are embedded there.

A more detailed description of the embedding follows. Let the N roots of these minitrees be denoted by $\mathcal{C}_m^s$. For any node $X \in \mathcal{P}_b^s$, the node $2X \in \mathcal{C}_m^s$ (and the entire *left* minitree rooted at $2X$) is embedded at the same RASOB node as node X. On the other hand, the node $2X + 1 \in \mathcal{C}_m^s$ (and the entire *right* minitree rooted at $2X + 1$) is embedded at $\frac{N}{2}$ columns away. As a result, only communications between the nodes in $\mathcal{P}_b^s$ and their right children in $\mathcal{C}_m^s$ require packet transfers. In particular, the P-to-C and C-to-P communications between the nodes in $\mathcal{P}_b^s$ and their right children will require $\frac{N}{2}$ packets be sent from $\mathcal{P}_b^s$ to their right children and *vice versa*. Accordingly, such communications can be accomplished in one row phase (the 3rd row phase after Phases 1 and 3).

Note that the above row phase may start as the fifth overall phase (at $t_0 = 4N$). However, the two column phases (Phases 2 and 4) described in Section 3 can be combined into one, enabling us to start the above phase as the fourth overall phase (at $t_0 = 3N$). Specifically, this is because in Phase 2, only the nodes in $\mathcal{P}_t$, which are at row N, will send packets. Hence, only the column train at row N is fully loaded, and those at all other rows are empty. Meanwhile, since in Phase 4, only the nodes in $\mathcal{C}_b$, which are at rows 0 through $N-1$, respectively, will send a packet, and hence the column train formed on row bus N will be empty. Clearly, inter-subtree P-to-C and C-to-P communications can share the bandwidth available in one column phase, which implies that the emulation of a $2l$-level tree can be accomplished in just three phases (two row phases and one column phase), and the emulation of a $(2l + k)$-level tree in four phases (three row phases and one column phases) or in one cycle. Note that no further bandwidth-sharing is possible, especially among the three row phases because

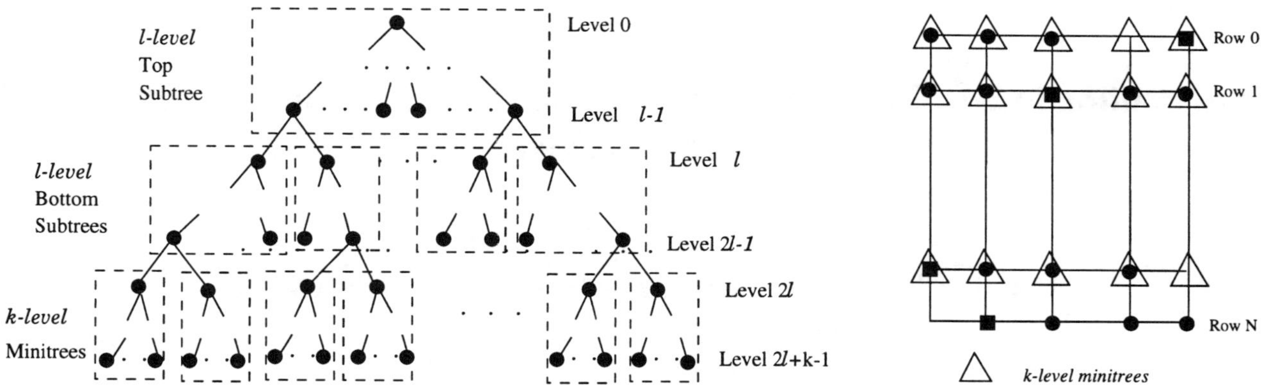

Figure 4. (a).A partitioned $(2l + k)$-level binary tree. (b). Its embedding

most of the row trains have already been heavily loaded.

5 Conclusion

An important step towards the development of novel architectures based on optical interconnects is to demonstrate that existing applications can be migrated into these architectures with improved performance. In this paper, we have demonstrated how to take advantage of the unique communication capabilities of the RASOB architecture in embedding binary trees. We have described an embedding of a $2l$-level binary tree of $N^2 - 1$ nodes (where $N = 2^l$) into a $(N + 1) \times N$ RASOB. Based on this result, we have also embedded a larger binary tree of $(2l + k)$ levels (for any $k > 0$) into the $RASOB$ with a good load balance. In both embeddings, all packet transfers for children-to-parents and parents-to-children communications in the binary trees can be accomplished in one bus cycle in the RASOB, which implies the optimum dilation cost of 1. Work on efficiently embedding binary trees into a square $N \times N$ RASOB is underway.

References

[1] R. Alferness, L. Buhl, S. Korotky, and R. Tucker. High-speed $\Delta\ \beta$-reversal directional coupler switch. In *Photonic Switching, OSA Tech. Digest*, volume 13, pages 77–78, 1987.

[2] R. Ballart and Y. Ching. SONET: now it's the standard optical network. *IEEE Communications Magazine*, Mar. 1989.

[3] D. Chiarulli et al. Optoelectronic buses for high performance computing. *Proc. of the IEEE*, 82(11):1701–1710, 1994.

[4] Z. Guo. Optically interconnected processor arrays with switching capability. *Journal of Parallel and Distributed Computing*, pages 314–329, 1994.

[5] Z. Guo et al. Array processors with pipelined optical busses. *Journal of Parallel and Distributed Computing*, 12(3):269–282, 1991.

[6] M. Hamdi and Y. Pan. Efficient parallel algorithms on optically interconnected arrays of processors. *IEE Proceedings-Computers and Digital Techniques*, 142:87–92, 1995.

[7] D. Kiefer and V. Swanson. Implementation of optical clock distribution in a supercomputer. Cray Research Inc., internal report, 1995.

[8] F. Leighton. *Introduction to parallel algorithms and architectures: arrays, trees, hypercubes*. Morgan Kaufmann, 1992.

[9] Y. Liu et al. Polymer optical interconnect technology (POINT) optoelectronic packaging and interconnect for board and backplane applications. In *Proc. 46th Electronic Components and Technology Conf.*, pages 308–315, 1996.

[10] R. Melhem, D. Chiarulli, and S. Levitan. Space multiplexing of waveguides in optically interconnected multiprocessor systems. *The Computer Journal*, 32(4):362–369, 1989.

[11] Y. Pan. Order statistics on optically interconnected multiprocessor systems. *Optics and Laser Technology*, 26(4):281–287, 1994.

[12] S. Pavel and S. Akl. On the power of arrays with reconfigurable optical buses. Technical report, Department of Computing and Information Science, Queen's University, 1995.

[13] C. Qiao. On designing communication-intensive algorithms for a spanning optical bus based array. *Parallel Processing Letters*, 5(5):499–511, 1995.

[14] C. Qiao and R. Melhem. Time-division optical communications in multiprocessor arrays. *IEEE Transactions on Computers*, 42(5):577–590, May 1993.

[15] S. Rajsekaran and S. Sahni. Sorting, selection and routing on the array with reconfigurable optical buses. Technical report, Department of Computer and Information Science, University of Florida, 1996.

[16] D. Sarrazin, H. Jordan, and V. Heuring. Fiber optic delay line memory. *Applied Optics*, 29(5):627–637, Feb. 1990.

[17] S. Tang et al. 1-GHz clock signal distribution for multiprocessor supercomputer. In *International Conference on Massively Parallel Processing Using Optical Interconnections (MPPOI)*, pages 186–191, 1996.

[18] C. Zhao, T. Oh, and R. Chen. General purpose bi-directional optical backplane: high-performance bus for multiprocessor systems. In *International Conference on Massively Parallel Processing Using Optical Interconnections (MPPOI)*, pages 188–194, 1996.

Self-routing in 2-D shuffle networks with dimension-dependent switches and interconnections

Josef Giglmayr
Heinrich-Hertz-Institut für Nachrichtentechnik Berlin GmbH
Einsteinufer 37, D-10587 Berlin, Germany
giglmayr@hhi.de

Abstract

In shuffle multistage interconnection networks ($MINs$), by increasing the size of the switches, the number of stages (NS) and in turn the attenuation of signals decreases. An interesting concept for self-routing in shuffle $MINs$ are dimension-dependent switches, i.e. switches of size $2^d \times 2^d$ (where $d \geq 1$ is the dimension of the interconnected data set) and dimension-dependent interconnections. Throughout the paper, the 1-D shuffle interconnections and $k \times k$-switches ($k \geq 4$) are replaced by d-dimensional shuffles ($d \geq 2$) and switches of size $2^d \times 2^d$ though the networks are still planar. In this way, given a data set, the original contribution of the paper is the presentation of (1) the number of topologically equivalent shuffle networks, (2) the complete concept of self-routing in (artificial) higher-dimensional shuffle networks (3) the solution of self-routing in 2-D shuffle networks not solvable by the common concept and (4) the decomposition of the input/output array into several small arrays without loss of functionality. The latter is important as presently reliable laser arrays have size of at most 8×8 and 16×16, respectively.

1. Introduction

In shuffle $MINs$, by increasing the size of the switches, the number of stages (NS) and in turn the attenuation of signals decreases. Beside the NS the self-routing capability is the major advantage of shuffle networks [10]. However, in 2-D shuffle networks with switches of size $\geq 8 \times 8$ the self-routing concept is more complicated, caused by the freedom of the placement of the switches (e.g. an 8×8-switch may be placed horizontally or vertically). Thus a complete concept for self-routing in shuffle $MINs$ is presented, which is aimed to consist of (1) the interconnected data/lines are mapped onto an equivalent d-dimensional cube, (2) the same operation, applied to a single mixed radix number (MRN) in a 1-D shuffle network, is applied to each coordinate of a MRN d-tuple, and the result ($\equiv$ destination routing) is assumed to be the same, (3) the concept of dimension-dependent switches, e.g. switches of size $2^d \times 2^d$ where $d \geq 1$ is the dimension of the interconnected data set, (4) the existence of switch-pattern preserving transformations, e.g. a 1-D shuffle is transformed into the topologically equivalent 2-D etc. shuffle (and vice versa), and (5) the independence of the permutation capability of shuffles from the dimension of the interconnection pattern, i.e. a 1-D shuffle network with 4×4-switches has the same permutation capability as the topologicallly equivalent 2-D etc. shuffle network with the same size of the switches.

(1) to (3) have been introduced in [1] and since this time the concept of dimension-dependent switches has been made transparent throughout several papers [3, 4, 8]. (4) has been presented for squares of data arrays and equivalent shuffles at each coordinate (symmetric generalized perfect shuffle, $SGPS$) in [5], and more generally, for the nonsymmetric generalized perfect shuffle ($NSGPS$) on squares (different shuffles are defined on different coordinates) and on rectangles (different or equivalent shuffles are defined on the coordinates). (5) is a major property of shuffle networks which is in contrast to other interconnection topologies [7].

Regarding the interconnection of d-dimensional cubes, for the 3rd coordinate of a 3-D cube, the frequencies/wavelengths may be assumed. Then, further dimensions are obtained by the factorization/decomposition of the 3rd coordinate and in turn by replacing the shuffle interconnections between the switching cubes by the Kronecker product (KP) of shuffles. In this way, higher-dimensional $MINs$ are obtained [1]. However, for their 2-D layout, the arrays of the cubes may be arranged in a certain way and interconnected according to the shuffle rules ($\equiv$ shuffling the arrays + shuffling the data/lines in Fig. 1). This procedure is made transparent and applied throughout the paper.

The paper is organized in the following way. In Section 2

0-8186-7974-3/97 $10.00 © 1997 IEEE

previous work of the author is briefly addressed, the original contributions of the paper are discussed with regard to this work and a basic example of the paper is presented. In Section 3 the transformation of a 1-D shuffle network into its higher-dimensional counterparts (and vice versa) is shown. Additionally, the existence/non-existence of transformation paths (TPs) is shown. In Section 4 the complete information for self-routing [structure of the routing tag (RT) etc.] in higher-dimensional shuffle networks is provided. In Section 5 the advantage of the presented concept with regard to self-routing is discussed.

2. Previous work, research objective and example

2.1. Previous work

Self-routing in 1-D shuffle networks with the number of N inputs/outputs and $k \times k$-switches works by setting the switches according to the MRN representation of the destination address where the number of $\log_2 k$ bits are applied at each switch and stage, respectively. Thus the complete RT adds up to $\log_k N \times \log_2 k$ bits (blocking) or to $(2\log_k N\text{-}1)\times \log_2 k$ bits (rearrangeable nonblocking), respectively. [For the upper bound of NS being $3\log_2 N\text{-}4$ [9] no self-routing algorithm exists yet.] The 1-D and 2-D shuffle networks for the rearrangeable non-blocking interconnection of $8 \times 8 = 64$ and $16 \times 16 = 256$ data/lines are defined in Tables 1 and 3.

The interconnection of 8×8 and 16×16 data by rearrangeable nonblocking 2-D shuffle networks has been presented, together with two routing algorithms, one based on single $MRNs$ and on the concept of switch-pattern preserving transformation of shuffles, indicated by $\star$ in Table 4 and called method **A**, and one based on pairs of MRN, called method **B**, where the latter is the most general [8] which easily may be generalized to arbitrary dimensions [2]. The corresponding 1-D shuffle networks are collected in the following Table 1.

2.2. Research objective

Throughout the paper, shuffle networks are defined on d-dimensionale cubes. In this way, beside the common 1-D [10] and 2-D [8] self-routing concepts in the literatur, to any size of data (subscribers, lines), an additional set of shuffle networks is made available and a proper member of this set may be chosen dependent on the desired layout and the available/applied technology. The number of additional shuffle networks equals the number of proper mappings of the data vector into the equivalent d-dimensional cubes. However, the paper is restricted to 2-D layouts of higher-dimensional shuffle networks.

2.3. Example

The rearrangeable nonblocking interconnection of the number of 64 and 256 data (subscribers, lines) is considered for 4×4- to 16×16-switches (Tables 1 and 2). For this purpose, the blockstructures arising by the recursive definition of the middle stage of the corresponding 3-stage networks [6], until all stages have the same size of switches, are presented in Tables 1 and 3. The RTs, composed of the destination address (DA) and the RT complement (RTC), for the different cases are collected in Table 4 together with the RT of 1-D shuffle networks and networks transformed in a switch-pattern preserving way (the latter indicated by $\star$).

The notation of $\geq$ 2-D shuffles in Table 3 has been introduced in [1] and applied throughout several papers of the author [3, 4, 8]. However, the collection of RTs in Table 4 is a new contribution and explains the concept of self-routing based on the (artificial) higher dimensional interconnections of the paper and it complements Ref. [8]. In Table 4 the 1st row for each switch size relates to the self-routing method **B** [8] extended to several coordinates and the 2nd row for each switch size to the self-routing method **A** [8] indicated by a $\star$ in Table 4.

Throughout the Example, for small data sets, the principles of the presented concept have been made transparent. In particular, instead of the proper design of the 1-D network and its mapping into the 3-D physical space, which provides the topologically equivalent 2-D network and its control by single MRNs (rows are indicated by $\star$ in Table 4), we may apply (artificial) higher-dimensional interconnections, together with dimension-dependent switches, and establish the self-routing by d-tuples of MRNs (1st row of each switch size in Table 4).

The advantages of the presented architectural concept, made transparent throughout the paper, are

(A) Possible choice of the switch size and in turn of the dimension of the MIN

(B) Possible balance between local (electronic) and global (optical) interconnections

(C) Design of large systems/arrays by means of the composition of reliable small arrays

(D) Avoidance of the generalized mixed shuffle (GMS) interconnection patterns throughout the blockstructure of the common 2-D layout, which requires a more difficult control scheme.

Data	64		256	
Switch	4×4	8×8	4×4	16×16
1. Pattern	$S(16,4)$	$S(8,8)$	$S(64,4)$	$S(16,16)$
2.	$4{\times}S(4,4)$	$S(8,8)$	$4{\times}S(16,4)$	$S(16,16)$
3.	$4{\times}S(4,4)$		$16{\times}S(4,4)$	
4.	$S(4,16)$		$16{\times}S(4,4)$	
5.			$4{\times}S(4,16)$	
6			$S(4,64)$	

Table 1. Blockstructure of rearrangeable nonblocking 1-D shuffle $MINs$.

Data	64	256	Dimension
Switch	4×4	4×4	2-D
	8×8		3-D
		16×16	4-D

Table 2. Geometries of data and size of switches.

Data	64		256	
Switch	4×4	8×8	4×4	16×16
1. Pattern	$S_{2-D}(4,2;4,2)$	$S_{3-D}(2,2;2,2;2,2)$	$S_{2-D}(8,2;8,2)$	$S_{4-D}(2,2;2,2;2,2;2,2)$
2.	$4{\times}S_{2-D}(2,2;2,2)$	$S_{3-D}(2,2;2,2;2,2)$	$4{\times}S_{2-D}(4,2;4,2)$	$S_{4-D}(2,2;2,2;2,2;2,2)$
3.	$4{\times}S_{2-D}(2,2;2,2)$		$16{\times}S_{2-D}(2,2;2,2)$	
4.	$S_{2-D}(2,4;2,4)$		$16{\times}S_{2-D}(2,2;2,2)$	
5.			$4{\times}S_{2-D}(2,4;2,4)$	
6.			$S_{2-D}(2,8;2,8)$	

Table 3. Blockstructure of rearrangeable nonblocking 2-D, 3-D, and 4-D shuffle $MINs$.

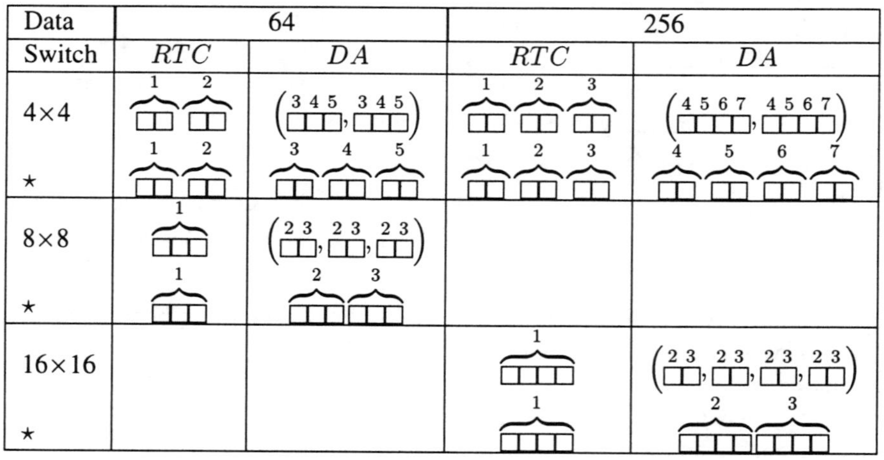

Table 4. RT for the blocking (restriction to the DA) and rearrangeable nonblocking ($RTC\&DA$) interconnection of 64 and 256 data. [$\star$ is the RT for the common self-routing concept. The numbers from 1 to 7 indicate the stages for rearrangeable nonblocking architectures. The numbering starting with 2, 3 and 4, respectively, indicates the RT ($\equiv DA$) for blocking interconnections.]

3. Realization principles

The d-dimensional interconnections and the dimension-dependent switches require the realization of the MIN in a way which is illustrated in Fig. 1 and which has been described throughout Section 1. In particular, the (2-D) arrays of the d-dimensional data and switching cubes are arranged within a large array requiring metallic traces between the 4×4-ports of larger (dimension-dependent) switches [Fig. 1 (b)]. Then, these arrays are interconnected by shuffling the order of the arrays (≡ shuffling of the 'pipes') and shuffling the single interconnections which cause their deflection [inserts in Fig. 1 (a)].

The resulting shuffle in Fig. 1 is $S_{3-D}(2,2;2,2;2,2)$ which will be analysed in the next Section. (The 3 coordinates are separated by semicolons, the 2 digits within a coordinate represent the algebraic bases a and b and thus the length of a coordinate is a×b, the 1st and 2nd coordinate relates to the array and the 3rd coordinate describes shuffling of the 'pipes'.) The balance between the local interconnections of switch ports (metallic traces) and the optical interstage interconnections (e.g. implemented by holograms) has been briefly analysed in [8].

4. Transformation of shuffles and transformation paths

The 1-D shuffle interconnections in Table 1 are aimed to be transformed into d-dimensional shuffles according to the desired size of the $2^d \times 2^d$-switches. For this purpose, first the geometries of the cubes for the d-dimensional shuffles have to be provided (Tables 2 and 6) though much more possibilities exist once rectangles are assumed.

Throughout this Section, minor results, indicated by **(1)** to **(6)**, are presented which are needed to understand the residual part of the paper.

4.1. Definitions

Let us assume a 1-D MIN with shuffle interconnections and with the number of M inputs/outputs.

(1) the M-vector may be mapped onto an equivalent cube/rectangle of size $\prod_{i=1}^{d} N_i$ where $N_i = n_1^{(i)} n_2^{(i)} \geq 4$ for i=1,2,...,d, $n_\mu^{(i)} \geq 2$ for μ=1,2, $d \geq 2$ and $M = \prod_{i=1}^{d} N_i$.

Remark 1: Simple examples of cubes are presented in Tables 2 and 6.

Definition 1: Let us denote the interconnected (source) array by A and the shuffles defined on the two coordinates by $S(n_1^{(1)}, n_2^{(1)})$ and $S(n_1^{(2)}, n_2^{(2)})$, respectively. Then a separable 2-D shuffle performs the matrix operation [12]

$$D = S(n_1^{(1)}, n_2^{(1)}) \times A \times S^T(n_1^{(2)}, n_2^{(2)}) \qquad (1)$$

where × is the ordinary matrix product and T is the transpose which, in the case of shuffles, simply interchange the arguments.

Remark 2: For a separable 2-D shuffle, rows of D are reordered according to S and columns of D are reordered according to S^T.

(2) A separable d-dimensional shuffle $S_{d-dim}(n_1^{(1)}, n_2^{(1)}; \ldots; n_1^{(d)}, n_2^{(d)})$ may be defined on any d-dimensional rectangle $\prod_i^d N_i$, where $N_i \geq 4$ and being a multiple of 2 is assumed, by a straight-forward extension of Eq.(1).

Definition 2: Let us assume the d-dimensional rectangle $\prod_{i=1}^{d} N_i$ and the numbering of the data (subscribers, lines) by numbers x between 0 and N_i-1 for any i, respectively. Then the d-dimensional shuffle may be defined by

$$S_{d-dim}^{NSGPS}(n_1^{(1)}, n_2^{(1)}; n_1^{(2)} n_2^{(2)}; \ldots; n_1^{(d)} n_2^{(d)}) = \prod_{i=1}^{d} \left(n_1^{(i)} \cdot x + \lfloor \frac{n_1^{(i)} \cdot x}{N_i} \rfloor \right) mod N_i \qquad (2)$$

where $\lfloor \cdot \rfloor$ means the largest integer less or equal to the argument.

4.2. Transformation

The following Eq.(3) has already been applied throughout Table 6 and will be further applied in Tables 7,8,9,10 and 11. Eq.(4) is needed to prove the existence of a TP (Sub-Section 4.3) and, moreover, for its particular construction.

(3) Let us assume rectangles of size $\prod_{i=1}^{d} N_i$ where $N_i = n_1^{(i)} n_2^{(i)} \geq 4$ and $d \geq 2$. Then the d-dimensional shuffle is transformed into the topologically equivalent 1-D shuffle (and vice versa) by

$$S_{d-dim}^{NSGPS}(n_1^{(1)}, n_2^{(1)}; n_1^{(2)}, n_2^{(2)}; \ldots; n_1^{(d)} n_2^{(d)}) \Longleftrightarrow S(\prod_{i=1}^{d} n_1^{(i)}, \prod_{i=1}^{d} n_2^{(i)}) \qquad (3)$$

Proof: A simple proof for the 2-D case has been presented in [8] which is easily generalized. In particular, the numbers $n_2^{(i)}$ describes the length of the blocks of MRN for the ith coordinate whereas $n_1^{(i)}$ describes the multiplicity of their occurrence. Thus, in order to arrive at the 1-D shuffle, the

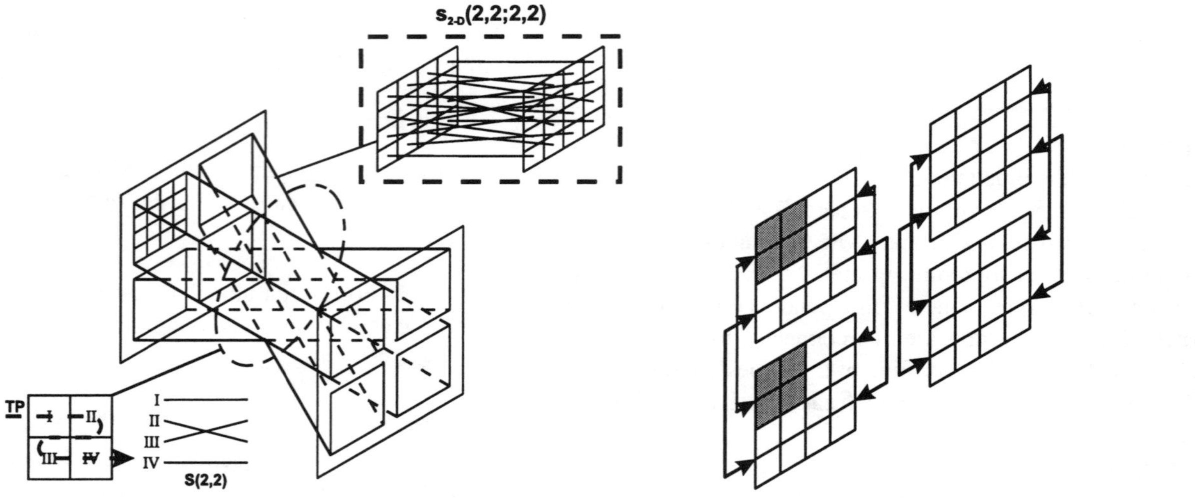

(a) (b)

Figure 1. (a) Shuffling of the 'pipes' of 4×4 interconnections (insert explains shuffling inside the pipes). (b) Input/output array of a 3-D cube of size 4^3 and interconnections within the 8×8-switches.

multiplicities $n_1^{(1)}, n_1^{(2)}, ..., n_1^{(d)}$ of blocks and the lengths $n_2^{(1)}, n_2^{(2)}, ..., n_2^{(d)}$ of blocks have to multiplied which provide the rhs of Eq.(3). □

(4) Let us assume a d-dimensional ($SGPS$, $NSGPS$) shuffle on rectangles of size $\prod_{i=1}^{d} N_i$ and its topologically equivalent 1-D shuffle according to Eq.(3) where the inputs/outputs of the latter are numbered by x between 0 and $\prod_{i=1}^{d} N_i$-1. Then the switch-pattern transformed 1-D shuffle may be described similar to Eq.(2) by

$$S\ (\prod_{i=1}^{d} n_1^{(i)}, \prod_{i=1}^{d} n_2^{(i)}) = \left(\prod_{i=1}^{d} n_1^{(i)} \cdot x + \lfloor \frac{\prod_{i=1}^{d} n_1^{(i)} \cdot x}{\prod_{i=1}^{d} N_i} \rfloor \right) mod \prod_{i=1}^{d} N_i \quad (4)$$

Remark 3: Proper self-routing in a d-dimensional shuffle network is restricted to inputs/outputs of size N_i=2^{m_i} where $m_i \geq 2$.

4.3. Transformation paths

The concept of the transformation path (TP) allows the complete design of shuffle networks in the 2-D domain (1-D design) or in a artificial dimension (mathematical space) and its transformation into the desired layout, respectively. The switch-pattern preserving transformation along a TP has been presented throughout several papers [3, 4, 5] and is briefly explained. The first part of the TP for a $SGPS$ pattern is shown in Fig. 2 (b) (dashed line).

For example, for the transformation of a 1-D shuffle network into its topologically equivalent 2-D shuffle pattern we simply have to run with the lhs of the 1-D shuffle network along the TP of the source array and with the rhs along the TP of the destination array. In this way, the 1-D shuffles of the various stages overlap to their topologically equivalent 2-D shuffles etc. In contrast, stretching the 2-D shuffles along the TPs generates the topologically equivalent 1-D shuffles [3, 4, 5].

The following definitions are due to [5].

Definition 3: A TP on the rectangle $\prod_{i=1}^{d} N_i$ is a polygon through the finite set of points $(x_1^{(i)}, x_2^{(i)}, ..., x_d^{(d)}; \nu)$ where $0 \leq i \leq N_i - 1$ and $1 \leq \nu \leq \prod_{i=1}^{d} N_i$; ν is a counting variable.

Definition 4: A TP on the rectangle $\prod_{i=1}^{d} N_i$ is called recursive if and only if

- the sequence (ν) addresses data elements e_1 (1st entity) and switch ports of size 2×2 (2nd entity e_2)
- the entities are recursively connected by one (and only one) of the six polygons possible through a 2×2-port.

(5) Let us assume 1-D shuffle on a M-vector and the equivalent d-dimensional ($d \geq 2$) $SGPS$ or $NSGPS$ pattern on the rectangle $\prod_{i=1}^{d} N_i$ which both are related according to

Eq.(3). Then there exists (at least) one TP through the d-dimensional rectangle which transforms the d-dimensional shuffle into its topologically equivalent 1-D shuffle (and vice versa).

Proof: The proof is a straight forward extension of the 2-D case in [8]. For the purpose of this proof, Eqs.(2) and (4) have to be applied. □

Definition 5: In the 2-D case a generalized mixed shuffle (GMS) has been assumed [3], where one coordinate is shuffled and the other coordinate is unshuffled [8]. For the GMS pattern we found the following result.

(6) Self-routing in a 2-D shuffle network by the TP concept ($\star$ in Table 4) can be established if and only if (iff) no GMS interconnection pattern occurs throughout the block-structure of the 2-D MIN. In the other case, where GMS patterns occur, a more general routing method by d-tuple RTs in Table 4 (**B** in [8] for the 2-D case) has to be applied.

Remark 4: The GMS pattern $S_{2-D}(4,2;2,4)$ cannot be transformed into $S(8,8)$ (no TP exists) though Eq. (3) is satisfied. For example the 2nd element at the lhs in Fig. 2 (b) (source array) is interconnected with the 5th element at the rhs (destination array). In contrast in $S(8,8)$ [Fig. 2 (a)] the 2nd element is interconnected with the 9th element, which contradicts the above.

5. The 2-D layout of d-dimensional shuffles versus common 2-D shuffles

Throughout this Section advantage **(D)** of Subsection 2.3 will be explained. For this purpose, the interconnected laser/detector arrays have to be extended to (at least) 32×32 and 64×64, respectively. Then the restrictions and difficulties of the common 2-D layout and the advantage of the presented concept can be made transparent. The main results are collected throughout **(7)** to **(10)**.

The 1-D shuffle networks for the possible interconnections of 64×64-data arrays are presented in Table 5, the geometries of the (artificial) higher dimensional interconnections are presented in Table 6 and the particular patterns of interest are collected throughout Table 7 (2-D and 4×4-switches, 3-D and 8×8-switches) and Table 8 (6-D and 64×64-switches), respectively.

The rearrangeable non-blocking interconnection of 4096 data/lines by a 1-D shuffle network with 8 × 8 switches in Table 5 and Fig. 3 is straight forward. However, its 2-D layout causes problems: for the arising GMS pattern no TP exists (Fig. 2) and thus it is not possible to design the 1-D network (Fig. 3) and map it into the 3-D physical space. Instead, the 2-D network has to be defined according to Eq. (3) and self-routing by means of the MRN d-dimensional tuples has to be applied [2, 8]. However, the assumption of 3-D switches (of size 8 × 8) and 3-D shuffles solves the self-routing problem completely (Table 7).

(7) Throughout the presented realizations, self-routing works properly in Table 5 (trivial) as well as in Table 7 and in Table 8.

Proof: Self-routing in Tables 7 and 8 is based on the validity of Eq.(3) and on the existence of a d-tuple RT (Table 4) or on the existence of a TP according to **(5)**, which generate results indicated by $\star$ in Table 4. □

In the following Tables 9 and 10 the corresponding 2-D shuffles on the square 64×64 and on the rectangle 8×32 will be presented. However, caused by space restriction, we will concentrate on those realizations which cause difficulties and conflicts throughout the self-routing of the common 2-D layout compared with the 2-D layout of the (artificial) higher dimensional architectures in Tables 7 and 8.

Remark 5: In Table 9 two equivalent realizations of the 3-stage network with 64×64-switches have been presented which have to be checked for proper routing.

(8) In Table 9 two GMS interstage interconnection patterns for 8×8-switches (3rd and 4th row) and all interconnection pattern for 64×64-switches are of the GMS type. Thus by means of **(6)**, in this case, self-routing is only possible by a d-tuple RT (Table 4). In Table 10 we also have two GMS interconnection patterns (1st column) which require self-routing by a d-tuple RT (Table 4).

(9) In Tables 9 and 10, for switches of size 32 × 32 (Fig. 4), two separable 2-D interconnection patterns exist, $S_{2-D}(2,2;2,16)$ on the rectangle 4 × 32 and $S_{2-D}(2,4;2,8)$ on the rectangle 8 × 16, between the stages 2 and 3 (2nd row) and between the stages 3 and 4 (3rd row). This layouts are explained in Fig. 5 for 64 × 64 and in Fig. 6 for 32 × 128.

Remark 6: In order to complete the results, one has to present the the d-tuple RT for Tables 7 and 8 similar to Table 4.

The foregoing results are completed by presenting the common 2-D layout for the interconnection of 32×32-arrays and the detection of similar difficulties.

Remark 7: From the comparison of the common 2-D self-routing concept for the interconnection of 32×32 and 64×64 arrays with the approach presented throughout the paper, we may conclude that the presented self-routing concept works properly for any appropriate size of the switches

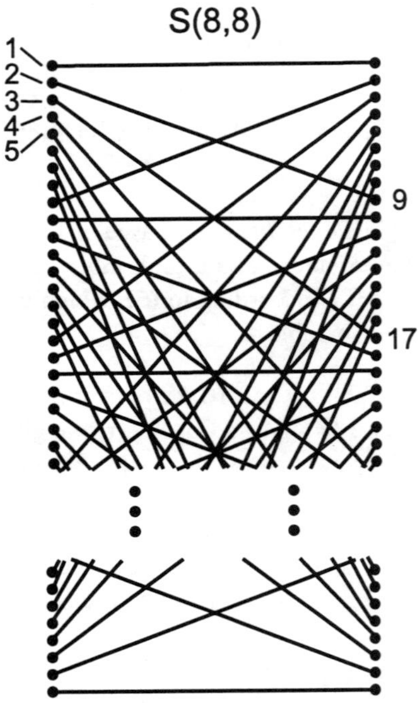

(a)

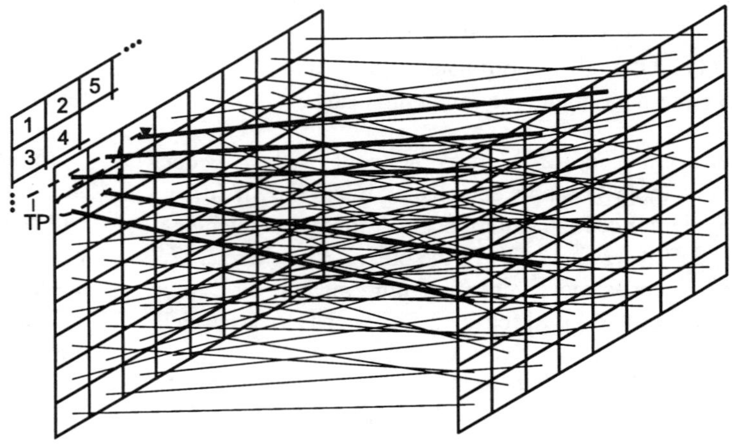

(b)

Figure 2. Impossibility to transform (a) $S(8,8)$ into (b) $S_{2-D}(4,2;2,4)$ (and vice versa) caused by the non-existence of the transformation path (TP).

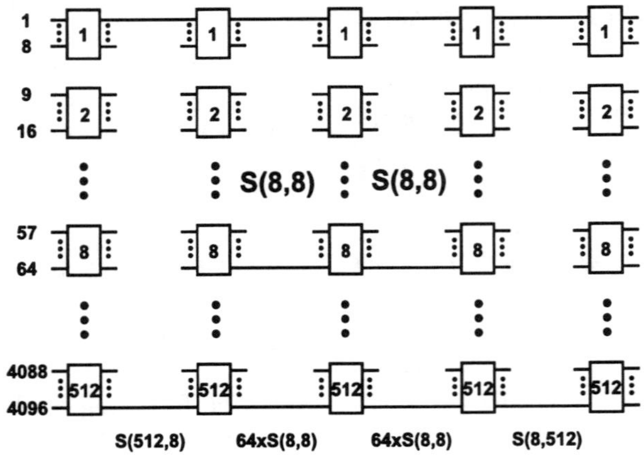

Figure 3. 1-D shuffle network with 8×8 switches for the rearrangle non-blocking interconnection of 4096 lines (for the transformation of $S(8,8)$ into the 3-D physical space see Fig. 2)

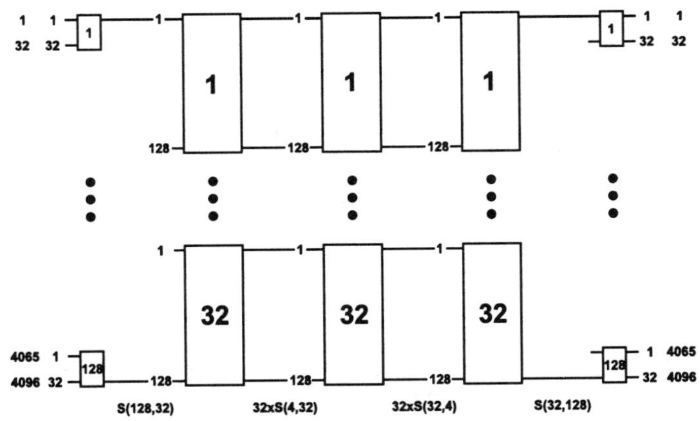

Figure 4. 1-D shuffle network with 32×32 switches for the rearrangle non-blocking interconnection of 4096 lines (for the transformation of $S(4,32)$ and $S(32,4)$, respectively, two 2-D shuffles exists, see (9))

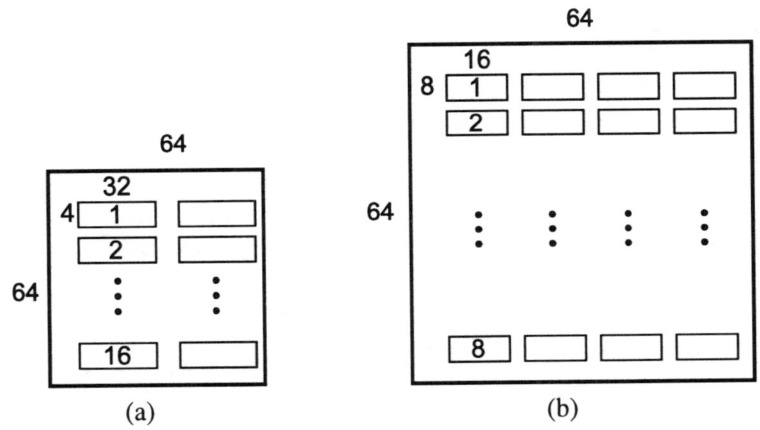

Figure 5. 2-D Layouts on 64×64 of $32 \times S(4,32)$ and $32 \times S(32,4)$, respectively, 2nd column in Table 9.

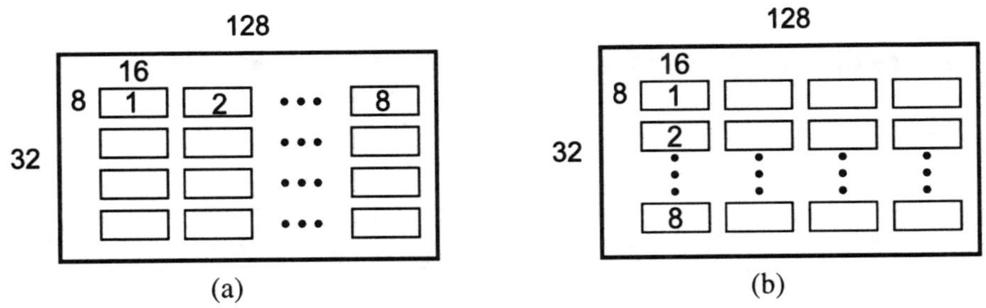

Figure 6. 2-D Layouts on 32×128 of $32 \times S(4,32)$ and $32 \times S(32,4)$, respectively, 2nd column in Table 10.

Data	4096				
Switch	4×4	8×8	16×16	32×32	64×64
1. Pattern	$S(1024,4)$	$S(512,8)$	$S(256,16)$	$S(128,32)$	$S(64,64)$
2.	$4\times S(256,4)$	$8\times S(64,8)$	$16\times S(16,16)$	$32\times S(4,32)$	$S(64,64)$
3.	$16\times S(64,4)$	$64\times S(8,8)$	$16\times S(16,16)$	$32\times S(32,4)$	
4.	$64\times S(16,4)$	$64\times S(8,8)$	$S(16,256)$	$S(32,128)$	
5.	$256\times S(4,4)$	$8\times S(8,64)$			
6.	$256\times S(4,4)$	$S(8,512)$			
7.	$64\times S(4,16)$				
8.	$16\times S(4,64)$				
9.	$4\times S(4,256)$				
10.	$S(4,1024)$				

Fig. 3 Fig. 4

Table 5. Blockstructure of rearrangeable nonblocking 1-D shuffle $MINs$ with 4×4- to 64×64-switches (the 2nd and 4th columns are illustrated in Fig. 3 and Fig. 4).

Data Set	4096				
Dimension	1-D	2-D	3-D	4-D	6-D
Geometry	4096	64×64	16×16×16	8×8×8×8	4×4×4×4×4×4

Table 6. Geometries of the data set.

Data	64^2=64×64=4096	16^3=16×16×16=4096
Switch	$2^2\times 2^2$=4×4	$2^3\times 2^3$=8×8
1. Pattern	$S_{2-D}(32,2;32,2)$	$S_{3-D}(8,2;8,2;8,2)$
2.	$4\times S_{2-D}(16,2;16,2)$	$8\times S_{3-D}(4,2;4,2;4,2)$
3.	$16\times S_{2-D}(8,2;8,2)$	$64\times S_{3-D}(2,2;2,2;2,2)$
4.	$64\times S_{2-D}(4,2;4,2)$	$64\times S_{3-D}(2,2;2,2;2,2)$
5.	$256\times S_{2-D}(2,2;2,2)$	$8\times S_{3-D}(2,4;2,4;2,4)$
6.	$256\times S_{2-D}(2,2;2,2)$	$S_{3-D}(2,8;2,8;2,8)$
7.	$64\times S_{2-D}(2,4;2,4)$	
8.	$16\times S_{2-D}(2,8;2,8)$	
9.	$4\times S_{2-D}(2,16;2,16$	
10.	$S_{2-D}(2,32;2,32)$	

Table 7. Blockstructure of rearrangeable nonblocking 2-D and 3-D shuffle $MINs$ with 4×4- and 8×8-switches.

Data	4^6=4×4×4×4×4×4=4096
Switch	$2^6\times 2^6$=64×64
1. Pattern	$S_{6-D}(2,2;2,2;2,2;2,2;2,2;2,2)$
2.	$S_{6-D}(2,2;2,2;2,2;2,2;2,2;2,2)$

Table 8. Blockstructure of a rearrangeable nonblocking 6-D shuffle MIN with 64×64-switches.

Data	4096=64×64			
Switch	8×8	32×32	64×64	
1. Pattern	$S_{2-D}(32,2;16,4)$	$S_{2-D}(32,2;4,16)$	$S_{2-D}(2,32;32,2)$	$S_{2-D}(4,16;16,4)$
2.	$8\times S_{2-D}(8,2;8,4)$	$32\times S(4,32)$	$S_{2-D}(32,2;2,32)$	$S_{2-D}(16,4;4,16)$
3.	$64\times S_{2-D}(4,2;2,4)$	$32\times S(32,4)$		
4.	$64\times S_{2-D}(2,4;4,2)$	$S_{2-D}(2,32;16,4)$		
5.	$8\times S_{2-D}(2,8;4,8)$			
6.	$S_{2-D}(2,32;4,16)$			

Table 9. Blockstructure for the interconnection of 4096 data by rearrangeable nonblocking 2-D shuffle $MINs$ with 8×8- to 64×64-switches on 64×64-arrays (for the layout of the 2nd column see Fig. 5).

Data	4096=32×128	
Switch	8×8	32×32
1. Pattern	$S_{2-D}(16,2;32,2)$	$S_{2-D}(16,2;8,16)$
2.	$8\times S_{2-D}(16,2;4,4)$	$32\times S(4,32)$
3.	$64\times S_{2-D}(4,2;2,4)$	$32\times S(32,4)$
4.	$64\times S_{2-D}(2,4;4,2)$	$S_{2-D}(2,16;16,8)$
5.	$8\times S_{2-D}(2,16;4,4)$	
6.	$S_{2-D}(2,16;2,32)$	

Table 10. Blockstructure for the interconnection of 4096 data by rearrangeable nonblocking 2-D shuffle $MINs$ with 8×8- and 32×32-switches on 32×128-rectangles (Fig. 6).

Data	1024=32×32				
Switch	8×8	16×16		32×32	
1. Pattern	$S_{2-D}(16,2;8,4)$	$S_{2-D}(8,4;8,4)$	$S_{2-D}(16,2;4,8)$	$S_{2-D}(16,2;2,16)$	$S_{2-D}(8,4;4,8)$
2.	$8\times S_{2-D}(8,2;2,4)$	$16\times S_{2-D}(2,4;2,4)$	$16\times S_{2-D}(2,4;2,4)$	$S_{2-D}(2,16;16,2)$	$S_{2-D}(4,8;8,4)$
3.	$64\times S(8,2)$	$16\times S_{2-D}(4,2;4,2)$	$16\times S_{2-D}(4,2;4,2)$		
4.	$64\times S(2,8)$	$S_{2-D}(4,8;4,8)$	$S_{2-D}(2,16;8,4)$		
5.	$8\times S_{2-D}(2,8;4,2)$				
6.	$S_{2-D}(2,16;4,8)$				

Table 11. Blockstructure for the interconnection of 1024 data by rearrangeable nonblocking shuffle $MINs$ with 8×8- to 32×32-switches.

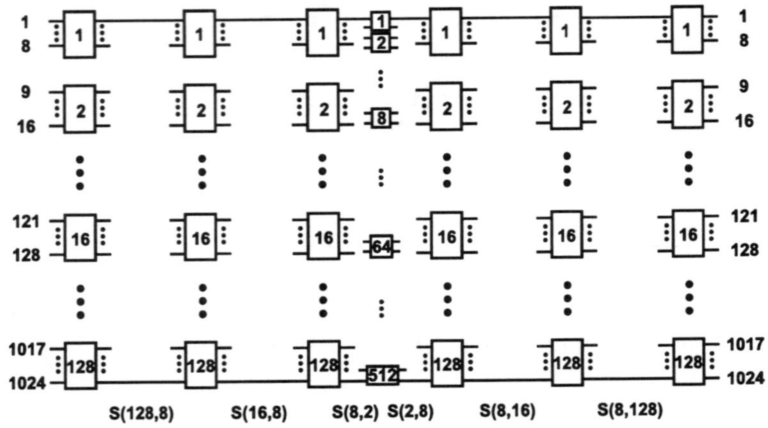

Figure 7. Impossibility to interconnect 1024 data with only 8×8 switches in a rearrangeable non-blocking manner (1st column in Table 11). The 2×2 switches in the center cause problems for the 2-D layout.

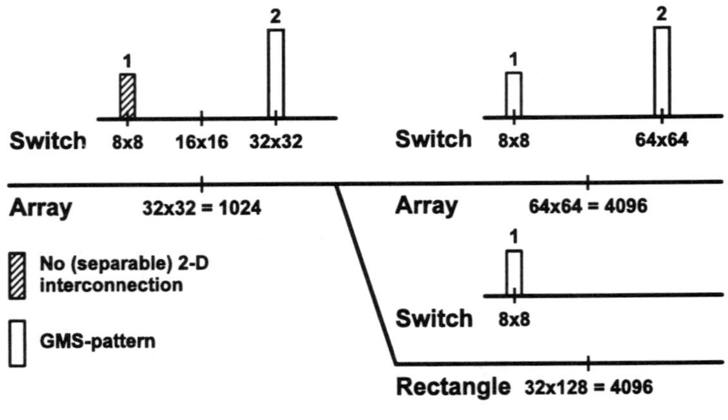

Figure 8. Review of the occurrence of GMS and non-separable 2-D shuffle interconnections.

even in the case the common 2-D self-routing fails.

(10) In Table 11 for switches of size 8×8 no separable 2-D interconnection pattern exists between the stages 3 and 4 (3rd row) and between the stages 4 and 5 (4th row).

6. Review of results

Throughout the paper, the interconnection of 32×32 and 64×64 arrays by d-dimensional shuffles has been analysed. The application of the concept of dimension-dependent switches and d-dimensional shuffles allows the proper operation of self-routing (Tables 7 and 8). However, once 2-D shuffles and large switches are applied (Tables 9, 10 and 11), two crucial problems have been observed

- Occurrence of GMS interconnection patterns and
- Non-separable 2-D interconnection patterns.

The GMS interconnection patterns in Tables 9 occur in the 1st column (3rd and 4th row) and in the 3rd and 4th column. In Table 10 they occur in the 1st column (3rd and 4th row) and in Table 11 GMS patterns occur in the 2nd to 5th column. These results are summarized in Fig. 8.

7. Conclusion

In multistage interconnection networks ($MINs$) by increasing the size of the switches the number of stages (NS) and in turn the attenuation of signals decreases. Therefore, throughout the paper, d-dimensional ($d \geq 2$) shuffle interconnections and dimension-dependent switches of size $2^d\times2^d$ have been applied to establish proper self-routing in shuffle networks with switches of size $\geq 4\times4$. Thereby, the 2-D layout of the presented shuffle networks, which provides several advantages (balance between local metallic traces and global optical interconnections), have been briefly considered.

By (1) mapping data vectors and data arrays onto higher dimensional cubes/rectangles, (2) the introduction of d-dimensional shuffles, and (3) the concept of dimension-dependent switches, in addition to the common 2-D self-routing concept, a further set of shuffle networks is established where all members are capable to do self-routing for any appropriate size of the switches. These networks are aimed to meet the needs of the optical technology. For example, large networks may be build simply by composing squares and rectangles of available wafers. Additionally, by means of this method, large reliable networks may be built although large reliable laser and detector arrays are not available.

Thus the presented architectures and self-routing principle extends the common 2-D self-routing concept and provides several topologically equivalent networks from which, for a certain situation and the available technology, the best may be chosen. Additionally, by means of the presented architectural and self-routing concept (higher artifical dimensions), difficulties, arising for the interconnection of large arrays, may be avoided without the application of complicated control schemes.

8. Acknowledgements

The work is supported by the "Bundesminister für Bildung, Wissenschaft, Forschung und Technologie" and the City of Berlin within the national PHOTONIK II program under contract 01 BP 4449/2.

The Figures were provided by A. Can, B. Feldhahn, and S. Fischer and the editorial work has been done by T. Kong, which is gratefully acknowledged.

References

[1] J. Giglmayr. Theoretical framework for 3-d rearrangeable mins and information on the appropriate control and application to optical computing. In *Int. Sympos.* Optics in Computing, *Toulouse, France*, pages 165–172, 17–18 October 1989.

[2] J. Giglmayr. Organization of $k \times k$ switches ($k \geq 4$) interconnected by d-dimensional ($d \geq 2$) regular optical patterns. *Appl. Opt.*, 30(35):5119–5135, December 1991.

[3] J. Giglmayr. d-dimensional ($d \geq 3$) shuffle interconnections. *Appl. Opt.*, 31(11):1695–1708, April 1992.

[4] J. Giglmayr. Properties of optically implemented shuffle interconnections. *Optics Commun.*, 93:112–125, 1992.

[5] J. Giglmayr. Basic building blocks for the switch-preserving transformation of shuffle interconnections. *Appl. Opt.*, 32(26):4992–5001, September 1993.

[6] J. Giglmayr. Locality and decomposition of regular optical interconnection patterns. *Appl. Opt.*, 33(26):6157–6167, September 1994.

[7] J. Giglmayr. Rearrangeability and connectivity of multistage interconnection networks with nearest-neighbour interconnections. *IEICE Trans. Commun.*, E77-B(12):1546–1555, December 1994.

[8] J. Giglmayr. Self-routing in 2-d shuffle networks. *IEICE Trans. Commun.*, E79-B(2):173–181, 1996.

[9] S.-T. Huang and S. K. Tripathi. Finite state model and compatibility theory: New analysis tools for permutation networks. *IEEE Trans. Comput.*, C-35(7):591–601, May 1986.

[10] K. Y. Lee. On the rearrangeability of 2($\log_2 n$)-1 stage permutation networks. *IEEE Trans. Comput.*, C-34(5):412–425, May 1985.

[11] H. R. Ramanujam. Decomposition of permutation networks. *IEEE Trans. Comput.*, C-22(7):639–643, July 1973.

[12] A. A. Sawchuk and I. Glaser. Geometries for optical implementations of the perfect shuffle. In *SPIE Proceedings* Optical Computing, 963, pages 270–282, 1988.

SESSION VII

Optoelectronics in MPP Computing Systems

Chair

A. Louri
University of Arizona

Optics Inside Future Computers

Craig Lund
clund@mc.com
Mercury Computer Systems, Inc.
199 Riverneck Road
Chelmsford, MA 01824-2820

Abstract

This paper discusses the potential role of optics in future COTS processors manufactured by Mercury Computer Systems. We conclude that high-end applications, particularly space time adaptive processing (STAP), benefit from a computing platform with an optical backplane.

1. System Area Networks

The heart of any parallel computer is the communications network used to tie that computer's processors together. Academics have many names for such a network, but "System Area Network", or simply SAN, is the most popular term today. SANs offer high bandwidth, low latency, and very low error rates. SANs sacrifice long cable runs and global scaleability.

There are almost as many SAN designs as there are parallel computing researchers. However, as markets mature, standards evolve. For example, the Internet Engineering Task Force (IETF) is developing a SAN internetworking protocol standard called PacketWay that will complement their TCP/IP standard.

RACEway Interlink[1], Scalable Coherent Interconnect (SCI), and the switched variant of Fibre Channel are among today's formal, international SAN hardware standards, each supported by multiple vendors. Of the three, RACEway is the only SAN focused on the unique challenges associated with hosting real-time applications in embedded environments. By volume, RACEway is also the most popular SAN standard today.

More than a dozen computer vendors use RACEway. Mercury Computer Systems invented RACEway and continues to play a leadership role on the ANSI/VITA committee responsible for its evolution. This paper describes Mercury's vision for the future of RACEway and the potential role of optics in that future.

2. Bandwidth

Historically, the bandwidth between any two points in a SAN has matched the bandwidth between a processor and its DRAM. RACEway evolved in this manner. The link bandwidth in today's RACEway is 160 megabytes per second, a common maximum for DRAM technologies available in 1993.

SANs stopped tracking memory bandwidth when memory chip designers switched to more exotic interfaces such as those used in Rambus and in synchronous DRAM. Fortunately, at about that same time, ASIC technology advances allowed SAN designers to affordably incorporate rate matching buffers which allowed SANs and associated processor memory systems to operate at different rates. SAN bandwidth today generally remains stalled at 1993 DRAM rates.

Mercury's defense and commercial customers appear satisfied with RACEway's existing link bandwidth. However, this does not mean that the RACEway community will stand still. RACEway will move beyond today's 160 MB/s port bandwidth as soon as higher rates become practical within the unique constraints posed by embedded applications.

The term "practical" includes "affordable." Thus any new link technology must have a volume driver outside the embedded computing niche. Few volume markets require extreme bandwidth over distances longer than an inch or two. Therefore, although Mercury would like to make a sudden leap to synchronous DRAM bandwidths, we predict a future where SAN bandwidth will remain below memory rates. To compensate, Mercury envisions SANs that incorporate an increasing number of moderate bandwidth links that offer multiple, simultaneous paths between arbitrary nodes. Special hardware can aggregate these SAN

1. Readers can purchase a copy of the ANSI/VITA 5-1994 RACEway Interlink standard for $17.00 from VITA; 7825 East Gelding Drive, Suite 104; Scottsdale, AZ 85260-3415; telephone: (602) 951-8866, fax: (602) 951-0720, internet mail: <lollie@vita.com>.

0-8186-7974-3/97 $10.00 © 1997 IEEE

ports to deliver higher rates in cases where offering more than moderate bandwidth over a single path is critical.

What will "moderate bandwidth" be in the year 2000? Given the movement towards gigabit local area network technologies like Gigabit Ethernet and Fibre Channel, it is likely that significant industry investment will go into driving a gigabit over wire pairs in a cost effective manner. Gigabit bandwidth is actually a little lower than today's RACEway bandwidth. However, RACEway ports use 37 wires. Tomorrow's gigabit delivers almost the same bandwidth over only two wires.

Future, higher bandwidth, SAN ports might employ multiple gigabit wire pairs operating in parallel. Unfortunately, controlling signal skew between parallel, gigabit lines remains challenging. The SCI community, for example, has set its goal at half gigabit rates to help manage skew.

There are electrical signalling technologies in research labs that show promise. In particular, Mercury is tracking ongoing research by Dr. William J. Dally at MIT and Dr. John W. Poulton at UNC. These researchers are cooperating to, in a laboratory, drive four gigabits over a wire pair, at moderate distance, using low power, and with manageable skew.

3. Corner Turn Performance

It is important to note that, in many embedded computing applications, particularly space time adaptive processing (STAP), critical multiprocessor performance bottlenecks occur during data transpose, or "corner turn" operations. This is when applications really stress memory systems and SANs. There are two problems. First, during a data transpose, every processor suddenly needs to communicate with every other processor. Topological contention is the result. Second, during a transpose, memory access patterns are not sequential. Thus memory systems generally cannot drive a transpose operation at anything close to maximum DRAM bandwidth.

Therefore, in the real-world of embedded applications, the scatter/gather performance of end point memory systems, and the topology of the SAN, are more critical performance factors than the bandwidth of individual links within a SAN. This is the primary reason why RACEway users are comfortable with a SAN in which the port bandwidth is less than the peak DRAM rate.

4. San as a Commodity

When one talks about SAN technology becoming commodity, it becomes important to differentiate between requirements associated with a multiprocessor communications fabric and associated with an I/O fabric. Commodity versions of ANSI RACEway offered by vendors such as Cypress Semiconductor are I/O fabrics. This is because, to achieve commodity sales goals, SAN chips must interface with processors in a manner that is broadly applicable and stable. The PCI I/O bus meets this requirement. Processor-specific memory busses do not.

Mercury continues to build RACEway SAN chips that interface directly with a processor's native memory bus. In contrast, the Mercury/Cypress SAN chips interface at the longer lived, more common, PCI level. Mercury will continue to play both sides of this issue. Mercury will still build processor-specific chips for its own use. However, Mercury's chips will continue to share a SAN infrastructure with commodity chips from trend setting companies like Cypress.[2]

5. Error Detection and Correction

Today's RACEway does not detect nor correct errors that theoretically could be encountered on its communication links. This is because the signalling technology that RACE uses today delivers error rates low enough that Mercury treats links as if they are completely error free. There is a user advantage here that is not immediately obvious. Every SAN we know of, except RACEway, tolerates noticeable error rates in order to offer a little extra performance. Such SANs rely upon error correction circuits and thus cannot be fully deterministic. This is due to the unpredictable number of retries a SAN might make in its effort to deliver an arbitrary information packet.

Unfortunately, this particular RACEway advantage will fade a little in future versions. Leading edge signalling technologies generally have lower noise margins than RACE is accustomed to. Future RACEs must detect and correct errors. When this switch occurs, RACEway will remain uniquely deterministic, but less so than it has been.

6. Specific RACEway Plans

Mercury has three significant RACEway enhancements in progress. The first enhancement, which we call RACE Multiport, is already shipping. It involves getting more RACEway ports off the edge of a standard VMEbus board; introducing RACEway into standard PCI environments;

2. RACEway remains the most successful commodity SAN in today's market. However, alternatives such as SCI occasionally appear. If a SAN technology ever overtakes RACE in commodity applications, Mercury reserves the right to switch.

creating RACE-only backplanes for use in thousand processor RACEway configurations; and increasing options for users who wish to configure RACEway systems that involve multiple chassis.

Mercury's next RACE enhancement carries two code names "RACE 1.5", and "RACE++". It will ship about one year from now. Here Mercury will introduce a denser router (crossbar). We will also speed up RACEway channel bandwidth within installations that do not include VME-bus.

Mercury's biggest plan for RACE is called "RACE 2.000". This is where Mercury will change RACE's fundamental signalling technology. We will use an aggressive electrical technology on our circuit boards. We will use either electronics or optics between boards (details follow).

DARPA ETO is supporting the optical aspects of the RACE 2.000 effort through its OMNET program. Mercury's SAN technology is a demonstration target for two OMNET contractors, HP Labs and Honeywell Technology Center. In even more exotic terrain, Mercury is a member of two DARPA ETO Free Space Optical Interconnect (FSOIA) teams led by BDM Federal and UCSD.

7. Stap Contention Forces Optics

From a performance perspective, the best topology for any SAN is a fully connected network where all nodes can communicate simultaneously (multiple paths between nodes would be even better). However, a fully connected topology is usually impractical for large configurations. Thus, real world configurations compromise on connectivity. The resulting compromises have names like "hypercube", "fat tree", or "mesh".

For many defense applications, these compromises are not troublesome. For example, vendors often configure RACEway in a Clos fat tree topology. Data distribution solutions for the SAR algorithm exist that allow a fat tree to host SAR without performance compromise[3].

Data distribution solutions exist for today's STAP algorithms as well. However, the STAP problem is more challenging, particularly as the volume of data flowing into STAP grows within future missions. To face that challenge, Mercury has prepared a Large Systems Plan that significantly increases connectivity between boards and between chassis using today's RACE® Multiport technology.

Mercury's Large System Plan requires physically large, "9U", circuit boards in order to provide a long enough card edge to pass four independent RACEway paths between each circuit board and the active backplane. However, a 9U chassis is too big for many UAV applications. This is where optics can play a role. Delivering identical functionality using smaller, "6U" circuit boards may not be possible without optics because of connector density challenges.

3. Most of the programming effort in a parallel environment focuses on finding an optimal data distribution. Therefore, SAN contention, and Mercury's hierarchal bandwidth idea, impact programmer productivity.

8. Connector Density

Today's RACE uses 37 parallel wires to pass each data channel (we clock the channel at 40 MHz). This number of wires limits RACE systems to about two data channels off each 6U board. This is because wiring an active backplane becomes very difficult in a twenty board system with anything more than two channels in 6U, or four channels in 9U. A passive backplane is practical, but to achieve the same level of performance, a passive backplane requires significantly more board edge channels. In the passive case, electrical connector density quickly becomes the limitation (the 6U card edge is about nine inches long).

Fortunately, optical systems offer the potential of significantly more connector density at a circuit board's edge. This potential excites us. With enough edge channels, RACEway users can fully connect the boards within a single chassis, while also supporting multiple links between chassis.

9. Optics in RACE 2.000

Today's commercially available, high-performance optical technologies are expensive in terms of dollars and power consumption. However, both obstacles will erode with time. We believe that, as optics technology continues to evolve, optics will replace copper at lower and lower levels of integration. Right now Mercury can justify optics for interchassis connections. In addition, due to connector density advantages, we see a requirement for optics within a chassis evolving over the next few years.

Our plan for integrating optics is therefore incremental. Mercury's vision of RACE 2.000 focuses on a new electrical signalling technology (one needs fast electronics in order to drive fast optics). We will use the new signals to quickly move data between processors collocated on a single circuit board. When connector density is not an issue, we may also use the new signals to move data between circuit boards.

Today Mercury uses optics when interconnecting multiple RACEway chassis. We make the connection using a bridge chip that connects one RACEway channel to a single optical channel. In RACE 2000 we want the option of moving optics into the backplane. Thus, with support from Honeywell's contract within DARPA's OMNET program,

Mercury plans to develop an optical router (crossbar) MCM to replace today's bridge chip. This specialized router will have electrical and optical ports. The electrical ports, which will use parallel signalling, will service the on-board nodes. The optical ports will pass data between chassis, and optionally between boards. Ideally, the optical bridging crossbar chip will require only a tiny optical connector at the card edge, giving board designers the option of squeezing many such ports onto an edge. Of course, we will also need some kind of passive optical backplane.

With such a router chip and backplane technology, the RACEway community can build topologies that are not possible today. Specifically, five optical ports will allow a sixteen board hypercube, with 16 free channels for use as paths to other chassis. Although not fully connected, any board will be able to communicate with any other board (in the same chassis) the help of no more than one intermediate board. The resulting contention will be better than what users achieve today using a single electrical channel and an active backplane. The contention will not be quite as good as four channels into an active backplane (our 9U Large Systems Plan), but the passive backplane is a maintenance advantage. Using two such crossbars on each board can reduce contention further. With five such chips on each board we can fully connect a 21 slot chassis.

The resulting crossbar technology must support all functionality common in electrical crossbars. We refer here to things like priority routing for deterministic behavior, error detection with reporting, adaptive routing, as well as logic that supports performance analysis and program debugging.

The optical crossbar must also meet embedded market constraints. For example, the existing RACEway crossbar uses less than one square inch of board space and one watt of power.

10. Conclusion

Contention challenges within applications like STAP are driving Mercury towards optics, particularly in smaller form factors like 6U. Although there is little market pull today, increasing bandwidth requirements may also force Mercury into optics.

The embedded market niche is not large enough to drive technical innovation within the optical domain. Therefore, by default, the RACEway community must wait until a larger market expresses similar requirements.

Mercury's RACE 2.000 plan includes optics.

References

1. Bradley C. Kuszmaul, "The RACE Network Architecture", 9th International Parallel Processing Symposium.

Systolic Processing Architectures Using Optoelectronic Interconnects

Sek Meng Chai, Abelardo López-Lagunas,
D. Scott Wills, Nan Marie Jokerst, Martin A. Brooke
School of Electrical and Computer Engineering
Microelectronics Research Center
Georgia Institute of Technology
Atlanta, Georgia 30332-0250

Abstract

Systolic arrays have traditionally provided efficient, high performance execution for computation intensive applications. Despite the extensive research in systolic arrays, system designers must continually incorporate new technological advances to improve node communications, I/O bandwidth, and programmability. This paper presents optoelectronic interconnect as a communication method for systolic arrays in early image processing applications. Optoelectronic interconnects provide potentially high I/O bandwidth required to maintain high utilization rate for systolic arrays. In addition, optoelectronic interconnects provides a two-dimensional focal-plane topology ideal for systolic image processing systems. This paper introduces two new systolic architectures that incorporate integrated optoelectronics to provide an extremely compact, high performance, highly efficient image processing system. Several important early image processing applications developed for these architectures are also described.

1. Introduction

A new emerging class of computational structures, "smart pixels", integrates optoelectronic devices, typically in a plane, with processing electronics. Traditional smart pixel systems are used for image processing where a small array of pixels is mapped to a processing node. Each node, illustrated in Figure 1, contains three components: optical inputs, "smart" electronics, and optical outputs. Optical inputs deliver electronic signals to the processing electronics. The processing electronics consist of either digital or analog functionality for processing images. Results from the processing electronics are then output as optical signals.

The integrated optoelectronic devices offer a potentially lower cost, higher density alternative to traditional wire-based I/O. For image processing applications that require high off-chip bandwidth, these devices provide compact, low latency focal-plane processing that is more difficult to achieve with traditional perimeter wire bonding. Integrated optoelectronics also provide a closer coupling between optical devices and processors for lower noise, higher sensitivity operations.

Despite the potential of integrated optoelectronics, smart pixel systems generally provide simple processing functions compared to general purpose microprocessors and digital signal processing chips that provide much greater generality at lower performance and efficiency per silicon area. The ideal smart pixel architecture provides not only computational versatility but also an efficient operation. SIMD (Single Instruction Multiple Data) and MIMD (Multiple Instruction Multiple Data) architectures incorporating optoelectronic devices have been reported [4,14,16], but are more versatile than needed for most early vision applications. Systolic computation for early image processing provides excellent fundamental design methodologies for smart pixel systems. Unlike SIMD and MIMD architectures, systolic processing provide compact, efficient, high throughput computation. In addition, systolic design methodologies establish localized communication that allows better scalability for larger image processing applications.

This paper presents a systolic architecture and its compatibility for early image processing in smart pixel systems. A focal plane topology incorporating integrated optoelectronics is introduced as an ideal topology for systolic image processing systems. Focal plane processing provides a three-dimensional computing structure (a two-dimensional computational mesh with data flow in the third dimension) [5]. Two new systolic architectures for early vision image processing, being developed at Georgia Tech, PAMSAC and GT-VISTA, are presented. These systems rely on optoelectronic devices integrated on the focal plane that provide high I/O bandwidth for systolic computation. They use integrated thin film optoelectronic devices interfaced with CMOS analog amplifiers to provide inter-connectivity among systolic elements in a three-dimensional processing structure [7,11].

2. Early image/vision processing systolic array smart pixel systems

Systolic architectures were introduced by H. T. Kung in 1978 as an architectural approach to exploit the promise of

0-8186-7974-3/97 $10.00 © 1997 IEEE

VLSI technology [13]. The design methodologies were set to alleviate communication penalties by using modular cells without global interconnects, and to decrease design time by reducing complexity. H.T. Kung stressed scalability, high degree of concurrency, and repetitive use of data to efficiently utilize the increasing number of transistors per integrated chip. His landmark paper forms the fundamental basis for early research in systolic architectures. The following describes the three basic design principles of systolic arrays.

- *Modular Cells.* The first design principle to use simple modular cells was set to cope with increased design complexity. For special purpose systems, this is an attractive guideline to reduce the design time by reusing common building blocks. These common building blocks can be optimized for area, power, and speed to create the overall speedup for the entire system.
- *Localized Communication.* Long interconnections consume more power and chip area, and have high latency. The second design principle establishes simple, regular communication to maintain short communication paths. By incorporating the communication flow into the overall design, the outcome may be an efficient, regular implementation without long communication paths.
- *Balanced Computation.* A VLSI computation is feasible only for compute-bound algorithms where there is more computation to be performed than available inputs and outputs. A good systolic design should therefore ensure that for every I/O operation, multiple operations are performed to obtain maximum throughput.

Systolic execution model allows for extremely efficient implementation of systems that solve computational intensive applications. These computations are pipelined in many dimensions in order to obtain high computational throughput. Systolic arrays maximize the processing performed on a datum once it has been obtained from I/O or memory by reusing the datum as it moves through the pipelines in the array. Unlike a regular pipeline structure, however, the input data as well as partial results flow through the array at varying speeds and in multiple directions [10].

Systolic arrays work well with algorithms that require high processing and high throughput, such as early image processing applications. The key components of these image processing algorithms include: large amounts of input data, complex algorithms, and high data rate requirements [15]. These algorithms involve simple operations with the output at each pixel relying on neighborhood pixel values. Examples of early vision algorithms include contrast enhancement, convolution, edge detection, and other simple filtering operations.

Smart pixel systems map image elements to a processing node, and therefore exhibit neighborhood dependency indicative of early vision algorithms. Consequently, traditional applications for smart pixel systems include early vision algorithms. Hence systolic design methodologies of modular cells, localized communication, and balanced computation are naturally consistent for smart pixel systems. By modifying an image processing application for a smart pixel system as a systolic algorithm, and designing the smart pixel system with systolic design methodologies, a designer can further the smart pixel capabilities with systolic characteristics of high computation rate and high throughput.

In higher level image processing applications, complex operations must be performed on collection of data, usually separated by large distances in terms of memory location or processor nodal location. These operations involve decisions or interpretations based on the relationships between the image data and databases or mathematical models [8].

3. Systolic arrays with integrated optoelectronics

Traditional two dimensional systolic arrays rely on perimeter input to feed data into its inner core. The performance of such configuration is limited by the I/O bandwidth, and thus the ultimate performance should be a computation rate that balances the available I/O bandwidth with external devices or memory [13]. Existing research has been focused on the systolic mappings of algorithms that limit the number of I/O rate per computation. In these systems, data items and interim results are stored and used repetitively to alleviate external I/O bandwidth. Figure 2(a) illustrates a two-dimensional mesh of systolic processors with perimeter input.

In a perimeter I/O limited system, the image data is often segmented into small scan-line rows. Each row of cells processes only a portion of the scanned image. Consequently, the processed image typically flows through neighboring rows in order to reach the output boundary cells at the opposite edge of the mesh of processing elements. The algorithm is usually pipelined in rows of cells in order to increase the throughput of the system.

New technologies, such as flip-chip bump bonding and through-wafer optoelectronic devices [7,11], provide additional communication accesses to the inner cells in the 2-D mesh topology. Figure 2(b) shows the focal plane topology with immediate communication access to the inner core [3]. This focal-plane configuration allows an additional dimension of I/O compared to the perimeter I/O. As in the perimeter I/O limited system, this focal-plane topology can be pipelined such that each layer of processing nodes operates on the entire image at an instance. There is no need to segment the image into smaller sub-images for processing. In addition, the systolic computation rate can

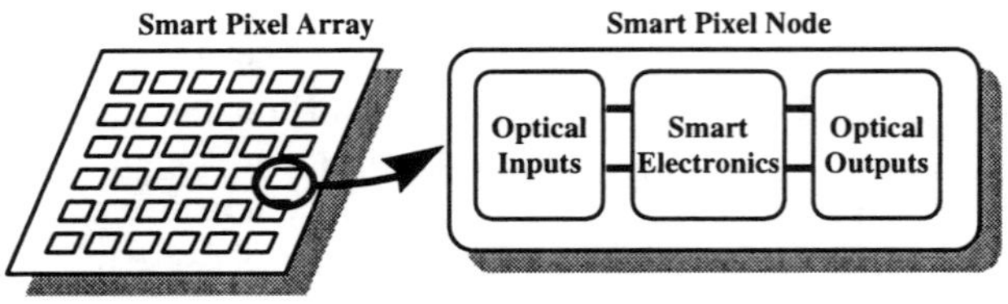

Figure 1. Smart pixel nodal components

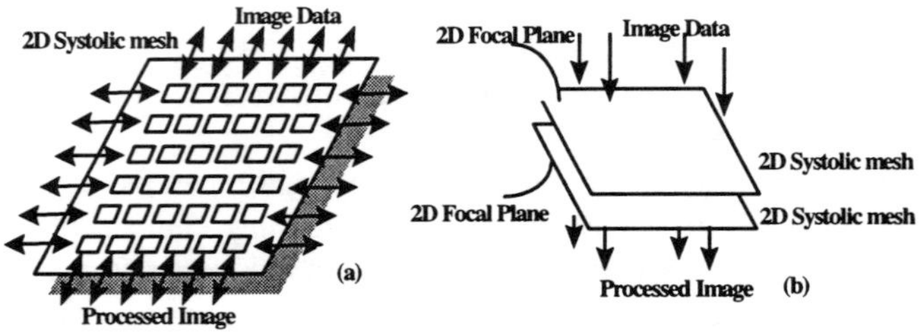

Figure 2. (a) Perimeter I/O via boundary cells and (b) Increase I/O bandwidth with focal plane topology

rise accordingly to match the already increased I/O rate instead of being limited by the I/O rate in a perimeter I/O limited system.

While this focal-plane topology is common in image processing systems [4,5], our intent is to assert that this topology is the ideal configuration for systolic image processing system. These configurations can provide the short communication path and scalability that are consistent with the systolic design principle. This section will proceed to describe the consistency of systolic design with characteristics of focal plane topology utilizing optoelectronic devices in systolic smart pixel systems.

- *Short Communication Path.* The focal plane topology provides short communication paths among cells between layers of systolic 2D meshes. These cells no longer have to transmit the processed image data along intermediate rows to reach the boundary cells to transmit the output, but rather in a vertical flow towards a new 2D VLSI systolic smart pixel plane.
- *Scalability.* The smart pixel system maintains scalability by incorporating the optical input and output into a cell. The I/O path no longer depends on boundary cells, but instead, individual cells can transmit or receive data. Each cell is modularized since the optical capabilities are granted to every cell. This property of scalability is important for extensibility, since for a large image size, the system only needs to add additional cells to fit a larger problem size.
- *Balance Computation.* The systolic mesh can perform at a higher computation rate to match the increased I/O bandwidth in the inner cells. As a result, the focal plane topology increases the overall system throughput. In addition, programming is simplified since the boundary cells in the systolic mesh no longer have to perform special routines for I/O transmission. The overall processing can be distributed more evenly through the systolic mesh to produce a more balanced computation.

With this focal plane topology for systolic arrays, new programming methodologies are needed for smart pixel algorithms. Algorithm mapping, problem partitioning and cell synchronization for applications such as early image processing must be reviewed in order to utilize desirable characteristics provided by this new topology. For example, pairs of cells in different layers of the systolic mesh can be coupled to form a processing node. This node, comprised of two systolic cells in two different layers, has more computational capabilities than a single node and may lead to a better algorithmic mapping, partitioning, and synchronization for the application. However, the re-mapping and re-partitioning tasks must be performed for each application in order to achieve better performance.

The 2D systolic mesh can be pipelined in a similar way to the perimeter I/O limited system. In the focal plane topology, an instance of the image is situated in a systolic mesh and is allowed to propagate in a pipeline fashion to the next systolic layer. Instead of processing at a scan row image in the perimeter I/O limited system, the focal plane topology allows pipelining of an entire image.

4. Two systolic array smart pixel systems

The following section describes current systolic smart pixel research at Georgia Tech. The first architecture, PAMSAC, is a fixed function systolic array that performs perfect pattern matching. While PAMSAC has modest computational power and limited programming flexibility, it demonstrates the realization of optical interconnection with integrated silicon detectors. The systolic processing core in PAMSAC illustrates the compact, highly efficient computational power of a systolic architecture. The second architecture, GT-VISTA, is multi-layered systolic array with a programmable pixel node. GT-VISTA focuses on early vision processing and provides an optimized, compact datapath to provide programming flexibility while maintaining a degree of efficiency.

4.1 The PAMSAC architecture

Figure 3 is the layout and floorplan of PAMSAC [16], a pattern matching chip that incorporates direct optical input of image data via eight on-chip silicon detectors and amplifiers. This 2252μm x 2222μm chip was implemented through the MOSIS foundry in 2.0μm CMOS technology and operates at 33MHz. Digital logic testing of the systolic core has been completed; the interface to the optoelectronic devices is currently in progress.

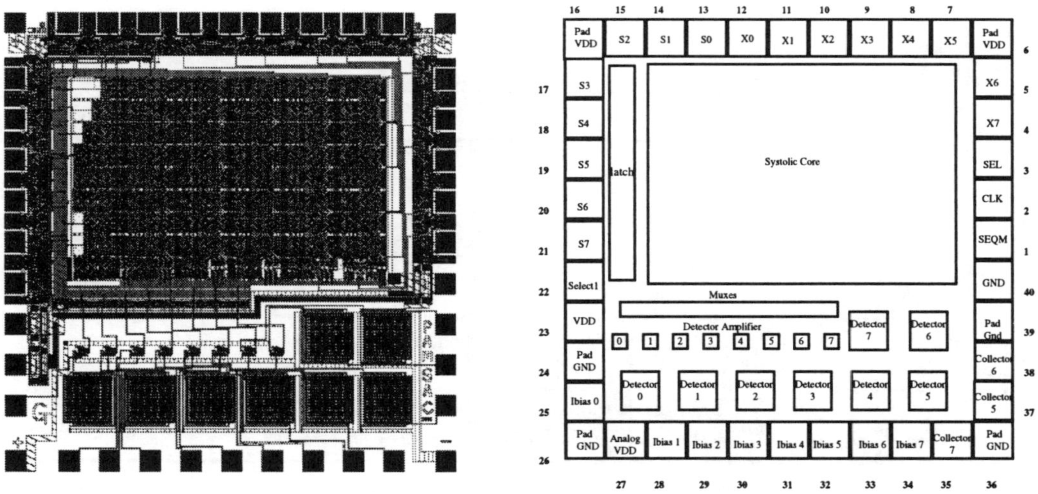

Figure 3. VLSI layout and floorplan of the PAMSAC chip

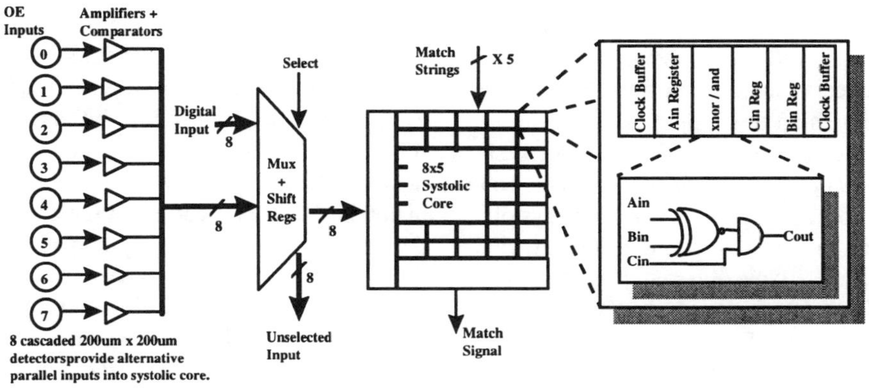

Figure 4. Block diagram of the PAMSAC chip

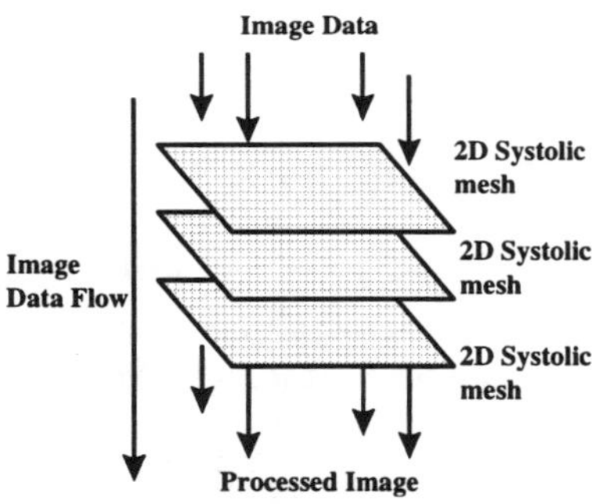

Figure 5: GT-VISTA multi-layer structure

Figure 4 illustrates the block diagram of the PAMSAC chip with a systolic cell logic operation consisting of an XNOR and an AND gate to detect perfect pattern matches. Although the programmability of PAMSAC is fixed, a different digital set of *Match Strings* can be loaded into each cell for comparison to a stream of optical inputs. The systolic core consists of 40 cells to match 40 input bits simultaneously. The system can be scale to match larger number of optical input bits with additional systolic cells and detectors.

The PAMSAC system demonstrates the realization of optical inputs to provide the high I/O bandwidth requirements. As a systolic system, PAMSAC can maintain a high computational and throughput rate once the system is configured. Each systolic cell is dense, and the overall system size is very compact. PAMSAC utilized localized communication to maintain scalability of the system.

4.2 GT-VISTA system overview

The GT-VISTA system consists of multiple layered two-dimension meshes of systolic processors. Each of these layers works collectively to perform low level vision processing. Figure 5 illustrates the proposed 3D topology for the GT-VISTA system. This multi-layered topology is common in image processing, but to the best of our knowledge, GT-VISTA presents the first multi-layered systolic mesh with optoelectronic interconnects. The motivation of the GT-VISTA system came from the desire to harness the capabilities of systolic computation with focal-plane processing.

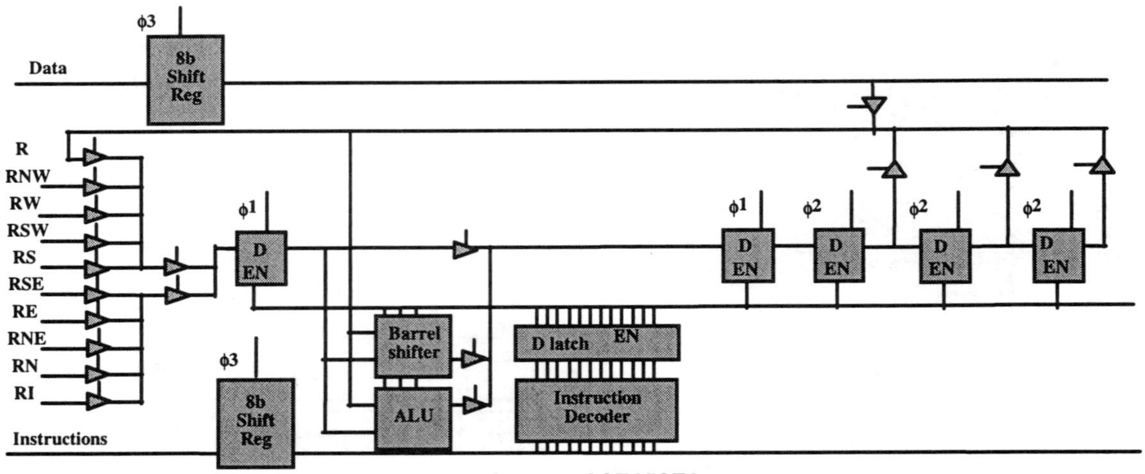

Figure 6: Block diagram of GT-VISTA processor

Communication between systolic layers is achieved with through wafer optoelectronic devices. In the first version of the GT-VISTA system, inter-layer communication is limited to image data flow. Because of the multi-layer topology, high throughput can be achieved by pipelining the image through each 2D systolic mesh. Each pixel is directly mapped onto a systolic element. This mapping is possible because each GT-VISTA systolic element is designed to be small. In addition, the targeted early vision applications typically require per pixel processing. Inter-nodal communication is enabled for all the nearest neighbors: North, East, West, South, North East, North West, South East, and South West. This neighborhood communication is unlike existing NEWS communication because it provides more access than just North, East, West, and South. These neighborhood pixel values require extra clock cycles to load data into the communication registers. Figure 8 illustrates the inter-nodal communication for a systolic node within the mesh.

4.3 GT-VISTA microarchitecture

The communication network allows nearest neighbor communication only. Each GT-VISTA node can read the pixel value of its 8 immediate neighbors. The datapath of a node consists of an 8-bit integer ALU, a barrel shifter, and special pipeline registers. This architecture is similar to the single bit MIP morphological system [6], but modified in GT-VISTA with 8 bit data words and a more powerful ALU and barrel shifter. The ALU and shifter will allow enough processing capabilities for early vision processing. Figure 6 illustrates a single node block diagram.

Each GT-VISTA node is mapped to a single thin film detector to form the focal plane processing architecture. Because most detectors generate analog signals from light intensities, an analog to digital converter (A/D) is required to convert the intensities into digital values [3,7,11]. The prototype GT-VISTA system has light input arriving at a node as a serial sequence of bits that is combined to form an 8 bit data word. Figure 7 illustrates the thin film integration with a GT-VISTA node. Although through-board wiring can be used to maintain the focal plane topology and the 3D structure, the prototype GT-VISTA system is demonstrated with optoelectronic devices as a means of interconnect.

The memory controller is set on the boundary of the 2D systolic mesh. The controller sends program instructions and data only to the boundary of the mesh. This information propagates through each column in the mesh in a systolic fashion. The idea of propagating instructions with moving data sets was introduced in [9], and is utilized here for cell scalability.

4.4 GT-VISTA applications

GT-VISTA is designed to perform repetitive neighborhood pixel access operations. Figure 9 illustrates a program segment for a convolution program with a low pass filter mask [2]. The following calculation shows a per node processing capability for a LPF convolution program operating at 100MHz.

Notice that the GT-VISTA instruction set is unlike traditional instruction sets in that many operations such as calculation and register data movement can be performed in a single cycle.

$$\frac{100\ \text{Mop}}{\text{sec}} \times \frac{\text{pixel}}{15\text{ops}} = \frac{6.67\text{Mpixel}}{\text{sec}}$$

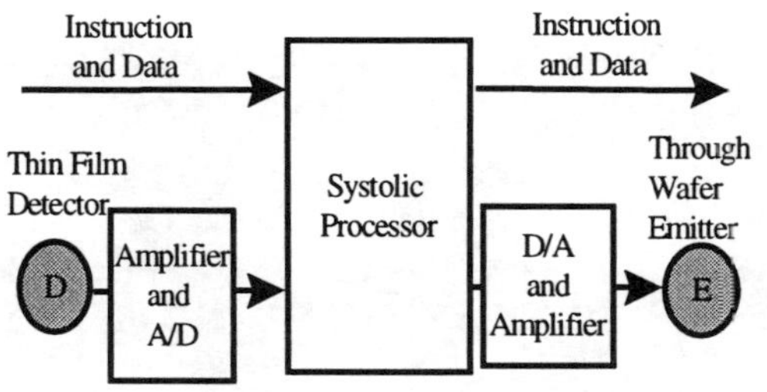

Figure 7: Detector and Emitter pair with systolic processor

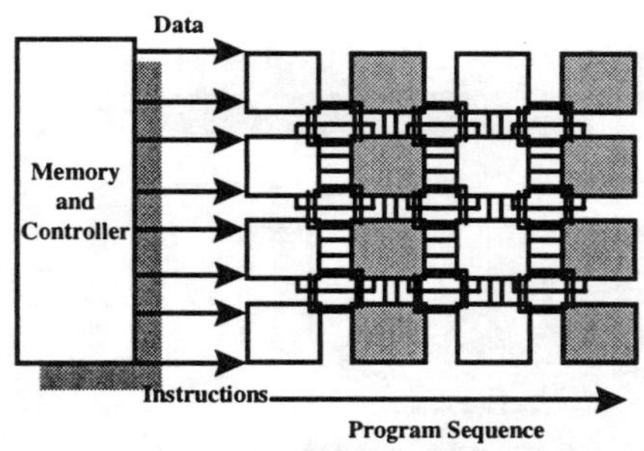

Figure 8. GT-VISTA Neighborhood Communication

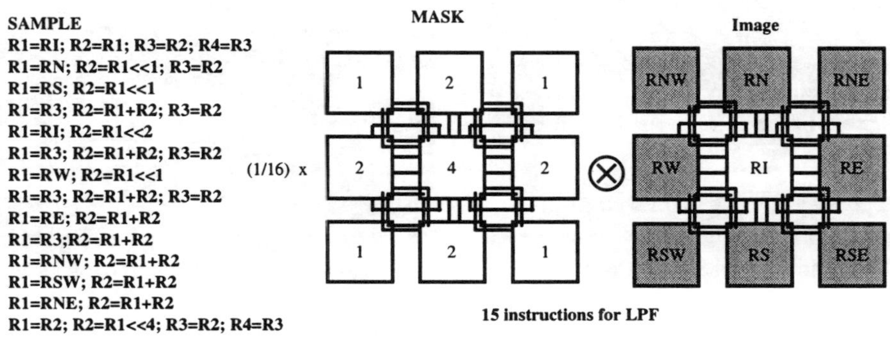

Figure 9: Convolution program with LPF mask

The high frame rate capability of GT-VISTA is derived from the pixel-to-node mapping of a systolic element. For example, if a systolic element is mapped to an image pixel, then an overall frame rate of 6.67Mframe/sec can theoretically be achieved. An array of image pixels can be mapped to a systolic element for lower frame rates. Although off-the-self general purpose processors provide an alternative for the processing core, they do not offer efficient operation and scalability of a GT-VISTA node.

4.5 GT-VISTA VLSI implementation

A completed VLSI design of a GT-VISTA element includes an ALU and barrel-shifter. Figure 10 illustrates the ALU and barrel-shifter units in a 2252μm x 2222μm chip fabricated through the MOSIS foundry in 2.0μm CMOS technology. The functional units operate at a maximum of 21MHz. Table 1 shows the component unit areas (in λ units) and the simulated maximum frequencies of operation. Figure 11 illustrates the VLSI layout for a GT-VISTA systolic processor chip. The functionality of the prototype chip is a limited version of the systolic node shown in Figure 6, but the node is a proof of concept chip, and will be used as a basis of comparison for future systolic designs. The chip will be submitted to the MOSIS foundry (2.0μm CMOS) for fabrication. With optoelectronic devices shown in Figure 7, this single node systolic processor will serve as a building block for larger system.

Table 1. Component unit area and maximum operational frequency

	Height (λ) x Width (λ)	IRSIM Simulated Freq. (0.8μm Feature Size)
ALU	752 x 396	140 MHz
Barrel Shifter	1472 x 1059	105 MHz
GT-VISTA Node	1841x1797	100 MHz

The ALU design is built upon the Manchester carry chain adder [17]. It has the ability to perform ADD, SUB, AND, OR, and XOR operations. The barrel shifter is capable of both arithmetic and logic shift operations as well as right and left rotations. These operations are sufficient to perform most early vision algorithms efficiently. Both designs were optimized for area and not speed because systolic arrays favor multiple computing elements to obtain higher throughput.

5. Conclusion and future work

In this paper, we described the union of systolic arrays and integrated optoelectronic interconnect for early image processing. Current research in systolic smart pixel architectures, including PAMSAC and GT-VISTA architectures, were introduced. PAMSAC is a special purpose system that demonstrates the realization of optical interconnection with integrated silicon

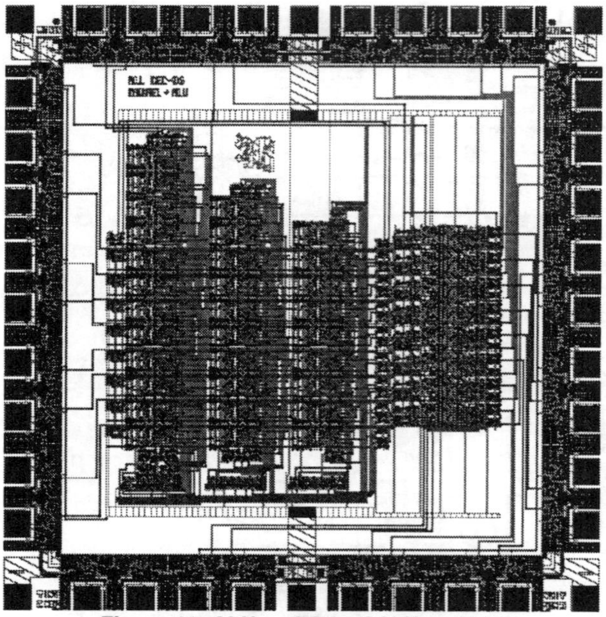

Figure 10. ALU and Barrel Shifter Chip

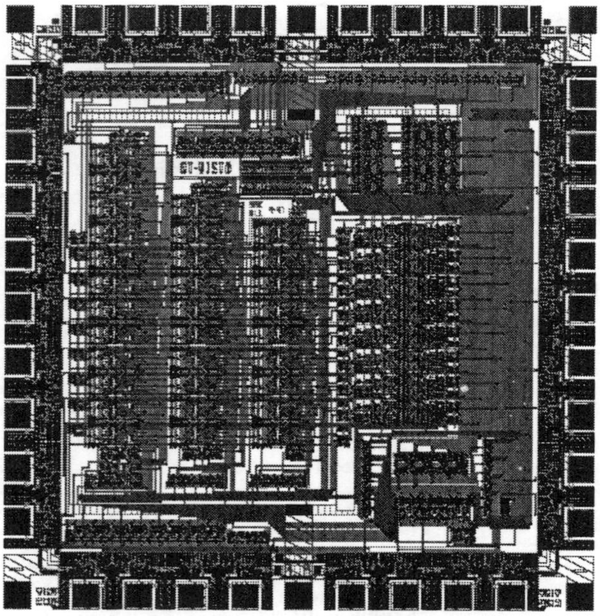

Figure 11. Prototype GT-VISTA VLSI Chip

detectors. PAMSAC advances systolic design methodology of modular cells and localized communications to promote efficient and high throughput operations.

GT-VISTA is a more flexible system for early vision processing, providing modest programmability for high throughput applications. A prototype system is being implemented, beginning with a series of VLSI chips, that have already been fabricated and evaluated, demonstrating both the architecture and optoelectronic interface functions. A complete GT-VISTA node will be submitted for fabrication later this year. Future goals of this project include developing additional programming methodologies for the system in the multi-layer topology and increasing the computational power efficiency and packaging density in a multi-node system.

6. References

[1] J.Basille and S.Castan, "Multilevel Architectures for Image Processing", Architectures and Algorithms for Digital Image Processing (1985), v.595, p.46-52

[2] G.A. Baxes, *Digital Image Processing: Principles and Applications*, John Wiley & Sons Inc., 1994

[3] B.Buchanan, et. al., "High Density Focal Plane Signal Processing Using 3-D Vertical Interconnects", Midwest Symposium on Circuits and Systems, 1994, p.191-194

[4] H.H.Cat, et. al., "SIMPil: An OE Integrated SIMD Architecture for Focal Plane Processing Applications," *MPPOI*, 1996, p.44-52.

[5] E.S. Eid and E. Fossum, Real-time focal-plane array image processor, *Proc. of The International. Society for Optical Engineering*, 1989, v.1197, p.2-12

[6] W.C. Fang, et. al., "VLSI focal-plane array processor for morphological image processing" *Proceedings of the Fifth Annual IEEE International ASIC Conference and Exhibit*, p.423-6, September 1992.

[7] S.M. Fike, et. al., "8*8 array of thin-film photodetectors vertically electrically interconnected to silicon circuitry," IEEE Photonics Tech. Let., v.7 n.10, p.1168-70, Oct. 1995

[8] T.J. Fountain, "The Use of Linear Arrays for Image Processing", *International Conference on Systolic Arrays*, May 1988, p.183-192

[9] R.Hughey and D.P.Lopresti, "Architecture of a Programmable Systolic Array", *International Conference on Systolic Arrays*, May 1988, p.41-49

[10] K.T. Johnson, A.R.Hurson, B.Shirazi, "General-purpose systolic arrays," Computer, v.26, Nov 1993, p.20-31

[11] N. M. Jokerst, et. al, "Communication Through Stacked Silicon Circuitry Using Integrated Thin Film InP-based Emitters and Detectors," IEEE Photonics Tech. Let., v.7 n.9, p.1028-1030, Sept. 1995.

[12] J.Jolion and A.Rosenfeld, *A Pyramid Framework for Early Vision*, Kluwer Academic Publishers, 1993.

[13] H.T. Kung, "Why systolic architectures?," Computer, p.37-46, Jan.1982

[14] W.S.Lacy, et. al., "A Fine-Grain, High Throughput Architecture Using Through-Wafer Optical Interconnect" *MPPOI*, p.27-36, April 1994

[15] R.M.Lougheed and C.W.Swonger, "An Analysis of Computer Architectural Factors Contributing to Image Processor Capacity", Architectures and Algorithms for Digital Image Processing (1985), v.595, p.3-13

[16] D. S. Wills, et. al., "Processing Architectures for Smart Pixel Systems", *IEEE Journal of Selected Topics in Quantum Electronics*, v.2 n.1, April 1996, p.24-34

[17] N.H.E. Weste and K. Eshraghian, *Principles of CMOS VLSI Design*, Addison-Wesley Pub. Co., 2nd ed., 1993

Free-Space Optical Interconnections
Within SIMD Massively Parallel Computers

Patrick Scheer, Thierry Collette
LETI (CEA-Technologies Avancées)
DEIN - CEA Saclay
F91191 GIF-SUR-YVETTE Cedex FRANCE
E-mail: {pscheer, collette}@gaap.saclay.cea.fr

Pascal Churoux
ONERA CERT / DERO
2, avenue Edouard Belin, BP 4025
F31055 TOULOUSE Cedex FRANCE
E-mail: Pascal.Churoux@onecert.fr

Abstract

Multi-level electronic integration of massively parallel computers leads to latency effects and I/O bottlenecks. A new implementation scheme using MCM-to-MCM free-space optical interconnects is discussed in terms of architecture enhancement, system modeling and technical challenges. Building blocks of an experimental demonstrator including zero-biased-VCSEL with hybridized microlenses are also presented.

1. Introduction

The use of computers in industry, research centres, telecommunications and at home is growing very quickly. When the applications are time consuming, such as image or signal processing, embedded processing or CAD software, the use of powerful parallel computers becomes a necessity. For this reason, we began to design, in 1987 a parallel computer, named SYMPATI2, dedicated to the low level image processing. Six years later, we designed another parallel computer, so-called SYMPHONIE, which is well suited for the iconic and symbolic data processing.

We are now working on a new generation of parallel computers which will use fast electronic ASIC based on 0.25 µm standard cell technology. However, if the clock frequency can be very high inside those components, it is not the case for the speed of the inputs and outputs. In order to fully take advantage of powerful components within parallel architectures, we started two years ago a research project named SYNOPTIQUE in which we are studying the interests of optical interconnects in our domain.

In this paper, the limitations encountered in SIMD massively parallel computers are illustrated and the motivations for using optics are presented in the first section. Then, a theoretical insight is given on the feasibility of free-space optical interconnections. Lastly, some experimental results are reported whose aim is to validate the new technological concepts involved in the design of massively parallel computers using optical interconnections.

2. Optics for SIMD massively parallel computers

2.1 Performance issues

In massively parallel calculators, the efficiency of the interconnection networks is as important as the powerfulness of each Processing Element (PE). When the system is based on a Single Instruction Multiple Data (SIMD) architecture, this point is more crucial since all the processing nodes are synchronous and work at a frequency determined by the timing performance of the global system. Hence, any variation of a transmission time during an exchange of data between two PE or during an instruction broadcasting is handled by introducing latency in the calculator cycle, which results in relatively low operation frequency of SIMD computers [1]. Especially, if the bandwidth of PE-to-PE communications is too small, the processing performance will be limited by the time required to access the data. Since the bandwidth is the product of the transmission rate of a single link with the number of links, a physical implementation which provides both high data rates and high Inputs/Outputs density (I/O) is desirable.

The following paragraphs give a practical illustration of the previously mentioned issues which results from an analysis performed on the two SIMD massively parallel calculators developed at CEA/DTA/DEIN: SIMPATI2 [2,3] and SYMPHONIE [4,5].

0-8186-7974-3/97 $10.00 © 1997 IEEE

2.2 Multi-level integration

Massively parallel computers have inherently a high number of elementary processors which must be tightly coupled together to ensure a efficient operation of the system. Even with the progress in microelectronics, the integration capability is not sufficient to implement all the PE in a single chip, and even on a single electronic board. All the PE which form the system are thus spatially distributed, and the interconnection path between two PE varies within the system. In fact, the interconnection length consists of the physical length of the link plus the number of buffers required to preserve the signal integrity along the interconnection path. In the case of the calculator SYMPHONIE, three levels of integration are present. First, an ASIC including four PE was realised in a 0.5 μm Standard Cell technology. Each ASIC integrates 250 000 standard cell gates and 64Kbytes memory (each PE is connected to a 128 Kbit Static-RAM). Then, four ASIC are integrated in a ceramic Multi-Chip Module (MCM), providing more efficient electrical links between the ASIC than a solution based on single ASIC packages interconnected on a Printed Circuit Board (PCB). A gain of integration is also achieved. The last level is the electronic board, which supports four MCM (Figure 1). Hence, 16 boards are needed for implementing the top level configuration with 1024-PE. The UC is integrated within a single ASIC located on a specific board.

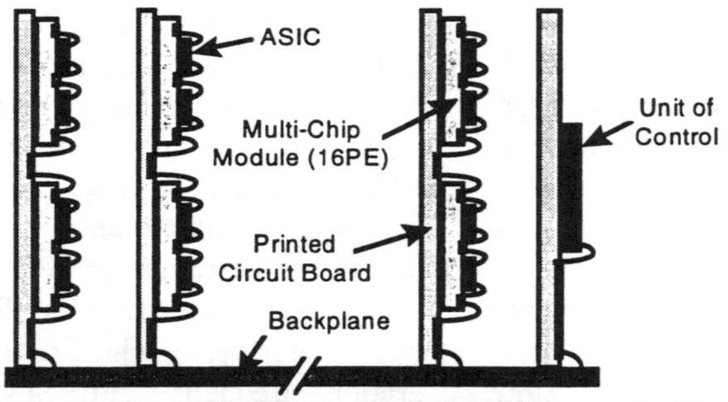

Figure 1: Multi-level integration of the massively parallel system SYMPHONIE.

2.2.1 Impact on the computer frequency

SYMPHONIE's architecture is based on a 1D-nearest-neighbor network, where the PE are arranged in a ring array. Due to the multi-level integration, the ring is implemented by using intra-chip, MCM level, board level and backplane level interconnections. This leads to interconnection paths with different loads and parasitic capacities and with a varying number of buffers. Since the system is synchronous, the longest data path (i.e. most time consuming) will determine the frequency of operation. On Figure 2, we have reported an estimation of the maximum transmission delay at the different levels of a system like SYMPHONIE. It results that the contribution of a propagation delay on the transmission time is all the more important that the considered level is loosely integrated. In particular, the Printed Circuit Boards (PCB) and the backplane are responsible for a large amount of the latency.

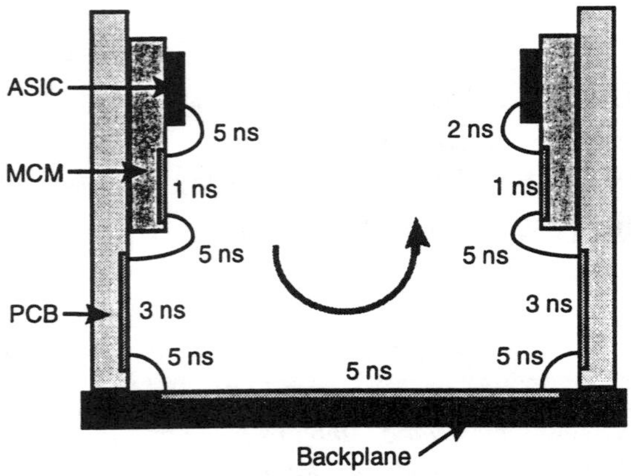

Figure 2: Latency timing of a board-to-board interconnection.

2.2.2 Impact on the number of I/O

I/O count is a major issue in the design of massively parallel computer: the efficiency of the system widely depends on the connectivity of the PE network. The current implementation of electronic systems limits the number of I/O at different levels:

- at the ASIC level, the number of links (pads) is a function of the size of the die (geometric constraint),
- at the MCM level, the type of the packaging determines the number of pins,
- at the board level, standard backplane connectors restricts the number of I/O.

In SYMPATI2, the number of I/O of the ASIC is restricted because of packaging limitations (the die is embedded in a 220-pin PGA). As a result, only 40 pins are dedicated to communications with the control unit, and a multiplexed bus was required. Data exchanges with the memory and the neighbouring ASIC are handled with 80 pins. In SYMPHONIE, the number of I/O per ASIC is 420, with 70 pins used for ground and power supply, 100 pins used for communications between the control unit and the processors, and 175 pins dedicated to interconnections with the neighbouring ASIC. The inflation in the number of pins dedicated to data exchanges between neighbouring ASIC is first caused by an increased format of data words (16 bits in SYMPATI2 versus 32 bits in SYMPHONIE), and also by the multiplication of networks. In SYMPATI2, only one network interconnects the ASIC, whereas in SYMPHONIE, three different networks tightly couple the ASIC: one for direct interconnections (32-bit wide), one for intercommunications (45-bit wide) and one for the loading/unloading of data (16-bit wide). However, the duplication of certain links would have be highly desirable but was incompatible with the I/O count at the ASIC and backplane connector levels.

Because the processors are more and more powerful, they are able to support more complex image processing operations. But to feed those new processors, new means of communication must be integrated. In SYMPHONIE, the intercommunication network has been implemented to improve the processing capabilities of the system, allowing the system to efficiently support the low and intermediate levels of image processing [5]. In the future, taking into account the computing capabilities of the next generation of processors used in massively parallel computers will further increase the volume of communications. We can expect for instance that it will be necessary to have a 32-bit wide network dedicated to the data loading/unloading operations, possibly two 64-bit wide direct interconnection networks and two 80-bit wide intercommunication networks. In other respects, the cycle time of future processors will scale down to the 10 ns range, and thus the processors will have an aggregate I/O throughput of 35 GBit/s, considering that the 10 ns period can be supported by the I/O. In Table 1, we compare this throughput and other figures with the ones of SYMPHONIE and SYMPATI2.

Present technologies of integration have in fact a great influence on some of the final architecture features. In the case of SYMPHONIE for instance, the fact that the system was physically split into several boards implied that any signal coming out of a board had to pass through a backplane connector which had only 320 pins. This source of bottleneck appeared in the early design of the system and solutions had to be found, as the expense of a few changes in the original architecture. Thus, we foresee that innovating technologies of interconnection must be developed before new massively parallel computers with increasing demands in speed and I/O are built. This is also a necessary condition to make the possibilities of implementation closer to the architecture requirements (and designer wishes).

2.3 Partitioning of electrical and optical interconnections

An important step is thus the determination of the integration level which will first preserve electrical interconnections, and secondly support the interface of the optical links. To date, the MCM level can provide relatively high frequency electrical links, up to several hundreds of MHz. Therefore, we may assume that the ASIC will not be frequency limited by communications at the MCM level in the next few years. New technologies based on 3D electrical interconnections [6] are also studied to increase the MCM integration density. Hence, MCM may support an increasing number of chips with efficient interconnections.

In other respects, the MCM is recognised as an efficient platform for hybrid integration of optoelectronics with electronics [7]. In particular, some MCM substrates such as silicon can integrate micro-structures realized by using standard microelectronics processes. These micro-structures are useful for the alignment of optoelectronic and optical devices [8]. Finally, optical interconnections between MCM are already under study in several laboratories [9,10]. Research is also performed to implement intra-MCM optical interconnections [11], which opens the way to systems with all-optically-interconnected electronic chips.

According to these considerations, the implementation of massively parallel computers with optically interconnected MCM is an attractive solution. This partition will ensure that the processing performance of electronic nodes is not quenched by a lack of efficiency of the surrounding interconnections.

		SYMPATI2 processor	SYMPHONIE processor	Future processor
Number of links with the neighbourhood	- for data loading and unloading - for direct communications - for intercommunications	16 I/O 32 I/O -	32 I/O 64 I/O 90 I/O	64 I/O 2 x 128 I/O 2 x 160 I/O
Period of the I/O: current for SYMPATI2 and SYMPHONIE and ideal for the future processor		120 ns	80 ns	10 ns
I/O processing capabilities		0.4 GBit/s	2.3 GBit/s	35 GBit/s

Table 1: I/O throughputs achieved with SYMPATI2 and SYMPHONIE processors and desirable for the future processor of a new massively parallel calculator

2.4 Free-space optical interconnections

The choice of the optical technology is made by taking into account the following features:

1. the MCM have to be ring interconnected, with as much as possible homogeneous interconnection paths within the system,
2. modularity must be preserved in order to allow the adjustment of the number of PE with the performance requirements, and to provide a maintenance-friendly system,
3. compactness is desired for embedded applications.

Free-space optical interconnections are well suited for high density point-to-point OI within massively parallel computers [12,13]. One of the reasons is that they fully exploit the third dimension offered by optics without requiring a guiding interconnection medium. A possible implementation scheme using free-space optical interconnections is outlined in Figure 3 [14].

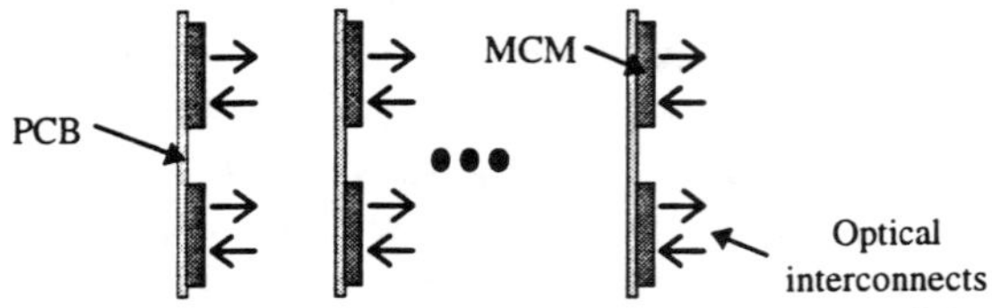

Figure 3: Concept of double-side optoelectronic planes.

With this new implementation of the ring interconnection networks, we expect the following improvements:

1. Free-space optical interconnections between MCM will reduce the length of the data paths, while providing a smaller dispersion of the transmission delays. As a result, the latency of a given PE-to-PE communication will be reduced and the frequency of the whole system will be increased.
2. MCM-to-MCM communications will have homogeneous performances all over the system, leading to a operation frequency independent of the number of MCM (i.e. the number of PE). A real scaleability of SIMD massively parallel computers in terms of performance may thus be achieved.
3. The density of 3D optical interconnections is assumed high enough to face the growing I/O density of the PE.

2.5 Trade-off in the design of optical interconnections

Using optics within massively parallel computers imposes some requirements on the technology to be used. First, the need of modularity together with the assembling constraints of a distributed system suppose that free-space optical interconnections are tolerant toward source-to-detector misalignments. Consequently, the optical interconnection density has to be compatible with the accuracy of the mechanical assembling.

Another important point concerns the optoelectronic interface which is added in each MCM. A massively parallel computers is built by replicating a elementary chip which may contains several PE. In a MCM for instance, some of the ASIC will be interconnected with electrical links while others will have to drive optoelectronic devices. In terms of reliability and cost, the minimisation of the number of chips required for building a given function is sought. Hence, it would be interesting to handle optical interconnections as their electrical counterparts, without inserting specific circuits to drive the optoelectronic front end components. As a result, parallel optical links operating at the PE frequency are preferable to high speed serial optical communications, even if, at first sight, the potentiality of optics is not fully exploited. However, it is assumed that the optical interconnection density is high enough to provide the required bandwidth.

The two points mentioned above show that a trade-off between the mechanical constraints and the complexity of the electronic interfaces must be found. This requires a precise study of the optical interconnection system in order to identify the parameters which determines the interconnection density and the misalignment immunity. A theoretical insight is introduced in the next section. Then, the first experimental results which illustrates some of the previous concepts are presented.

3. Feasibility of free-space optical interconnections

3.1 Contribution to the optical interconnection modeling

Free-space optical interconnections have been modeled by several authors during the last five years [15-17 and references included]. These studies are either based on the optical system itself or on the whole interconnection, taking into account the conversion performance of the front end optoelectronic components. The subject of this section refers to the first class of studies, since it deals with the effects of misalignment on the power transmission efficiency of the free-space optical interconnections. More precisely, we first propose a new formalism of the clipping effect which occurs in the microlens plane when the beam size is too large with respect to the aperture diameter. Then, taking into account the optical crosstalk in the detection plane, some analytical guidelines are derived to assess the misalignment immunity of a given configuration, which is known as one of the most important parameters for free-space interconnections.

A free-space optical interconnect can be outlined as follows:

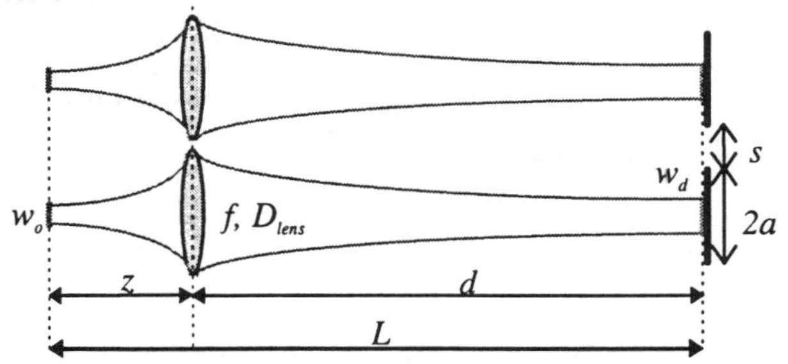

Figure 4: Outlines of a parallel free-space optical interconnect.

We assume that the parallel optical interconnections consists of Vertical-Cavity Surface-Emitting Laser (VCSEL), refractive or diffractive microlenses, and PIN photodetectors. The microlens are designed in order to minimize each beam size in the detection plane, and thus improve the misalignment immunity of the system. The dimensions of the reception window determines the positioning margin once the incident beam size is known. This detection window is either the detector itself or a second microlens used to focus light onto small detector elements. Here, we consider that the window is the sensitive area of the detector and that this area can be made large enough to fit the alignment requirements. This configuration minimizes the number of components and thus the sources of misalignment.

3.2 Influence of beam clipping on the detected optical power

The calculations are performed under the following assumptions:
- the VCSEL is single transverse mode at wavelength λ_0,
- the intensity distribution of the VCSEL is gaussian with a $1/e^2$ radius of w_o, and presents a circular symmetry,
- the microlens is assumed aberration free,
- the small angle diffraction theory of Fresnel applies.

The $1/e^2$ intensity beam radius in the detection plane, w_d, is derived in two steps. First, the classical formulas describing the propagation of gaussian beams in free-space are used to calculate the $1/e^2$ beam radius, w_z, and the radius of curvature, R_z, of the incident beam in the microlens plane, at distance z from the beam waist. Then, a reduced form of the Fresnel diffraction integral, the Fourier-Bessel integral which applies in the case of circularly symmetric pupil function, is used to derive the radius w_d in the detection plane [18]. Hence, the finite aperture diameter of the microlens, D_{lens}, can be taken into account in the calculations. Another advantage is that the beam radius is derived for any location beyond the microlens plane, and not only at the waist location.

In a first evaluation, we assume that the influence of the aperture diameter, D_{lens}, is negligible (infinite aperture). If d is the distance from the microlens to the detection plane and f the focal length of the microlens (see Figure 4), one obtains:

$$w_d = w_z d \sqrt{\left(\frac{1}{f} - \frac{1}{R_z} - \frac{1}{d}\right)^2 + \left(\frac{\lambda_0}{\pi w_z}\right)^2} . \quad (1)$$

The form of the previous expression shows that an optimal focal length, f_{opt}, can be found for which the spot size is minimum. These optimal values writes:

$$\frac{1}{f_{opt}} = \frac{1}{d} + \frac{1}{R_z} \text{ and } w_d^{opt} = \frac{\lambda_0 d}{\pi w_z} . \quad (2)$$

w_d^{opt} is very close to the beam waist conjugated of w_o by the microlens.

Under the far field approximation $z >> \pi w_0^2/\lambda_0$, the expression of the optimal focal length and of the corresponding $1/e^2$ beam radius reduce to:

$$\frac{1}{f_{opt}} \approx \frac{1}{d} + \frac{1}{z} \text{ and, } w_d^{opt} \approx w_o \frac{d}{z} \quad (3)$$

respectively, which are the expressions given by the theory of geometrical optics.

Expression (3) shows that one can increase z to reduce the spot size. However, the clipping ratio $k = D_{lens} / 2w_z$ will then be a relevant parameter, since it governs the losses due to the beam truncating at the microlens aperture (see the formula below).

$$Loss\,(\%) = 100 \times \exp\left[-2\left(\frac{D_{lens}}{2w_z}\right)^2\right] = 100 \times \exp\left(-2k^2\right) . \quad (4)$$

In fact, because of diffraction effects due to the limited aperture of the microlens, the clipping ratio k has an influence on the spot size in the detection plane. The role of k in a microlens-based optical system has already been studied in previous papers [19-22]. In all these studies, the effect of clipping was represented by a correction factor applied to the source beam waist, which did not provides direct information on the spot size modification in the observation plane. Here, we use the initial and more general formulation of the clipping effect depicted in [18] in order to directly derive an analytical expression of w_d in presence of clipping. Using the Fourier-Bessel integral mentioned in the previous paragraph with a finite value of D_{lens}, one obtains an amplitude distribution which may be approximated by a gaussian distribution if the clipping is not too severe. As in [19], the derivation of a equivalent $1/e^2$ beam radius, w_d, relies on the equivalence between the real incident power in the detection plane and the one of a ideal gaussian intensity profile. After several calculation steps, one obtains:

$$w_d = \beta w_z d \sqrt{\left(\frac{1}{f} - \frac{1}{R_z} - \frac{1}{d}\right)^2 + \left(\frac{\lambda_0}{\pi w_z^2}\right)^2}, \tag{5}$$

where β is a correction factor due to the clipping effect:

$$\beta = \sqrt{\frac{1-\exp(-2k^2)}{1-2\cos\left[\frac{\pi w_z^2}{\lambda_0}\left(\frac{1}{f}-\frac{1}{R_z}-\frac{1}{d}\right)k^2\right]\exp(-k^2)+\exp(-2k^2)}} \tag{6}$$

This factor is similar to the one which appears in [19] for correcting the source beam waist. However, the distance d between the observation plane and the microlens is here not neglected, and the circular aperture is replaced by a microlens of focal length f, which justifies the presence of the $1/f$ term in the expression of β. Consequently, the sinusoidal dependence of the radius w_d is quite different from the one depicted in [20]. Moreover, the above expression of w_d gives the spot size of the truncated beam in the same observation plane as for the unclipped case. Thus, a direct comparison of the clipped and unclipped beam sizes is possible.

The optimized case still corresponds to the focal length f_{opt} derived above, for which we obtain the following minimum beam radius:

$$w_d^{optimal} = \frac{\lambda_0 d}{\pi w_z}\sqrt{\frac{1+\exp(-k^2)}{1-\exp(-k^2)}}. \tag{7}$$

Figure 5 represents the increase of the minimum beam radius versus the clipping losses in the microlens plane (the varying parameter is the microlens diameter). The parameters are set to: λ_0 = 850 nm, f = 850 µm, w_o = 2.5 µm, d = 3900 µm and z = 1100 µm (L = 5 mm). One notices that a 1 % clipping loss induces an increase of 10 % of the beam radius in the detection plane. This variation may have an impact on the performance of the system as significant as the clipping loss itself.

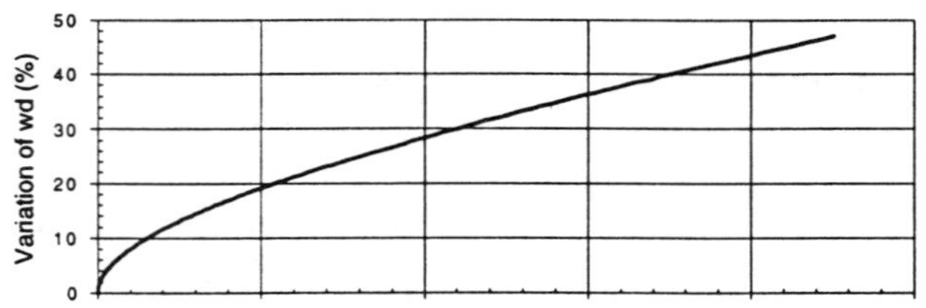

Figure 5: Relative variation of the waist in the detection plane vs. clipping losses.

Another way to modify the clipping ratio is to change the source-to-microlens distance z, while D_{lens} and the interconnection length L are kept constant. According to (3), the beam radius w_d decreases when z increases, but the correction factor β modifies this variation as shown in (5). As a result, the gain in size reduction is lower than one would expect in the case of no clipping.

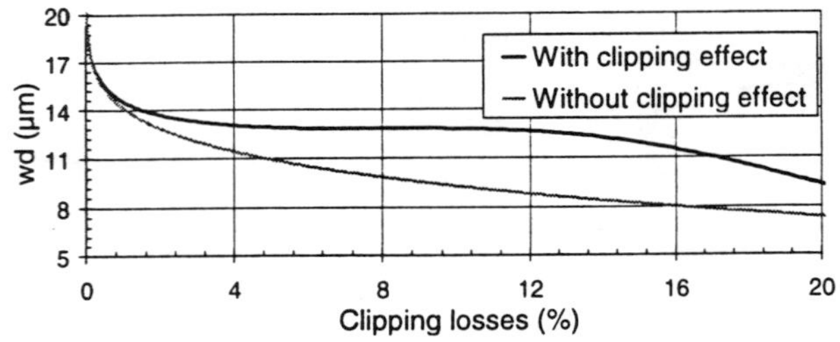

Figure 6: Waist in the detection plane vs. clipping losses.

Figure 6 depicts the evolution of the beam radius w_d for a given microlens diameter, when the source-to-microlens distance z varies, leading to various clipping losses. The parameter values are the same as before, except that the microlens diameter, D_{lens}, is set to 247 µm. The steep slopes of both curves for clipping losses lower than 2 % shows that a small clipping may be advantageous in terms of beam size. The clipping effect on the beam radius in the detection plane is also clearly demonstrated.

3.3 Power transmission efficiency

The optical system has a power transmission efficiency η_{opt} defined by the ratio of the power coupled to the detector, P_{coupl}, to the power emitted by the VCSEL, P_{opt}. For free-space optical interconnections, the factors responsible for a degradation of the transmission efficiency are the clipping losses due to the finite aperture of the microlens, the Fresnel reflection losses due to index mismatch, the diffraction efficiency if diffractive optics is used, and the coupling losses in the detection plane due to the finite size of the photosensitive area. These factors are represented by two transmission efficiencies η_{lens} and η_{coupl} respectively. In the case of refractive microlens, the transmission efficiency writes:

$$\eta_{lens} = \left\{1-\exp\left[-2\left(\frac{D_{lens}}{2w_z}\right)^2\right]\right\} \times \left[1-\left(\frac{n_l-1}{n_l+1}\right)^2\right]^2, \tag{8}$$

where w_z is the irradiance $1/e^2$ radius of the beam falling on the microlens, D_{lens} and n_l are the aperture diameter and the refractive index of the microlens, respectively.

We assume that the elements of the detector array have a rectangular active area of dimensions $2a$ x $2b$, with a spacing zone of width s and a pitch p of $2a+s$.

The incident beam has an irradiance 1/e² radius w_d. The power P_{coupl} coupled to a detector element is the integral of the beam intensity profile over the active area. The coupling efficiency writes:

$$\eta_c = erf\left(\frac{a}{w_d}\sqrt{2}\right)erf\left(\frac{b}{w_d}\sqrt{2}\right). \quad (9)$$

Since the optical interconnections are parallel, another important figure of merit is the optical crosstalk. To evaluate this figure, we only consider the parasitic power which is emitted by the first two neighboring sources and falls on the detector element under consideration (we neglect the sources which are not directly at the left and right sides of the useful one because of the exponential decrease of the intensity with the distance). With the same notation as before, the parasitic power writes:

$$\begin{aligned} P_{parasitic} &= I_d\int_{-a}^{a}\int_{-b}^{b}\exp\left(-2\frac{(x-p)^2+y^2}{w_d^2}\right)dxdy \\ &+ I_d\int_{-a}^{a}\int_{-b}^{b}\exp\left(-2\frac{(x+p)^2+y^2}{w_d^2}\right)dxdy \\ &= I_d\frac{\pi w_d^2}{2}\left[erf\left(\frac{a+p}{w_d}\sqrt{2}\right)+erf\left(\frac{a-p}{w_d}\sqrt{2}\right)\right]erf\left(\frac{b}{w_d}\sqrt{2}\right) \end{aligned}, \quad (10)$$

3.4 Misalignment immunity

Once the spot size w_d is derived, a criterion must be defined to quantify the tolerance of the optical interconnection. In the case of a NRZ transmission of the information, the bit error rate is function of the power swing defined by the difference between the optical power received when a "1" is transmitted and the one received when a "0" is sent. In the presence of crosstalk, this swing is reduced to a residual power which equals the useful coupled power minus the parasitic power defined above. The criterion we are using here is that this residual power must keep a constant value in order to minimize the dynamic of the receiver.

The source of the misalignment may be an offset between the center of the emitter and the center of the microlens, or between the emitter and the receiver modules. In the former case, a leverage effect occurs which dramatically increases the offset in the detection plane. When a misalignment occurs, the incident beam onto the detection area is shifted by an amount x_d in the direction of a and y_d in the direction of b, which modifies the coupling efficiency in the following way:

$$\begin{aligned} \eta_c &= \frac{1}{2}\left[erf\left(\frac{a-x_d}{w_d}\sqrt{2}\right)+erf\left(\frac{a+x_d}{w_d}\sqrt{2}\right)\right] \\ &\times\frac{1}{2}\left[erf\left(\frac{b-y_d}{w_d}\sqrt{2}\right)+erf\left(\frac{b+y_d}{w_d}\sqrt{2}\right)\right] \end{aligned}. \quad (11)$$

Simultaneously, the parasitic power is also modified. The figure below shows the evolution of the residual power with a misalignment in the x direction, normalized to the nominal residual power (with no misalignment). The parameter is the spacing width s of the detector array. The pitch is set to 250 µm and the beam radius in the detection plane equals 15 µm (corresponding to the optimal case for L = 5 mm).

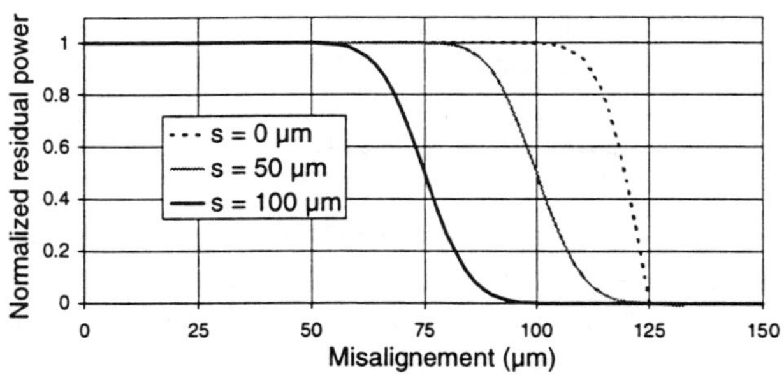

Figure 7: Normalized residual power vs. misalignment.

We notice that the residual power is best maintained in the case of no spacing and provided the shift x_d satisfies the relation:

$$\frac{a-x_d}{w_d} \geq 1.4. \quad (12)$$

Hence, a shift of the incident beam will not affect the coupling efficiency if the relevant half dimension of the detector is larger than the shift plus 1.4 w_d. In other words, the misalignment immunity (or positioning margin) can be defined as the difference between the half size of the detector (a or b with our notations) and 1.4 w_d, where w_d is the 1/e² irradiance radius of the beam in the detection plane.

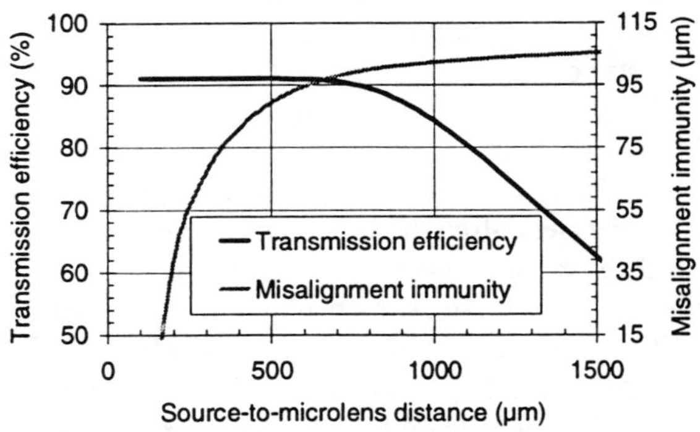

Figure 8: Transmission efficiency and misalignment immunity vs. source to microlens distance.

The influence of the clipping on the misalignment immunity is illustrated on Figure 8 for a given interconnection length of 5 mm. The detector size is 240 µm x 200 µm with a spacing zone of 250 µm and the microlens diameter is 250 µm. The evolution of the transmission efficiency is also reported. The curves show that the misalignment immunity can be improved without significantly decreases the transmission efficiency. In particular, considering that only 1 % of clipping losses must be tolerated (which corresponds here to z = 750 µm), may be a too drastic assumption if more transmission losses can be accepted. Indeed, relaxing the positioning margin by 10 or 20 µm may allow the designer to choose a simpler assembling procedure of the system.

4. Experimental approach

The aim of our experimental approach is to validate the technological choices that were made in the design study. First, the building blocks corresponding to the different concepts involved in the system are separately tested. Then, the system assembling is performed to demonstrate a complete OI between two electronic modules. The results given below concern the free-space OI and more precisely the emission module. Two building blocks have yet been studied: the hybridization of a microlens array in front of a linear VCSEL array, and the direct modulation of the VCSEL with digital signals provided by standard electronic circuits. The reception module and the mechanics are currently under investigations.

4.1 Hybridization of refractive microlenses with VCSEL

4.1.1 Different techniques

Collimated sources are a major concern in the realization of free-space OI. As far as VCSEL sources are concerned, monolithic integration of microlenses on the substrate of VCSEL arrays has been reported by several laboratories with both refractive [23] and diffractive [24] optical elements. The main advantage of this technique lies in the lithography process which is used to precisely align the microlenses with the VCSEL. Up to date, the microlenses are etched on the back side of the GaAs substrate, which requires bottom-emitting VCSEL operating at a wavelength for which GaAs is transparent, typically 980 nm. A shorter wavelength would be desirable for diffraction purpose, and thermal management may be more difficult if the substrate surface can not be fully used as a thermal contact. In other respects, the features of the optical system are such that the output beams generally focus a few hundreds of µm toward the substrate, which considerably limits the interconnection length.

Hybrid integration does not present the drawbacks mentioned above but requires additional alignment and mounting steps which must be carefully handled. An effective technique of passive alignment has been proposed in [25], based on micro-machining of a polysilicon layer deposited on a silicon substrate. The side-mounting of the VCSEL array is however an inadequate configuration for a 3D optical interconnection scheme. Passive alignment of the two substrates has also been achieved with an accuracy better than 2 µm by using reflowed solder bumps [26]. Here, we consider the case of two elements, a microlens array and a VCSEL array, which are not specifically designed for solder bumps assembling. As a result, a macroscopic technique must be developed to align and hybridize the two elements with an accuracy in the micrometer range.

4.1.2 Experimental evaluation of an assembling technique

To align two elements, six degrees of freedom must be controlled: three translations (x,y,z) and three rotations (θx,θy,θz). In our case, the VCSEL array is fixed (except in the direction z) and micro-controllers are used for the displacement of the microlens array over the VCSEL array. The two components and the micro-controllers are fixed on the plate of a microscope.

The angular alignments are realized with a passive method (without activating the VCSEL) by controlling the orientation of the component surface. An accuracy of ± 2 mrad is achieved in the three directions. The z position monitoring relies on the field depth of the microscope. Whereas the z-translation had a sub-micrometer resolution, the precision on z was estimated to ± 2.5 µm with the objective used. The x and y positions are controlled through the microscope using a CCD-camera and a monitor. Since the observed objects (refractive microlenses) are relatively large, the magnification of the microscope must be small. As a result, this visual control has an accuracy limited to a few microns. A fine adjustment is then performed by exploiting the presence of a significant feedback effect due to reflections on the microlens substrate. For this purpose, the VCSEL on the microscope bench are biased just below threshold. When the microlenses are aligned with the active area of the VCSEL, the weak emitted light is reflected on the plane side of the microlens substrate and re-injected into the laser cavity. Hence, the threshold current is apparently reduced and the biasing is finally high enough for the VCSEL to lase, resulting in a high increase of the optical power detected by the CCD-camera. This method is found very sensitive to x- and y-translations and sub-micrometer resolutions are achieved.

We validated this technique by assembling a commercially available 1x8 VCSEL array provided by Vixel Corp. with a refractive microlens array designed by NPL. The pitch of both arrays is 250 µm and the operating wavelength is 850 nm. The VCSEL array was only available in a DIL-package, which prevented us from building a highly integrated system. Moreover, the depth of the DIL package was such that mounting the plane side of the microlens toward the VCSEL to minimize aberration effects was not possible. This reverse mounting is responsible for the feedback effect previously mentioned, since all the light reflected on the plane side was re-focused in the VCSEL active window through the microlenses.

Once the alignment was performed, we deposited four small bumps of epoxide resin under each corner of the microlens substrate (see Figure 9). The polymerization of the epoxide resin was achieved at ambient temperature to avoid any heating of the refractive microlenses.

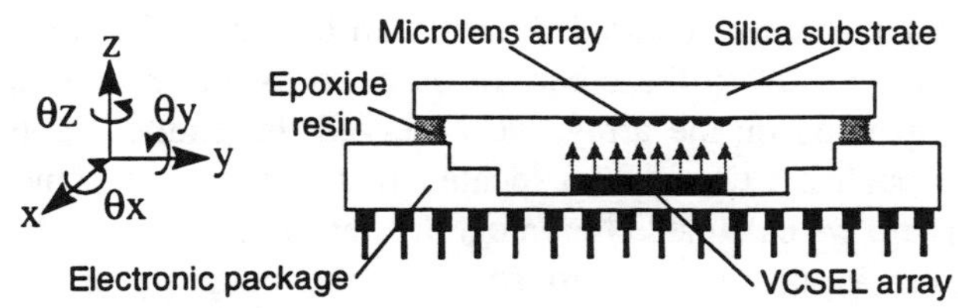

Figure 9: Outlines of the hybrid VCSEL/microlens subsystem.

The beam spots and profiles in the detection plane are shown in Figure 10 and Figure 11, respectively. Some aberration effects can be noticed (side lobes).

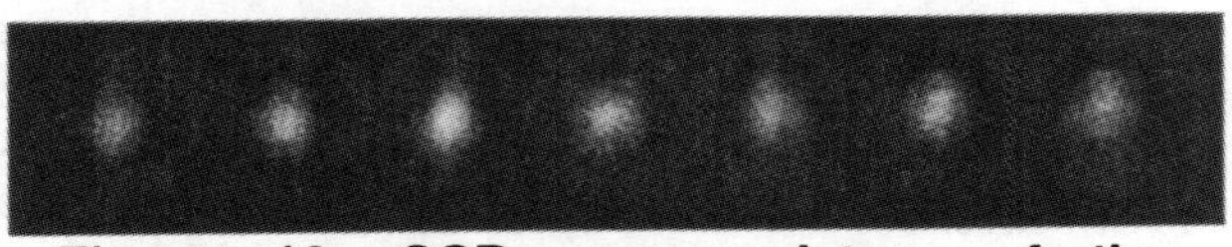

Figure 10: CCD-camera picture of the detection plane.

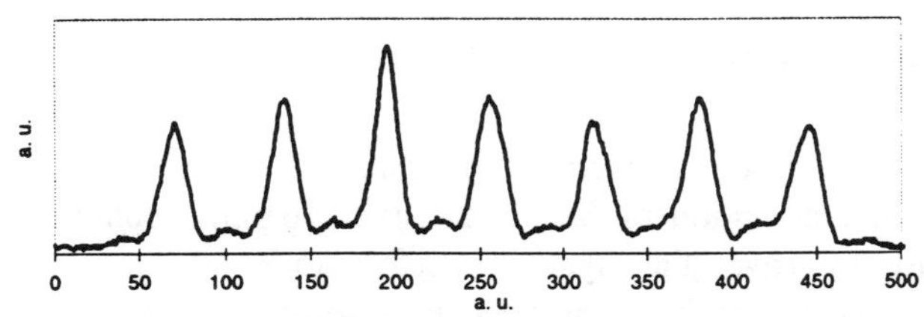

Figure 11: Intensity profile of the beam array in the detection plane.

By observing the shift of the spots between the microlens plane and the detection plane 15 mm further, we assessed that the misalignment between the VCSEL and the microlens arrays does not exceed 2 μm in both x and y directions.

4.2 Zero-bias VCSEL modulation

The principle of zero-bias modulation of laser diodes is not new and has already been demonstrated with edge-emitting laser diodes [27]. However, the advent of VCSEL with low threshold current and voltage increased the interest of direct modulation, and several authors have recently studied or experimented it [9,28-31]. Zero-bias modulation may be preferable for high density optical interconnections since it does not require bias monitoring and feedback control. Then, if digital signal transmissions are considered, direct modulation is particularly attractive since the operating current and voltage of the VCSEL are now compatible with the output characteristics of logical gates. This section presents our first experimental results of a direct modulation of the hybrid VCSEL/microlens array.

4.2.1 Importance of the output drive characteristics of the logical circuit

The VCSEL we used have a threshold voltage of ~ 2.8 V and a threshold current of ~ 4.8 mA. Because of the relatively high threshold voltage, we used 5 V CMOS logical circuits instead of more advanced 3.3 V CMOS devices.

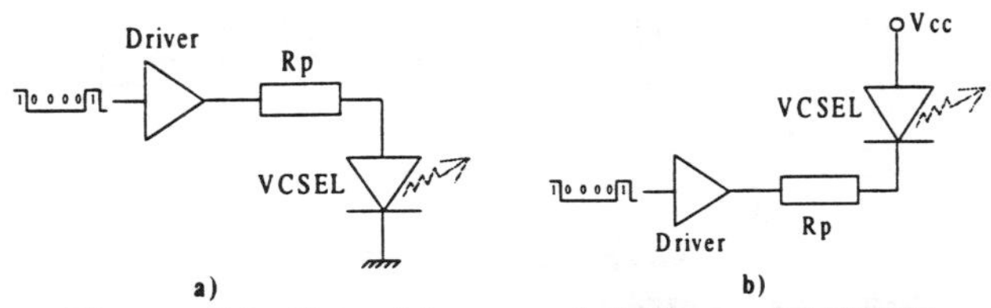

Figure 12: Zero-bias modulation of VCSEL with standard logical circuits.

In a first experiment, the VCSEL array was directly driven by the outputs of a 5 V Field-Programmable Gate Array (FPGA). Each VCSEL was connected to a FPGA output through a small resistance in order to adjust the input current (see Figure 12.a). Unfortunately, the output drive characteristics of the FPGA were such that the output voltage at high level (which corresponds to a "1" transmission) decreased from 4.4 V to less than 3 V for an output current in the range of 8 mA, leading to an incorrect operation of the VCSEL. Measurements of the output drive characteristics of the FPGA for a logical "0" showed that the FPGA outputs could be used with inverted logical signals, where VCSEL would be lasing when "0" are transmitted (Figure 12.b). Unfortunately, because of their common cathode, it was impossible to independently drive the VCSEL in this configuration.

In a second experiment, we inserted a CMOS circuit between the FPGA and the resistance array. The circuit was a hex inverter NS74AC04 presenting better output drive characteristics than the FPGA. Namely, the output voltage in the high level state remained above 4.95 V for a range of output current of 0-10 mA. We used this configuration for the test of a dynamic operation, where the eight VCSEL are driven by eight different digital signals coming from the FPGA. The FPGA simulates a counter and provides eight outputs at 16, 8, ..., 0.125 Mbit/s, respectively.

4.2.2 Signal delay evaluation

A fast avalanche photodiode (0.5 ns rise time) was put in front of the VCSEL driven at 16 Mbit/s, which was the fastest achievable data rate of our evaluation board. Figure 13 shows the output voltage of the photodiode together with the voltage across the VCSEL. The aim of this acquisition was to evaluate the turn-on delay due to the zero-bias modulation. Assuming that there is no turn-off delay, the delay introduced by the measurement chain was estimated to 1 ns maximum according to the relative position of the falling edges (this is not noticeable on the curves of Figure 13).

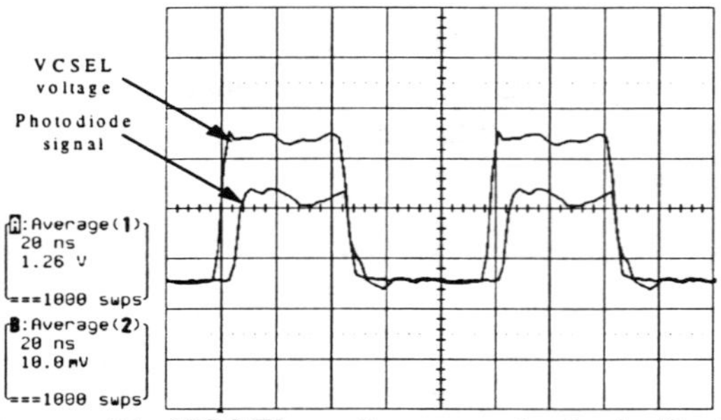

Figure 13: VCSEL voltage and photodiode signal at 10 Mbit/s.

The overall signal delay at midpoint was 6 ns, as shown in Figure 14. This delay is composed of the rise time of the electrical signal and of the turn-on delay of the laser. The latter was estimated at 2-2.5 ns, between the instant of the threshold voltage is reached and the onset of the optical power increase, taking into account the propagation in the acquisition chain.

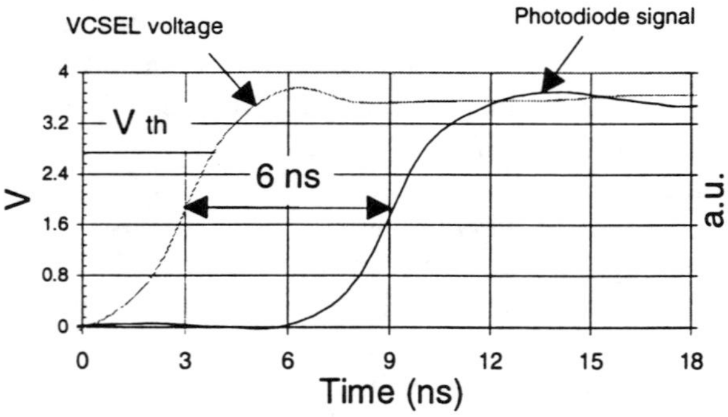

Figure 14: Propagation delay of the free-space optical interconnection.

This value is larger than the one measured in [9,31] but the laser drive current was here twice smaller (10 mA). The following formula gives some information on the influence of the drive current I on the turn-on delay, t_d [28]:

$$t_d = \tau_e \ln \frac{I}{I - I_{th}}, \tag{13}$$

where τ_e is the carrier lifetime in the laser cavity (usually in the 1-3 ns range). This delay only accounts for the time required to achieve the threshold population of carriers. Using this formula, a 20 mA drive current would reduce our turn-on delay by almost 60 %, down to 1 ns. A more precise modeling of the turn-on delay would include the rise time of the applied voltage and the RC time constant of the VCSEL/series resistance system.

4.2.3 Homogeneity of the parallel optical emissions

In parallel optical interconnections, it is important that the power emitted do not significantly differ from one channel to the other. In order to assess the power dispersion on the array, we observed the emitted spots through a CCD-camera located in the detection plane. Then, we calculated the integral of each intensity profile over a square area to simulate the coupling of the emitted beams on the elements of a detector array. The acquisition of the profiles was performed at different instants, and the temporal average power was calculated for each channel. The spatial average over all the channels was then computed and used as the reference value. Rather good results were obtained: a maximum dispersion of 23 % is noticed on the average power per channel. This value includes the dispersion due to the CCD-camera, the output voltage fluctuations of the CMOS inverter and the dispersion of the resistance values. The effects of thermal variations on the coupling power is currently under study.

5. Conclusion

We have presented the role that optics can play in the implementation of SIMD massively parallel computers to improve the system performance. A particular attention has been paid on the alternative provided by free-space optical interconnections to tightly couple the processing elements embedded in multi-chip modules. A necessary trade-off between the achievable bandwidth including the interconnection density and the mechanical constraints of the system assembling was pointed out. A trade-off analysis is required and we have presented the guidelines of a feasibility study which will be illustrated by several experimental building blocks. Some of these experimental validations have been presented in this paper, and other are under development. In particular, the demonstration of a mechanical assembling compatible with both the alignment requirements and the system constraints is an important step in the acceptance of free-space optical interconnections by designers of massively parallel computers.

6. References

[1] C. Weems. The next generation image understanding architecture. *ARPA IUW, Monterey, CA*, pp. 1133-1140, 1994.

[2] D. Juvin *et al.*. Sympati2, a 1.5D Processor Array for Image Applications. *Signal Processing IV: Theory and Applications*, Elsevier Science Publishers B.V., North Holland, 1988.

[3] K. Preston. The Abingdon Cross Benchmark Survey. *IEEE computer*, 22(7), July 1989.

[4] T. Collette *et al.*. Symphonie, calculateur massivement parallèle : modélisation et réalisation. *Proceedings of Journées Adéquation Algorithme Architecture en Traitement du signal et images, Toulouse (France)*, pp. 279-286, January 1996 (in French).

[5] T. Collette *et al.*. SympatiX: a SIMD computer performing the low and intermediate levels of image processing. *Future Generation Computer System*, 10(1), April 1994.

[6] R.C. Eden. Capabilities of normal metal electrical interconnections for 3D MCM electronic packaging. *SPIE Vol. 2153*, pp. 132-145, 1994.

[7] L.A. Hornak and S.K. Tewskbury. A generic VLSI platform for system-level optical interconnection insertion. *SPIE Vol. 2153*, pp. 3-13, 1994.

[8] K.P. Jackson *et al.*. A high-density, four-channel, OEIC transceiver module utilizing planar-processed optical waveguides and flip-chip, solder-bump technology. *J. Lightwave Technol.*, 12(7):1185-1191, 1994.

[9] R.F. Carson *et al.*. Low-power modular parallel photonic data links. *Proc. of the 46th ECTC Conference, Orlando*, pp. 321-326, May 1996.

[10] D.S. Wills *et al.*. A three-dimensional high-throughput architecture using through-wafer optical interconnect. *J. of Lightwave Technol.*, 13(6):1085-1092, 1995.

[11] M. Feldman *et al.*. Holographic optical interconnects for VLSI multi-chip modules. *IEEE Trans. Components, Packaging, and Manufact. Technol., Part-B*, 17(2):223-227, 1994.

[12] M.R. Feldman *et al.*. Comparison between optical and electrical interconnects based on power and speed considerations. *Appl. Opt.*, 27(9):1742-1751, 1988.

[13] J-M. Wang *et al.*. High-speed free-space interconnect based on optical ring topology: experimental demonstration. *Appl. Opt.*, 33(26):6181-6187, 1994.

[14] P. Scheer *et al.*. A massively parallel SIMD multi-processor system using optical interconnects: SYNOPTIQUE. *Optical Computing Conference, Sendai, Japan*, pp.120-121, April 1996.

[15] R.K. Kostuk *et al.*. Distributed optical data bus for board-level interconnects. *Appl. Opt.*, 32(26):5010-5021, 1993.

[16] A. Louri and S. Furlonge. Feasibility study of a scalable optical interconnection network for massively parallel processing systems. *Appl. Opt.*, 35(8):1296-1308, 1996.

[17] D. Zaleta *et al.*. Tolerancing of board-level-free-space optical interconnects. *Appl. Opt.*, 35(8):1317-1327, 1996.

[18] L.D. Dickson. Characteristics of a propagating Gaussian beam. *Appl. Opt.*, 9(8):1854-1861, 1970.

[19] P. Belland and J.P. Crenn. Changes in the characteristics of a Gaussian beam weakly diffracted by a circular aperture. *Appl. Opt.*, 21(3):522-527, 1982.

[20] F.B. McCormick *et al.*. Optical interconnections using microlens arrays. *Opt. and Quantum Electron.*, 24:S465-S477, 1992.

[21] F.B. McCormick *et al.*. Corrigendum: 'Optical interconnections using microlens arrays'. *Opt. and Quantum Electron.*, 24:1209-1212, 1992.

[22] C.J. Kuo *et al.*. Wavelength-division microlens interconnection using weakly diffracted Gaussian beam. *Opt. and Quantum Electron.*, 28:381-394, 1996.

[23] E.M. Strzelecka *et al.*. Monolithic integration of vertical-cavity laser diodes with refractive GaAs microlenses. *Electron. Lett.*, 31(9):724-725, 1995.

[24] T. Du *et al.*. Directional beam control by using on/off-axis high-efficiency diffractive optics, integrated on substrate-emitting vertical-cavity lasers. *Proceedings of CLEO/QELS'95*, paper CWF15, 1995.

[25] S.S. Lee *et al.*. Passively aligned hybrid integration of 8x1 micromachined micro-Fresnel lens arrays and 8x1 vertical-cavity surface-emitting laser arrays for free-space optical interconnect. *IEEE Photon. Technol. Lett.*, 7(9):1031-1033, 1995.

[26] J. Jahns *et al.*. Hybrid integration of surface-emitting microlaser chip and planar optics substrate for interconnection applications. *IEEE Photon. Technol. Lett.*, 4(12):1369-1372, 1992.

[27] K.Y. Lau *et al.*. High-speed digital modulation of ultralow threshold (<1 mA) GaAs single quantum well lasers without bias. *Appl. Phys. Lett.*, 51(2):69-71, 1987.

[28] D.M. Curter and K.Y. Lau. Ultralow power optical interconnect with zero-biased, ultralow threshold laser - How low a threshold is low enough?. *IEEE Photon. Technol. Lett.*, 7(1):4-6, 1995.

[29] K. Obermann *et al.*. Turn-on jitter in zero-biased single-mode semiconductor lasers. *IEEE Photon. Technol. Lett.*, 8(1):31-33, 1996.

[30] H. Karstensen *et al.*. Parallel optical interconnection for uncoded data transmission with 1 Gb/s-per-channel capacity, high-dynamic range, and low power consumption. *IEEE J. Lightwave Technol.*, 13(6):1017-1030, 1995.

[31] R.F. Carson *et al.*. Low-power, parallel photonic interconnections for multi-chip module applications. *45th ECTC, Las Vegas*, pp. 380-386, May 1995.

Three-dimensional Optoelectronic Architectures for Massively Parallel Processing Systems

H. Van Marck and J. Van Campenhout
University of Ghent
Department of Electronics and Information Systems
St.-Pietersnieuwstraat 41, B-9000 Gent, Belgium
{hvm,jvc}@elis.rug.ac.be

Abstract

Advances in optical interconnection technology create the potential of constructing three-dimensional systems. This has a profound impact on the performance of the designs implemented in such a way. Using the average interconnection length and the interconnection length distribution as performance measures, we will show that three-dimensional architectures are much more suitable for the implementation of massively parallel processing systems than traditional two-dimensional architectures. For optoelectronic three-dimensional architectures, we have to take into account the physical and geometric differences between optical and electrical channels. The main consequences of these differences on system performance will be discussed.

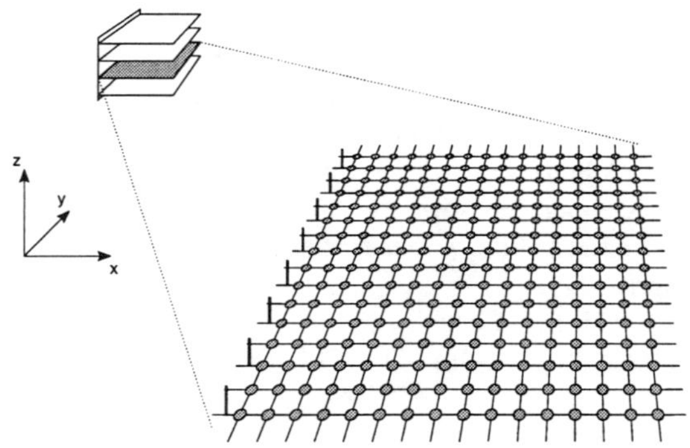

Figure 1. Physical architecture of a traditional electronic backplane system.

1. Introduction

Traditional electronic systems are inherently two-dimensional. The physical architecture[1] consists of a number of two-dimensional grids, loosely interconnected by some sort of backplane (see figure 1). Although such systems occupy a three-dimensional volume, they are essentially two-dimensional from a systems point-of-view. Recent advances in the field of optical interconnection technology are providing us with the building blocks to extend two-dimensional physical architectures into the third dimension. Parallel electronic boards, interconnected by large numbers of free space optical channels could yield three-dimensional optoelectronic processing systems. A representation of the physical architecture of such a system is shown in figure 2. Notice that this is not the same as having a lot of routing layers. Each board is an active component layer, rather than just a passive interconnection plane! Although still in a developmental stage, such systems are expected to be built in the near future. The focus of this paper is to sketch the impact that the use of three-dimensional physical architectures may have on the layout properties of massively parallel processing systems, and the consequences on their performance compared with traditional two-dimensional implementations.

A popular way to compare the performance of VLSI circuits is to determine the average interconnection length of the routing interconnecting the logic circuits. It is well established that this measure is an important factor in other performance measures such as area requirement, routability and maximum clock frequency. Techniques to determine the average interconnection length for implementations in two-dimensional physical architectures are described by Donath [1][2]. These techniques are based on the partitioning properties of electronic designs. We have extended Donath's techniques to optoelectronic three-dimensional architectures [6][7]. Among other things, this involves taking into account the different nature of optical channels compared to electrical ones. The results presented in this paper have all

[1] Description of the physical space a design is implemented in.

0-8186-7974-3/97 $10.00 © 1997 IEEE

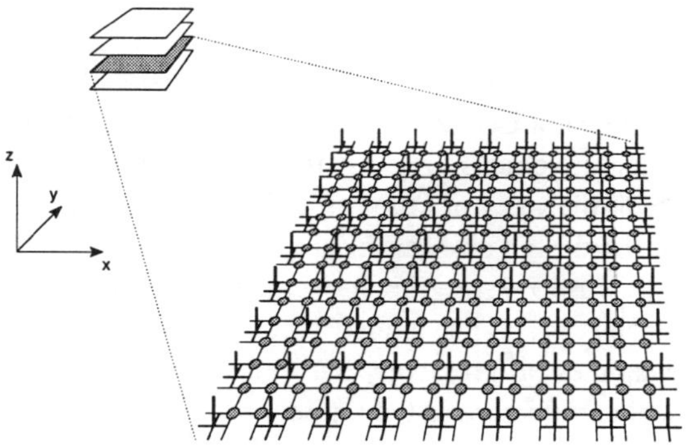

Figure 2. Physical architecture of a three-dimensional optoelectronic system, where free space optical channels interconnect parallel electronic boards.

been derived by applying these extended techniques. For a description of the underlying mathematical techniques used we refer to [4].

This paper is structured as follows. First we analyse the partitioning properties that characterize massively parallel processing systems. Then we show that these properties make them especially suited for implementation in three-dimensional physical architectures. Finally, we present the main effects of the physical and geometric differences between optical and electrical channels in an optoelectronic architecture.

2. Massively Parallel Processing Systems

The main idea behind massively parallel processing is to do as much processing as possible at any given time. In particular in non-trivial problems (i.e. problems that are hard to parallellize), this involves large amounts of communication between the parallel activities of the application. To achieve this goal a vastly complex interconnection structure is needed. A quantitative measure for the complexity of the interconnection structures in a design can be derived by studying its partitioning properties. Consider, for example, the partitioning of a logic circuit design into two subdesigns, minimizing the number of interconnections between the two parts. The more complex the interconnection structure of this design, the more interconnections there are between the subdesigns.

A quantitative description of these partitioning properties is given by Rent's rule. It states that when partitioning a design, there is a relationship between the size of a subdesign B and the number of interconnections P interconnecting it to the outside world or other subdesigns:

$$P \sim B^r,$$

where r is a parameter of the design called the *Rent exponent*. It ranges from 0.4 for designs with a simple interconnection structure (like memory circuits), up to 0.75 for designs with a complex interconnection structure [3][5]. Massively parallel processing systems invariably have high Rent exponents around 0.7.

3. Three-dimensional Physical Architectures

Let us now turn towards the implications that designs with complex interconnection structures (high values of r) have on the physical layout properties of their implementations. First, let us consider some properties of design implementations in a two-dimensional physical architecture.

Figure 3 shows the interconnection length distributions[2] of implementations of designs with different interconnection complexities. It is clear that designs with a higher r have a proportionally larger number of long interconnections, and thus a larger average interconnection length $\bar{l}$.

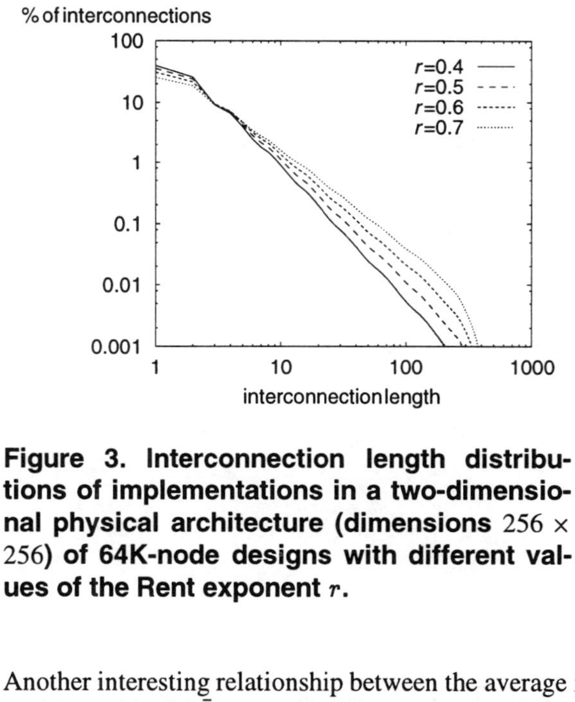

Figure 3. Interconnection length distributions of implementations in a two-dimensional physical architecture (dimensions 256×256) of 64K-node designs with different values of the Rent exponent r.

Another interesting relationship between the average interconnection length $\bar{l}$ and the interconnection complexity of a design is shown in figure 4. It shows the asymptotic behaviour of $\bar{l}$ as the size of a design increases. For designs with a Rent exponent r lower than a threshold value r_c, the average interconnection length $\bar{l}$ converges to a constant $l_\infty(r)$. For designs with $r > r_c$ the value of $\bar{l}$ runs off to infinity, at a rate proportional to the design size raised to the power $r - r_c$. The threshold r_c can thus be interpreted as the capacity of the physical architecture to hold a certain design with a Rent exponent r. The larger the difference $r - r_c$,

[2]For clarity, the discrete distributions are shown as continuous ones.

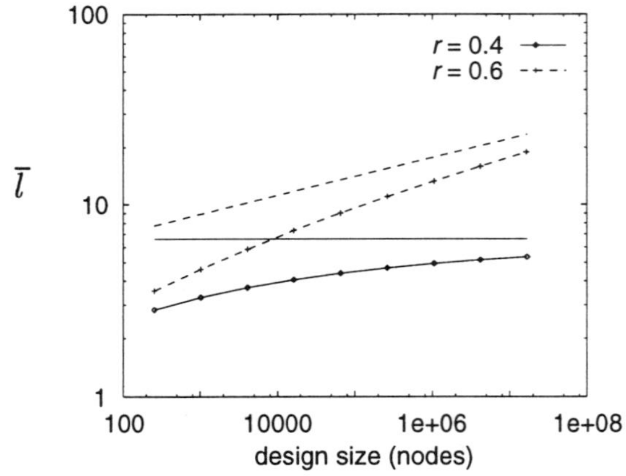

Figure 4. Asymptotic behaviour of the average interconnection length $\bar{l}$ for different values of r in a two-dimensional physical architecture.

the harder it is for the architecture to contain the design. For two-dimensional physical architectures $r_c = 0.5$.

We are now ready to determine the impact of using a three-dimensional physical architecture. Figure 5 shows the influence of the dimension on the interconnection length distribution of an implemented design (with $r = 0.6$). It is clear that in the three-dimensional physical architecture the interconnections are shorter. This implies that the same design will be faster when implemented in 3D instead of 2D.

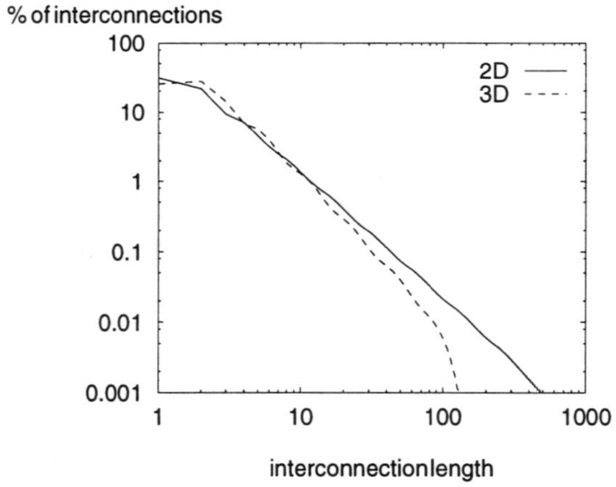

Figure 5. A comparison of interconnection length distributions for a 256K-node design ($r = 0.6$) implemented in a two-dimensional versus a three-dimensional physical architecture.

Another implication of using a three-dimensional physical architecture is shown in figure 6. It shows that the capacity to hold a design is higher for a three-dimensional physical architecture than for a two-dimensional one. In fact, the threshold value r_c for a three-dimensional physical architecture equals $2/3$. Again, we note that for designs with $r > r_c$ the value of $\bar{l}$ runs off to infinity at a rate proportional to the design size raised to the power $r - r_c$. Notice that in the case $r < r_c$ the convergence rate decreases as r approaches r_c. This is also a consequence of the fact that it becomes progressively harder to contain a design in a physical architecture as the interconnection complexity of the design increases.

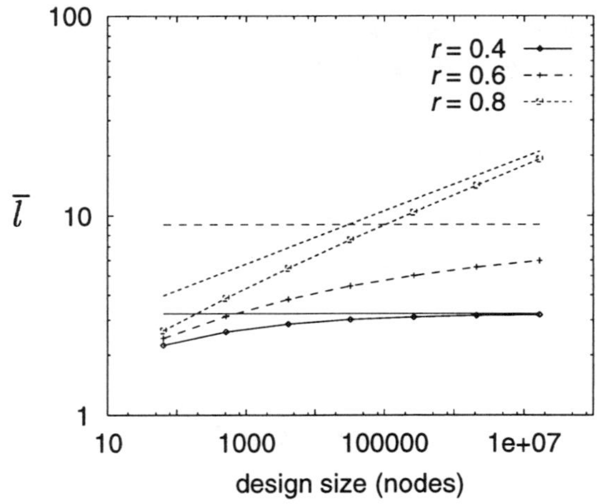

Figure 6. Asymptotic behaviour of the average interconnection length $\bar{l}$ for different values of r in a three-dimensional physical architecture.

The comparison between two- and three-dimensional physical architectures clearly shows that the latter are more suited to be used for the implementation of complex systems such as massively parallel processing systems. The relative advantage of three-dimensional architectures increases with growing problem size.

4. Optoelectronic Three-dimensional Architectures

Using optical technology to interconnect parallel electronic boards enables us to build three-dimensional physical architectures. However, there are significant differences between the electrical channels within the boards, and the optical channels that interconnecting the boards. First of all, they have different physical properties such as bandwidth, latency, etc. Secondly, there are significant differences concerning their geometric properties such as size, spacing, etc. As a result of all these differences, optoelectronic architectures have an *anisotropic* channel structure [7]. This means that the cost of an electrical channel differs from the cost of an optical channel. To account for these differences we introduce a relative cost c_z, specifying how much more expensive it is to use an optical channel instead of an electrical channel. This parameter strongly depends on both the electronic and optical technology used, as well as the properties considered.

Another limitation in opto-electronic architectures is that it is unrealistic to assume that we can stack as many boards on top of each other as we want. There are a multitude of factors limiting the number of boards.

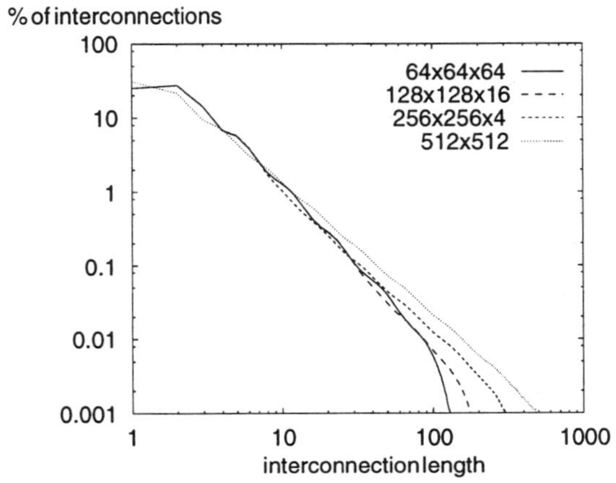

Figure 7. Interconnection length distributions of implementations of a 256K-node design ($r = 0.6$) in different physical architectures.

All these factors result in three-dimensional optoelectronic architectures being *pseudo 3D*. How does all this affect the analysis made earlier for 3D architectures? First let us examine the influence of limiting the number of boards. Figure 7 shows the interconnection length distribution of a 256K-node design realised in both a 3D architecture (dimensions $64 \times 64 \times 64$), a 2D architecture (dimensions 512×512) and two pseudo 3D architectures (dimensions $128 \times 128 \times 16$ and $256 \times 256 \times 4$, $c_z = 1$). Notice how the pseudo 3D architectures behave more and more like 2D architectures as the number of boards decreases.

The impact of the relative cost c_z on the average interconnection length $\bar{l}$ is shown in figure 8. As c_z increases, optimal implementations tend to use less and less optical interconnections. This results in interconnections that are 'squeezed' in ever fewer electrical planes, the architecture behaving more and more like a two-dimensional physical architecture instead of a three-dimensional one. It is clear that if c_z is large enough, it is no longer advantageous to implement a design in this pseudo 3D physical architecture. With current optical technology, the value of c_z with respect to inter-chip electrical interconnects does not warrant the use of optical interconnects. However, when compared to off-chip or off-board interconnects, at least for some cost measures, c_z is taking on values that open the door for optical inter-chip interconnects.

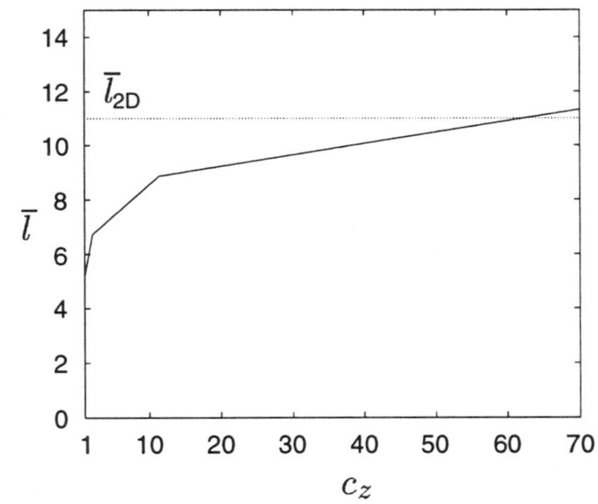

Figure 8. Average interconnection length $\bar{l}$ of an implementation of a 256K-node design in a pseudo-3D physical architecture (dimensions $128 \times 128 \times 16$) as a function of the relative cost c_z of an optical channel. For comparison, the average interconnection length $\bar{l}_{2D}$ of an implementation in a two-dimensional physical architecture (dimensions 512×512) is indicated.

5. Conclusion

Massively parallel processing systems are characterized by complex interconnection structures. We have shown that traditional two-dimensional physical architectures have a capacity that is too low to hold such complex designs without large degradation in performance. In terms of average interconnection length, optoelectronic three-dimensional architectures are much more suited to implement complex designs, provided that we can bring the relative cost c_z of an optical interconnection low enough.

6. Acknowledgements

This research is carried out at the Department of Electronics and Information Systems at the University of Ghent, Belgium. It is supported by an Inter University Attraction Poles research program (IUAP IV-13) on Photonic Interconnects initiated by the Belgian Government, Prime Minister's Service, Science Policy Office.

References

[1] W. E. Donath. Placement and average interconnection lengths of computer logic. *IEEE Trans. on Circ. & Sys.*, CAS-26:272 – 277, 1979.

[2] W. E. Donath. Wire length distribution for placements of computer logic. *IBM Journal of Research and Development*, 25:152 – 155, 1981.

[3] R. L. Russo. On the tradeoff between logic performance and circuit-to-pin ratio for LSI. *IEEE Trans. on Computers*, C-21:147 – 153, 1972.

[4] D. Stroobandt, H. Van Marck, and J. Van Campenhout. On the use of generating polynomials for the representation of interconnection length distributions. In G. Gielen, W. Sansen, and P. Wambacq, editors, *Proceedings of the 4th international workshop on Symbolic Methods and Applications in Circuit Design SMACD '96*, pages 70 – 78, Heverlee, Oct 1996. Katholieke Universiteit Leuven.

[5] H. Van Marck, D. Stroobandt, and J. Van Campenhout. Towards an extension of Rent's rule for describing local variations in interconnection complexity. In S. Bai, J. Fan, and X. Li, editors, *Proceedings of the Fourth International Conference for Young Computer Scientists*, pages 136–141. Peking University Press, 1995.

[6] H. Van Marck and J. Van Campenhout. Modeling and evaluating optoelectronic architectures. In R. T. Chen and J. A. Neff, editors, *SPIE PROCEEDINGS: Optoelectronic Interconnects II*, volume 2153, pages 307– 314. SPIE, 1994.

[7] H. Van Marck and J. Van Campenhout. Modeling signal delay distribution in optoelectronic architectures. In R. T. Chen and H. S. Hinton, editors, *SPIE PROCEEDINGS: Optoelectronic Interconnects III*, volume 2400, pages 267–276. SPIE, 1995.

SESSION VIII

Optical Interconnect Modeling and Experimentation

Chair

James G. Grote
WPAFB

Fundamentals of Optical Interconnections—a Review

Haldun M. Ozaktas
Bilkent University, Department of Electrical Engineering
TR-06533 Bilkent, Ankara, Turkey

Abstract

We review some of the relatively fundamental work in the area of optically interconnected digital computing systems. We cover comparisons of optical interconnections with other interconnection media in terms of energy and interconnection density, studies determining the optimal combination of optical and electrical interconnections that should be used, work on free-space optical interconnection architectures, complexity studies, and work on physical and logical system architectures and algorithms. We exclude work on devices, components, materials, and manufacturing.

1. Introduction

Following publications such as [1], a substantial amount of effort has been invested to determine whether, when, and how the use of optical interconnections may lead to improvements in digital computing systems. These efforts have been multi-faceted, ranging from the development of materials, devices, and components; to system-level studies comparing the relative strengths and weaknesses of optical interconnections; to the development of novel optical and system architectures.

In this work we attempt to provide a review of some of the relatively fundamental work in this area. We exclude fundamental work on devices, materials, and manufacturing techniques. We also limit our attention to digital systems, excluding analog systems and neural networks. We further exclude other important topics such as computer-aided design of optoelectronic or optically interconnected systems.

We cannot claim to be comprehensive, neither in terms of content nor in terms of the authors cited. Space limitations has allowed us to include only a sampling of references. We will be grateful for omissions brought to our attention, as well as suggestions regarding the organization of this paper. An attempt will be made to incorporate these in the full version of this paper.

2. General considerations

The following considerations are not specific to optically interconnected systems but apply to all digital computers.

2.1. Heat removal limitations

The nonlinear elements (switches or gates) of which digital computing systems are universally made of, dissipate a certain amount of energy E_d per switching event. Furthermore, each bit of information that is sent from one point to another is represented by an amount of energy E, which is consequently dissipated. The value of E_d may very well be in the fJ range. On the other hand, the value of E will more likely be of the order of a pJ or more. Smaller values may be attainable for very short interconnections, but for systems whose overall size is of the order of 1 m, it seems fair to take $E + E_d \approx E \sim 1$ pJ as an appropriate average for the energy per switching/transmission event.

If we let N denote the number of elements (switches or gates) in our system and k the average number of interconnections per switch, then the total power dissipated is $\mathcal{P} = kNEB$, where B is the bit-repetition-rate; the rate at which bits of information are being emitted into each interconnection. With $N = 10^8$, $k = 5$, $B = 2\,\mathrm{Gb/s}$, we obtain $\mathcal{P} = 1\,\mathrm{MW}$. If this system occupies a volume of $\mathcal{L}^3 = (10\,\mathrm{cm})^3$, then it becomes necessary to remove $10^8\,\mathrm{W/m^2} = 10\,\mathrm{kW/cm^2}$ through the system. This seems to be the very upper limit of what can be achieved by fluid convection [2], and would probably be very difficult to achieve. Notice that the amount of power we can remove from a system is proportional to the *cross-sectional area* (not the surface area) of the system [2].

Simple calculations will show that the space occupied by the elements and even the interconnections is small in comparison. The moral is that heat removal will be the most important consideration in high performance future computing systems. It will be of paramount importance to employ the most aggressive heat removal methods and integrate heat removal into system design from the onset [3].

0-8186-7974-3/97 $10.00 © 1997 IEEE

2.2. Confining active devices to planes

For highly interconnected circuits, the following result is of relevance [4, 5, 6]: Provided the interconnections are allowed to be routed through three-dimensional space, there is no disadvantage in restricting the active devices to a plane. That is, the overall volume and signal delay and thus clock rate of a highly interconnected three-dimensional system in which the active devices are restricted to a plane will not be inferior to a system in which the active devices can be situated freely throughout the volume. This is because the volume is primarily determined by heat removal limitations or the space occupied by the interconnections, so that additional restrictions on the active devices are of little or no significance. This result, which is based on purely geometrical considerations, is valid for all types of interconnections.

2.3. Globally interconnected systems

Globally interconnected systems are better than locally interconnected systems because global connections allow flexible and fast global transfer of information. Global interconnections take up much more space, but since heat removal considerations imply large separations between the elements anyway, this does not result in larger system size and delays [7].

3. Energy comparisons

Having concluded that heat removal limitations will become one of the most important, if not the most important consideration, it follows that reducing the energy per transmitted bit of information E is of primary importance. Various studies comparing E for isolated optical and electrical lines indicate that optics becomes more profitable for interconnections shorter than some break-even distance, estimated between 0.1 mm and 10 cm [8, 9, 10]. (These comparisons assume that the energy received is large enough to charge the receiver capacitance to the nominal logic level—area consuming amplifier circuits as used in long-distance communications would be unacceptable.)

Studies which account for a very large number of parameters exist, but the essence of the comparison can be captured by a simple argument. Since attenuation in optical media is very low (as evident from the distance information is able to travel in telecommunications fibers), the energy per transmitted bit can be assumed to be constant in optical systems. On the other hand, the energy for an unterminated (lumped RC) conducting interconnection is proportional to ℓ^2, where ℓ is the length of the line. Thus, beyond a certain value of ℓ, optical interconnections are deemed favorable. If terminated lines are used, the energy is proportional to the length T of the shortest pulse that can propagate on the line with acceptable attenuation, which is in turn proportional to ℓ^2/W^2, where W is the width of the line. The only way to prevent the energy from increasing with length is to increase $W \propto \ell$, but this increase in the thickness of lines and subsequent crowding will eventually result in an increase in the size of the system, increasing the line lengths ℓ, which will require a further increase in W, and so on, thwarting the attempt to circumvent the intrinsic limitations associated with line resistance.

Miller has given an intriguing physical interpretation of the fact that optical interconnections are energetically more advantageous [10]. Other fundamental works in this area include [11, 12, 13]. The effect of fan-in and fan-out is discussed in [14].

It has been shown that the energy per transmitted bit with superconducting interconnections is also constant and comparable to what may be achieved with optical interconnections, for a nominal voltage level of 1 V. It may be further reduced if lower nominal voltages are employed at lower temperatures [4].

4. Interconnection density

4.1. Comparisons with other technologies

A fairly common misconception is that optical channels do not occupy any volume and are "free" in this sense. Whereas it is true that separate optical channels can cross through each other with little or no interference, optical channels nevertheless have a volume cost: The *minimum* volume occupied by an optical interconnection system with total interconnection length ℓ_{total} is $\sim \lambda^2 \ell_{\text{total}}$, where λ is the wavelength of light [15]. Thus, each independent spatial channel can be thought to have a constant transverse area of λ^2.

On the other hand, the cross-sectional area of conducting interconnections must increase with length to maintain acceptable attenuation. Thus beyond a certain length, optical interconnections become favorable. The break-even lengths cited are comparable to those obtained from energy considerations [4, 8, 16, 17].

Two-dimensional integrated optical guided wave circuits are not able to support a surface density of one spatial channel per wavelength because of the larger separations implied by crosstalk considerations. Such systems will probably not be favorable until extremely large system sizes [18, 19].

4.2. Topological considerations for optics

The word "minimum" appearing above is of significance. Indeed, it was first thought that a strong tradeoff between topological flexibility (the ability to implement arbitrary patterns of connections) and volume existed: that greater flexibility came at the cost of greater volume. However, it was later understood that these tradeoffs applied only to a broad class of architectures which may be referred to as multi-facet architectures, but that other architectures free from these limitations are possible. Thus arbitrary circuit diagrams (graphs) can be realized with an effective interconnection density of $\sim 1/\lambda^2$. This result assumes optical systems whose f-numbers (analogous to the F-stop on a camera) approach unity. In practice, it seems realistic to expect this density to be achieved within an order of magnitude. In most cases this will be sufficient, since heat removal and not interconnection density will be the limiting factor.

Publications investigating these issues include [20, 21, 22, 23, 24, 25, 26, 27, 28, 29]

4.3. Architectures for free-space optics

A large variety of free-space optical interconnection architectures have been proposed and studied. In this section we mention works that deal with the optical interconnections only, without consideration of the overall computing system architecture [30, 31, 32, 33, 34, 35, 36, 37, 38, 39, 40, 41]. These studies concentrate primarily on optical systems to image arrays of sources onto arrays of detectors in an efficient manner. Several authors have discussed the ultimate limitations of these systems; others have been led to investigations of mathematical and combinatoric issues regarding permutation and other types of networks. Shuffle-based systems are by far the most commonly studied both because they have efficient optical implementations and because of their versatility.

"Planar free-space" systems also deserve mention in this context [42].

5. System-level studies

5.1. Area-volume-time complexity studies

Here we are referring to area-volume-time studies either in the spirit of classical VLSI complexity theory [43], or the closely related pin-out/line-length distribution based studies [44, 45]. Work on three-dimensional complexity theory includes [4, 5, 6, 46, 47, 48]. Some of these works are classical complexity studies, being based on purely geometrical considerations and ignoring all constants of proportionality. Others have reintroduced physical constants and order-of-magnitude accuracy in an attempt to obtain results which are more physically relevant [4].

5.2. System-level technology comparisons

These studies typically assume an array of elements of some degree of complexity (usually ranging from transistors to processors) and compare performance and cost measures resulting from the use of different interconnection media. These works differ from the comparison studies mentioned earlier in that they compare systems, rather than isolated interconnections [4, 49, 50, 51].

Based solely on fundamental physical considerations, optical and superconducting interconnections are comparable to each other and superior to normally conducting interconnections, even when aggressive use of repeaters is made to circumvent capacitive and resistive problems. The possibility of three-dimensional circuits and freedom from termination problems seems to give optics an edge over superconductors.

The use of normally conducting interconnections results in severe limitations in large scale systems. Even with arbitrarily small scaling and arbitrarily fast devices, with or without termination, the maximum bit rates that can be supported sharply decrease with increasing system size. Likewise, the bisection-inverse delay and bisection-bandwidth products are bounded from above. This is in contrast with the other media with which it is possible to arbitrarily increase B and the bisection-bandwidth product for any given N. The use of repeaters alleviates, but does not change the inferiority of normal conductors, while at the same time greatly increasing manufacturing complexity because of the need to support active devices at all levels of the interconnection hierarchy. The use of optics is comparably even more advantageous when large bandwidths are required.

5.3. Optimal combination of optical and electrical interconnections

These studies discuss how optical and electrical interconnections can be used together. They essentially address the question: Beyond what level of the interconnection hierarchy should optics be used? Or, how should a large circuit be partitioned into optically interconnected electronic chips? That is, what is the optimal grain size? [19, 52, 53, 54]

The general indication is that the system should be partitioned into clusters of $\sim 10^4$–10^6 transistors; for instance, in the form of an optically interconnected array of chips with this many transistors on each. It has been argued that the use of optical interconnections allows one to access points in performance space unachievable otherwise, however possibly at a significant cost of space and/or power [19]. The increase in performance may take the form of smaller signal delay and/or larger bandwidth in comparison to an all-electrical system. If minimization of the cost associated with size and power is the primary objective, rather than the maximization of performance, then the use of optics does not become beneficial until extremely large system sizes.

5.4. Multi-faceted system-level studies

Here we mention some studies which deal with many or all aspects of an optically interconnected system simultaneously, rather than concentrating on only one part (such as the smart pixel array or the optical interconnection architecture). Some of these studies are part of a specific development effort, but the results nevertheless have general applicability or implications. [55, 56, 57, 58, 59]

Figure 1 depicts the tree of alternative optical interconnection architectures. In [60] we started from the top of this tree and by offering arguments that allow us to prune suboptimal branches, we finally arrived at the boxed alternative shown at the bottom as the basis for an optimal architecture.

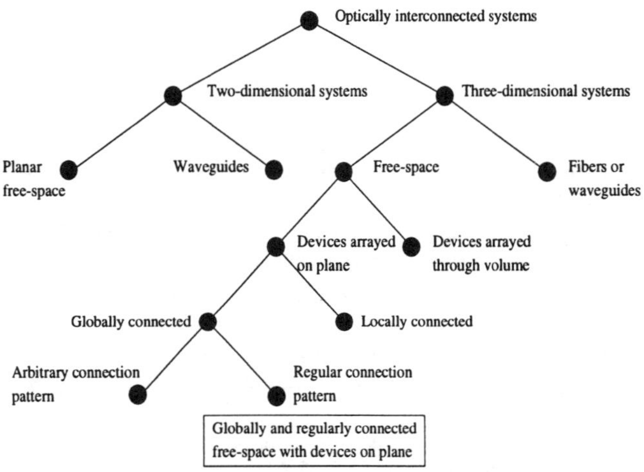

Figure 1.

5.5. Physical system architecture and technology platform development

Many different systems employing optical interconnections in one form or another have been or are being developed. Although these specific development efforts may not be considered fundamental, they are important because they represent novelties or breakthroughs in design, architecture, packaging, or systems engineering [61, 62, 63, 64, 65, 66, 67, 68, 69, 70].

It should be noted that considerable subjectivity is involved in determining what should be included in this or the preceding subsection.

5.6. Algorithms and logical architectures

The different physical architectures supported by optics has created interest in different logical architectures and associated algorithms which better match the abilities of optical interconnections. These often involve massive parallel flows of information [71]. In addition to exploration of various different paradigms (systolic architectures, connectionist systems, cellular systems, etc.), there has also been a revival of work in switching networks [62, 72, 73, 74].

5.7. Components and devices

While we have excluded components and devices from the scope of this paper, a number of studies deserve inclusion because of their fundamental implications from a systems viewpoint. For instance, we may mention device comparison studies such as [75, 76], and studies analyzing the scaling properties of refractive and diffractive lenses [77, 78].

Other publications deal with the design of optical components specifically for optical interconnection applications. These include the design of diffractive optical components [79], microoptical assemblies, and spot array generators.

6. Technology evolution studies

These studies may help track the evolution of optoelectronic technology in the context of the history of development of digital computing systems in general, and may also shed light on why a technology with fundamental credentials as strong as optics, is nevertheless not easily able to find its way into mainstream systems [80, 81, 82].

7. Conclusion

Although a consolidated body of knowledge and understanding has emerged in several areas, this is particularly not the case for full-blown system-level studies. The different starting points and assumptions makes it difficult to compare the many studies on a common footing. This may be viewed as a strength as much as a weakness, as the community has not been locked into a specific direction which may be suboptimal.

References

[1] J. W. Goodman, F. J. Leonberger, S.-Y. Kung, and R. Athale. Optical interconnections for VLSI systems. *Proc IEEE*, 72:850–866, 1984.

[2] H. M. Ozaktas, H. Oksuzoglu, R. F. W. Pease, and J. W. Goodman. Effect on scaling of heat removal requirements in three-dimensional systems. *Int J Electronics*, 73:1227–1232, 1992.

[3] W. Nakayama. Heat-transfer engineering in systems integration—outlook for closer coupling of thermal and electrical designs of computers. *IEEE Trans Components, Packaging, and Manufacturing Technology, Part A*, 18:818–826, 1995.

[4] H. M. Ozaktas and J. W. Goodman. The limitations of interconnections in providing communication between an array of points. In *Frontiers of Computing Systems Research, Volume 2*, Plenum Press, New York, 1991, pp 61–130.

[5] A. L. Rosenberg. Three-dimensional VLSI: a case study. *J ACM*. 30:397–416, 1983.

[6] F. T. Leighton and A. L. Rosenberg. Three-dimensional circuit layouts. *J Computer and System Sciences*, 15:793–813, 1986.

[7] H. M. Ozaktas and J. W. Goodman. Comparison of local and global computation and its implications for the role of optical interconnections in future nanoelectronic systems. *Opt Commun*, 100:247–258, 1993.

[8] R. K. Kostuk, J. W. Goodman, and L. Hesselink. Optical imaging applied to microelectronic chip-to-chip interconnections. *Appl Opt*, 24:2851–2858, 1985.

[9] M. R. Feldman, S. C. Esener, C. C. Guest, and S. H. Lee. Comparison between optical and electrical interconnects based on power and speed considerations. *Appl Opt*, 27:1742–1751, 1988.

[10] D. A. B. Miller. Optics for low-energy communication inside digital processors: quantum detectors, sources and modulators as efficient impedance converters. *Opt Lett*, 14:146–148, 1989.

[11] H. J. Caulfield and J. Shamir. Wave particle duality considerations in optical computing. *Appl Opt*, 28:2184–2186, 1989.

[12] H. J. Caulfield, J. Shamir, J. E. Ludman, and P. Greguss. Reversibility and energetics in optical computing. *Opt Lett*, 15:912–914, 1990.

[13] H. M. Ozaktas and J. W. Goodman. The optimal electromagnetic carrier frequency balancing structural and metrical information densities with respect to heat removal requirements. *Opt Commun*, 94:13–18, 1992.

[14] J. W. Goodman. Fan-in and fan-out with optical interconnections. *Optica Acta*, 32:1489–1496, 1985.

[15] H. M. Ozaktas and J. W. Goodman. Lower bound for the communication volume required for an optically interconnected array of points. *J Opt Soc Am A*, 7:2100–2106, 1990.

[16] M. R. Feldman, C. C. Guest, T. J. Drabik, and S. C. Esener. Comparison between optical and electrical interconnects for fine grain processor arrays based on interconnect density capabilities. *Appl Opt*, 28:3820–3829, 1989.

[17] D. A. B. Miller and H. M. Ozaktas. Limit to the bit rate capacity of electrical interconnects from the aspect ratio of the system architecture. *J Parallel and Distributed Computing*, to appear.

[18] G. Önal, A. Altıntaş, and H. M. Ozaktas. Computer-aided analysis and simulation of complex passive integrated optical circuits of arbitrary rectilinear topology. *Opt Eng*, 33:1596–1603, 1994.

[19] H. M. Ozaktas and J. W. Goodman. Elements of a hybrid interconnection theory, *Appl Opt*, 33:2968–2987, 1994.

[20] J. Shamir. Fundamental speed limitations on parallel processing. *Appl Opt*, 26:1567, 1987.

[21] R. K. Kostuk, J. W. Goodman, and L. Hesselink. Design considerations for holographic optical interconnects. *Appl Opt*, 26:3947–3953, 1987.

[22] M. R. Feldman and C. C. Guest. Interconnect density capabilities of computer generated holograms for optical interconnection of very large scale integrated circuits. *Appl Opt*, 28:3134–3137, 1989.

[23] A. W. Lohmann and A. S. Marathay. Globality and speed of optical parallel processors. *Appl Opt*, 28:3838–3842, 1989.

[24] C. W. Stirk and D. Psaltis. Comparison of optical and electronic 3-dimensional circuits. In *Proc SPIE 1389*, 580–593, 1990.

[25] H. M. Ozaktas, Y. Amitai, and J. W. Goodman. Comparison of system size for some optical interconnection architectures and the folded multi-facet architecture. *Opt Commun*, 82:225–228, 1991.

[26] A. W. Lohmann. Image formation of dilute arrays for optical information processing. *Opt Commun*, 86:365–370, 1991.

[27] G. E. Lohman and K.-H. Brenner. Space-variance in optical computing. *Optik*, 89:123–134, 1992.

[28] H. M. Ozaktas and D. Mendlovic. Multi-stage optical interconnection architectures with least possible growth of system size. *Opt Lett*, 18:296–298, 1993.

[29] H. M. Ozaktas, K.-H. Brenner, and A. W. Lohmann. Interpretation of the space-bandwidth product as the entropy of distinct connection patterns in multifacet optical interconnection architectures. *J Opt Soc Am A*, 10:418–422, 1993.

[30] A. W. Lohmann. What classical optics can do for the digital optical computer. *Appl Opt*, 25:1543–1549, 1986.

[31] A. Lohmann, G. Stucke, and W. Stork. Optical perfect shuffle. *Appl Opt*, 25:1530–1531, 1986.

[32] K.-H. Brenner and A. Huang. Optical implementations of the perfect shuffle interconnection. *Appl Opt*, 27:135–137, 1988.

[33] C. Stirk, R. A. Athale, and M. W. Haney. Folded perfect shuffle optical processor. *Appl Opt*, 27:202–203, 1988.

[34] Q. W. Song and F. T. S. Yu. Generalized perfect shuffle using optical spatial filtering. *Appl Opt*, 27:1222–1223, 1988.

[35] J. Jahns and M. J. Murdocca. Crossover networks and their optical implementation. *Appl Opt*, 27:3155–3160, 1988.

[36] J. Shamir, H. J. Caulfield, and R. B. Johnson. Massive holographic interconnection networks and their limitations. *Appl Opt*, 28:311–324, 1989.

[37] M. W. Haney and J. J. Levy. Optically efficient free-space folded perfect-shuffle network. *Appl Opt*, 30: 2833–2840, 1991.

[38] J. Giglmayr. Generation and evaluation of d-dimensional ($d \geq 3$) optical shuffle patterns. *Appl Opt*, 31:4662–4675, 1992.

[39] G. C. Marsden, P. J. Marchand, P. Harvey, and S. C. Esener. Optical transpose interconnection system architectures. *Opt Lett*, 1083–1085, 1993.

[40] J. Giglmayr. Locality and decomposition of regular optical interconnection patterns. *Appl Opt*, 33:6157–6167, 1994.

[41] P. S. Guilfoyle and J. M. Hessenbruch. Reconfigurable N^4 optical interconnects using the PROMAC architecture. *Int J Optical Memory and Neural Networks*, 3:99–109, 1994.

[42] J. Jahns. Planar packaging of free-space optical interconnections. *Proc IEEE*, 82:1623–1631, 1994.

[43] J. D. Ullman. *Computational Aspects of VLSI*. Computer Science Press, Rockville, Maryland, 1984.

[44] R. W. Keyes. *The Physics of VLSI Systems*. Addison-Wesley, Reading, Massachusetts, 1987.

[45] H. M. Ozaktas. Paradigms of connectivity for computer circuits and networks. *Opt Eng*, 31:1563–1567, 1992.

[46] R. Barakat and J. Reif. Lower bounds on the computational efficiency of optical computing systems. *Appl Opt*, 26:1015–1018, 1987.

[47] M. M. Eshaghian, D. K. Panda, V. K. P. Kumar. Resource requirement for digital computations on electrooptical systems. *Appl Opt*, 30:928–935, 1991.

[48] S. Pavel and S. G. Akl. Area-time trade-offs in arrays with optical pipelined buses. *Appl Opt*, 35:1827–1835.

[49] F. E. Kiamilev, P. Marchand, A. V. Krishnamoorthy, S. C. Esener, and S. H. Lee. Performance comparison between optoelectronic and VLSI multistage interconnection networks. *J Lightwave Tech*, 9:1674–1692, 1991.

[50] T. J. Cloonan. Comparative study of optical and electronic interconnection technologies for large asynchronous transfer mode packet switching applications. *Appl Opt*, 33:1512–1523, 1994.

[51] L. J. Camp, R. Sharma, M. R. Feldman. Guided-wave and free-space optical interconnects for parallel-processing systems: a comparison. *Appl Opt*, 33:6168–6180, 1994.

[52] A. V. Krishnamoorthy, P. J. Marchand, F. E. Kiamilev, and S. C. Esener. Grain-size considerations for optoelectronic multistage interconnection networks. *Appl Opt*, 31:5480–5507, 1992.

[53] H. M. Ozaktas and J. W. Goodman. Implications of interconnection theory for optical digital computing. *Appl Opt*, 31:5559–5567, 1992.

[54] J. Fan, B. Catanzaro, V. H. Ozguz, C. K. Cheng, and S. H. Lee. Design considerations and algorithms for partitioning optoelectronic multichip modules. *Appl Opt*, 34:3116–3127, 1995.

[55] F. Kiamilev, S. C. Esener, R. Paturi, Y. Fainman, P. Mercier, C. C. Guest, and S. H. Lee. Programmable optoelectronic multiprocessors and their comparison with symbolic substitution for digital optical computing. *Opt Eng*, 28:396–409, 1989.

[56] D.-T. Lu, V. H. Ozguz, P. J. Marchand, A. V. Krishnamoorthy, F. Kiamilev, R. Paturi, S. H. Lee, and S. C. Esener. Design trade-offs in optoelectronic parallel processing systems using smart-SLMs. *Optical and Quantum Electronics*, 24:S379–S403, 1992.

[57] T. J. Drabik. Optoelectronic integrated systems based on free-space interconnects with an arbitrary degree of space-variance. *Proc IEEE*, 82:1595–1622, 1994.

[58] M. P. Y. Desmulliez, B. S. Wherrett, J. F. Snowdon, and J. A. B. Dines. Optical, algorithmic and electronic considerations on the desirable "smartness" of optical processing pixels. In *Optical Computing*, Proceedings of the International Conference, Edinburgh, 1994, Inst Phys Pub, Bristol, U.K., 1995, pp 489–492.

[59] D. R. Rolston, B. Robertson, H. S. Hinton, and D. V. Plant. Analysis of a microchannel interconnect based on the clustering of smart-pixel-device windows. *Appl Opt*, 35:1220–1234, 1996.

[60] H. M. Ozaktas. Towards an Optimal Foundation Architecture for Optoelectronic Computing, Part I: Regularly Interconnected Device Planes; Part II: Physical Construction and Application Platforms. *Appl Opt*, to appear.

[61] H. S. Hinton, T. J. Cloonan, F. B. McCormick, A. L. Lentine, F. A. P. Tooley. Free-space digital optical systems. *Proc IEEE*, 82:1632–1649, 1994.

[62] H. S. Hinton. *Introduction to Photonic Switching Fabrics*. Plenum, New York, 1993.

[63] T. H. Szymanski and H. S. Hinton. Reconfigurable intelligent optical backplane for parallel computing and communications. *Appl Opt*, 35:1253–1268, 1996.

[64] K. S. Huang, C. B. Kuznia, B. K. Jenkins, and A. A. Sawchuk. Parallel architectures for digital optical cellular image processing. *Proc. IEEE*, 82:1711-1723, 1994.

[65] P. S. Guilfoyle. Digital optical computing architectures for compute intensive applications. In *Optical Computing*, Proceedings of the International Conference, Edinburgh, 1994, Inst Phys Pub, Bristol, U.K., 1995, pp 285–288.

[66] V. N. Morozov, J. A. Neff, H. Temkin, A. S. Fedor. Analysis of a three-dimensional computer optical scheme based on bidirectional free-space optical interconnects. *Opt Eng*, 34:523–534, 1995.

[67] L. J. Irakliotis, S. A. Feld, F. R. Beyette, Jr., P. A. Mitkas, and C. W. Wilmsen. Optoelectronic parallel processing with surface-emitting lasers and free-space interconnects. *J Lightwave Tech*, 13:1074–1084, 1995.

[68] A. Louri and S. Furlonge. Feasibility study of a scalable optical interconnection network for massively parallel processing systems. *Appl Opt*, 35:1296–1308, 1996.

[69] P. J. Marchand, A. V. Krishnamoorthy, G. I. Yayla, S. C. Esener, and U. Efron. Optically augmented 3-D computer: system technology and architecture. *J Parallel and Distributed Computing*, to appear.

[70] G. I. Yayla, P. J. Marchand, and S. C. Esener. Energy and speed analysis of digital electrical and free-space optical interconnections. In *Optical Interconnections and Parallel Processing: The Interface*. Kluwer Academic Publishers, Dordrecht, The Netherlands, to appear.

[71] A. V. Krishnamoorthy and D. A. B. Miller. Firehose architectures for free-space optically-interconnected VLSI circuits. *J Parallel and Distributed Computing*, to appear.

[72] R. Paturi, D.-T. Lu, J. E. Ford, S. C. Esener, and S. H. Lee. Parallel algorithms based on expander graphs for optical computing. *Appl Opt*, 30:917–927, 1991.

[73] H. M. Ozaktas and J. W. Goodman. Organization of information flow in computation for efficient utilization of high information flux communication media. *Opt Commun*, 89:178–182, 1992.

[74] T. J. Cloonan, G. W. Richards, A. L. Lentine, F. B. McCormick, Jr., H. S. Hinton, and S. J. Hinterlong. A complexity analysis of smart pixel switching nodes for photonic extended generalized shuffle switching networks. *IEEE J Quantum Electronics*, 20:619–634, 1993.

[75] D. A. B. Miller. Device requirements for digital optical processing. *Digital Optical Computing*, SPIE Critical Reviews, 1990.

[76] C. Fan, B. Mansoorian, D. A. Van Blerkom, M. W. Hansen, V. H. Ozguz, S. C. Esener, and G. C. Marsden. Digital free-space optical interconnections: a comparison of transmitter technologies. *Appl Opt*, 34:3103–3115, 1995.

[77] H. M. Ozaktas, H. Urey, and A. W. Lohmann. Scaling of diffractive and refractive lenses for optical computing and interconnections. *Appl Opt*, 33:3782–3789, 1994.

[78] D. T. Neilson and C. P. Barrett. Performance trade-offs for conventional lenses for free-space digital optics. *Appl Opt*, 35:1240–1248, 1996.

[79] K. S. Urquhart, P. Marchand, Y. Fainman, and S. H. Lee. Diffractive optics applied to free-space optical interconnects. *Appl Opt*, 33:3670–3683.

[80] A. V. Krishnamoorthy and D. A. B. Miller. Scaling optoelectronic-VLSI circuits into the 21st century: a technology roadmap. *IEEE J Selected Topics Quantum Electronics*, 2:55–76, 1996.

[81] H. M. Ozaktas. Levels of abstraction in computing systems and optical interconnection technology. In *Optical Interconnections and Parallel Processing: The Interface*. Kluwer Academic Publishers, Dordrecht, The Netherlands, to appear.

[82] N. Rosenberg. *Exploring The Black Box: Technology, Economics, and History*. Cambridge University Press, Cambridge, 1994.

We acknowledge the support of NATO under the Science for Stability Program.

Realisation of a Smart-Pixel Parallel Optoelectronic Computing System

N. McArdle, M. Naruse, T. Komuro, and M. Ishikawa
Department of Mathematical Engineering and Information Physics,
University of Tokyo, Hongo 7-3-1, Bunkyo-ku, Tokyo 113, Japan
Tel: +81.3.5800.6569 Fax: +81.3.5800.6969 Email: neil@k2.t.u-tokyo.ac.jp

Abstract

Initial experimental results will be presented from the realisation of a smart-pixel based general purpose parallel optoelectronic processor. A single chip array of integrated processing elements and photodetectors is optically interconnected with a vertical cavity surface-emitting laser array. We give examples of some algorithms the system can perform. Compact gradient index lenses are utilised and we compare their performance with conventional imaging systems.

1. Introduction

Recent rapid advances in technologies such as modulators, vertical cavity surface-emitting laser (VCSEL) arrays, smart-pixel processing elements (PEs) integrating electronic circuitry with optical input/output channels, and micro-optic components has allowed the construction of parallel optoelectronic computing systems. These systems utilise the high bandwidth, high density and global nature of optical communication paths to overcome some of the limitations of conventional metallic interconnections in current computing hardware.

Such globally optically interconnected parallel processing systems are suitable for computationally intensive applications such as sorting, fast fourier transforms, and signal processing. Moreover the inherently parallel flow of 2D optically addressed arrays in pipelined systems is ideally suited for the processing of images. One of the main application areas in our laboratory is high-speed image processing for machine vision. However we can achieve high flexibility of operation due to the programmability of the PEs and the reconfigurability of the optical interconnections. We can therefore implement a variety of operations on our system: image processing, arithmetic, matrix operations, sorting, and signal processing.

We have previously described the design of our system architecture and the main components in detail [1]. We shall present initial results from the experimental realisation of our system. Section 2 briefly describes the architecture of our system. The single chip integrated version of our smart pixel processing element array is described in Section 3. In Section 4 we describe an a comparison of gradient index (GRIN) rod lenses and conventional relay imaging systems for imaging optoelectronic device arrays. Section 5 describes some algorithms which can be implemented on our system, including locally connected low-level image processing and globally connected algorithms such as matrix-vector multiplication and sorting. We conclude with a discussion of the current state of our work.

2. System architecture

Our system is based on the pipelined architecture shown in Fig. 1 [2, 3]. Two-dimensional arrays of smart-pixel processing elements are connected in free-space by optical sources (VCSELs) and detectors.

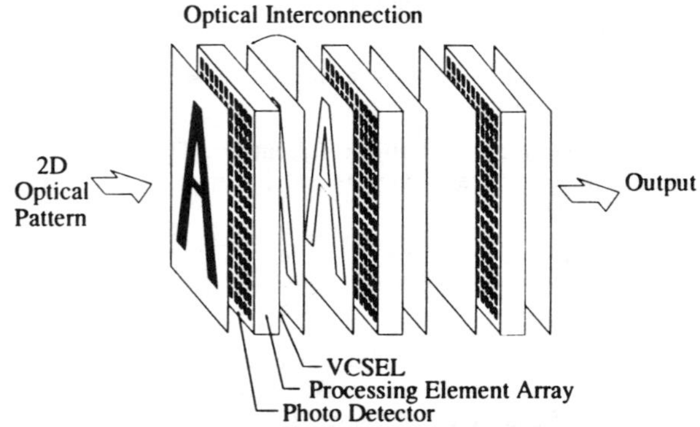

Fig. 1. Pipelined or hierarchical optically interconnected parallel processing architecture.

In the experimental system we utilise a single smart-pixel PE array in a feedback configuration shown schematically in Fig. 2. We consider both types of configuration in our analysis of suitable algorithms in Section 5 and previously in reference [1].

0-8186-7974-3/97 $10.00 © 1997 IEEE

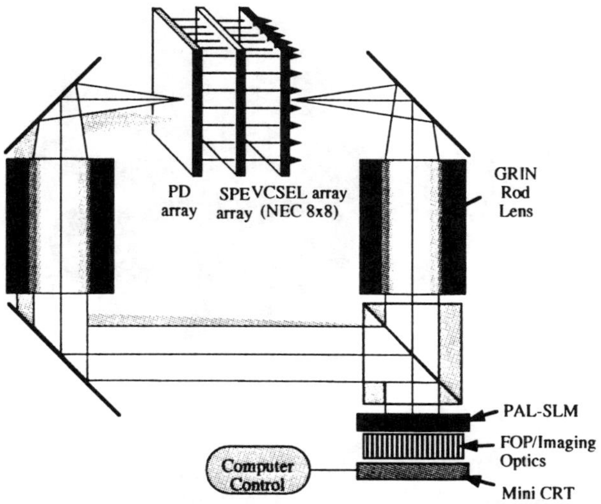

Fig. 2. Single stage of pipelined architecture in feedback configuration.

We consider the ideal system to have complete generality of operation. Thus the processing elements in out system are programmable. In addition the optical interconnections between planes of PEs should be reconfigurable. This allows the machine to use an interconnection topology that is best suited to the data-flow structure of the algorithm being performed. However, current nematic liquid crystal device characteristics severely limit the rate at which these connections can be reconfigured. Other technologies have the potential to improve the rate [4] and we are also investigating the use of fixed interconnection modules for useful topologies such as the perfect shuffle (either one-dimensional or two-dimensional) and butterfly connections .

The most important feature of the above architecture is its programmability and flexibility, enabling the system to perform a variety of algorithms. This is in contrast to many special-purpose optoelectronic computing machines such as FFT processors [5] and sorters [6, 7].

3. Smart Pixel Technology

As already mentioned, the functionality of the processing elements in the smart-pixel array should be high. Therefore we have designed each PE to consist of an arithmetic logic unit (ALU) and local memory. The smart-pixel array is a single instruction multiple data-stream (SIMD) type processor which can be programmed by micro-instructions via interfacing to a host computer. The design was described in detail in [1]. Each PE is electrically connected to its four nearest-neighbouring PEs. For optical input there is an integrated silicon photodetector at each pixel.

Each PE consists of approximately 700 transistors and is fabricated in 0.8μm CMOS. We will present initial experimental results of the operation of the PE array, together with details of the receiver circuitry and its characteristics.

4. Optics

4.1 Comparison of Imaging Systems

To connect in free-space large two-dimensional arrays of optoelectronic devices requires high performance and cost effective imaging systems. Whether the devices used are modulators, such as arrays of symmetric self-electrooptic effect devices (S-SEEDs), or arrays of optical sources (such as VCSELs) and detectors the imaging requirements are crucial to overall system performance. Typical window sizes for smart-pixel photodetectors, modulators and laser diodes are of the order of 5-20 μm. The pitch between pixels can vary from ~20μm to 250μm and typical array sizes can be from 8×8 to 64×64 devices although larger arrays may be required for image processing applications. To ensure maximum system speed and performance, the imaging systems must be diffraction limited over substantial field sizes, for example up to 8×8 mm^2 or larger. In addition, the cost of the lenses must be kept low and their size should be compact.

Various options exist for imaging between planes of devices. These fall into three main categories: (i) micro optics; (ii) macro optics; and (iii) hybrid systems. Microlens arrays have been successfully used in systems however the interconnection distance between planes is severely limited by diffraction effects. Hybrid lens systems which use both microlenses and large macro-optic lenses have also been successfully used [8].

Macro-optic systems can utilise the enormous breadth of experience of classical optical design. Strict imaging requirements sometimes demand custom designed multi-element lenses which are costly and require much time and effort. However careful use of a combination of off-the-shelf optical components is often sufficient for many systems.

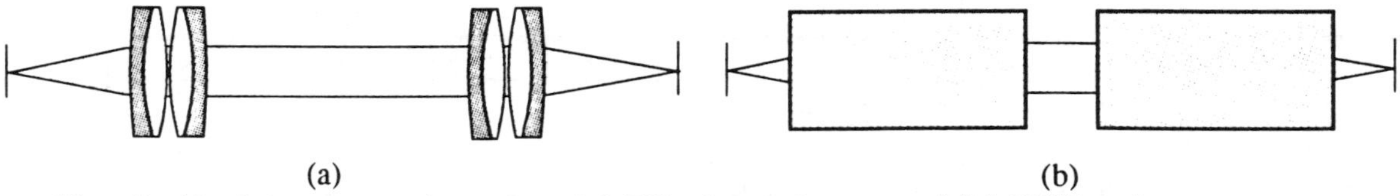

Fig. 3. 4f relay systems based on (a) Plössl eyepieces, and (b) GRIN rods.

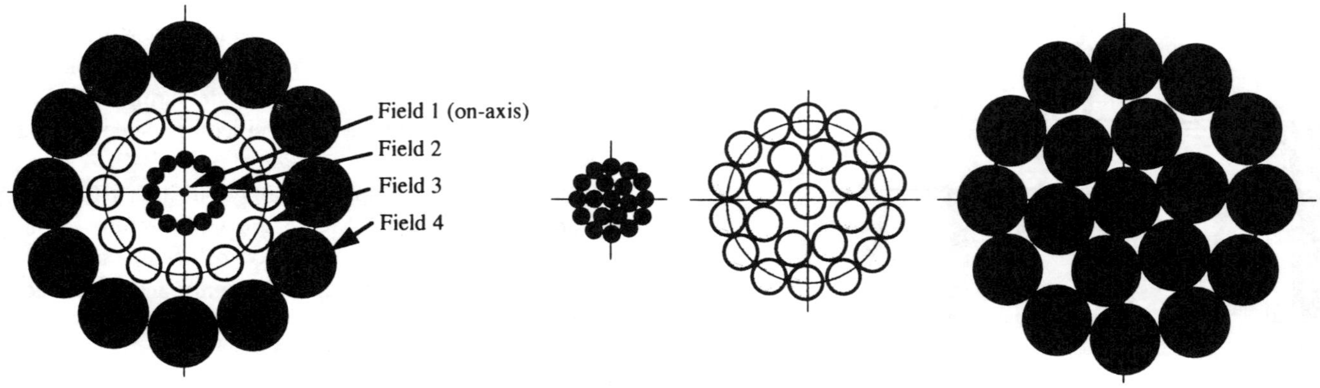

(a) SBWP=37 (b) N=19 (c) N=23 (d) N=19

Fig. 4. (a) schematic representation of image plane. The SBWP=37 is the number of spots. (b) shows N=19 for field position 2. (c) N=23 for field position 3. (d) N=19 for field position 4.

Gradient index (GRIN) rod lenses fall somewhere between the micro-optics and macro optics categories. Previously they have been available in diameters from 1mm to 3mm, but recent advances in manufacturing have allowed lenses as large as 5mm and 8mm to be made. They have been successfully used in parallel interconnection systems in our laboratory and elsewhere [1, 9].

We compare two types of imaging systems which are 4f relays based on: (i) achromatic doublets in a Plössl eyepiece configuration; (ii) GRIN rod lenses. We compare the systems based on the resolution, the information density, compactness, complexity and cost.

4.2 Description of Imaging Systems

A Plössl eyepiece is easily constructed from two identical achromatic doublets with their crown elements facing each other. It has low distortion and wavefront aberrations and the ability to adjust the focal length by changing the distance between the achromats. Due to its relative ease of construction and low cost it has been successfully used in several free-space interconnected systems [10, 11]. GRIN rods are commercially available from Nippon Sheet Glass Co. and Gradient Lens Corporation. Both types of system are shown in Fig. 3. We have used GRINs with a pitch length of less than 0.25 to allow some working distance between the device plane and the lens surface.

By performing a diffraction-based ray-tracing analysis on CodeV, we calculated the spot diameters in the image plane for various off-axis object field positions. From this data we determined the *useful* resolution of the lens systems which we define as the quantity N. This value is different from the space bandwidth product (SBWP) as described below.

The SBWP is a measure of the **total** number of spots which can be resolved by a lens system. In general the spot size will vary across the image field, and typically becomes larger as the field becomes larger (Fig. 4(a)). For imaging optoelectronic devices where we desire a uniform and isotropic resolution across the field N is a more useful measure. It is given by the area of the field divided by the

Table I. Summary of comparison of Plössl eyepiece and GRIN rod relay systems.

Lens type	Lens Diam. (mm)	Total Track (mm)	Maximum N	Field size (mm)	Inform. Density (mm^{-2})	Number elements	Approx cost (US$)
4f Plössl (Melles Griot LAL001)	4.5	26.25	14428	1.6	907	4	1400
4f Plössl (Melles Griot LAO007)	8	40.29	18822	1.8	374	4	600
4f Plössl (Melles Griot LAO011)	10	49.46	22813	2.4	290	4	520
4f Plössl (Melles Griot LAO068)	19	123.12	39211	4.0	138	4	400
NSG SELFOC (W18E23)	1.8	9.31	5214	0.86	2049	2	40
NSG SELFOC (W20E23)	2.0	10.38	5876	0.9	1870	2	40
Grad. Lens Corp (BG30)	3.0	41.83	37489	2.55	5303	2	200
Grad. Lens Corp (BG40)	4.0	55.8	59488	3.2	4734	2	200
Grad. Lens Corp (BG50)	5.0	69.06	77399	3.6	3942	2	250
Grad. Lens Corp (BG80)	8.0	114.35	97430	5.4	1938	2	1600

worst-case spot area for that field size since the detector window size is determined by the maximum spot in the field. *N* is calculated for increasing field sizes as depicted in Fig. 4(b-d). and we then maximise *N* over all field positions. In this example field size 3 would provide the maximum *N*.

We also define the *information density* as the maximum value of *N* divided by the cross-sectional area of the lens system [12]. This is an important figure of merit for systems where the overall size must be reduced.

In our experimental free-space interconnected system we use arrays of surface emitting lasers. They have a full divergence angle of 12° [13]. Therefore in this analysis we have assumed an object space numerical aperture of 0.096. This corresponds to an f-number of about 5.2 for all the lenses we have analysed. We have used object plane field sizes up to 85% of the lens diameter. The image spot size was assumed to be a circle which enclosed 84% of the energy in the image plane. The wavelength in all calculations was 633nm.

4.3 Results of Comparison

The above procedure was carried out for various lens systems. The Plössl eyepiece systems were constructed with Melles Griot achromatic doublets. We used two types of GRIN rod lenses from Nippon Sheet Glass (SELFOC lenses) and Gradient Lens Corporation (BIG GRINs). The results are summarised in the Table I. The approximate costs are the prices in Japan given in US$.

Comparing the 4.5mm Plössl lenses to the 5mm BIG GRIN, observe that the maximum *N* is 14428 and 77399 respectively. These correspond to information densities of 907 and 3942 respectively. Note also that the BG50 has a larger field size than the Plössl lens.

Experimental observations for the BG50 lenses and the NSG SELFOC lenses verify the predicted field sizes and resolution [1].

Therefore comparing lenses of similar diameter (around 5mm) we observed approximately a five times greater value of *N* and information density in the case of the GRIN system. Additional benefits of the GRIN system is its relatively low cost, simplicity, ease of alignment and flat end faces which ease integration with other microoptic components and device arrays.

It is important to note that the actual number of useful data channels which can be imaged by the lens system will be less than the value of *N*. The number of channels in a given system will depend on the spacing between device windows and the crosstalk which can be tolerated.

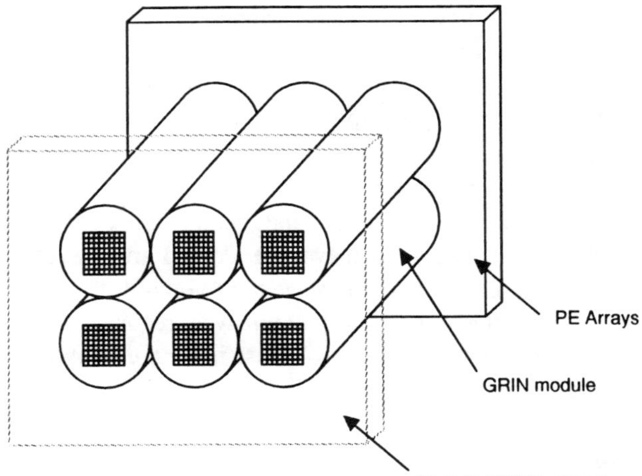

Fig. 5. Using an array of GRIN rods to increase the channel capacity.

4.4 Scalability of GRIN-Based Systems

When it is required to image larger and larger arrays of devices, the requirements of the imaging system become more demanding. If bulk macro-optics were used then the lens system would become intolerably large and expensive as the object field sizes increased.

On the other hand, however, if it is possible to partition a large number of PEs and optical channels into several smaller arrays then an array of GRIN rods or other mini-lenses could be constructed for direct 1-to-1 imaging between planes. (Fig. 5) [14].

From the above analysis it becomes apparent that the *information density* is an important parameter for such systems. As the number of channels increases, the overall system track length remains constant.

5. Programming and algorithms

5.1 Neighbourhood-connected Algorithms

The on-chip neighbourhood connectivity of our PE array is ideally suited to a range of image processing applications, for example early visual processing including edge detection and smoothing. Some examples of the applications and their execution times were shown in [1].

5.2 Globally-connected Algorithms

By utilising the ability to perform connections beyond the neighbourhood of a PE our system can efficiently implement operations which are inherently globally connected. These include various signal processing functions, such as the fast fourier transform, and sorting problems. We can achieve the necessary global connections in the optical domain (which can be either reconfigurable or fixed). There follows a brief description of some globally connected algorithms our system can perform.

Matrix-vector multiplication

The details of the algorithm were described in [1]. Optical connections between rows and columns can efficiently perform the *broadcast* and *summation* operations which are required to achieve the desired matrix-vector multiplication. At various stages throughout the algorithm the interconnection pattern was required to be changed by changing the CGH phase pattern displayed on the phase modulating spatial light modulator.

Sorting

We are developing a theory by which an arbitrary application can be embedded into optically connected hierarchically architecture of the type shown in Fig. 1. We have analysed such 3-dimensional systems from an algorithmic viewpoint [15], and evaluated some basic tendencies considering both the performance of optical interconnections and the calculation time for an application [1].

Here we describe a sorting algorithm. Recently, a few optically interconnected sorting machines have been developed but they are special purpose machines and can perform only sorting applications [6, 7]. In contrast to these special purpose systems, the sorting application is simply an example algorithm for our system to demonstrate its flexibility and programmability.

The algorithm is briefly described as follows :

1. Broadcast the data on base row -> data A (Fig. 6(a))
2. Broadcast the data on right hand column -> data B (Fig. 6(b))
3. Make a flag if data A is bigger than data B.
4. Sum the number of flags along each row.
5. The summation of each row shows the order of the data.(Fig. 6(c))

These algorithms could be implemented in a pipeline fashion where each stage is implemented in a processing element layer which is connected to the next layer by optical interconnections as shown in Fig. 6(d) [16].

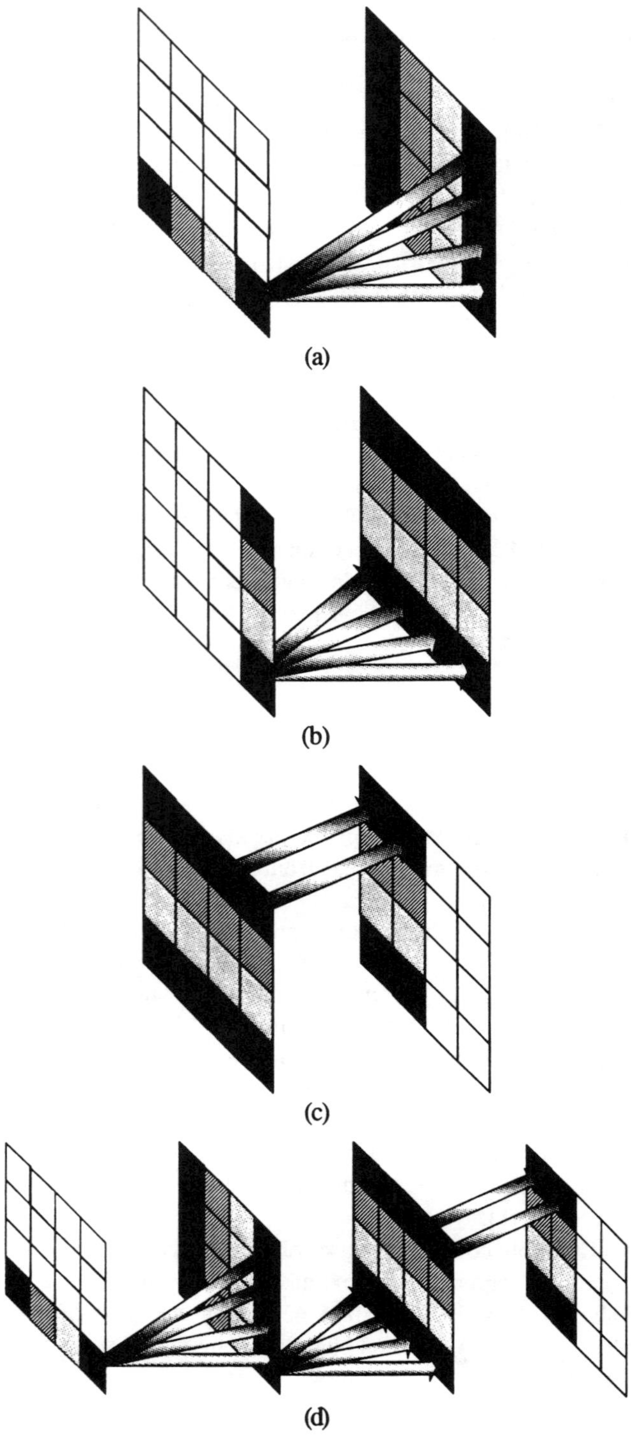

(a) (b) (c) (d)

Fig. 6. Sorting algorithm.

6. Discussion and Conclusion

A single chip smart pixel array has been designed which integrates processing elements and photodetectors. Initial results of its operation and performance will be presented., including details of the receiver circuitry and its characteristics.

The currently available maximum VCSEL size is 8×8 devices. This is presently limited by heat dissipation factors. Efforts are underway to reduce the threshold current and drive voltage of VCSELs in order to reduce the thermally dissipated power [17]. This should allow fabrication of much larger arrays and together with low power receiver circuitry [18-19] will aid the integration of detectors, emitters and processing circuitry into single units.

We have obtained GRIN rods with diameters up to 8mm. The imaging quality of the BIG GRIN lenses is excellent, and easily satisfy the requirements of the present demonstrator systems which have limited field sizes and number of channels. An analysis of GRIN rods and conventional imaging systems based on ray tracing confirms that GRIN rods are an excellent candidate for imaging arrays of two-dimensional optoelectronic devices. System scalability issues have been addressed and GRIN rods have the potential to provide high quality, compact imaging with high parallelism

By compactly integrating smart pixel processing elements, optical communication paths, VCSEL arrays, and free space interconnection components, we can demonstrate a compact, general purpose parallel optoelectronic processing system. This system is capable of performing a variety of tasks from low-level image processing to globally interconnected signal processing and sorting operations.

Acknowledgements

The authors thank K. Kasahara of NEC Optoelectronics Research Laboratories for supplying the VCSEL arrays used in these experiments. We thank T. Hara, Y. Kobayashi, and H. Toyoda of Hamamatsu Photonics for supplying the PAL-SLM used in some experiments. One of the authors (N.M.) is supported by the Japan Society for the Promotion of Science through a postdoctoral research fellowship.

References

1. N. McArdle, M. Naruse, T. Komuro, H. Sakaida, M. Ishikawa, Y. Kobayashi, and H. Toyoda, "A smart-pixel parallel optoelectronic computing system with free-space dynamic interconnections", in Proceedings of the Third International Conference on Massively Parallel Processing Using Optical Interconnections, A. Gottlieb, Y. Li, and E. Schenfeld, eds., (IEEE Computer Society Press, 1996), pp146-157.
2. M. Ishikawa, "System architecture for integrated optoelectronic computing", Optoelectronics - Devices and Technologies 9 (1), pp29- (1994).
3. M. Ishikawa, "Optoelectronic parallel computing system with reconfigurable optical interconnection", in Critical Reviews Vol. CR62, (SPIE Press), pp156-175 (1996).
4. J.S. Powell, J.A. Trezza, M. Morf, J.S. Harris, Jr., "Veertical cavity x-modulators for reconfigurable optical interconnection and routing", in Proceedings of the Third International Conference on Massively Parallel Processing Using Optical Interconnections, A. Gottlieb, Y. Li, and E. Schenfeld, eds., (IEEE Computer Society Press, 1996), pp352-359.
5. R.G. Rozier, F.E. Kiamilev, and A. Krishnamoorthy, "Design of a parallel photonic FFT processor", *ibid.* pp36-43.
6. A.C. Walker et al., "InGaAs/CMOS smart pixel arrays and their application to data sorting", in Technical Digest of IEEE/LEOS Summer Topical Meeting on Smart Pixels, pp109 (1996).
7. P.J. Stanko, F.R. Beyette, Jr., E.M. Hayes, R.D. Snyder, S.A. Feld, P.A. Mitkas, and C.W. Wilmsen, "Performance of a silicon CMOS/VCSEL smart pixel for a recirculating sorter", in Technical Digest of IEEE/LEOS Summer Topical Meeting on Smart Pixels, pp34-35 (1996).
8. F.A.P. Tooley, S.M Prince, M.R. Taghizadeh, F.B. McCormick, M.W. Derstine, and S.W. Wakelin, "Implementation of a hybrid lens", Applied Optics **23**, pp6471-6480 (1995).
9. A. Kirk, A. Goulet, H. Thienpont, N. McArdle, K.-H. Brenner, M. Kuijk, P. Heremans, and I. Veretenicoff, "A compact optical imaging system for arrays of optical thyristors", Optics Letters, in press.
10. F.B. McCormick, A.L. Lentine, R.L. Morrison, S.L. Walker, L.M.F. Chirovsky, and L.A. D'Asaro, "Parallel Operation of a 32x16 symmetric self-electrooptic effect device array", IEEE Photonics Technology Letters **3**, pp232-234 (1991).
11. F.A.P. Tooley and S. Wakelin, "Design of a symmetric self-electro-optic-effect-device cellular logic image processor", Applied Optics **32**, pp1850-1862 (1993).
12. H.M. Ozaktas, H. Urey, and A.W. Lohmann, "Scaling of diffractive and refractive lenses for optical computing and interconections", Applied Optics **33**, pp3782-3789 (1994).
13. M. Kajita, T. Kawakami, M. Nido, A. Kimura, T. Yoshikawa, K. Kurihara, Y. Sugimoto, and K. Kasahara, "Temperature characteristics of a vertical-cavity surface-emitting laser with a broad-gain bandwidth", IEEE Journal of Selected Topics in Quantum Electronics **1**, pp654-660 (1995).
14. H. Thienpont, A. Kirk, I. Veretennicoff, P. Heremans, B. Knupfer, G. Borghs, M. Kuijk, and R. Vounckx, "Optical thyristor based subsystems for digital parallel processing: demonstrators and future perspectives", in Proceedings of the Second International Conference on Massively Parallel Processing Using Optical Interconnections, (IEEE Computer Society Press, 1995).
15. M. Naruse, N. McArdle and M. Ishikawa, "An algorithmic approach to hierarchical parallel optical processing systems", Proceedings of International Topical Meetings on Optical Computing, pp102-103 (1996).
16. M. Naruse and M. Ishikawa, "Three dimensional systolic array architecture with optical interconnections", Proceedings of Japan Optics '95, pp215-216 (1995).
17. P.D. Dapkus, M. MacDougal, G.M. Yang, and Y. Cheng, "Ultralow threshold VCSELs for application to smart pixels", in Smart Pixels Technical Digest, p5, IEEE/LEOS Summer Topical Meetings, Keystone, Colorado, August 5-9 (1996).
18. T.K. Woodward, "VLSI-compatible smart-pixel interface circuits and technology", in Smart Pixels Technical Digest, p65, IEEE/LEOS Summer Topical Meetings, Keystone, Colorado, August 5-9 (1996).
19. C.Fan, D.A. Van Blerkom, and S.C. Esener, "Optimisation of transmitter and receiver design for optoelectronic computing", in Smart Pixels Technical Digest, p72, IEEE/LEOS Summer Topical Meetings, Keystone, Colorado, August 5-9 (1996).

A Pipelined TDM Optical Bus with Conditional Delays

Yueming Li †, Yi Pan ‡ and S.Q. Zheng †§

†Department of Computer Science, Louisiana State University, Baton Rouge, LA 70803

‡Department of Computer Science, University of Dayton, Dayton, OH 45469

§Department of Electrical and Computer Engineering, Louisiana State University, Baton Rouge, LA 70803

Abstract

A new pipelined time-division multiplexing optical bus for implementing a linear array parallel computer architecture is proposed. In this bus system, switches are introduced on the receiving segment of the bus to control the signal delays on the optical waveguide. The states of switches are dynamically programmable under the control of processors according to computation needs. The linear processor arrays based on such buses can be used as building blocks to construct parallel architectures of higher dimensions to achieve improved scalability and performance.

Key Words: Fiber optics, linear processor array, optical interconnection, optical switch, parallel computing.

1. Introduction

In parallel computing, time complexities of many computation problems are constrained by data movement among processors. Designing high-bandwidth interconnection networks has long been a focus in parallel computing research. Due to the bandwidth limit of electronic interconnections, researchers have turned their attention to optical interconnections. Several approaches, such as free space optical devices, wavelength-division multiplexing (WDM) and time-division multiplexing (TDM), of constructing optical interconnections for multiprocessor systems have been studied, and the advances in optical devices and fiber optic communications have made the optical interconnections feasible.

Optical waveguides can be used to implement a bus. Signal propagation in an optical bus is unidirectional and has predictable delay per unit length. Furthermore, an optical bus can connect more processors than an electrical bus. Processors connected by an optical bus are linearly ordered. Such a bus system is considered as a one-dimensional parallel computer architecture — a linear processor array. It is important to investigate linear arrays because they can be used as building blocks to construct parallel architectures of higher dimensions to achieve improved scalability and performance.

One class of promising parallel architectures are the distributed-memory SIMD (Single Instruction Stream Multiple Data Stream) computer systems equipped with pipelined optical buses using TDM access protocols. In such a system, the transmission latency between furthest processors is the end-to-end propagation delay of light over a waveguide. Since messages are transmitted concurrently in a pipelined fashion on a bus, this latency is hidden. Due to their remarkable advantages, such optical bus systems have received much of attention (e.g. [3, 4, 8, 9, 11, 13, 14]). More powerful multidimensional processors arrays connected by such optical bus systems have also been proposed recently (e.g. [12, 14]).

In this paper, we propose a modified pipelined TDM optical bus for implementing a linear array parallel computer architecture. In this bus system, switches are introduced on the receiving segment of the bus to control the signal delays on the waveguide. The states of switches are dynamically programmable under the control of processors according to computation needs. In conjunction with coincident pulse processor addressing technique, the reconfigurability of signal delays becomes an integral part of parallel computation. We show that using this linear array architecture several fundamental parallel communication and computation operations, which include broadcasting, multicasting, binary prefix sums, processor reordering, compaction, partition and concurrent subarray computation, can be carried out efficiently. These operations constitute a set of powerful tools for designing parallel algorithms.

We would like to note that the idea of programmable

0-8186-7974-3/97 $10.00 © 1997 IEEE

delays using electrooptically switched fiber loops has been used in the designs of TDM time slot interchangers (e.g. [6, 7, 15, 16]). Also, two optical bus structures with conditional delays have been proposed in [3] and [11], both are more complicated than the one presented in this paper. In the bus structure of [3], switches are on the transmitting segment of the bus, and because of this parallel computation on subarrays, if not possible, is difficult. To solve this problem, an optical bus with considerable more switches was proposed in [11]. Such a bus can be physically partitioned into several buses for parallel subarray computation. Our bus structure is more powerful than the bus of [3], and more cost-effective than the bus of [11].

2. Pipelined Optical Bus

The two properties of light, unidirectional propagation and predictable propagation delay per unit length, make it possible to have synchronized concurrent access of an optical bus in a pipelined fashion [4]. A pipelined optical bus consists of three waveguides, the message waveguide, the reference waveguide and the select waveguide, as shown in Figure 1. The message waveguide is used for carrying messages. The reference waveguide and the select waveguide together are used for carrying address information encoded using the *coincident pulse technique* [2, 8].

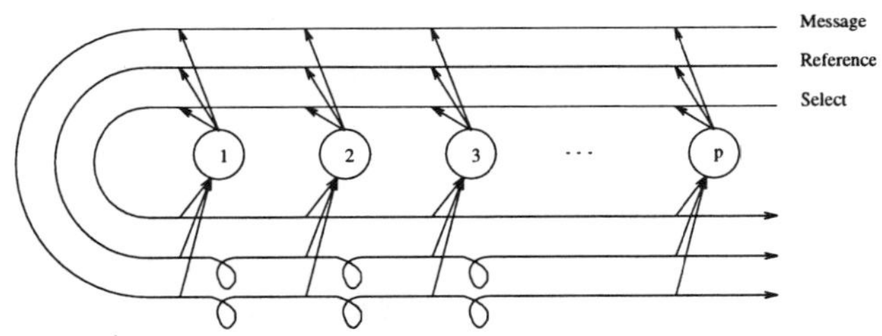

Figure 1. A pipelined optical bus system.

A pipelined optical bus is a *folded bus*. It is divided into two segments, the *transmitting segment*, which is the upper half of the bus, and the *receiving segment*, which is the lower half of the bus. Note that all previous proposed pipelined optical buses have loops on the receiving segments of the reference waveguide and the message waveguide. Each loop, which has spatial length of a single optical pulse, causes the light in the waveguide a unit delay. When a source processor sends a message to a destination processor, it also sends a reference pulse and a select pulse. The select pulse is transmitted later by an appropriate amount of time than the reference pulse. The two pulses will arrive at the destination processor at the same time since the reference pulse is delayed during the propagation on the receiving segment. That is, the coincidence of the two pulses occurs at the desired destination. Whenever a processor detects a coincidence of a reference pulse and a select pulse, it starts to read from the message waveguide. More specifically, consider that a processor is going to send a message to processor j. We use t_{ref} to denote the time when the processor transmits its reference pulse and t_{sel} to denote the time when it transmits its select pulse. The two light pulses will coincide at processor j if and only if $t_{sel} = t_{ref} + j\omega$, assuming that each pulse takes ω time.

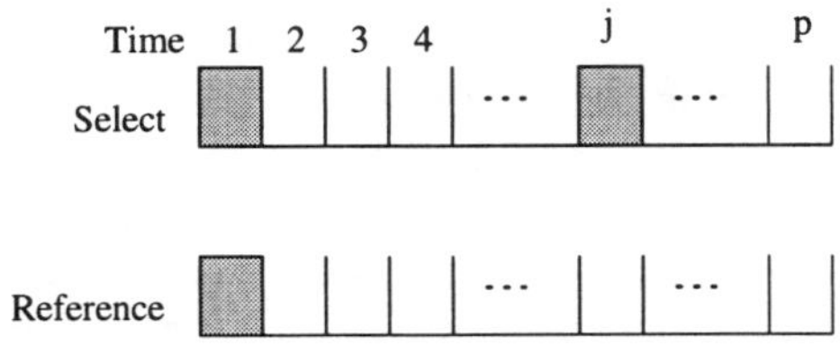

Figure 2. An address frame.

Let p denote the number of processors attached to the bus; p is the size of the bus. We call the duration of each light pulse a *pulse slot*. Then, a sequence of p pulse slots is called an *address frame*, as shown in Figure 2. Note that the presence of a select pulse at pulse slot j means that a message is to be sent to processor j. Messages are organized as *message frames*, which have a fixed length.

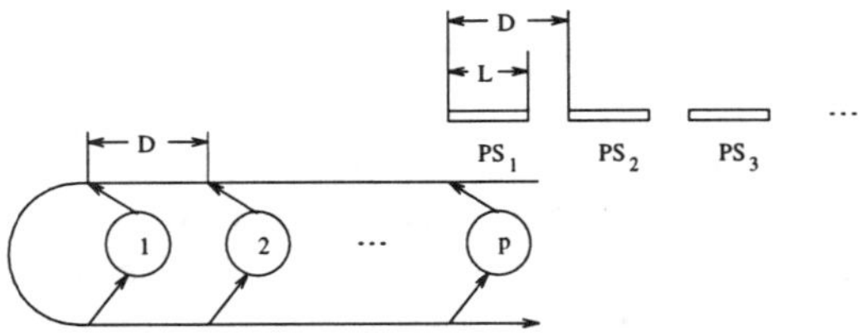

Figure 3. A train of p packets when initialized.

It is assumed that adjacent taps on the select waveguide have a fixed spatial distance D (see Figure 1). The reference and message waveguides are the same as the select waveguide except that an extra unit (i.e. a loop) is added between any two adjacent taps on their receiving segments (refer to Figure 1). According to [14], a collection of a message frame and an address frame is called a *packet*, whose length is denoted by L. A message frame and an address frame can be sent over different waveguides, and they propagate along the waveguides synchronously. Let L_{AF} and L_{MF} be the length of an address frame and a message frame, respectively. Then, $L = \max\{L_{AF}, L_{MF}\}$, and $D \geq L$. A time slot that consists of L pulse slots is called a *packet slot* (PS). A packet slot is used to transmit a message. When a processor detects a coincidence of a reference pulse and a select pulse, it reads the message frame. A sequence of p packet slots can be viewed as a train. Usually, the time-division source-oriented multiplexing approach (TDSM) is used to assign each packet slot to a processor; that is, there is a one-to-one mapping between a sending processor and a packet slot. Messages are loaded to the train such that the $(kp+i)$-th packet slot, PS_{kp+i}, is assigned to a message originated from processor i, for $k \geq 0$ (see Figure 3).

The pipelining use of packet slots discussed above and shown in Figure 4(a) has a problem. Since the address frame and its corresponding message frame overlap in time, it is possible that when a processor j detects that a message is addressed to it, part of the message has already passed processor j. To avoid incomplete message, we cannot overlap a message frame with its address frame. This problem has not been addressed before. A simple way to get around is to let a packet have length $L_{AF} + L_{MF}$, and the address frame is sent L pulse slots ahead of its corresponding message frame so that once a processor detects a pulse coincidence, it reads a message (see Figure 4(b)). The advantage of this method is that, in addition to enforcing complete message transmissions, two waveguides are sufficient instead of three. The selection waveguide is eliminated, since selection pulses can be sent over the message waveguide. For such a bus to function properly, detection of coincident selection and reference pulses is enabled only when an address frame passes by a processor. The major drawback of this method is that a packet size increases from $\max\{L_{AF}, L_{MF}\}$ to $L_{AF} + L_{MF}$, and D must be at least $L_{AF} + L_{MF}$. Consequently, the waveguides are not effectively used, and the system is less scalable.

Figure 4. Packet transmission: address frame AF_i corresponds to message frame MF_i. (a) Overlapping scheme. (b) Non-overlapping scheme. (c) Offset overlapping scheme.

We propose to use the following scheme. As before, we use three waveguides, and assume that $D \geq L$. The address frame and its corresponding message frame do not overlay in time; however, the message frame of the current packet overlaps with the address frame of the next packet. The pattern of this pipelined address and message transmissions is shown in Figure 4(c). In effect, this mode of transmission is equivalent to the one shown in Figure 4(a). For easy reference, we call this method the *offset message transmission scheme*. As a consequence of this correction, we can simplify the bus by eliminating the loops on the message waveguide because without them the synchronization of message transmission can still be enforced. Note that this fact is useful for reducing the number of switches that are needed in a bus with conditional delays.

The time for an optical signal to propagate distance D is τ. The communication of processors are performed in terms of bus cycles. A *bus cycle* consists of end-to-end transmission of p consecutive packet slots. Despite of the remarkable effect of pipelined data transmission, we still need to be careful when we assess the performance of such an optical bus. To avoid misleading time complexity claims of a linear array of processors connected by such a pipelined optical bus, it is necessary to separate the communication time from computation time. As in sequential algorithm analysis, we assume that each parallel computation step takes constant time. The communication time is measured in terms of bus cycles. When p is small, a bus cycle can be assumed taking constant time. However, as p becomes larger, the time for a bus cycle increases proportionally.

3. Pipelined Optical Bus with Conditional Delays

Our new bus architecture is shown in Figure 5. On the receiving segment of the reference waveguide, we introduce p 2×2 optical switchs, S_i, $1 \leq i \leq p$. Switch S_i can be set to one of two states, *straight* and *cross*, by processor i. When a switch is set cross, ω time delay occurs when a signal passes the switch, in comparison to the case when the switch is set straight, because of the extra traversed distance. The Ti:LiNbO3 switches of [1] can be used for this purpose. We use the new offset message transmission scheme proposed in the previous section to avoid incomplete message read. The setting of the address frame for any processor to send a packet to processor j is shown in Figure 6, assuming that all switches are in the cross state. Note that the address frame for this bus system requires one more pulse slot with respect to the bus system discussed in the previous section.

The adjustable delays on the receiving segments of

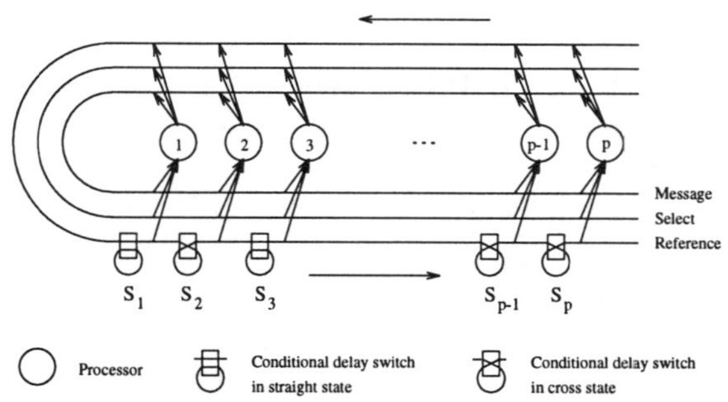

Figure 5. An optical bus with conditional delays.

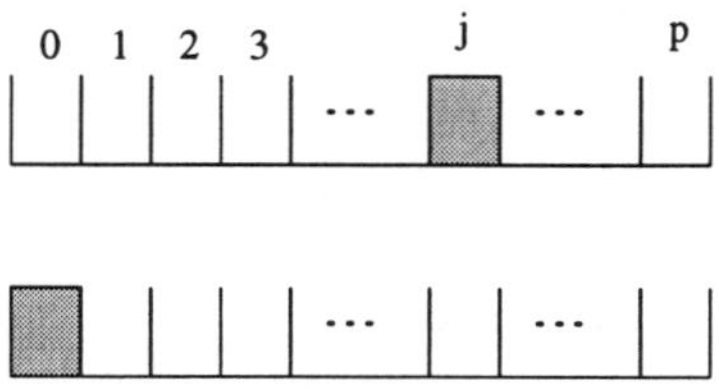

Figure 6. An address frame of the bus with conditional delays, assuming that all switches are in the cross state.

the reference and message waveguides make our bus system more powerful. Previously, two pipelined optical buses with conditional delays were proposed in [3] and [11], both buses require more hardware. Our bus requires p switches[1]. Compared with the bus of [3], our bus, which has half the number of switches, is more powerful. The bus proposed in [11] has $2(p-1)$ 2×2 switches, $3(p-1)$ 1×2 switches, and $3(p-1)$ 2×1 switches. It is believed that the additional reconfigurability of this bus, which has about eight times the number of switches, does not exhibit additional power compared with our bus design. In what follows, we show that our bus architecture supports several useful fundamental operations.

Broadcast and Multicast In a multicast operation, each processor may send a packet to a group of processors, and each processor receives at most one packet. In a broadcast operation, which is a special case of multicast, a packet is sent from one processor to all other processors. There are different ways to carry out a broadcast operation. One way is to set all switches to the cross state and let the source processor use the address frame shown in Figure 7(a). Another way is to set all switches to the straight state and let the source processor use the address frame shown in Figure 7(b). Similarly, there are more than one way to perform a multicast operation. Assuming that all switches are in the cross state, Figure 8 shows the address frames for a multicast operation with three source processors, each sending a packet to a group of three destination processors. Clearly, one bus cycle is sufficient for either a multicast or a broadcast operation.

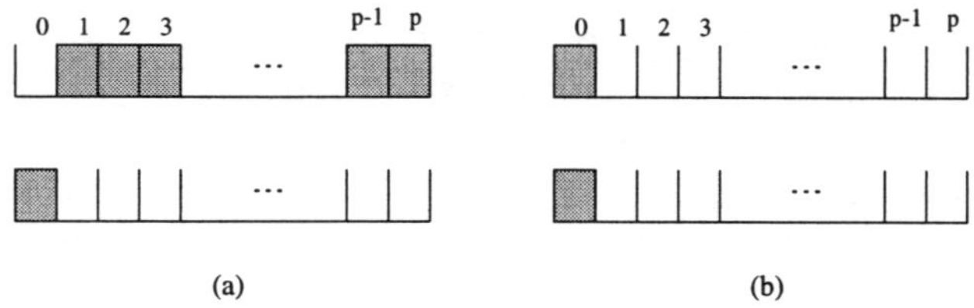

Figure 7. Address frames for broadcasting. (a) All switches are in the cross state. (b) All switches are in the straight state.

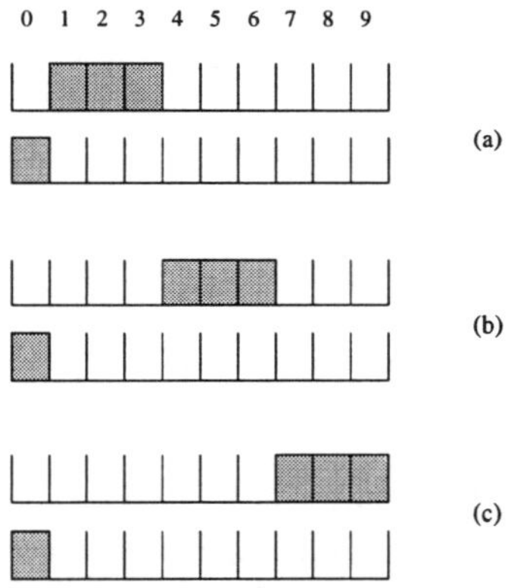

Figure 8. Address frames for multicasting, assuming that all switches are in the cross state. Three source processors send messages to three subsets (a), (b) and (c), of destination processors.

Binary Prefix Sums and Processor Reordering Given p one-bit values, b_j, $1 \leq j \leq p$, the binary prefix sums (BPS) problem requires the computation of $s_j = b_1 + b_2 + \cdots + b_j$ for all $1 \leq j \leq p$, where "+" is the addition operation. This operation can be done as follows. Processor j sets its switch S_j to the cross state if $b_j = 1$; otherwise S_j is set to straight state by processor j. An empty message is broadcast from processor p. Assume that the bus cycle in which the broadcasting occurs starts at t_0. It takes $(p+j-1)\tau$

[1] Actually, $p-1$ switches are sufficient if we slightly modify all operations discussed in this section. We choose to use p switches for the simplicity of our discussions.

time for the reference light pulse to arrive at processor j if no delays caused by switches are involved, where τ is the time delay corresponding to distance D. If some switch delays occur, the reference light pulse will arrive at a later time, say t_j, at processor j to cause coincidence with a broadcast select pulse. The number of unit delays can be computed by

$$i = \frac{t_j - t_0 - (p+j-1)\tau}{\omega}. \quad (1)$$

We call the value computed by Equation (1) the i-value of processor j. Clearly, the i-value of processor j is s_j.

We say that a processor is *active* if it will participate in the next computation step; otherwise, we say that it is *inactive*. Processor reordering is to assign active processors indices in such a way that the i-th active processor is assigned a new index i. The operation for processor reordering is almost the same as that for BPS. If a processor is active, it sets its switch to the cross state; otherwise, it sets its switch to the straight state. After a broadcast operation, the i-value obtained for an active processor j is its new index. Thus, both the BPS problem and the processor reordering problem can be solved using one bus cycle and $O(1)$ computation time.

Compaction and Partition Suppose that each processor has one data item. Using processor reordering method, in one bus cycle the active processors can be assigned new ordered indices starting from 1, and the total number of active processors can be determined by the i-value of processor p, regardless whether or not it is active. Suppose that the number of active processors is s. Then, each active processor j with its new index i sends its data item to processor i. In one additional bus cycle, the s data items of active processors can be packed in the first s processors, each having one item; furthermore, the compacted data items preserve their original order. Such an operation is called an ordered compaction operation.

A partition operation is to partition p data items, one per processor, into two subsets, one contains s items, and the other contains $p-s$ items. The first subset of items are moved to the first s processors, whereas the second subset of items are moved to the remaining processors. After the partition operation, each processor contains one original item. This operation can be carried out in two phases. The first phase employs a processor reordering operation followed by a compaction operation to move s items in the first subset to the first s processors. Then, in the second phase, active processors and inactive processors switch their roles, and another pair of processor reordering and compaction operations are performed on the $p-s$ items in the second subset. Therefore, a partition operation can be performed in four bus cycles and $O(1)$ computation time.

Parallel Operations on Subarrays For parallel computation, it is often convenient to consider a linear array connected by a pipelined bus as several subarrays, each consisting of a sequence of consecutive processors. If the processors are controlled properly, the operations on subarrays can be performed in parallel. Parallel computation on subarrays is an important feature for supporting parallel algorithms based on divide-and-conquer design paradigm. In a divide-and-conquer algorithm, the initial problem is partitioned into several subproblems, and each subproblem, which can be further recursively partitioned, is solved independently. The combination of subproblem solutions yields a solution to the initial problem.

Let us refer to the processor with the smallest index and the largest index in a subarray as the *head* and *tail processor*, respectively, of the subarray. In a divide-and-conquer algorithm, processors in a subarray are notified the identities of head and tail processors of the subarray in the problem partition step. Knowing the head and tail processors of a subarray, a processor in the subarray can broadcasting a packet to all processors in the subarray in one bus cycle using a sequence of select pulses targeted at processors in the subarray (see Figure 8). Obviously, concurrent broadcasting on all subarrays is a special case of multicast.

Other operations can also be performed in parallel on subarrays. Consider the BPS problem on subarrays. We set switch S_j to the cross state if $b_j = 1$, and set it to the straight state if $b_j = 0$. After one broadcast operation, each processor computes its i-value. For a head processor of a subarray, we compute its i' value as follows: $i' = i - 1$ if this processor is active; otherwise, $i' = i$. Then, we use a multicast operation to send the i'-value of the head processor of a subarray to all remaining processors in the subarray, for all subarrays. The binary prefix sum of a processor in a subarray is obtained by subtracting i' from the i-value of the processor. Therefore, The BPS problem on subarrays can be carried out using two bus cycles and $O(1)$ computation time. Consequently, the processor reordering problem for all subarrays can be done in same amount of time.

It is not difficult for a reader to be convinced that, if the head and tail processors are known to all processors in a subarray, for all subarrays, then concurrent compaction and partition operations on all subarrays can be carried out using $O(1)$ bus cycles and $O(1)$ computation time. For brevity, we omit detailed discussions.

4. Conclusions

Optical buses offer much larger bandwidths than electronic ones. Among available optical interconnection technologies for parallel computing, optical buses are probably the easiest to implement. Designing a bus-based parallel computer architecture requires taking both computation and communication aspects into consideration. We proposed a linear array architecture based on a pipelined TDM optical bus. We showed that using the conditional-delay and coincidence pulse techniques, several fundamental operations can be carried out very efficiently on our bus system. We also demonstrated how to design parallel algorithms on our linear architecture. Our bus structure is simpler and more powerful than the one proposed in [3], and much simpler than and as powerful as the bus of [11]. All algorithms presented in [11] can be ported to our architecture with the same performance. For brevity, we omit additional algorithm design examples.

Our linear array can be used as building blocks to construct processor arrays of multiple dimensions to achieve better scalability and performance. For example, Pavel and Akl proposed to use pipelined TDM optical buses of [3] to implement a two-dimensional reconfigurable array [10]. They call this architecture an array with reconfigurable optical buses (AROP). They showed that an AROP is a powerful parallel computing architecture. In order to achieve their claimed reconfigurability, they require each processor to be equipped with several high-speed counters to determine the processor ordering after the buses are reconfigured by switches. Such a counter is used to count the number of a sequence of optical pulses. It would be impractical for an electronic processor to match the bit rate of an optical waveguide, and using optical counters would increase the system cost significantly. Our optical bus provides a simple optical solution to the reconfigurability of AROP.

Acknowledgements

This research is supported in part by US NSF grants ECS-9626215 and CCR-9503882, Louisiana grant LEQSF(1996-99)-RD-A-16, and Ohio Board of Regents Investment Fund Competition Grant.

References

[1] A. F. Benner, H. F. Jordan, and V. P. Heuring. Digital optical computing with optically switched directional couplers. *Optical Engineering*, 30(12):1936–1941, 1991.

[2] D. Chiarulli, R. Melhem, and S. Levitan. Using coincident optical pulses for parallel memory addressing. *IEEE Computer*, 20(12):48–58, 1987.

[3] Z. Guo. Sorting on array processors with pipelined buses. *Proceedings of 1992 International Conference on Parallel Processing*, pages 289–292, 1992.

[4] Z. Guo et al. Array processors with pipelined optical buses. *J. Parallel Distributed Comput.*, 12(3):269–282, 1991.

[5] M. Hamdi and Y. Pan. Efficient parallel algorithms on optically interconnected arrays of processors. *IEEE Proceedings - Computers and Digital Techniques*, 142(2):87–92, 1995.

[6] D. K. Hunter and D. G. Smith. New architectures for optical TDM switching. *J. Lightwave Technol*, 11:495–511, 1993.

[7] H. F. Jordan, D. Lee, K. Y. Lee, and S. V. Ramanan. Serial array time slot interchangers and optical implementations. *IEEE Trans. on Computers*, 43(1):1309–1318, 1994.

[8] S. Levitan, D. Chiarulli, and R. Melhem. Coincident pulse techniques for multiprocessor interconnection sturctures. *Applied Optics*, 29(14), 1990.

[9] R. Melhem, D. Chiarulli, and S. Levitan. Space multiplexing of waveguides in optically interconnected multiprocessor systems. *Computer Journal*, 32(4):362–369, 1989.

[10] R. Miller, V. Prasanna-Kumar, D. Reisis, and Q. Stout. Meshes with reconfigurable buses. In *MIT Conference on Advanced Research in VLSI*, pages 163–178, 1988.

[11] Y. Pan and K. Li. Linear array with a reconfigurable pipelined bus system – concepts and applications. *Proceedings of 1996 International Conference on Parallel and Distributed Processing Techniques and Applications*, pages 1431–1442, 1996.

[12] S. Pavel and S. G. Akl. On the power of arrays with optical pipelined buses. *Proceedings of 1996 International Conference on Parallel and Distributed Processing Techniques and Applications*, pages 1443–1454, 1996.

[13] C. Qiao, R. Melhem, D. Chiarulli, and S. Levitan. Optical multicasting in linear arrays. *International Journal of Optical Computing*, 2(1):31–48, 1991.

[14] C. Qiao and R. G. Melhem. Time-division optical communications in multiprocessor arrays. *IEEE Trans. on Computers*, 42(5):557–590, 1995.

[15] S. V. Ramanan, H. F. Jordan, and J. R. Sauer. A new time domain, multi-stage permutation algorithm. *IEEE Trans. Inform. Theory*, 36:171–173, 1990.

[16] R. A. Thompson and P. P. Giordano. An experimental photonic time slot interchanger using optical fibers as reentrant delay-line memories. *J. Lightwave Technol.*, 5:154–162, 1987.

Four Multiplexed, 8x8-bit 2-D Parallel Transmission based upon Space-CDMA

Moriya Nakamura and Ken-ichi Kitayama
Yasunori Igasaki *, and Keiji Kaneda **

Communications Research Laboratory
Ministry of Posts and Telecommunications
4-2-1, Nukui-kita, Koganei, Tokyo 184 JAPAN
Tel. +81-423-27-7499 Fax. +81-423-27-7035
E-mail: moriya@crl.go.jp
* Hamamatsu Photonics K.K.
** Fujikura Ltd.

Abstract

4 channel multiplexing for 64 bit two dimensional (2-D) parallel optical data link based upon optical space-CDMA is experimentally demonstrated by using newly developed modules of optical spatial encoder and decoder. Each 8x8 bit-plane (64 bit parallel data) is optically encoded with an 8x8 2-D optical orthogonal signature pattern. The encoded bit-planes are spatially multiplexed, and it is transmitted through an image fiber having 10^5 cores. Each receiver can recover the intended input bit-plane via the optical decoding process. Total error-rate is 2.73%. This result will encourage the application of optical space-CDMA to future high-throughput 2-D parallel data links connecting massively parallel processors.

1. Introduction

Code division multiple access (CDMA) is an asynchronous, random access protocol. The features include addressability using signature codes in the network, ability to support bursty data traffic, and natural increase in communication security. In conventional time-domain optical CDMA, each data bit is encoded into a waveform which corresponds to a signature code sequence. All the encoded signals from the transmitters are multiplexed. The multiplexed signal is broadcast to the receivers, and each receiver regenerates the intended data among the multiplexed signals by using its own signature [1]-[4].

For massively parallel computer networks as well as for data transfer from optical page-oriented memories to another memories or to processors [5], two-dimensional (2-D) parallel reconfigurable optical data links based upon an innovative optical space-CDMA has been proposed [6]. This 2-D parallel optical links allows to transfer 2-D bit-planes without serial to parallel conversion, and hence, this will resolve "I/O bottleneck" of parallel processors caused by *wiring crisis*. Each receiver side can be linked to the intended bit-plane by selecting the corresponding signature pattern. It is possible to demultiplex these bit-planes which are shifted in position each other and multiplexed. Due to this space-invariant property of space-CDMA, we can resolve the difficulty of positioning in the practical system implementation. Using this space-CDMA, we have succeeded the preliminary experiment to multiplex 2 channel of 4x4 bit-planes [7]. Here, a bit-plane is defined that each binary bit is allocated on a grid which is regularly aligned in a plane.

In this paper, a significant upgrade of the throughput is experimentally demonstrated by four 8x8 bit-planes transmission based upon space-CDMA by using newly developed modules of optical spatial encoder and decoder. Each 8x8 bit-plane is optically encoded by 8x8 2-D *optical orthogonal signature pattern*, so-called OOSP. The encoded bit-planes are spatially multiplexed, and it is transmitted through an image fiber having 10^5 cores. Each receiver can properly recover the intended bit-plane via the optical decoding process.

2. Concept of Space-CDMA

The spatial encoding process is schematically shown in Fig. 1(a). In this example, two 2x2-pixel binary input bit-planes are encoded with two 5x5 OOSP's (weight w=3)

0-8186-7974-3/97 $10.00 © 1997 IEEE

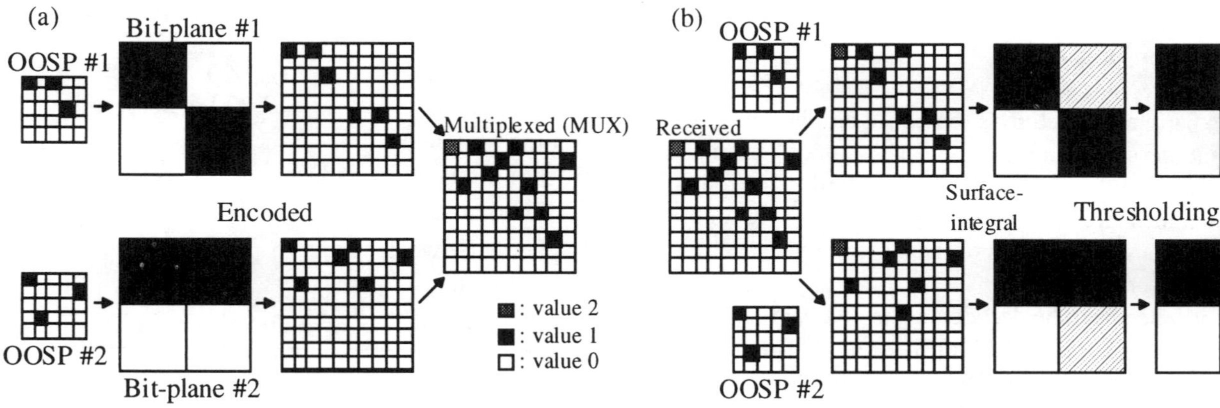

Fig. 1. Schematics of (a) spatial encoding and (b) spatial decoding.

into a 10x10 multiplexed encoded pattern. These OOSP's are orthogonal mutually, so that it's possible to demultiplex these patterns, even if these are multiplexed with some shift. The spatial decoding process is schematically shown in Fig. 1(b). The receiver correlates the received pattern with its own OOSP. The input bit-plane is regenerated after the thresholding is operated on the correlation output [6].

3. Optical implementation

Parallelism of optical computations is exploited for the spatial encoding and decoding. In Fig. 2, the optical implementation of the optical space-CDMA network is schematically shown. The transmitter consists of an optical spatial encoder. The receiver consists of the optical spatial decoder and the thresholding device. An image fiber is used as the transmission medium which has a large number of cores in a common cladding as shown in Fig. 3. The encoder and decoder consist of spatial light modulators (SLM's). It seems impractical to implement with a bunch of individual optical fibers. To realize the data link up to a few hundreds meters long, the compactness and the flexibility are one of the key requirements. For this distance, the loss of the image fiber will be acceptable.

In the encoder, an OOSP and input bit-plane are addressed electrically on the SLM1 and SLM2, respectively. By reading out SLM1 and SLM2 in order with the light beam, the encoding is accomplished. The pattern bearing readout beams are superimposed by MUX, the multiplexed bit-plane is launched into an image fiber and transmitted in parallel. At the receiver side, the multiplexed bit-plane is broadcast to every decoder by DEMUX. In Fig. 2, there is only one decoder. The decoder performs correlation between the received one and its own OOSP addressed on the SLM3. After performing the surface-integral and thresholding by using the desktop computer, the intended input bit-plane is regenerated.

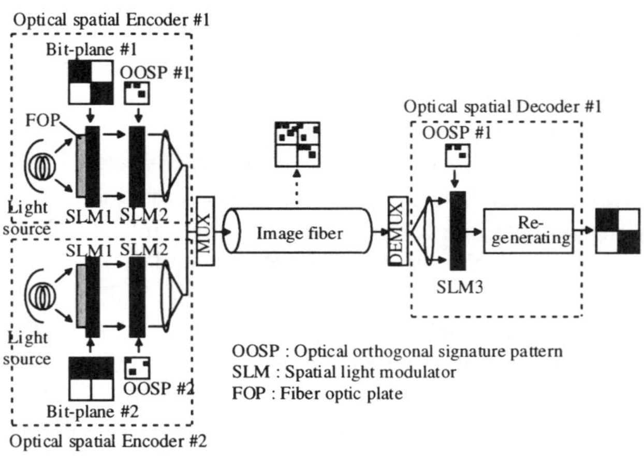

Fig. 2. Optical implementation of space-CDMA network.

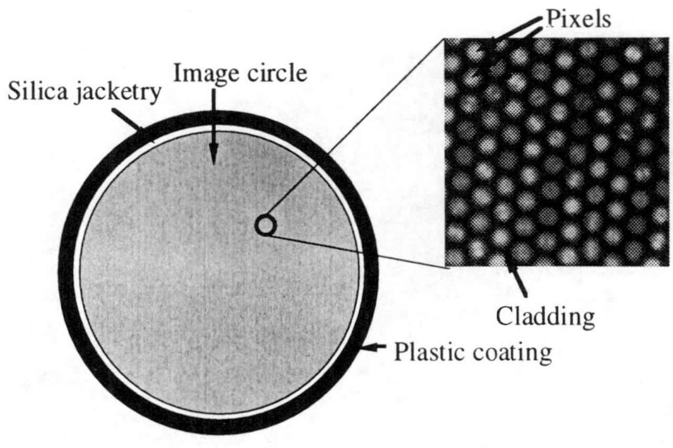

Fig. 3. Cross-sectional view of test image fiber.

4. Experiment

4.1. Experimental setup

The experimental setup is based upon the optical implementation shown in Fig. 2. The optical spatial encoders and decoders are fully modularized. The four encoder modules are shown in Fig. 4. By using this modules, the transfer functions of the system is drastically improved as described below.

In the encoders and the decoder, a commercial twisted-nematic liquid-crystal(LC) SLM's [8] are used. The beam is intensity-modulated by passing through the SLM. The average value of the contrast ratio between ON and OFF was measured to be approximately 50. Xe lamps are used as the light sources. Fiber-optic plates (FOP's) are placed in front of SLM's1. FOP's are used as diffusers so that the SLM's are illuminated uniformly. The image processor is used to grab the readout pattern detected by CCD camera.

A test silica-based image fiber was newly prepared. The fabrication process is as follows. A preform rod is drawn into the core fiber. A number of the core fibers are bundled and inserted into a silica tube, and a preform of the image fiber is prepared. The preform is heated and drawn into an image fiber. This fabrication method is more suitable for manufacturing long image fibers compared with that of the conventional multi-component image fibers.

The fiber length is 0.5 m-long. In Table 1 the specifications of the prepared image fiber are summarized. It has 10^5 cores. The spectral optical loss of the test image fiber measured by the cut-back method is shown in Fig. 5. The optical loss in the spectral region from 500 nm to 900 nm is less than 0.10 dB/m. In Fig. 6, the measured contrast is shown as a function of spatial frequency in lp/mm (lp: line pairs). The contrast ratio of the contrast ratio is given in the graph. The contrast value of over 0.5 is obtained at the spatial frequency of 5 lp/mm.

Fig. 4. Optical spatial encoder modules.

Table. 1. Specifications of test image fiber.

Number of pixels	100,000
Fiber diameter	3,200 μm
Picture diameter	3,000 μm
Minimum bending radius	500 mm
Numerical aperture	0.2
Spacing between pixels	9 μm
Core diameter	6.8 μm
Core material	Ge-doped silica glass

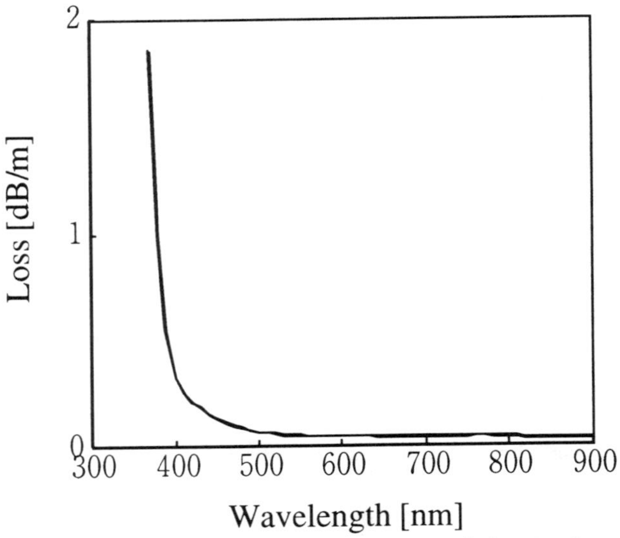

Fig. 5. Measured optical loss of the test image fiber s a function of wavelength.

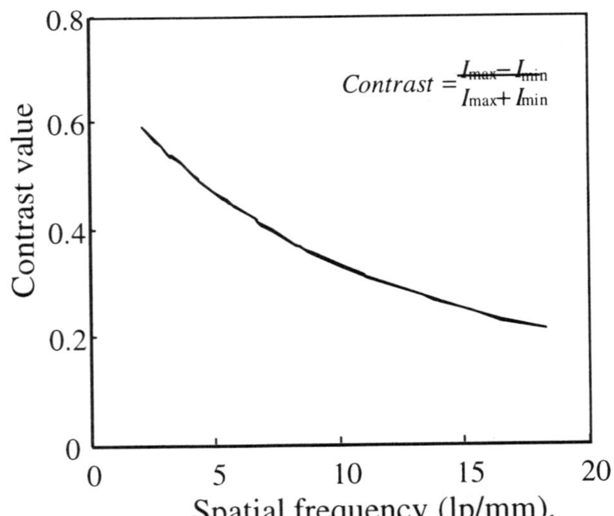

Fig. 6. Measured contrast of the test image fiber as a function of spatial frequency in lp/mm (lp: line per millimeter). I_{max} and I_{min} are the maximum and minimum optical intensities, respectively.

4.2. Experimental results

Four prepared 8x8 bit-planes and the 8x8 OOSP's are shown in Fig. 7. Bit-planes #1, #2, #3 and #4 are encoded by OOSP's #1, #2, #3 and #4, respectively. The multiplexed and transmitted image is shown in Fig. 8.

The receiver can recover intended bit-plane by correlation process with the corresponding OOSP followed by the thresholding process to cut off the mutual interference noise of the codes. The image after the correlation process with OOSP's #1, #2, #3 and #4 are shown in Figs. 10(a), (b), (c) and (d), respectively. Table 2 shows the values of the decoded Bit-plane #1. The shaded values correspond to "0". Each value of these bit-planes are obtained by the surface integral of the pixel values. The minimum value of "1" must be larger than maximum value of "0" to decode properly by thresholding. However, some errors are found. For example, the pixel (2,1) value which should be "1" is smaller than the pixel (3,5) value which should be "0". The values indicated by italic type are the pixels in error. The total error rate was 6.64%.

The error will be presumably analyzed by investigating the 2-D nonuniformity of transmission characteristics. Uniform plain patterns are transmitted from the four transmitters. The plain patterns at the exit of the optical decoder and their intensity distributions are shown in Figs. 10(a) and (b), respectively. The 2-D distribution of brightness of the output pattern gradually decreases toward the off-center area. The nonuniformity is due to the intensity distribution of the light sources and the transfer function of the image fiber and the lenses. Moire is also seen in Fig. 10(a) which is due to the interference between the fiber endface and the LC-panel of the SLM. The intensity value scatters to some extent around 0.6. These nonuniformity makes it difficult to set the thresholding level, and thus this causes the errors, especially in off-center area as shown in Table. 2.

To improve the discrimination of the pixel value, the nonuniformity of the intensity is compensated. The pixel values of the multiplexed bit-planes after the propagation are normalized by the value of the plain pattern in Fig. 10 so that the nonuniformity of the intensity of the overall system is canceled. The computation is made by the desktop computer for the decoded bit-planes shown in Fig. 9. Table 3 shows the result. Consequently, the total error rate is reduced to 2.73%. If the compensation was made correctly, the error free transmission should have been realized. However, each encoder has a different nonuniformity. This will be one reason why the error is not perfectly recovered.

In this experiment, for simplicity, we used still image as data to be transmitted and desktop computer for some processing in decoding process. However, it should be mentioned that the processing at the decoder can be implemented either optically or electrically. Slow SLM's and Xe lamps which are used for addressing the data bit-plane, can be replaced by 2-D LD array. This will allows to transmit at the frame rate at least up to mega-frame per second and even more. Eventually, the latency problems of the decoding can be resolved.

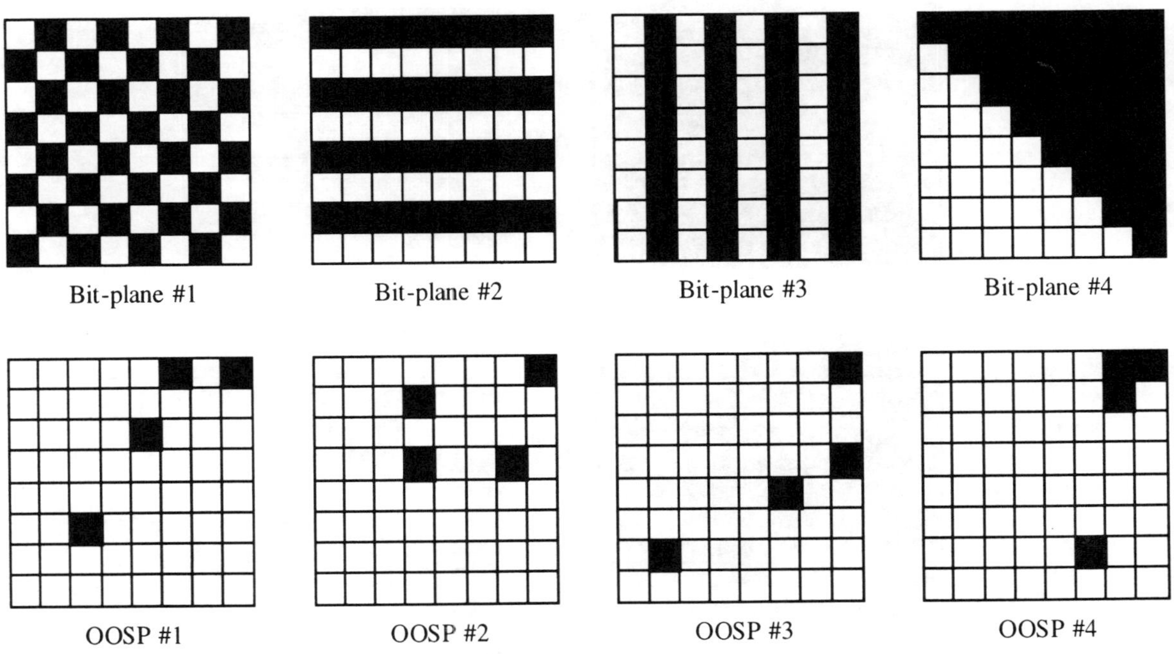

Fig. 7. Prepared bit-planes and OOSP's.

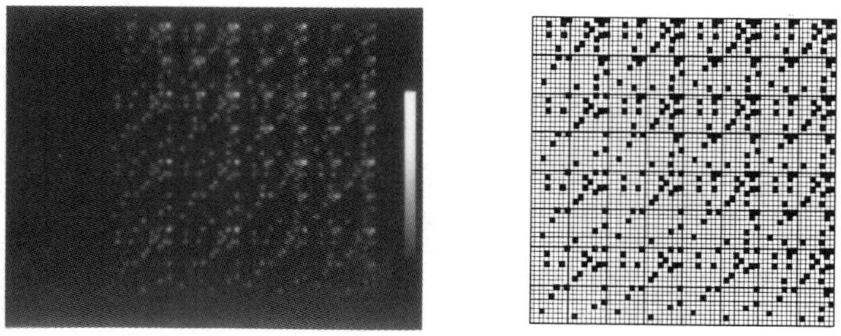

Fig. 8. Encoded and multiplexed bit-planes after propagation through image fiber.

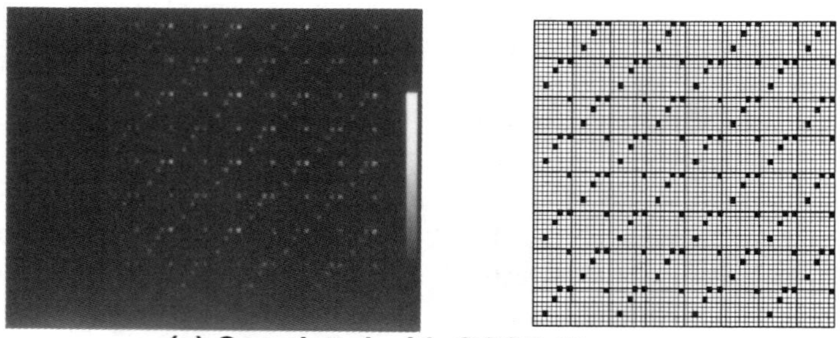

(a) Correlated with OOSP #1.

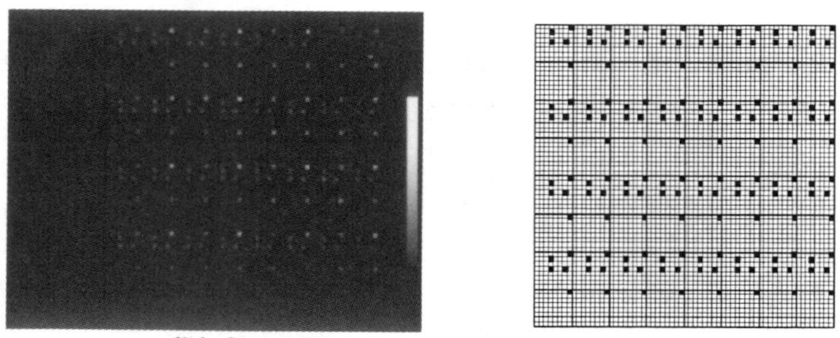

(b) Correlated with OOSP #2.

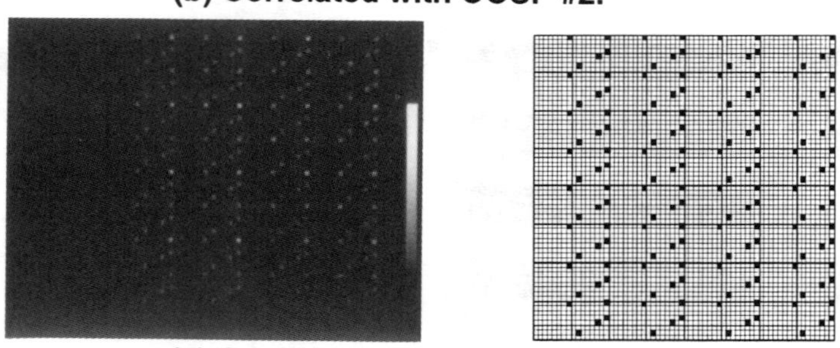

(c) Correlated with OOSP #3.

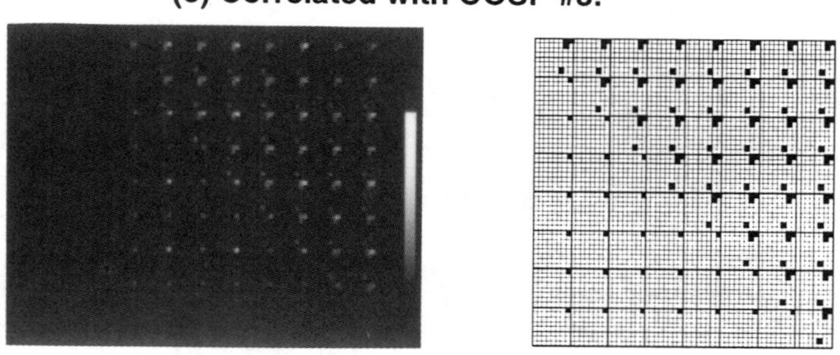

(d) Correlated with OOSP #4.

Fig. 9. The image after the correlation process with OOSP's #1 (a), #2 (b), #3 (c) and #4 (d).

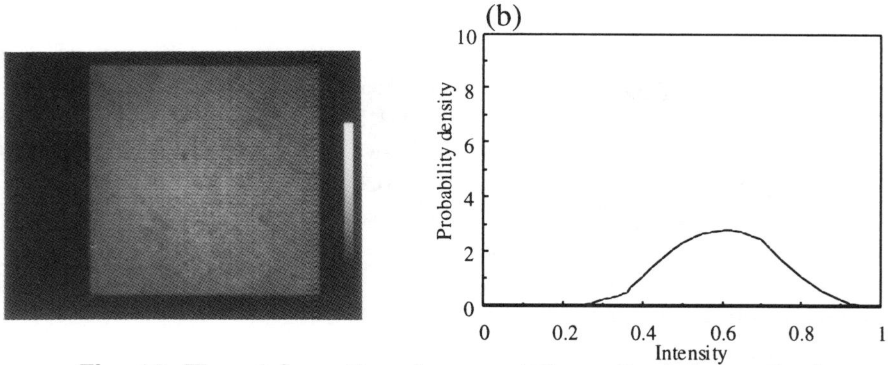

Fig. 10. The plain pattern image at the exit of the optical decoder (a) and its intensity distribution (b).

Table 2. Bit-plane #1 decoded with OOSP #1 (without normalization).

1569	6069	2384	6599	2258	5347	1538	***2974***
2073	1743	5082	2982	4859	2655	3708	2452
1371	6066	3025	8675	3305	6515	2386	6402
3775	1038	4650	2781	8236	2941	6405	2297
1026	7323	1570	8268	3128	8844	3056	7869
3694	1207	5098	1773	6818	2303	6228	1827
1220	5829	1342	6818	1305	5513	1709	5991
2227	802	***2910***	640	3631	481	3422	1144

Table 3. Bit-plane #1 decoded with OOSP #1 (normalized)

41.29	127.7	44.83	122.9	44.69	112.9	34.95	80.98
50.23	34.73	88.87	53.75	89.56	51.58	79.32	56.31
28.61	107.1	51.12	147.7	58.07	124.5	47.01	132.4
86.92	18.9	79.54	48.08	134.5	50.36	115.9	48.19
22.89	134.9	26.36	141.1	51.98	158.7	58.17	168.9
79.53	22.77	95.16	32.41	123.5	45.09	136.6	47.48
28.09	120.1	28.79	131.1	27.41	121.4	42.54	171.9
62.6	20.5	74.94	16.71	91.66	12.88	109.6	41.3

5. Discussion

Another solution to the error-free transmission is to improve the interference property of OOSP's. In this experiment, OOSP's with the weight w=4 are used for the number of encoder N=4. The thresholding level Th has to be $N-1<Th<w$ ($3<Th<4$ in this experiment) to threshold off the interference noise [9]. As w becomes larger, the larger the margin of the thresholding increases, resulting in the enhancement of the robustness to noise and we would be able to decrease error rate. However, a higher contrast ratio of the system is required for OOSP's with a larger weight. To achieve the error rates less than 10^{-9} which are expected for actual processor links, we have to investigate code theory which guarantees less interference and improve the spatial resolution of the system which are determined by the contrast of image fiber and SLM's. This will be discussed in detail in a forthcoming paper [10].

The relation of code definition MxM, weight w and number of code (or encoder) N is written by

$$N \le \frac{M^2 - 1}{w(w-1)} \ .$$

The maximum weight is 4 for 8x8 (M=8) bit-plane which is used in this experiment. The weights w=5, 6 becomes available for M=9, 11, respectively. As the size of OOSP becomes larger, the bit-error-rate is improved due to the enhancement of the robustness to the interference noise, and the addressable number of the users increases, while, on the contrary, the transmission capacity per channel decreases. The calculated transmission capacity and the number of users are plotted as a function of the weight w in Fig. 11. To increase the throughput which is defined by the product of the transmission capacity and the number of users, an image fiber with higher contrast ratio is required.

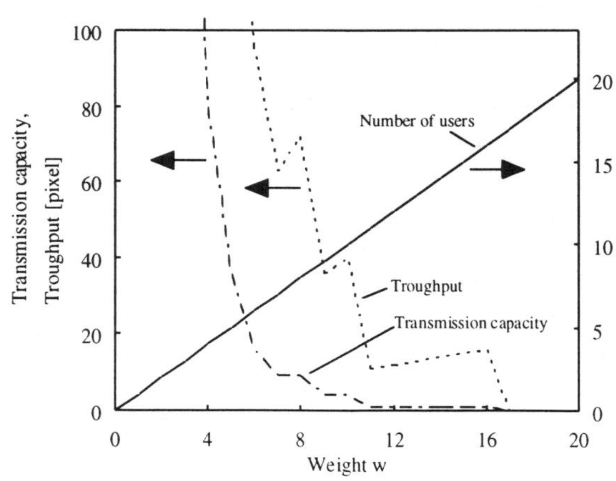

Fig. 11. Calculated transmission capacity, throughput and number of users as a function of the weight *w* in the condition of system definition 64x64.

6. Conclusion

4 channel multiplexing for 64 bit 2-D parallel optical data link based upon space-CDMA has been experimentally demonstrated by using newly developed modularized optical spatial encoders and decoder. Error-rate 2.73% has been achieved by using 8x8 binary OOSP's and by compensating the brightness nonuniformity. This result will encourage the application of optical space-CDMA to future high-throughput 2-D parallel data link connecting massively parallel processors[11].

In the presentation, we will also show the results of the transmission experiment using a 100 meter long image fiber.

Acknowledgment

The authors wish to thank T. Hara and Y. Kobayashi of Hamamatsu Photonics K.K. and T. Tsumanuma of Fujikura Ltd. for their useful discussions. Their thanks are also due to T. Shiomi and Y. Furuhama of Communications Research Laboratory for their encouragement.

References

[1] P. Prucnal, M. A. Santoro, and T. R. Fan, "Spread spectrum fiber-optic local network using optical processing," *IEEE J. Lightwave Tech.*, LT-4, NO. 5, pp. 547-554, 1986.

[2] S. Tamura, S. Nakano, and K. Okazaki, "Optical code-multiplex transmission by gold sequences," *IEEE J. Lightwave Tech.*, vol.LT-3, pp. 121-127, 1985.

[3] J. A. Salehi, "Emerging optical code-division multiple access communications systems," *IEEE Network*, pp. 31-39, 1993.

[4] P. E. Green, Jr., *Fiber optic networks*, New Jersey: Prentice-Hall, Inc., 1993.

[5] W.-F. Hsu and A. A. Sawchuk, "Design of smart pixel interfaces for volume optical memories," Technical Digest of *1996 International Topical Meeting of Optical Computing (OC'96)*, OWB3 (April, Sendai, Japan).

[6] K. Kitayama, "Novel spatial spread spectrum based fiber optic CDMA networks for image transmission," *IEEE J. Selected Areas in Commun.*, vol. 12, pp. 762-772, 1994.

[7] K. Kitayama, M. Nakamura, Y. Igasaki and K. Kaneda, "Image fiber-optic two-dimensional parallel links based upon optical space-CDMA: Experiment," to be published in *IEEE J. Lightwave Technol.* vol. 15, Feb. 1997.

[8] J. Neff, R. A. Athale, and S. H. Lee, "Two-dimensional spatial light modulators: A tutorial," *Proc. of the IEEE*, vol. 78, pp. 826-855, 1990.

[9] J. A. Salehi, "Code division multiple-access techniques in optical fiber networks - Part I: Fundamental principles," *IEEE Trans. Commun.*, Vol. 37, No. 8, August 1989 pp. 824-833.

[10] M Nakamura and K Kitayama, "Performances of optical space-CDMA based 2-D parallel data link," to be submitted.

[11] M. Ishikawa, "Optoelectronic parallel computing system with reconfigurable optical interconnection," *SPIE*, vol. CR62, pp. 156-175, 1996.

Author Index

Notes

Notes

IEEE COMPUTER SOCIETY

Press Activities Board

Vice President:
I. Mark Haas
Managing Partner
Haas Associates
P.O. Box 451177
Garland, TX 75045-1177
m.haas@computer.org

Editor-in-Chief
Advances in Computer Science and Engineering Board
Pradip Srimani
Colorado State University
Dept. of Computer Science
601 South Hows Lane
Fort Collins, CO 80525
Phone: 970-491-5862 FAX: 970-491-2466
srimani@cs.colostate.edu

Jon T. Butler, Naval Postgraduate School
James J. Farrell III, Motorola
Mohamed E. Fayad, University of Nevada
I. Mark Haas, Haas Associates
Ronald G. Hoelzeman, University of Pittsburgh
Gene F. Hoffnagle, IBM Corporation
John R. Nicol, GTE Laboratories
Yale N. Patt, University of Michigan
Benjamin W. Wah, University of Illinois
Ronald D. Williams, University of Virginia

Editor-in-Chief
Practices for Computer Science and Engineering Board
Mohamed E. Fayad
Computer Science, MS/171
Bldg. LME, Room 308
University of Nevada
Reno, NV 89557
Phone: 702-784-4356 FAX: 702-784-1833
fayad@cs.unr.edu

IEEE Computer Society Executive Staff
T. Michael Elliott, Executive Director
Matthew S. Loeb, Publisher

IEEE Computer Society Publications

The world-renowned Computer Society publishes, promotes, and distributes a wide variety of authoritative computer science and engineering texts. These books are available in two formats: 100 percent original material by authors preeminent in their field who focus on relevant topics and cutting-edge research, and reprint collections consisting of carefully selected groups of previously published papers with accompanying original introductory and explanatory text.

Submission of proposals: For guidelines and information on Computer Society books, send e-mail to cs.books@computer.org or write to the Acquisitions Editor, IEEE Computer Society, P.O. Box 3014, 10662 Los Vaqueros Circle, Los Alamitos, CA 90720-1314. Telephone +1 714-821-8380. FAX +1 714-761-1784.

IEEE Computer Society Proceedings

The Computer Society also produces and actively promotes the proceedings of more than 130 acclaimed international conferences each year in multimedia formats that include hard and softcover books, CD-ROMs, videos, and on-line publications.

For information on Computer Society proceedings, send e-mail to cs.books@computer.org or write to Proceedings, IEEE Computer Society, P.O. Box 3014, 10662 Los Vaqueros Circle, Los Alamitos, CA 90720-1314. Telephone +1 714-821-8380. FAX +1 714-761-1784.

Additional information regarding the Computer Society, conferences and proceedings, CD-ROMs, videos, and books can also be accessed from our web site at http://computer.org/cspress

4/15/97